Reading by Touch

How people come to understand ideas from touching marks on paper is a fascinating question. It raises new issues about the relationship of perceptual, linguistic and cognitive processes, yet touch has been studied very little compared to vision. This book considers evidence on how reading by touch takes place.

Susanna Millar draws on her research with young beginners, fluent braillists and adults who have learned braille late in life. She examines how people initially process small raised dot patterns which lack distinctive features, and how skill with sounds, words, and meaning influence such processes. By filming hand movements from below transparent surfaces, she obtained detailed new data on components of normal prose reading. Does processing by young beginners differ from fluent readers? Is there a best hand for braille? Do words that consist of single characters alter processes in reading and spelling? How far do models of visual reading apply to reading by touch?

The book focuses on braille, the script most widely used by visually impaired people throughout the world. But findings on the 'Moon' script, vibrotactile devices, maps and 'icons' are also considered in the context of practical implications of the findings and access to computer technology.

Reading by Touch will be of interest to all teachers and students of braille and other tactual reading systems, and makes a significant contribution to theories in cognitive and developmental psychology.

Susanna Millar is at the Department of Experimental Psychology, University of Oxford, and author of *Understanding and Representing Space: Theory and Evidence from Studies with Blind and Sighted Children* (1994).

Reading by Touch

Susanna Millar

London and New York

First published 1997
by Routledge
11 New Fetter Lane, London EC4P 4EE

Simultaneously published in the USA and Canada
by Routledge
29 West 35th Street, New York, NY 10001

Typeset in Times by Florencetype Ltd
Printed and bound in Great Britain by Biddles Ltd, Guildford and King's Lynn

British Library Cataloguing in Publication Data
A catalogue record for this book is available from the British Library

Library of Congress Cataloguing in Publication Data
Millar, Susanna
    Reading by Touch / Susanna Millar.
        p. cm.
    Includes bibliographical references and index.
    1. Braille–Psychological aspects.   2. Touch–Psychological aspects.
    3. Cognitive psychology.   4. Developmental psychology.
    I. Title.
    HV1672.M55 1997
    411–dc20   96–36571
                        CIP
ISBN 0-415-06837-1
        0-415-06838-x (pbk)

Contents

Figures

Tables

Acknowledgements

My gratitude is due to a number of people and institutions. Foremost is the Department of Experimental Psychology of the University of Oxford for providing the stimulating intellectual climate and facilities without which it would not have been possible to write this book. A research grant from 'Blindness: Research for Learning, Work and Leisure' contributed financial support which is gratefully acknowledged. The Birmingham University Centre for the Education of Visually Handicapped Children has been an indispensable source of information. I was honoured to be awarded the title of Honorary Senior Research Fellow by that Department. The experimental research on which this book is based was supported throughout by the Economic and Social Research Council, formerly the Social Research Council.

My particular thanks are due to the children and young people who participated in my studies, and to their teachers and head-teachers, for their unfailing cooperation and interest. I am greatly indebted also to the adult braillists and former print readers who gave their time so generously. Relatively few people work on touch. The interchanges with colleagues and their studies in this field have been invaluable, as has the communication with other developmental and cognitive psychologists. The book is dedicated to Fergus for his constant support and encouragement.

1 Introduction and layout of the book

How people come to understand ideas and stories from sensing meaningless physical marks is a fascinating topic as well as being of practical importance. It addresses the relations between perceptual, linguistic and cognitive processes which are at the heart of the question how the human cognitive system operates. To ask how we read by touch opens a further window on these connections, because we know relatively little as yet about how touch works and how it transmits information. The question is not only of scientific interest. Reading by touch is an important alternative and additional source of information when sight is absent, or is lost later in life.

Reading has been called 'visible language' or 'visible speech'. The phrase is interesting, because it emphasizes the linguistic nature of reading. But it also suggests that to read is to understand language by means of vision. There is no comparable phrase such as 'tactile language' or 'felt speech', although reading by touch is the most important means of written communication for blind people. Visual reading is, of course, more common. But there is also a tacit assumption that touch is perceptually much the same as vision, if less clear, and that lower level perceptual processes do not, in any case, need to be included as factors in models of how reading takes place.

The studies on which this book is based suggest an almost opposite view on both points. The studies were motivated originally by research on intersensory processes which showed that touch produces poor spatial and shape information for perception and memory. Such findings raised questions about the basis of perception by touch, and particularly how it relates to language, to which I could find no easy or simple answer. To read means to understand heard language through another sense modality, and involves much the same language skills. But braille takes a relatively long time to learn, and tends to be slow. Nevertheless, reading can become fast and fluent. How does this come about? What makes reading by touch difficult? In what respect does it matter that language is conveyed by touch rather than by vision, and whether the physical inputs are composed of raised dot patterns or of shapes made up of lines and curves? How does 'low level' tactual perception relate to the 'higher order' processes whereby we construe the gist of stories, the meaning and sounds of words, and how they are spelled, combined and pronounced? The studies which are reported here were carried out to explore these questions, and to try to understand how the physical patterns of braille are initially perceived by touch, how tactual processes relate to the semantic, phonological and orthographic skills that reading involves, whether and how this changes with experience, and how the processes involved in the acquisition of reading and in fluent reading should be described. The aim of the book is to draw the findings together, and to propose a tentative explanatory model which suggests some testable predictions and practical implications.

Braille is not the only system of reading by touch. Raised line scripts such as 'Moon' are also used to some extent. A very successful device, known as the 'optacon', provides information about print letters by means of vibrators. Reading by touch also embraces reading maps and graphs which use raised line configurations to symbolize spatial and quantitative information rather than language. These systems are described briefly in discussing what kind of working model is needed for shape perception by touch, and in considering practical implications.

The main focus of the book is on braille. It is the most widely used script by blind people throughout the world. But the system also needs special consideration in order to understand the tactual information that it provides. Touch is an intersensory system. It is a shorthand expression for information that actually comes from touch, posture and active exploring movements. The balance of information from these sources differs with the size and composition of objects. Processing is, therefore, not precisely the same for all tactual scripts. Braille has some unique features that need quite detailed analysis if we are to understand the perceptual and orthographic basis of that reading system, how it relates to processing language, and what implications that has for learning and reading.

The empirical research was conducted in what can broadly be described as an information theory framework with a developmental bias. I take it for granted that maturation influences and is influenced by incoming and past information. But more precise theoretical descriptions must depend on what that information is, and how it is processed during acquisition and in fluent reading.

The language of English braille is the same as for print, and the reading system mainly uses the same imperfectly alphabetic orthography. But braille is unique in three important respects: the modality of input, the compositions of the symbols, and in some orthographic conventions. The ostensible modality is touch, but the intake of information occurs during movement. The symbols are raised dot patterns that are based on a single matrix. The orthographic conventions differ, because they include logographs (single characters that represent whole words), contracted forms, and mandatory rules for using these contractions as words and within words. How these aspects of braille influence and are influenced by the acquisition and deployment of linguistic knowledge and processing skills are, therefore, recurring themes in this book.

The fact that braille is linguistically identical with print means that models and findings on processes in decoding sounds, meaning and gist from print can be used for testing hypotheses about braille. But direct empirical comparisons between reading braille and print are not possible; not can it be assumed *a priori* which model applies, or that perceptual processes can be excluded from the description of reading by touch. The most influential braille theory, and one that has been an extremely important starting point for my studies, is the view that braille is read letter-by-letter, and is based on the perception of the global outline-shape of the letters. The theory does not specify in detail how processing relates to the phonological and semantic aspects of reading. But analogous models in visual reading assume a strict invariant sequence of processing from perception to cognition. The issue was particularly important for thinking about the acquisition and further development of braille.

The present findings seem to me to fit in better with the general assumptions of more recent 'connectionist' models which can accommodate more complex relations between processes, although the connections that I am assuming have to include innate and maturational biases as well as biases due to the nature of the input and task demands.

The working model that I am proposing specifies some of the connections that seem to me to describe how braille is processed during acquisition and in fluent reading, and suggests hypotheses that need further study and testing in practice.

1   SOME ASPECTS OF METHOD, SUBJECTS, DESIGNS AND PROCEDURES

The book centres mainly on the empirical studies which I carried out over many years with young beginners, competent younger and older readers, slow young readers, and with adults who learnt braille later in life after being fluent print readers. It will become evident that specific task conditions are often extremely important in interpreting findings. Many of the findings that I shall be discussing have been published previously, but other studies have not yet been published or are not easily available. In both cases my aim is to present the empirical evidence in sufficient detail for the reader to judge the basis on which my inferences and explanations are based. I am, therefore, describing specific materials, tasks and details of designs in the relevant studies. Where relevant, and in the case of as-yet unpublished studies, I am also providing the statistical results, including degrees of freedom (df) and levels of significance (usually in parentheses).

They are thus available for assessment by colleagues and students who are working in similar fields, but can easily be skipped.

The apparatus that was used to obtain data on continuous reading of texts is also described in detail. It films the fingers and text from underneath transparent surfaces, and was developed specifically to obtain accurately-timed data on character-by-character finger movements during normal reading of texts.

The children and young people who took part in my studies were being educated in schools for the blind whose teachers had been trained in braille and in the education of visually handicapped children. Except where stated otherwise, the young children and young people were totally or near totally blind, either from birth or before the start of education. Some young people who took part in later studies, and had not been seen by me before, had rather more residual vision than earlier groups, but did not have sufficient sight to learn to read visually. The conditions of blindness were distributed over the whole range of causal conditions, but care was taken not to include children with known brain damage, severe multiple handicaps, or children who would have needed special education for reasons other than visual handicap. That is not because their education is less important, but because these conditions require studies that focus on the relevant conditions. Details about levels of reading proficiency are reported as they are relevant to particular studies. But details that could identify individuals who took part in the studies, including the specific conditions causing blindness, have been kept to a minimum. Most children who took part in my studies knew me well, and I was able to follow the school careers of some over a period of years.

Some further general points should be mentioned here. The children who participated in the studies over the years formed a changing population. The varying compositions of age and/or proficiency groups are reported in describing particular studies. The number of people who are available at any one time to take part in particular studies is relatively small. That makes it impossible to use experimental designs that require matched control samples. To overcome the problem, I generally used (within-subject) designs in which every subject performs in all experimental and control conditions. The method that was used to eliminate bias due to the order of presentation was to present every condition in several blocks of trials which could then be randomly ordered for each subject. The testing conditions were relatively uniform. Subjects were always tested singly in a quiet room of their school or college, or, in the case of the adult braillists who were kind enough to take part, testing was carried out either in their own homes or in the laboratory, if they so chose. Every one was familiarized beforehand with the recording device. Explanations of the purpose of specific experimental conditions or texts were given after the test series was completed. All subjects were informed beforehand that the general purpose of the studies was to find out more about how braille reading takes place as a means of improving the conditions of learning. For young children and slower readers the reading exercises also provided additional practice in braille.

2 LAYOUT AND ISSUES CONSIDERED IN THE BOOK

Reading uses most or all of the language skills that are needed to understand and to produce speech, and it involves additionally the processing of arbitrary perceptual symbols in a modality that differs from heard speech, and using the orthographic rules and conventions that link heard and read speech. The main theme of this book is how perceptual, phonological, lexical and semantic procedures and knowledge interrelate both during the acquisition of reading, and in fluent reading. But evidence about how 'low-level' perceptual variables in touch relate to 'higher order' linguistic and cognitive factors cannot be presented all at once. Each chapter in this book therefore focuses primarily on a particular form of processing in turn. The chapters respectively emphasize issues in tactual perception, the role of scanning movements, phonological recoding, lexical and semantic processes, and the influence of contractions on spelling, reading and writing. The role of individual differences is discussed in a separate chapter. But the order in which chapters are presented is not an indication of sequence of acquisition of the processes they describe, nor of the importance of those processes in reading.

The perceptual basis of touch is, nevertheless, the first problem that confronts the investigator. The main reason is that we know very little about the basis of tactual form perception. The issue for me was, therefore, first of all, to investigate how shapes are actually perceived by touch.

The second chapter therefore begins by addressing some very general issues in perception. The discussions turn on the reasons why shape coding in touch has to be considered in terms of intersensory processes, and the implications which that has for shape perception by touch. The description of intersensory processing in touch for which I have argued previously (Millar, 1981 a, 1994) implies that the spatial organization of tactual shapes depends on the balance of converging cues from touch, movement and posture, and that the balance varies with the size and compositions of patterns. Examples are presented which show that the different types of tactual objects and forms provide a different balance of converging information from touch, posture and movement.

Some of the peripheral tactual and cerebral systems that are involved in processing information from touch, movement and proprioceptive sources are then described briefly, and they are considered also in relation to the problem of tactual acuity. Some exciting recent findings on the plasticity of some of the relevant brain regions are discussed briefly in terms of their potential implications for responses to learning and experience. A further section centres on distinctions between various forms of spatial reference frames, and refers to evidence on the convergence of multi-sensory inputs in some of the central regions that are concerned in spatial organization.

The remainder of the chapter concentrates on the perception and coding of small raised dot patterns, and specifically of braille characters. The composition of the patterns is described first. The main issue in the sections that follow is the evidence for and against the traditional view that the outline shape of braille patterns is the basis of recognizing the characters. The aim of the initial studies was to probe the assumption that braille patterns are perceived as global outline shapes, as a means of understanding the basis of coding braille patterns. The alternative hypothesis is that the perception of braille patterns depends initially on dot density disparities, and that shape coding depends on adequate reference information for spatial organization which is not available in these conditions prior to learning. The empirical methods that were used to converge on the question are described as they become relevant to particular issues. Effects of dot density disparities, and of the orientation and symmetry of raised patterns are considered, and are then related to previous findings. The final section proposes that haptic perception of braille patterns involves the progressive constructive organization of dot density cues, and that it involves cognitive processes from the start.

The main issue in the third chapter turns on the fact that the intake of information in braille reading occurs during scanning movements. That is important for understanding the processes that underlie braille reading. The on-line recording device mentioned earlier is described in detail first, because it provided accurately-timed data on minute changes in scanning movements in relation to the text. Photographs of actual frame-by-frame transcriptions of movement times for each character in the text are presented to give a concrete notion of the details of the time-course of the fingers over the braille text. Methods of scoring and criteria for assessing proficiency levels are discussed in separate sections.

Hypotheses on the functions of the hands in reading connected texts are considered next. The first issue is the suggestion that the left hand should be used for braille on the grounds that there is a lefthand / right hemisphere superiority in braille reading. The notion is discussed in relation to contradictory findings, and to the different tasks and levels of proficiency that have been used in various studies. Two-handed reading has intrigued researchers for a long time, and a number of hypotheses have been put forward to explain how the two hands function in reading connected braille texts, and what advantages the deployment of both hands may have. The discussion centres first on the hypothesis that fast readers read different portions of text in parallel. That is contrasted with the view that the hands process information from different domains in fluent reading. Findings from frame-by-frame timing of the fingers of the two hands are examined for evidence that the fingers simultaneously touch different new letters of words in different portions of text. The wider implications of the findings, that parallel processing occurs for information from different (verbal and spatial) domains rather than from the same verbal domain, are left to discussions in the final chapter. The evidence that is examined next depends on experimental manipulations of the texts. These are used to explore further hypotheses about the perceptual information that braillists pick up with increased proficiency in reading. The evidence shows that the actual pick-up of perceptual information by proficient readers differs as a function of the type of reading task that subjects are asked to undertake. That is not so for beginning readers. The finding is important because we tend to think of perceptual information as 'given' by the external patterns, and assume that there is an unchanging substrate 'out there' which itself imposes limits on tactual perception. The detailed time-course of patterns of hand-movements in reading for meaning by fluent readers, by beginners and by slow readers is examined for further evidence on the functions that the right and left hands perform in two-handed reading. The findings have several implications for the conditions under which parallel processing is achieved, and also for the notion of a 'perceptual unit' in braille reading. The results suggest that there is a progressive organization and differentiation of scanning movements with proficiency, which produces highly skilled pick-up of the spatial as well as the verbal aspects of reading. Some of the factors which mediate this development are discussed in later chapters in relation to individual differences and to the practical implications this has for learning to read.

The focus of the fourth chapter is on phonological processes. The relation between coding by sound and coding by touch involves a number of important issues. They include questions about modality-specific tactual coding, and phonological recoding in short-term memory and reading, the acquisition of alphabetically defined phonemic sounds in association with braille patterns, speech-based coding in reading difficult texts, and the question of inner speech during fluent silent reading.

The question how braille patterns are coded in short-term memory is considered first. Tactual coding can indeed be demonstrated, but produces small memory spans. The much larger spans for items that are recoded phonologically are associated with fast naming, and this has a number of implications, including developmental issues that are taken up in Chapter 7. The findings also relate to questions about the basis of the 'word superiority' effect in braille, because meaningful words are processed faster than nonsense words in braille, as in print. The explanation that the effect is mediated by the recognition of the global shape of braille words is ruled out. Findings show that the effect is associated with word length and with proficiency in braille. The discussion turns on the question whether theories which propose an invariant sequence of processes from perception to understanding can explain the findings adequately.

The remaining sections centre on phonological coding in relation to tactual effects in reading connected texts at different levels of proficiency. Phonic teaching methods which start by associating letter sounds with braille patterns are necessarily used more in braille – in contrast to visual reading, which often starts by associating pictures of written words with pictures of the objects that are named. Many of the models of how sighted adults read single words have centred on the question whether words are coded by their sound before or after their meaning is recognized. The very multiplicity of theories and findings suggests that phonological coding is not all of the same kind. However, the traditional braille model which assumes letter-by-letter reading also has implications about the sequence of processing in beginning and fluent reading. Evidence from four main methods in reading connected texts is considered: the suppression of covert speech output during silent reading of easy and difficult texts at different levels of proficiency; semantic judgments by beginners and competent readers of sentences with contracted and less contracted homophones that make sentences sound correct when they are not; silent reading by the same subjects of texts that contain words which differ in the number of syllables as opposed to the number of letters they contain; and finally, differences between oral and silent reading by beginning and competent readers. Evidence on pre-lexical phonemic recoding, consistent with letter-by-letter processing by beginners, and on undue reliance by beginners on the sounds of words in memory is compared with findings on proficient readers and in tasks which compare scanning latencies for words that differ in the number of syllables but contain the same number of letters, and vice versa. The discussion turns on distinctions between different forms of phonological coding and how these relate to tactual length effects. The effects are considered in relation to theories about the basis of increased proficiency in braille reading. It is suggested that different types of reading task, and the semantic structure of materials have to be included in explaining the effects. Explanations of the time course of different forms of phonological effects with reading proficiency in braille are discussed in the final chapter.

The relation between word meaning, the semantic context and perceptual factors in tactual reading is explored in the fifth chapter. An important issue in braille is the role of semantic context and word familiarity when scripts lack perceptual clarity. Hypotheses about the extent to which the semantic context can be used to make it easier to recognize perceptual features are briefly described. Several studies are reported which tested hypotheses based on different models of visual reading and a braille theory. Two sections are concerned with the question how far related semantic context can compensate for lack of perceptual clarity in the materials, by using stories that contained some physically degraded words that were either preceded by compatible context or by contextual changes. Issues on semantic priming legibility are also tested as a function of braille experience with beginning and experienced adult readers. Lack of braille experience had similar effects in that respect as lack of legibility. The practical implications of the findings on the effect of braille experience, especially in combination with word familiarity and semantic priming, are potentially important. The fact that such factors may well override problems caused by decreased acuity with age is taken further in considering individual differences.

Scanning latencies are examined for further evidence on how readers process words in reading for meaning. The question is whether there are differences with proficiency in processing words letter-by-letter, or in terms of syllables, or in segmenting compound words into meaningful sub-units. The discussion focuses on the question whether the strategy of construing words by decomposing them into segments is determined by semantic difficulties, or can be considered as a habitual effect of covert or inner speech.

Finally, processes in the integration of perceptual, lexical and semantic information are explored by using scanning latencies, patterns of regressions and spontaneous comments by braille readers. The findings suggest that competent braillists use not only prior semantic context, but also make inferences from the length of words, and from the preceding grammar, and also use their knowledge of spelling to decipher partly legible words.

Some of the issues that are posed by the fact that braille contains contractions and mandatory rules for their use are explored in Chapter 6. The most obvious of these concern the relation of contractions to spelling and writing. But contractions and contraction rules also raise questions about their influence on processing words in text reading. The studies that are discussed in this chapter do not by any means tackle all the relevant issues. But they serve to pinpoint some of the factors which need further investigations both for practical purposes and as tools for understanding reading processes.

The first section introduces some of the more frequent contractions. Perhaps the most interesting for understanding 'whole word' processes are single character contractions which stand for whole words when flanked by spaces, but also have to be used within words when the relevant letter clusters occur. A study is reported that compares the time it takes to scan contractions when they occur as words and when the same contractions occur as mandatory parts of words. The fact that contractions within words take longer to scan than when they represent whole words is discussed in relation to perceptual, phonological and semantic processes and combinations of these.

Contractions are also explored in the context of spelling. The typical spelling mistakes by young children who learn to write contractions and also learn oral spelling are very similar to those found for young print readers. Both tend to spell phonetically, or at least spell the sounds that they think they hear. Words that are written in normally contracted braille are scanned proportionately more quickly than in uncontracted form, presumably because the former are learnt first. In fact, writing by means of a machine which produces single braille patterns, including contractions, by a combination of finger presses is actually easier than recognizing the patterns in the early stages of braille learning. Recognizing words which contain contractions is proportionately faster than recognizing the same words in uncontracted form. But such findings also depend on the frequency or familiarity of words and their contracted forms. In dealing with contractions as with orthographically irregular forms, the frequency and length of exposure of the reader to the form in question seems to be the most important factor in determining the speed with which they are recognized and produced.

Contracted forms were also used as tools to answer questions about their effect on orthographic and phonological habits and strategies in reading for meaning. Words with the same mandatory contraction, but at different locations within words, were used. The results suggested that familiarity was probably more important than the locus of segmentation in determining scanning latencies by experienced braillists. Findings showed the importance of long-term orthographic/phonological habits by former print readers. Differences in effects of auditory and tactual primes were found. Hearing the target word before scanning it reduced the overall scanning time. But tactual priming had the added advantage of reducing adverse effects of different orthographic habits by former print readers. The implications for the processes that underlie reading are discussed in the final chapter. The findings on contracted forms demonstrate the importance of long-standing orthographic/phonological associations in processing braille materials. They also suggest that they can be altered quite quickly even in later life. However, far more work is needed to understand the role of different types of contractions in reading braille, and what they indicate about the involvement of orthographic–phonological habits and semantic processes in reading.

Three aspects of individual differences that affect learning to read are merely mentioned in passing in the previous chapters, and are considered in more detail in Chapter 7. They concern developmental aspects of language acquisition in the absence of vision, factors in retardation in braille reading, and the role of linguistic experience and of developmental factors in the intake and processing of information by young children and by older adults.

The sections on language review some aspects of phonological and semantic skills that can be presupposed for learning to read braille and dispel some perennial misconceptions about language in conditions of congenital total blindness for children who have no additional handicaps. The section on phonological coding suggests that attention to sounds and speech is more necessary in blind than in sighted conditions, and this seems to facilitate phonological coding. Although the detection of some sounds is aided by vision, preference for phonological coding and play with sounds is, if anything, greater in blind than sighted children. Reasons for the apparently greater incidence of speech impediments among blind children are also considered briefly.

Previous findings on the extent of the vocabulary that congenitally totally blind children acquire and their semantic competence are briefly reviewed next. The notion that they use empty 'verbalisms' is shown to be unjustified. Findings show that perfectly reasonable inferences can be made about the meaning of words without direct sensory experience of the quality or object to which they refer. That applies even to colour words and terms that refer to visual experience. There is no reason to believe that children have specific difficulties in understanding stories or texts simply because they are blind. However, blind children do require more assisted learning in acquiring an adequate vocabulary. The importance of a wide vocabulary, and of familiarity with words, for learning to read braille are among the topics discussed in Chapter 8.

In order to consider the problem of reading retardation in braille, various forms of acquired dyslexia, alexias and developmental phonological dyslexia are distinguished first. It is suggested that the notion of reading retardation is best used as an umbrella term for retardation in braille. A number of findings on children who have difficulties in learning braille are reviewed. The general picture of reading retardation in braille differs to some extent from that for retarded print readers. Although serious verbal and phonological impairment, including slight deafness, is associated with poor reading, as in print, not all retarded braille readers are mainly or solely impaired in sound detection, and some show a preference for relying on sound while neglecting the tactual and spatial skills that are also needed. Most children who were found to lag behind in reading showed more than one difficulty in learning braille. Some of the implications of having to learn to associate difficult new sounds with tactual patterns that are difficult to code tactually are discussed also in Chapter 8. Braille learning by older adults who were previously fluent in print is considered next, and it is suggested that here too some prevalent stereotypes need to be dispelled.

Developmental factors in learning are considered in relation to factors that limit the immediate memory span of young children, and produce slower processing speeds. The familiarity of items that need to be remembered in the short-term, and their organization in terms of useful output strategies, as well as the more restricted word and world knowledge of young beginners are considered as contributing factors. The difficulties are probably greatest at the point when young children learn to associate phonemic segments that are difficult to detect in speech with tactual patterns that have not yet been spatially organized in terms of systematic movements. It is argued that considerable redundancy is consequently needed in the information that is presented to young children.

The chapter on practical implications is intended to highlight the practical questions that the findings and proposed explanations raise and which need to be studied in the field. One of the main issues in relation to braille learning by young children turns on the integration of the multiple verbal and spatial demands that reading by touch demands. It is suggested that further studies are needed which compare prior training of subsidiary skills in isolation, with teaching the conjunction of sound, meaning and tactual/spatial scanning skills from the start. Two sections briefly discuss effects on learning braille of residual vision, and of convergent auditory information from listening to tapes. A slightly different question concerns the use of the very useful 'optacon' (optical to tactual conversion) device as an additional or substitute reading device which involves learning print letters and literal letter-by-letter reading, but allows the user to scan printed materials.

The last section briefly discusses some issues in reading tactual maps, graphs, and the use that congenitally totally blind children can make of raised line analogues of 'icons'. It is argued that raised line configurations which illustrate descriptions can be extremely useful aids to learning, and can, in principle, also serve as 'windows' in computers for blind users. Some reasons why the symbols in tactual maps, graphs and other raised line drawings do not seem to be as immediately 'transparent' in touch as in vision are considered, and means of using organized movement outputs as additional nonverbal aids to mental representations are briefly outlined.

The final chapter presents a working model for reading by touch. Some reasons for describing human information processing in terms of active connections that converge in a number of combinations are discussed. The evidence which suggests particular interrelations between haptic and verbal processes is then used to specify the development of specific links between language processes and spatially organized inputs from touch and movement during acquisition and in fluent reading.

The proposed working model is by no means an exhaustive or complete description. It is intended rather as an overall framework which makes some predictions that can be falsified. The studies that I shall be discussing in the remainder of the book are by no means sufficient to do justice to these issues. The findings so far present a coherent picture, but they raise a number of questions that need to be investigated further, both for practical purposes and because they also have wider implications.

3   DO WE NEED TO READ AT ALL?

It is possible to envisage a world without books. Knowledge can increasingly be stored on tiny high density discs, can be called up by icons on the screens of monitors, and conveyed by listening to the radio, to talking books, or to the speech output of computers. Communication can take place by direct speech into the system. Only a few cherished manuscripts of literature will survive, lovingly preserved from too much handling for posterity for their antiquarian interest, and read by specialists who have learned to read for that purpose. No one else needs to learn to read fluently, although it may be useful to be able to make out labels on discs.

I do not actually believe that people will cease to read, that books will go out of fashion, or that anyone seriously envisages a world without the written word, at any rate as yet. Devices for viewing and listening are increasingly sophisticated and useful aids to communication, especially when vision is impaired. But sensory impairments decrease not only the inputs for which a given sensory source is specialized, they also reduce the overlap with other forms of information. Visual impairments are likely to increase as the population ages. The ability to read by touch, even if it is slower than visual reading, restores some of the informational redundancy that is lost. But for those who read for pleasure and instruction, auditory aids are not really adequate substitutes for books. The point which I hope this book will make is that reading is a pleasure and a source of information of which people need not be deprived when vision fails, or that cannot be acquired by visually handicapped young children.

2 Towards a theory of tactual shape perception

Shape perception by touch is not yet well understood. This is partly because it has been studied much less than vision. But there is also another reason. The information we receive about the features of tactual forms comes from a number of sources. That is not unique to touch. But in touch the relative influence of these sources differs with the size, depth and composition of the forms. That is important. The processes that underlie the recognition of characters in one tactual reading system may not apply to the recognition of the characters in a reading system that uses symbols with characteristics that provide a different balance of perceptual information. In reading by touch, therefore, the question how perceptual processes affect and are affected by the linguistic and cognitive aspects of reading is an integral part of the questions that need to be answered in order to understand language through touch.

I am proposing that tactual shape perception has to be understood as intersensory processing. As such, processing depends on the balance of complementary information from touch, posture and movement. These converge to produce the reference organization on which shape coding depends. The size, depth and composition of the shapes, as well as prior knowledge and task conditions, determine the balance of information from the complementary sources.

I shall first discuss the reasons for regarding shape perception by touch as a form of intersensory processing which differs for different types of shapes. It is argued that at least six categories of tactual configurations have to be distinguished in terms of the range and type of inputs they require for spatial coding. Some neuropsychological aspects of sensory acuity and movement processing are presented next. Another section deals briefly with three broad classes of spatial reference that can be involved in the perception of shape.

The remainder of the chapter focuses on the perception of single small raised dot patterns, and more particularly on braille characters. The hypothesis that the small size, lack of salient features, and the paucity of reference cues make shape coding difficult is tested against the traditional assumption that braille patterns are perceived initially and directly as global forms. Evidence from studies using different methods to assess global shape perception is reviewed in some detail. Apparent discrepancies in the findings on orientation and symmetry can also be explained by the hypothesis that tactual perception of small dot raised patterns initially hinges on dot density ('texture') cues and that coding in terms of shape depends on the presence of cues that permit systematic scanning and spatial organisation. The corollary of this view is that shape coding by touch occurs when relevant frame cues for systematic scanning and spatial organization are available.

Taken together, the findings suggest that shape perception of small raised dot patterns is initially a constructive process. Before learning has taken place, discrimination depends on the 'texture' or dot density cues that are produced on the forefinger pad by moving across the pattern. Shape coding occurs when relevant frame cues for systematic scanning and spatial organization are available.

The final section summarizes the argument for regarding shape coding by touch as a constructive, intersensory process that depends on the balance of converging inputs from different specialized sources, and discusses some practical implications.

1   SHAPE PERCEPTION BY TOUCH AS INTERSENSORY PROCESSING

Tactual shape perception is often tacitly regarded as simply an inferior form of vision. Shape perception by touch is less accurate, takes longer and is less efficient than vision. Discrepancies between findings for touch and vision are therefore attributed to differences in sensory acuity and to the fact that vision can take in more information in one glance than is possible by one touch. Touch is thus seen as providing impoverished information. But apart from this limitation, processing is assumed to be the same. Visual shape perception is certainly more efficient in normal conditions. It is also possible to reduce visual efficiency to levels that are more typical of touch, by reducing brightness contrast in visual displays so that perception is blurred, and by restricting the view to a small tunnel (e.g. Apkarian-Stielau and Loomis, 1975; Loomis, 1990; but see Loomis, 1993). But the fact that similar levels of error and speed can be produced in two systems does not, of course, entail that the underlying processes are identical.

The view of touch as a form of impoverished vision contrasts sharply with an older notion that touch is the basis of perception. That was assumed by the eighteenth-century philosopher Bishop Berkeley (1709), and by the Russian school of psychology in the early part of this century who suggested that 'touch teaches vision' and that it is the main modality that mediates between the different sense modalities (e.g. Zaporozhets, 1965). The idea that touch is an impoverished modality is also at variance

with the detailed observations by Katz (1925), who described the rich
world of information that is provided by touch. Katz suggested that it is
actually misleading to speak of a 'sense of touch'. Touch conveys information about a number of different, although often overlapping, skin
sensations. Inputs can arise from vibration or temporally spaced pulses,
from pressure which gives impressions of hardness or softness, from shear
patterns that convey impressions of rough and smooth surfaces, dry or
wet textures. Hot and cold temperatures are also sensed. The impressions
can all be used to identify objects. Moreover, touch can also provide spatial
information about extended surfaces and the spatial relations between
them. For instance, the hand can be used with the fingers spread out to
touch different points simultaneously on an extended surface. Using the
two hands together provides even better spatial information. Complementary movements of the two hands which encompass an object from
different sides yield simultaneous information about the features on either
side. Alternatively, one hand or finger can remain stationary to provide a
spatial reference anchor while the other hand can locate other features
in relation to that reference. Katz entitled his work *The Construction of
the World of Touch* (*Der Aufbau der Tastwelt*, 1925). The title makes an
important point to which I shall return.

It is one of the fascinations of touch that we are confronted from the
outset with such instructive contradictions. On the one hand, we find touch
a slow, impoverished modality compared with vision; on the other, it is
an expert system by which we can identify small objects with great accuracy (e.g. Katz, 1925, 1989; Klatzky *et al.*, 1985). It is a conglomeration of
partly overlapping sensations rather than a single sense modality. At the
same time, the hand has been considered a unitary sense organ like the
eye (Katz, 1925).

Contradictory descriptions usually indicate that underlying distinctions
have been glossed over too easily. One such distinction is between identifying objects and specifying their spatial orientation, features and locations. For vision, there is evidence that processes differ for tasks that ask
about the nature and function of an object compared with tasks that
require specification of its location or shape (Humphrey and Weiskrantz,
1967; Trevarthen, 1968; Schneider, 1967; Weiskrantz 1986). People fail to
see objects that fall on blind portions in their field of vision resulting from
damage in the primary visual cortex. But when pressed to guess where
they appeared they can point to the correct location. A similar difference
between 'what' and 'where' has been found for touch (Paillard, 1971,
1991). A patient who was unable to report what object had touched her
arm or whether her arm had been touched at all, was nevertheless able
to point accurately to the place on her arm which had been touched
(Paillard, 1971; Paillard *et al.*, 1983). The opposite type of deficit also
occurs. People with brain damage to areas concerned with spatial
processing (see Section 2) seem to be able to identify objects, but have

difficulties in coping with their spatial properties. The neural pathways that are involved in processing information about the nature and function of objects are not precisely the same as in processing information about their shape and spatial location (e.g. Weiskrantz, 1986).

The distinction between identifying objects by their nature and function and identifying the spatial properties of shapes is relevant to the apparent contradiction that touch is simultaneously an impoverished modality and a rich source of information. Descriptions of touch as an expert system almost all refer to tasks that involve identifying objects. People lift, shake, poke, palpate and explore manipulable objects to obtain information about their size, hardness, surface texture and temperature, edginess and prominent features in order to recognize objects by their categories and function (Lederman and Klatzky, 1990). On the other hand, although knowing the shape of an object can help to determine its function, some of the spatial aspects of objects – for instance, their location and orientation – may actually have to be disregarded to recognize a displaced or rotated object.

Shape perception, by contrast, depends on spatial organization. To code a configuration spatially as a shape, felt features within a pattern have to be located by reference to each other or to so some external or internal frame. The distance, angle and direction of a feature relative to others within a pattern, or its location relative to a background or to some other spatial frame has to be detected. The perception and name of geometric forms can differ crucially simply in virtue of their orientation relative to the frame of reference (Rock, 1973, 1983). A square is seen as a diamond when rotated by ninety degrees. But the rotations only makes sense in relation to some coordinate frame.

When sight is excluded, the informational conditions for perceiving small, unfamiliar raised line or dot patterns afford few, if any, concomitant reference cues. It is no accident that the findings which suggest that touch is an impoverished modality compared to vision almost all refer to the recognition of unfamiliar, small raised dot or line patterns in conditions that lack spatial reference cues. It is in this respect that the conditions resemble the type of tunnel vision that was mentioned at the beginning. Among the crucial parameters which determine whether and how tactual patterns are coded as shapes are the type and immediacy of reference cues that are available for systematic exploration and spatial organization.

Another instructive contradiction is that though touch and vision patently perceive the same shapes, their receptor systems differ radically in the stimulus qualities that they are specialized to sense. How we get from the specialized analyses of stimulation by different receptor systems to global perception is at the heart of some of the oldest theoretical controversies in perception. Helmholz (1866) solved the problem by explaining perception as a process of (unconscious) inductive inference from sensations engendered by stimulation of the sense receptors. Similarly, Gregory

(1970) describes perception as a process of testing hypotheses based on sensory information and experience, and Rock (1983) argued that perception involves (unconscious) deductive logic. Marr (1982) proposed a computational model of visual 3-D shape perception which assumes three levels of representation: an initial 'primal sketch' or 'image'; a 2½-D representation based on retinal spatial coordinates; and a 3-D representation based on spatial coordinates that are centred on the object. By contrast, Gibson (1966, 1979) argued that perception is not based on inference from sensations and memory, or mediated by cognitive processes. Perception of objects, shapes and spatial relations is direct. The environment and the state of the individual 'afford' all the information that is perceived. If you see depth in a flat drawing, that is because the drawing affords three-dimensional information. Instead of asking how stimulation of sense receptors gets transformed into perception of objects, we should analyse what information is necessary and sufficient for the perception to take place. The crucial information for perceiving that two objects are colliding, for instance (e.g. Runeson, 1977), is the relative velocity difference of two moving patches before and after contact. Gibson (1966, 1979) denied that perception involves memory. Shape is not inferred from sense data and recollection of past instances. The information is there and is merely picked up with greater or less efficiency with development, in touch as well as vision.

Theories differ in the questions and the level of analysis on which they focus. Marr's (1982) questions were about what is computed in visual perception, what algorithm best describes the computation, and how that algorithm can be implemented to simulate such processing (Bruce and Green, 1990). His use of terms such as 'representation' and 'image' is thus primarily relevant to levels of theoretical analysis rather than to the information that is available to the perceiver, although evidence which shows that visual depth perception occurs without mediating imagery (e.g. Howard and Rogers, 1995) makes the analysis less relevant. Gibson's theory stresses the analysis of the information which produces perceptual phenomena. The theory includes the state of the individual in the 'affordances' to deal with the obvious objection that recognizing a character in a writing system must include prior knowledge of the relevant alphabet, whether or not the perceiver is aware of that knowledge, or of retrieving it from memory. The theory thus redescribes rather than excludes the operation of experience and previous knowledge. However, the model (Gibson, 1966, 1979) also stresses the unity of the senses. That can only apply at the level of geometric description. In terms of Euclidean coordinates, a square has the same angular relation to the sides, whether it is perceived by touch or by vision, or is formed by a 6 millimetre dot pattern, or by a table top. The sources from which the information is derived are irrelevant at that level of description. Gibson considered 'amodal' perception its most important aspect. The model implies that 'low level' specialized processes are almost irrelevant. If so, it is rather odd that evolution has provided us with so many of them.

Gibson's notion of direct perception contrasted designedly with theories of intersensory perception, which start from the assumption that the senses are separate sources of different types of information, and that special translation or mediating mechanisms account for the cross-talk between them. Touch was considered one such a mediating modality (e.g. Zaporozhets, 1965). More often that role has been assigned to vision (e.g. Warren, 1977; Worchel, 1951). Cognitive and linguistic systems have also been invoked as mediating processes. Intersensory and crossmodal effects were explained by translating between modalities via some form of learned verbal (e.g. Ettlinger, 1967) or nonverbal mental dictionary (e.g. Connolly and Jones, 1970). On the Gibsonian view, on the other hand, the sensory systems are unitary and give the same higher order amodal information, except about some relatively unimportant modality-specific aspects (e.g. colour) of the stimulation (e.g. E.J. Gibson, 1969; J.J. Gibson, 1979). What is in common between the sense modalities is the direct perception of amodal, abstract relational properties that are invariant across the sensory systems, although they are picked up more or less well by different sensory modalities. The theory implies that vision and touch give exactly the same invariant information about shape, except that touch is less efficient.

However, the empirical findings on crossmodal coding cannot be described adequately by assuming either learned translations between separate sensory inputs, or by focusing on a common abstract description (Millar, 1975 a, 1981 a, 1988 a, 1994). Intersensory coding is better described by the convergence and partial overlap of inputs from specialized but complementary sources (Millar, 1981 a, 1994). Moreover, outputs from specialized analysing systems normally also converge and partly overlap, thus providing important further redundancy (Millar, 1994). The evidence from behavioural and neurophysiological studies which suggests the convergence and partial overlap of intersensory information has been reviewed previously, and I shall only mention some of these briefly here. Behavioural studies have shown that matching shapes or lengths across modalities is not necessarily worse than matching them within modalities, as would be expected if an additional learnt process were involved. Similarly, crossmodal coding does not improve more steeply with age than coding within the constituent modalities, as would be expected if it depended on learned translations between separate modalities (e.g. Millar, 1971, 1972 a, 1975 a, Rudel and Teuber, 1964). Discrimination can be improved by adding a different dimension redundantly. For instance, judging size and shape can be improved by adding texture that varies redundantly with these dimensions (e.g. Millar, 1971, 1986). But crossmodal effects are not necessarily symmetrical. Seeing a line and recognizing it from touch produces a different effect from feeling it first and judging it from vision (e.g. Connolly and Jones, 1970; Millar, 1975 a). Inputs from different sources can produce amalgams that differ from either. If two different syllables are presented simultaneously to hearing and sight, they may be heard as a syllable that differs from both (Campbell, 1987; Dodd, 1980, 1983; McGurk, 1976), indicating that both visual and auditory information contribute to the perception. The neurophysiological evidence makes the case for the convergence of inputs from different sources even more convincing. Multimodal cells in the brain respond to stimulation from more than one type of sensory source and this presumably contributes to intersensory processing. More processing capacity seems to be invested in specialization, not merely in receptor systems, but in the cerebral areas to which they project. Nevertheless, inputs that have been analysed by different specialized systems converge in the same cerebral areas, often in single neurones (Sakata and Iwamura, 1978). Moreover, the multisensory inputs converge in areas of the cortex (Section 6) that are specialized for spatial coding (Stein, 1991, 1992).

The point is that the convergence and partial overlap of multisensory inputs provides the reference on which the spatial organization of shape depends. I am assuming that convergent inputs are evaluated by a process akin to the 'fuzzy logic' model of perception (Massaro, 1989; Massaro and Friedman, 1990; Massaro *et al.*, 1993). The reference frames which the spatial organization of shape requires are determined by the balance of convergent information from all sources.

I suggest that this account of intersensory processing applies also within modalities. It is particularly important for explaining shape coding by touch. Touch is not the only modality that depends on inputs from more than one modality. It also applies to vision (Berthoz *et al.*, 1992). Visual perception depends crucially on the primary specialized areas of the cerebral cortex which process previously analysed (exteroceptive) inputs from the retinae of the eyes and from intermediate (geniculate) bodies in the thalamus. But proprioceptive inputs from the head, neck and eye-muscles and from the vestibular system contribute to knowledge of eye, head and body position (e.g. Berthoz *et al.*, 1992). Nor is it the case that tactual shape perception necessarily develops later than visual shape perception. Infants visually discriminate two- and three-dimensional shapes virtually from birth (e.g. Gibson and Spelke, 1983). But they can also discriminate three-dimensional smooth, round objects from objects with edges by mouthing them (e.g. Meltzoff and Moore, 1989). The convergence between touch sensations and tongue movements seems to occur very early. An example of convergent processing of specialized information from different sources in shape perception by touch without vision is the perception of the shape of small three-dimensional objects (Sakata and Iwamura, 1978). Monkeys can discriminate round from straight objects by grasping them in one hand. Single unit (neurone) recording showed that the discrimination depends on the convergence of inputs from skin receptors in the hand with inputs from the joint receptors in the grasping (bent) fingers into single neurones in the cerebral cortex (Section 6).

But that is not the case for all types of tactual shapes. The recognition of small three-dimensional shapes through systematic exploration by the hands by children lags behind visual perception (Millar, 1971), and occurs much later than the coordination of hand and eye in reaching for visual targets. Shape perception by touch is not always unlearned or immediate, ahead of learning. For some tactual patterns particularly, the notion that shape perception is 'direct', rather than that it becomes so with learning and experience, will not do. An example is the poor recognition of braille shapes by newly blind adults (Chapters 6 and 7). The 'hypothesis testing' proposed by Gregory (1970) is often a more appropriate description in these instances. As the title of the work by Katz (1925) implies, shape perception by touch is initially a constructive process.

One reason why the notion of construction and hypothesis testing seems more convincing for touch than for vision is the involvement of movement in shape coding by touch. The importance of movement for coding shapes by touch was already noted by Weber (1834/1978), as well as by Katz (1925), by Revesz (1950) who used the term 'haptics' to make the point, and by Gibson who used the notion of 'active touch' (1962, 1966). Gibson (1962) explained differences in the efficiency of tactual recognition by contrasting active with passive touch. Active touch includes kinaesthetic information from exploratory movements (inputs from the muscles, joints and tendons) in tracing around the raised outline of an object, while in 'passive touch' the skin is being touched, possibly by a flat object placed on the skin, so that the information comes mainly from the skin (cutaneous) receptors.

But the division into active touch that requires movement, and passive touch that does not, is not sufficient. Active touch is not always superior. It may convey little in the absence of prominent features or prior information that can provide anchor cues for systematic exploration. By contrast, prior information can produce efficient recognition also by passive touch. What Gibson's analysis exemplifies clearly is the difference in information needed to code different types of shape by touch.

The point is that the complementary information from proprioceptive sources in touch depends on the type of exploratory movement that the shape affords. Imagine having to make out the shape of a large square object in the dark when you do not know what the object is, or what category of object it might be. Compare this with having to make out the shape of a 4 millimetre square pattern made up of raised dots in the same conditions. Perceiving the large square requires large sweeps of arm movements, together with some information from the hands about edges. But fine tactual discriminations by the finger tip are usually irrelevant. The reverse is the case for perceiving a small dot pattern as a square. Tactual sensitivity becomes important, and large arm and hand movements are irrelevant. Weber (1834) gave a marvellous account of how the hands build up a picture of the shape of a large object by feeling around its contours. Recognition may well become immediate with experience. But it is not so without prior knowledge.

The importance of movement for the perception of the shape of large objects by touch is thus not merely a question of active versus passive touch. As Katz noted, it is often a process of construction, at least initially.

The fact that shape is perceived by touch as well as by vision is not in doubt. What is striking about shape perception by touch is that the range of complementary information from all sources that is actually available to the perceiver differs crucially with the size, depth and physical composition of the shapes (Millar, 1991, 1994).

The main reason for characterizing shape coding by touch as intersensory processing is that the convergence and overlap of concomitant inputs from different sources seems to be inherently less tightly organized than in vision. Spatial processing can differ quite radically with apparently irrelevant differences of size and composition. The amount or type of reference cues that are available is thus more variable for shape coding by touch.

Spatial coding can, in principle, depend on a number of different frames of reference (Paillard, 1991). They can be summarized under three main headings for convenience. External reference frames can be based on coordinate information from the wider or nearer environment. Object-centred frames are also based on cues external to the subject, but concern the spatial organization of features with respect to each other within a pattern as distinct from its relation to a surround. Self-referent or ego-centric frames are centred on information arising within the body of the observer and form another large category. The frames can be centred on the body midline, or on other anchor cues provided by the hands or fingers, or on cues from the position of the limbs in various conjunctions. In visual conditions, simultaneous information from vision, hearing, touch, smell, movement and gravitational information from body-centred sources coincides, and converges.

The assumption that visual shape perception depends on a number of reference frames is implicit in most theories (e.g. Marr, 1982; Marr and Nishihara, 1976; Palmer, 1991; Palmer and Hemenway, 1978; Pashler, 1990; Rock, 1983). Different frames can be isolated. A square can be seen as a diamond by rotating it by ninety degrees relative to an external surround, or we can tilt our heads. The square is a diamond relative to the body-centred retinal frame in that case.

In touch there are also multiple frames of reference for coding tactual patterns as spatially organized shapes in the absence of vision. An example is the description by Katz (1925) of perceiving extended surfaces. The hand with simultaneously extended fingers can sense an extended surface, and the shape of a small manipulable object can be felt by enclosing it simultaneously by the two hands. Moreover, one hand can be used as a reference anchor for features felt by the other hand. But in the absence of vision, information about external coordinates is greatly reduced. Coding depends on the balance of information from the remaining sources, and particularly on the redundancy and coordination of various forms of body-centred reference frames, and it varies far more with particular conditions.

The next section describes some of the differences in information that different tactual forms afford for shape coding.

2   CONVERGENT INFORMATION FOR DIFFERENT CATEGORIES OF TACTUAL SHAPE

The main parameters of information for coding shapes by touch can be summarized in terms of the degree of acuity that is required from skin receptors, the type and range of exploratory movements that are needed to gain information, and the amount and type of reference cues that are available from all sources for organizing the information spatially.

At least six types of tactual patterns can be distinguished in terms of the complementary inputs they require for shape processing (Millar, 1991, 1994). These include large stationary objects that have to be explored by sweeps of hand and arm movements, small three-dimensional objects that can be manipulated by hand, and flat shapes placed on the skin, which are not used as symbols in writing systems. But raised dot patterns, raised line configurations, and vibratory stimuli delivered to the skin are all used in different tactual reading systems. Although I have described the differences in the convergent information needed for shape coding for these different tactual forms in some detail before, I am listing them briefly again here to show that the detailed analysis of shape perception for the braille system cannot necessarily be generalized to other types of tactual shapes.

Consider large three-dimensional stationary objects (e.g pieces of furniture, trees and large artifacts) of the kind Weber described. They require large sweeps of hand and arm movements, although these are limited by the size of the object that can be encompassed. Shape coding is no problem. Both the object and the perceiver are in a gravitationally oriented environment. The top location, the vertical orientation of the object and the location of prominent and smaller features can, therefore, be determined in relation to the body-centred coordinates (e.g. body midline) of the perceiver. Spatially organized information about the direction and amplitude of the movements, as well as convergent inputs from the hand and fingers about edges and corners can also be based on other body-centred reference frames. But the acuity of skin receptors in the ball of the finger is hardly relevant for coding the shape of large pieces of furniture or trees. Acuity and other skin senses come into play if the task is not merely to perceive shape, but to identify the nature and material of the object. For shape, the crucial information depends on limb movements, and on body-centred spatial reference. It depends on touch receptors only for information about sequential contact or absence of contact.

By contrast, small manipulable three-dimensional objects that can be grasped in one or both hands do not require large arm movements. Descriptions of exploring small three-dimensional shapes actively by the two hands (Gibson, 1962, 1966; Revesz, 1950) suggest that information comes mainly from relatively small convergent articular motions by the two hands. Reference coordinates centred on the body trunk or midline can rarely be useful for locating the small protuberances or indentations on small objects relative to each other. The spatial frame is more typically object-centred. The description by Katz (1925), as well as the findings by Sakata and Iwamura (1978) suggest that the relevant information depends on the convergence of inputs from the skin and joints of the hand, by gauging extents through information from the thumb and fingers, or from small articulatory movements. A high degree of acuity is not generally needed unless important anchor features are very small. The features can be determined spatially by the simultaneous inputs to the skin receptors in the palms and fingers of the two hands, and by convergent inputs from the joint receptors from the bent fingers. Spatial reference for small three-dimensional objects thus depends on coordinates centred on the hand rather than on the body mid-axis. The extent to which the sensory acuity of the skin receptors is relevant depends on the size of the object and the size of its salient features.

A different range of complementary information is needed for coding the shape of objects placed passively on the skin (Gibson, 1962). Active movement, whether from limb movements or from the fingers, is irrelevant. Gibson (1962) compared a passive condition in which forms were placed in the subject's hand with an active condition in which the subject traced around the forms. Active tracing was superior for identification of the form. But shapes can be recognized from passive stimulation also (Krauthammer, 1968). Moreover, if passive stimulation occurs by moving forms under the finger so that the contour is felt simultaneously, it can be as efficient as active exploration when some prior knowledge is provided (Schwartz, Perey and Azulay, 1975). With prior information, the hand or finger can be used as a reference frame from the outset. The difference in shape coding between active and passive touch is partly a difference between being able to impose an organization on inputs or having it imposed, but also between having an anchor point for systematic exploration and having no spatial reference. Similarly, large arm or hand movements are irrelevant to perceiving extended surfaces by placing the palm and fingertips on the surface. Simultaneous inputs to the palm and finger tips are needed because they can be coded relative to each other or to other skin surfaces. But the density and acuity of skin receptors in that portion of skin, and the length, strength and intermittency of stimulation are crucial if sensation is not to be lost altogether in passive touch.

The range of necessary concomitant information differs still further for physical forms that are used as symbols for characters in tactual scripts.

The Optacon (optical-to-tactile converter) has been one of the most useful and successful devices for reading print by touch. Vibrotactile stimulation is delivered to the skin via arrays of rounded pin-like vibrators ('benders'). The fingerpad rests passively on a rectangular (5 × 20 or 6 × 24) matrix of benders, while the subject scans a line of text with a hand-held camera that contains an electronic sensing device. The sensing device picks up the patterns of print letters and translates these into pulses that activate the relevant benders. These deliver the letter pattern in the form of vibrotactile pulses (230 Hz) via the benders to the fingerpad (Sherrick, 1991).

There have been other telesensory devices with relatively large arrays of vibrators that are either strapped to the back or to various other sites of the body. But the Optacon is used more generally, and is also taught in schools for the blind in conjunction with braille, usually (although not necessarily) to children who have some residual vision. The information is passive, but sensation is not lost because the stimulation depends on intermittent, changing pulses. Stimulus change is, of course, needed for perception by touch, as it is for other modalities. Without change, sensation is lost. However, the reader does not have to execute any active movement. Acuity of the skin receptors is the major parameter and limitation. Acuity depends on the distance between the pins and the time interval needed between pulses for these to be recognized as separate (Craig and Sherrick, 1982). The length, strength and intermittency of stimulation are important. Masking studies in which an irrelevant pattern supervenes (Craig, 1978, 1989) have shown that targets are easier to discriminate than to identify. This raises questions about what additional information is needed for identification to take place. In principle, the rectangular array of vibrators in the optacon also has the advantage that it provides an invariant, coordinate frame to which the successive pulses on the fingerpad can be referred in terms of relative locations (e.g. top/left; bottom/right). The optacon is often taught as well as braille, and the optacon, or optacon-like devices are also sometimes combined with computing devices. Some practical implications will be considered later (Chapter 8).

The Moon reading system uses small raised line configurations. The embossed characters are based on very simplified capital print letters. The shapes are larger overall (0.8 × 0.8 cm) than braille, and are composed of simple combinations of lines, curves and dots. They are clearer to feel and have more distinctive features, and are relatively easy to discriminate from each other. Tactual acuity is therefore not a major limitation. The raised line configurations require active scanning, most usually with one finger, but the characters have sufficient distinctive features to direct the small tracing movements which follow the lines and curves of a character. These features can, in principle, be spatially organized by the directions of the tracing movements. The system uses the same alphabet as print though it also has a few characters that are contracted forms. A writing ('moon-writer') system has also been developed (Gill, 1985; Tobin and Hill, 1984), so that it is possible to write as well as to read Moon. Since discrimination is clear and the symbols are based on print, the system is easy to learn. Some newly blind adults learn Moon before going on to braille. The system tends to be slow and produces rather bulky reading matter. The number of people who use it is relatively small. Unlike braille, Moon has not so far become an internationally used system.

Tactual maps, graphs and graphic illustrations also use raised line displays and configurations. Tactile maps vary in size and complexity. They generally require active arm, hand and finger movements to trace along the external surround and the raised lines that are used to symbolize roads and routes, or countries, or whatever information is needed in given maps. Recognition of line configurations requires learning or precuing in tactual conditions (Berla and Butterfield, 1977; Davidson, 1972). Some raised line systems also make demands on tactual acuity. Fine discriminations are needed to detect the texture differences between symbols for landmarks or other types of information, depending on the purpose for which the map is to be used (e.g. Gill, 1974). The most important information in maps is the coordinate references they provide. In principle, these larger raised line patterns of maps provide coordinate references that can be used to specify locations within the contour of the map. They can also be coordinated with projected body-centred (e.g. midline) coordinates, or in terms of directional movements, or by using the relation between the two hands as anchor points for coding features spatially. Learning the relevant symbols, and training in coordinating reference information is important for reading tactual maps (James, 1982), as it is indeed for map reading in sighted conditions. Practical aspects of using the optacon, maps and graphs and other raised line configurations as additional aids will be discussed in Chapter 8.

The final category consists of small raised dot patterns, and particularly braille. The patterns are very small and lack distinctive features. The small size makes tactual acuity an important factor (but see later). The lack of distinctive features means that there are few anchor points for spatial coding and systematic exploration which could organize the patterns spatially. There is no external coordinate frame to which they could be related, and the details of the patterns are too small to be located accurately relative to body-centred frames.

Despite these apparent disadvantages, braille is still the most widely used tactual reading system, not only in this country but throughout the world. The perception of braille patterns is, therefore, discussed in detail in the rest of this chapter, and the relation between the perceptual and language skills on which the acquisition of reading depends is the subject matter of all subsequent chapters.

The main sources of converging information which distinguish the six categories of tactual shapes can be summarized briefly in terms of three main parameters: the degree of tactual acuity of skin receptors that is required, the amount and type of movement input that is needed, and the reference cues that the converging inputs from current and prior information produce for spatial organization.

Some of the neuropsychological characteristics of these parameters are briefly described next.

3   TOUCH RECEPTORS, CEREBRAL SYSTEMS AND MEASURES OF SENSORY ACUITY

Language, touch and spatial coding are all needed for reading by touch. Some of the main cerebral centres that are involved are illustrated in Figure 2.1. The figure shows the left hemisphere of the human brain, and indicates two areas (Broca and Wernicke) that are specialized particularly for processing language (Chapters 4, 5, 6, 7). Spatial coding is more

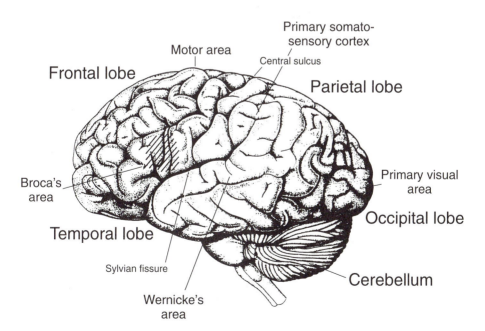

Figure 2.1 The left hemisphere of the human brain, seen from the outside. Adapted from S. Zeki (1993). *A Vision of the Brain*. Oxford: Blackwell Scientific Publications

specialized in the right hemisphere (not illustrated), particularly in parietal and frontal areas, but also in other regions (Section 4). The primary area for inputs from cutaneous receptors is the somatosensory region.

Questions about tactual acuity and how far this limits shape perception can be asked at several different levels. At the anatomical and neurophysiological level, the question turns on the number of touch receptors or end-organs that respond to mechanical disturbances of the skin by physical contact, and their connecting pathways and representation in the brain. These will be considered briefly first.

Four types of receptor cells which end in corpuscles (Meissner corpuscles, Merkel cell complexes, Ruffini endings, Pacinian corpuscles) have been distinguished in the skin. Non-corpuscular or 'free nerve endings' in deep cutaneous tissue have been associated with pain, and possibly also with cold in the case of free nerve endings that project into higher cutaneous tissue (Coran and Ward, 1989). It has been tentatively suggested that the four types of corpuscular receptor organizations may represent different functional units, starting with light touch for receptors nearer the surface of the skin, and pressure for endings organized in deeper subcutaneous tissue (Vallbo and Johansson, 1978). However, the older notion that each type of receptor cell is specialized for a different form of sensation (temperature, pain, pressure and touch) has not received much support.

In tactual tasks which involve scanning movements or posture information, inputs also come from end-organs in the muscles, tendons and joints. Haptic (touch and movement) tasks also involve the adjacent sensorimotor areas (see later). Two main pathways carry cutaneous information to the somatosensory areas of the cerebral cortex. The spinothalamic pathway is mainly concerned with pain, temperature and diffuse touch. The lemniscal pathways (Figure 2.2) mainly carry information from tactile and kinaesthetic receptors via the spinal cord and dorsal column and have synapses in the lower medulla. Most fibres cross over to the contralateral side when they reach the brain stem, ascend in the medial lemniscus to synapses in the thalamic relay nucleus, and project from there to somatosensory areas in the cortex. Although most fibres cross over to the contralateral side, there are probably also some ipsilateral fibres.

Evidence on the neurophysiology of tactual receptor systems and their cerebral representations is much sparser than for the visual systems. But it is known that tactual acuity is proportional to the density of the distribution of receptor organs in different areas of the skin. The somatosensory areas of the brain which receive cutaneous innervations via the lemniscal system are directly proportional in size to the distribution of receptor cells in the body (Thompson, 1967; Vallbo and Johansson, 1978; Weinstein, 1968). The proportion representing the finger as well as the mouth is large, corresponding to high degrees of tactual sensitivity in the mouth and finger-tip.

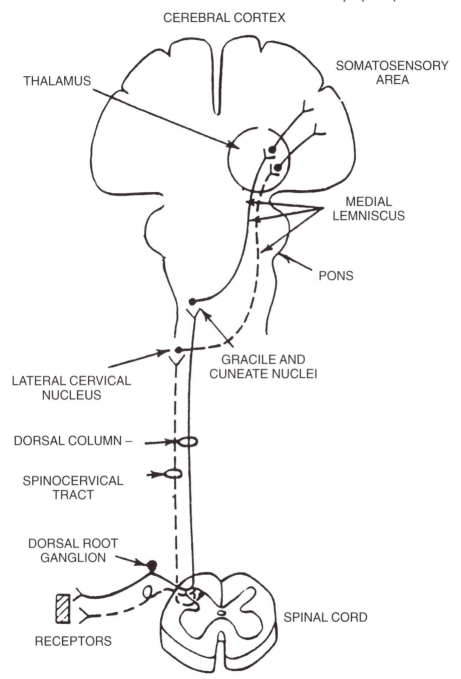

Figure 2.2 Schematic diagram of the lemniscal pathways to the somatosensory areas of the cortex. Adapted from R.F. Thompson (1967). *Foundations of Physiological Psychology*. New York: Harper & Row. Reprinted by permission of Addison-Wesley Educational Publishers Inc.

Tactile acuity can also be considered in terms of psychophysical threshold measures. Threshold measurements ascertain the point along a physical scale at which people just begin to notice a stimulus. The scales of these just noticeable differences may be in terms of differences in weight, in length, or in any other physical measure that can just be discriminated from the one below it. The main measure of tactual acuity has been in terms of the 'two-point' threshold. This threshold is the minimum (mm) distance at which people can feel the two points of a compass (aesthesiometer) which touch the skin simultaneously as separate points rather than as a single point of touch. Threshold measures correlate highly with the density of distribution of touch receptors at various sites on the skin, and the somatosensory areas of the cerebral cortex to which these project. Acuity in these terms is particularly crucial for passive touch (see earlier). Pressure is externally regulated, and feeling disappears or adapts unless there is movement (e.g. Sherrick and Craig, 1982). There is little doubt that, compared with vision, tactual acuity or the power of resolution by the skin tends to be relatively poor. However, threshold values which show how far apart two passively received stimuli must be before they can be told apart are not particularly informative about the basis of perceiving complex shapes. As we saw earlier, for some shapes the acuity of skin receptors is only marginally relevant, in any case. But even for the perception of small raised dot patterns acuity, measured in terms of the two-point threshold, fails to take into account that the perception involves active scanning. Accuracy in braille depends more on systematic exploratory movements than on passive perception (see Chapter 3).

The role of experience is perhaps even more important. Gibson (1969) showed long ago that visual patterns that could not be discriminated on the first trials became quite distinguishable with repetition. That is the case also for touch. Braille patterns that cannot be discriminated by touch early in learning are easily recognized by fluent readers (see also Section 5). Krueger (1982 a) cites the case of a deaf-blind girl described by Katz (1925) who was able to detect differences in print by touch.

4   TACTUAL EXPERIENCE AND PLASTICITY OF CEREBRAL REPRESENTATION

The implicit assumption in our thinking about the relation between brain and behaviour is that the structure of the central nervous system and brain determines behaviour. The specialization of the sensory systems and areas of the brain for different forms of information and skill is innately determined. At the same time, it has long been known that there is a good deal of plasticity in the brain, especially during the early childhood period (Adams *et al.*, 1990). Indeed, sensory stimulation is necessary for further development of the relevant specialized cortical areas (Shatz, 1992). Sensory deprivation at birth, or soon after, has deleterious effects on the number, sensitivity and specialization of cortical cells in, for instance, the primary visual areas in congenital blindness (Adams *et al.*, 1990).

But sensory deprivation also produces some differences in activity in the association areas around the primary specialized areas. This includes the parietal cortex (e.g. Hyvarinen and Poranen, 1978; Hyvarinen *et al.*, 1981) which receives multimodal inputs (see Section 5). Compensation by increased attention to visual stimulation for congenitally deaf adults has been reported (Neville, 1990; Neville and Lawson, 1987).

Exciting new evidence on touch suggests that there can be changes in brain architecture due to experience, activity and training. The importance of experience and learning for behaviour has, of course, long been demonstrated in experimental studies of behaviour. We have also known for some time that physical changes occur with repeated stimulation at synaptic junctions between neurones (e.g. Sur, 1995), and behavioural effects of experience and training have been associated with these. But recent advances in molecular and biochemical knowledge and from non-invasive techniques of investigating activity in the central nervous system and neuronal networks also now suggests some reorganization of cortical representation (Morris, 1989).

A study of the representation of the fingers in the somatosensory cortex (Wang *et al*, 1995) produced evidence for reorganization. The authors trained owl monkeys for several hundred trials over a 4–6 week period on stereotyped serial inputs that coincided in time across several fingertips. Electrophysiological neuronal mapping in the contralateral cerebral hemisphere showed changes to neuronal response specificity and to maps of the hand surfaces in the primary somatosensory cortical field, integrating the fingers that had received concurrent stimulation. This was in contrast to normal monkeys who had multi-digit topologies. The authors suggest a time-based mechanism for the reorganization.

Interesting in relation to the behavioural evidence on changes in the pick-up of haptic information with experience (Chapter 3) is the finding that prolonged stimulation of the finger pad of adult monkeys leads to considerable enlargement of the representation of that finger in the somatosensory cortex (Jenkins *et al.*, 1990). Changes are therefore not confined to very young animals.

Particularly relevant to the present topic is evidence that experience of (vibratory) stimulation with braille pattern is associated with the expansion of the sensorimotor cortical representation of the reading finger (Pascual-Leone and Torres, 1993). Subjects were experienced braille readers who only used the right index finger for reading. There was a highly significant difference in area for somatosensory evoked potentials for the reading finger of experienced braillists, compared with their non-reading (left) index finger and with the index fingers of control subjects who did not know braille. The sensory thresholds (i.e. peripheral tactual acuity) of the reading and non-reading fingers did not differ. Transcranial magnetic stimulation also blocked the detection of a vibratory stimulus eliciting movement in the areas representing the reading compared with non-reading fingers.

The findings thus suggested that experience of braille patterns did not increase peripheral tactual acuity, but that the enlarged cortical sensori-motor areas were associated with increased information processing. The fact that the effects of experience were shown in sensorimotor areas suggests that the increased processing may have been due more to move-ment than to somatosensory processes. But that is speculative as yet. However, the new findings challenge traditional concepts of brain and behaviour, and suggest the type of physiological underpinning there may be for the behavioural evidence that a braille pattern which the beginner finds impossible to identify presents no problem to a fluent reader.

Recent studies with positron emission tomography (PET) have reported activation of primary as well as secondary areas of the visual cortex in early blind braille readers when discriminating braille words and other tactile stimuli. In sighted subjects tactile discrimination tasks produced deactivation (Sadato *et al.*, 1996). Non-discrimination tasks did not activate the primary visual cortex in either the blind or in sighted subjects. It is not yet clear precisely what aspects of the task produce larger activation with braille than with non-braille tactile stimuli. Evidence that the primary visual area of the cortex may be activated by other, including somato-sensory inputs (Podreka *et al.*, 1993) needs further confirmation, however. Prolonged learning in the tactile modality seems to be a factor in the effects that have been reported.

5   CEREBRAL SYSTEMS IN SPATIAL CODING AND INFORMATION FROM TOUCH AND MOVEMENT

While the tactual receptor systems are relevant to questions of acuity, inputs from the modality systems end up not only in cerebral areas that are primary for their analysis, but typically converge also in association areas that are important in spatial processing. Spatial functions have multiple representations in the brain, with specialization of different inter-connections, and also some redundancy (Faglioni and Villa, 1977; Kornhuber, 1984; Paillard, 1991).

The posterior parietal area in the right hemisphere of the cerebral cortex is one of the most important, though not the only, area for spatial coding in man (De Renzi, 1982; Ratcliff, 1991). Visual and somatosensory inputs converge in that area (Robinson *et al.* 1978; Leinonen *et al.*, 1979). Signals from limb movements, gravitational cues from vestibular sources, moti-vational signals from subcortical regions, auditory, as well as visual and kinaesthetic inputs seem to be integrated in these areas for visually guided reaching movements, and updating cues for locomotion (Paillard, 1991;

Stein, 1991). Posterior parts of the parietal cortex have been identified in tasks of orientating oneself in the geographical environment (Semmes *et al.*, 1963), in aspects of visuospatial processing (Duhamel *et al.*, 1991), and body-centred spatial coding (e.g. Stein, 1992). Patients with brain damage in the right hemisphere (junctions of the posterior parietal, temporal and occipital association areas) not only show visual neglect of the left side of their bodies, but are evidently also unable to describe the left half of remembered images (Bisiach *et al*, 1981).

Sensory inputs from all modalities converge in the post-parietal area of the right hemisphere (Stein, 1991). Other cortical and subcortical regions are also involved in spatial functioning and interconnect reciprocally with the parietal regions. Of these, the prefrontal cortex, which lies anterior to the motor area, is concerned in spatial memory in man, and has large networks of (reciprocal) interconnections with the parietal regions as well as with hippocampal and limbic (Goldman-Rakic and Friedman, 1991) regions and with the rest of the neocortex. All modality-specific sensory areas also project into that region (Squire, 1987).

The convergence of processes from all modalities in the regions concerned with spatial processing suggests that it functions to provide the overlap and redundancy that is needed for spatial reference organization. Information from the visual system converges with proprioceptive inputs from the head and neck muscles. Inputs also come from the limbs and joints and from the vestibular (semicircular canals) system. Hearing provides further information about the direction of external locations, either from stationary sounds in the environment or from echolocation devices. Convergent information from touch receptors in the skin, kinaesthetic cues from limb and body-position can be supplemented by external directional sound cues. For vision the connection with information from touch and movement seems to be particularly well established. Graziano and Gross (1994) found bimodal visual–tactile neurones in parts of the frontal and of the parietal areas of the brain and the putamen. They suggest that these areas represent near (within reach) extrapersonal space in a body-part centred fashion.

These regions are also substrates for a multiplicity of reference frames for touch. Haptic as well as visuospatial tasks are impaired by lesions in the post-parietal area of the cortex (Stein, 1991). It has been shown that when the fibres connecting (corpus callosum) the two hemispheres are cut, the right hemisphere is superior for tactile shape recognition (Kumar, 1977; Milner and Taylor, 1972). Spatial coding in terms of body-centred coordinates that are based on somaesthetic cues from limbs and body posture and converging information from skin receptors (Paillard, 1971, 1991) can, for instance, provide information about the location of the top and sides of large objects when sight is excluded. Body-centred reference frames are sufficient for coding felt positions of external objects spatially (Howard and Templeton, 1966; Millar, 1985a, 1994). Converging stimulation from the skin of the hand and from proprioceptive information from the joints of bent fingers has been shown to provide information about three-dimensional straight and round objects even in passive touch (Sakata and Iwamura, 1978).

The description by Katz (1925) of information about extended surfaces from simultaneous stimulation of the hand and spread out fingers also suggests the convergence of tactual stimulation with proprioceptive cues, but also with additional information about the relation of the hand and fingers to the rest of the body. Kinaesthetic and proprioceptive cues from the head, body, limbs and joints can thus provide reliable reference cues for spatial coding in terms of body-centred frames. In principle, kinaesthetic information from the body, or any body-part, can act as a location anchor for starting or stopping a movement, and so provides information about distances and directions. Hand positions in touching external objects can be related to the body midline or arm position and can act as a coordinate reference frame to determine the location of a felt position.

However, not all movements are initially spatially organized relative to external locations in the absence of vision. In blind conditions, memory for movements can be distinguished experimentally from memory for locations (Laabs, 1973; Laabs and Simmons, 1981; Millar, 1979, 1981 b, 1985 a, 1994; Wallace, 1977). Laabs (1973) pioneered an important paradigm for separating movement and spatial coding. The basic task is a positioning movement which then has to be recalled from a different location. The task is to reproduce either the endlocation of the positioning movement or the extent or distance of the movement. Memory for movement distances that are not anchored spatially because they cannot be reproduced from the same anchor point as in presentation tends to be much less accurate than recall of the endlocation of the original movement, which (endlocation) can be determined by reference to body-centred coordinates. The fact that recognition of unfamiliar raised line configurations is poor and scanning is unsystematic (Berla and Butterfield, 1977; Davidson, 1972) is consistent with the notion of patterns of movements that have not yet been organized spatially. Furthermore, repeated blind movement sequences can be imagined or mentally rehearsed without actually moving (Finke, 1979; Johnson, 1982; Millar, 1985 b; Millar and Ittyerah, 1991). The evidence suggests that mental rehearsal of movements can be an important basis for nonverbal (movement and spatial) representation in blind conditions (Millar, 1991, 1994). A recent study by Smyth and Scholey (1996) shows further evidence for short-term memory for serial movements.

The spatial organization of touch and movement inputs is particularly important for shape coding of braille patterns. The patterns lack salient features which could anchor systematic exploration, and are too small to code by reference to body-centred frames in the absence of prior knowledge or vision. There is no doubt that braille patterns can be coded as shapes by touch with experience. The time course of scanning movements which are organized for systematic informational pick-up with practice and experience is presented in later chapters (Chapter 3 and 7).

But the basis of tactual perception of braille patterns needs to be examined first. The following three sections focus on such patterns.

6 THE COMPOSITION OF BRAILLE PATTERNS

The composition of braille is an extremely important factor in understanding the processes that underly its perception. The traditional assumption has been that braille patterns are perceived as global shapes by touch as they appear to be in vision, and that reading is slow simply because tactual acuity is poor. Indeed, braille is sometimes considered as too difficult and too slow to merit the allocation of adequate resources to its teaching.

It is therefore particularly interesting that Louis Braille, who invented the system early in the nineteenth century, was blind himself and was educated as a blind person. Louis Braille went blind at the age of about ten years and went to the Paris Institute for the blind where he learned to read by means of embossed letters. He evidently found these cumbersome. The system he invented was eminently logical and economical. It has certainly proved extremely successful in that it is still the main system of written communication for blind people throughout the world.

Braille characters are all derived from a six (2 × 3) dot matrix (the braille 'cell'). The cell is approximately 6.3 millimetres high. The characters are certainly small. The dots are just over a millimetre (0.06 inch) in diameter. The distance between the midpoints of two adjacent dots in a cell (0.16 inch, Nolan and Kederis, 1969) is approximately 1.5 millimetres. The advantage of the small size of the characters is that they take up much less space than embossed characters. In principle, they can, therefore, be scanned faster.

The small size of braille patterns is frequently considered the main limit on processing, because it presents problems for tactual acuity. As in vision, detecting the presence of a pattern is determined by the contrast between background and figure. In touch this depends on the height of the raised dots or raised lines of which the figure consists. In the standard braille format the height of the dots presents sufficient contrast, although in 'well-thumbed' books that height may be reduced to the point where there is insufficient contrast and consequent perceptual blurring.

The question of acuity was considered briefly in the section on touch receptors or end-organs that respond to mechanical disturbances of the skin by physical contact, and their connecting pathways and representation in the brain. In terms of the psychophysical measure of the two-point threshold, the ball of the finger tip is one of the most sensitive parts of the skin, and median values of between 2 and 3 mm have been reported.

The complete braille cell from which the characters derive is larger than this. In principle, therefore, it should be possible to feel the global outline shape of most of the letters on the ball of the passive finger. Considered in terms of the two-point threshold, the separation of dots in the braille cell borders on that limit. More important, threshold tasks only require that two points are felt as separate. They do not demand the localization of each dot in relation to the others or to external features, which is necessary for shape coding.

At the same time, the two-point threshold is not necessarily the most appropriate measure for the legibility of braille patterns. The finger in braille is by no means confined to passive touch. Braille involves active scanning movements. The speed and type of movement, as well as the pressure that is exerted, are determined by the reader. Movement cues are extremely important for the recognition of braille patterns and enter the acquisition of reading from the start. As we shall see later, although acuity of the fingerpad in terms of threshold measures produces limitations, practice and experience in scanning braille patterns is a more important factor in discriminating braille than is often assumed.

Rather less attention has been paid in the literature to the lack of redundancy of braille letters. The fact that the presence or absence of any dot denotes a different character means that the system lacks the redundancy of print letters, which can be recognized by the salient features that different spatial combinations of straight lines and curves provide. Braille letters differ from each other in the presence or absence of a dot in one of six possible locations. As we shall see later, the lack of redundancy and differences in dot density turn out to be important aspects in the initial perceptual processing of braille patterns by touch. The braille alphabet and some contractions (characters that stand for more than one letter in English braille) are shown in Figure 2.3.

The size and the composition of dot patterns that derive from a single matrix have an important bearing on perception because they determine the reference information that is available for spatial coding. Millar (1978 a) argued that the combination of small size and lack of salient features in patterns that vary only along one dimension makes shape coding difficult. When shapes have salient features, these can be used as anchor cues for systematic scanning to locate other features within a pattern. But braille patterns lack prominent features. The patterns are too small to determine the locations of dots or gaps within the shapes by reference to body-centred frames, and external reference cues have to be sought.

At the same time, the idea that braille characters are perceived as global shapes has been a powerful assumption in studies of braille reading. Evidence on this question is important for understanding how braille should be taught, and what methods would improve reading speeds. How this is best achieved depends very much on knowing the initial basis of perception, how far this may differ with experience and in speeded scanning.

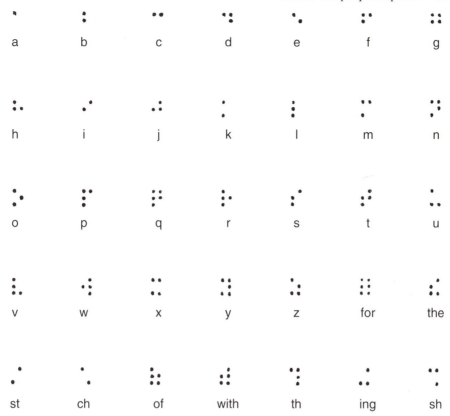

Figure 2.3 The braille alphabet and examples of some single character contractions

The question is therefore whether it can be assumed that tactile perception of braille patterns is based on the outline shapes of the characters. Evidence on the perceptual basis of processing small raised patterns by touch is therefore considered in some detail in the next three sections.

7 ARE SMALL RAISED DOT PATTERNS CODED INITIALLY AS GLOBAL SHAPES?

Early on in my research I witnessed a competent braille teacher tell a young boy not to rub constantly over the braille letter that he was trying to identify, but to keep his finger still. All that I had ever learned about the superiority of active over passive touch (e.g. Gibson, 1962) was at variance with that injunction. At the same time, it was also obvious to me that the better readers did not 'rub' over the raised dot patterns. What did the competent readers perceive that was not immediately obvious also to the boy who evidently found the task difficult?

The observation made me question perhaps for the first time whether braille characters are initially perceived as global shapes by touch, which had been the general assumption.

The idea that braille letters are perceived holistically goes back at least to Burklen (1932). It probably stemmed initially from the 'Gestalt' theory of perception (Boring, 1942), which assumed that the perceptual system is organized to perceive 'good' forms which make up global or 'whole' configurations. The Gestalt laws describe phenomena such as the tendency to see circles even if they have a gap, or outline shapes even if they are made up of discontinuous dots. It seemed reasonable to assume that global shape is also the unit in perception by touch. The question is whether this is in fact the case.

Viewed individually, braille characters certainly look like very simple patterns (see Figure 2.3). The view that tactual perception is also based on their global outlines was supported by Nolan and Kederis (1969) who argued that mistakes which occurred in naming braille letters were due to the similarity of the letters to each other in their global outline shape. But they also suggested that these errors could be due to the lack of redundant features in the system. As we shall see later, this is extremely important.

Braille characters are bound to be similar to each other since they all derive from the same (2×3) matrix. Indeed, this would be a reason for not using outline shape as the basis of perception. The actual findings will be compared with the results of other studies in more detail later.

Another finding which apparently supports the global letter shape view derived from a study which showed that error and speed levels similar to braille can be obtained for print by blurring print letters (Apkarian-Stielau and Loomis, 1975). It was suggested that poor tactile acuity produces a blurred global image, rather like seeing a shape through frosted glass. However, arguments based on finding that comparable levels of efficiency can be achieved in touch and vision by blurring the latter does not actually constitute evidence that the basis of recognition is the same in both systems. Identical levels of accuracy or speed in any two systems may be achieved by quite different means. Moreover, a high degree of accuracy with raised patterns is found quite frequently, especially in tactual discrimination tasks, even for beginners or people who are unfamiliar with the shapes (e.g. Katz, 1925; Millar, 1977 a, b). This does not accord with the analogy of touch to blurred vision.

The global shape view served as the initial hypothesis for investigating shape perception by touch. The hypothesis was tested in a series of studies with a variety of different methods. The reason for using different experimental methods to converge on the same problem is that it eliminates artifacts arising from the use of any one particular method, and raises the probability of correct interpretations.

Briefly summarized, the studies all showed that small raised dot patterns are not initially coded in terms of their global outline shape. The methods and findings are described in some detail, because they have an important bearing on the perception of braille patterns. A detailed examination shows that previous, apparently conflicting, findings are in fact consistent with the present results in showing that the initial perception of small raised dot patterns which lack salient features because they derive from a single matrix is not based on holistic spatial organization.

The first experiments used the fact that identical visual shapes are usually matched faster than shapes that differ. It has been suggested that this is because identical patterns can be compared quickly by their global shape, while an exhaustive scan of features is needed to establish whether they differ (Bamber 1969, Krueger 1973). An alternative explanation has been that the first stimulus 'primes' the identical test stimulus (e.g. Nickerson, 1965).

The assumption that the same findings obtain for touch was not borne out. Blindfolded sighted children who had never seen or felt braille patterns before (Millar, 1977 a) were asked to judge by touch alone whether pairs of braille letters were identical or different in shape. The pairs were presented on a display tray which was linked to a separate timing and programming unit, housed in a closed unit with sleeved (right and left hand) openings, so that subjects did not see the stimuli at any time. Ten letters that had previously been found to be least confusable by touch or sound were brailled in normal raised dot format on (2.25 × 2.5 cm) braille paper, and fixed to perspex shanks, mounted on metal pins to fit into adjacent spring contacts on the display tray. Subjects used either the right or left hand (in counterbalanced order) to scan the standard for 2 (signalled) seconds, and then moved (1 s interstimulus interval) to the test stimulus. Response times were recorded automatically from first touch of the test shape to lifting it for the (same/different) response which broke the circuit. The results showed that identical pairs of shapes had no advantage over pairs of different shapes in either accuracy or response time. Neither the explanation that identical shapes are judged faster because they are perceived holistically, nor the assumption that identical shapes prime each other was borne out for touch.

Accuracy in discriminating the letters by touch was surprisingly high (less than 11 per cent errors) even on first test for these children who had never seen the shapes before. This is important, because it shows clearly that the lack of advantage for identical pairs was not a question of discrimination difficulty. Further tests were run to see whether familiarity with the shapes, or learning to name them, would produce faster judgments of identical pairs of stimuli. The same subjects were therefore trained on four of the letters until they could name these completely correctly in two runs. Discrimination accuracy had improved still further. The final tactual discrimination test showed an accuracy rate of over 90 per cent (94.5 per cent for girls; 86.25 per cent for boys).

A subsequent visual test showed the usual significant advantage for identical pairs. The stimuli and task conditions were precisely the same except that the stimuli were seen instead of touched. Shuttered windows, situated above the sleeved openings, were linked to solenoids, automatically activated by control circuits in the timing and programming unit (2 s presentation). Accuracy was at ceiling level in vision, but 'same' judgments were significantly (162 ms) faster. The findings were contrary to the hypothesis that tactual judgments are initially based on global shape comparisons. They also showed that this was not due to poor discrimination, since tactile discrimination accuracy was high, nor to the particular stimuli, because visual test produced the usual advantage with the same stimuli.

By contrast, a drawing test which was given immediately after the children had named the four trained shapes correctly and before the visual test, showed further that, despite their discrimination accuracy on the prior tactual test, very few of these intelligent nearly eleven-year-olds had any idea of these visually very simple shapes. Less than 30 per cent of the drawings were accurate reproductions, and most of these were of the letter K which consists of only two spaced dots. This could clearly not be attributed to poor discrimination of the patterns, because the accuracy of the final discrimination tests was high. The drawings (Figure 2.4) showed that the majority of the children had little idea of the global shape of the patterns, consistent with the finding that identical shapes did not have the advantage for touch that was found for vision.

I have since found very similar results in informal tests with University students. They had no difficulty in judging by touch whether two braille letters were the same or different. But they were quite unable to describe, or to draw, either of the two shapes. In fact, the students were surprised by the shapes when they subsequently saw what they looked like. The accuracy with which they were able to discriminate the letter shapes must have depended on some other aspect of the stimuli than global shape.

Another test of shape perception is that forms are recognized despite differences in size. The next experimental question was, therefore, whether the perception of small raised dot patterns by touch generalizes to examples that differ only in size. Reducing the already small size of braille characters further would make them difficult to perceive. But enlarging them without changing their configuration should make recognition easier if the characters are perceived as global shapes. This was tested with twelve blind braille readers who recognized braille letters without mistakes. The experiment used standard and enlarged formats of braille characters (Millar, 1977 b, experiment 1). Enlarged characters were produced by doubling the gaps between the dots in each braille character. This increased their size but preserved all aspects of the configurations. Before subjects were tested with enlarged letters, they were told that the patterns were enlarged braille letters, and that this had been done by making the gaps between dots twice the normal (standard) size, so that the letters

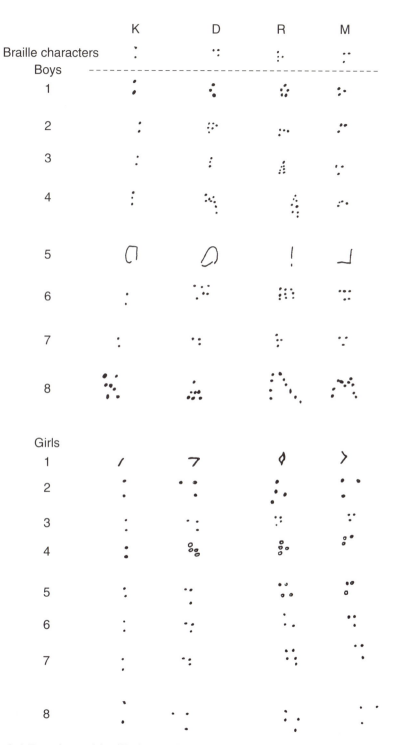

Figure 2.4 Drawings of braille letters from memory by eleven-year-old boys and girls who had previously discriminated the shapes very accurately by touch, but had never seen them. First published in *Perception*, 1977, 6, 333–343 by Pion Ltd, London

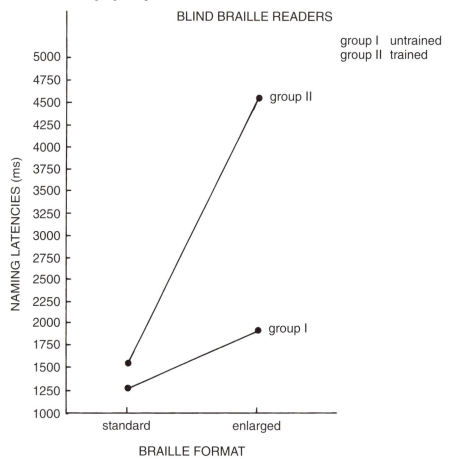

Figure 2.5 Naming latencies for braille letters in standard format and in enlarged format by young braille readers who required little or no training, and by slower young readers after they had been trained to name the enlarged forms

were larger but retained the same shape. Only two of the faster subjects were able to name the enlarged letters without mistake, and four were able to name the enlarged shapes after one training session (the 'untrained' group in Figure 2.5). The slower subjects needed an average of 8.2 training runs before they could name the enlarged letters correctly in two test trials (the 'trained' group in Figure 2.5). Mean naming latencies for completely correct naming runs, graphed in Figure 2.5, show that all subjects took longer to name the enlarged letters, and that the difference was significantly larger still for the slower subjects.

In a further test four conditions were compared. In one, the identical and different letter pairs were both in standard format. In another, the pairs of identical and of different letters were in enlarged format. In the third and fourth conditions, both identical and different letter pairs consisted of one standard format and one enlarged letter, on either the left or right hand side of the pair. Subjects used both hands to explore the letters in any way they wished. There were now relatively few errors, but they were all in the conditions in which either one or both the letters were in enlarged form. Latencies from first touch to the voiced decision showed that letters in the familiar normal format took significantly longer to judge as identical to the preceding standard if that standard was the same shape but enlarged. A similar result was shown by a third test in which subjects had to scan the two letters in a pair successively from left to right. The interesting findings were again for judging identical shapes. It took subjects significantly longer to judge the test letter as identical to the preceding standard if that standard was identical in shape but enlarged in size. Indeed, it took less time to judge different pairs in standard format than identical pairs which contained an enlarged form.

Direct tests with outline shapes of braille letters were also conducted (exp. 1 and 2, Millar, 1985 c). It was argued that if braille characters are perceived by their global outline shape, braille readers should find it easier to match letters in standard patterns to the outline shapes than to each other. The outline shapes were prepared by brailling the letters in normal format and connecting the raised dots by lines indented from the reverse side with a stylus that had the same diameter tip as the dots. The resulting configurations are shown in Figure 2.6.

One experiment tested two groups of ten-year-old braille readers. Half of the subjects scored reading ages on braille (Tooze, 1962) tests at a level that was appropriate to their age and (average) intelligence. The other group scored at levels that were two years below their age and (average) intelligence level. Both groups were significantly faster and more accurate when both the prime and test letters were in standard format, than when the outline shape was either the prime or the test letter. A second experiment with braillists at 3 levels of proficiency showed similar results. Braille readers who had average reading rates of 74 words per minute (wpm) made no mistakes on standard format letters, and had a relatively low error rate (from 4 to 7 per cent) also on the other matches. The youngest and slowest readers averaged a reading rate of 10 wpm and made significantly more mistakes (16 to 24 per cent) on matches that included outline shapes than in matching standard format letters (4 per cent). But all subjects were significantly faster in judging braille format letters than on all combinations which included the relevant outline shape either as the cue or as the test stimulus, or both. The results are contrary to the prediction that outline shapes of letters are the perceptual basis of braille letter recognition.

In considering what aspects of stimulation are used for accurate discrimination, and what conditions make shape coding effective also in touch, three types of findings stand out. One is that a high degree of accuracy is reported uniformly in studies of tactile discrimination even by people

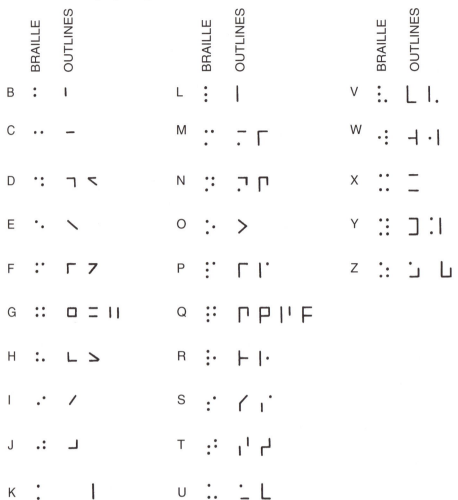

Figure 2.6 Examples of braille letters and outline shapes produced by connecting the dots in a cell. First published in *Perception*, 1985, *14*, 293–303, by Pion Ltd, London

who are not familiar with the patterns. This is particularly so for discrimination tasks in which subjects have to judge whether two tactual patterns are identical or different. The second is that the most effective discrimination cues are differences in dot density or numerosity, rather than spatial features such as dot locations, outline shape, or symmetry (Millar, 1978 a). Finally, poor accuracy and slow speeds are found more often in tasks that involve recognizing, naming, or drawing the patterns than in discrimination tasks.

If we now compare these findings with the careful reports by Nolan and Kederis (1969), there is, in fact, no conflict of evidence. Nolan and Kederis (exp. 1, 1969) tested 36 skilled braille readers on a device (tachistotactometer) that exposed braille characters for controlled (0.01 s steps) periods from 0.01 seconds to 10 minutes. The average time to name characters was 0.07 seconds for experienced braillists. Interestingly enough, the most significant factor in the analysis of the range (from 0.02 to 0.19 seconds) of speeds were the individual letters themselves. Subsequent further analyses showed that the time it took to name a letter increased significantly with the number of dots the letter contained, and with the spacing (intervals) between dots. Consistent with previous analyses of the types of errors braillists make, Nolan and Kederis (exp. 1, 1969) also found that the largest proportion of errors (86 per cent) were due to missed dots, particularly in the lowest (3rd and 6th) dot positions and more in the right-hand rows of the braille cell, suggesting a tendency to attend more to the upper left portion of the matrix. This will be discussed later in relation to scanning movements in reading. The important point here is that quantitative findings are entirely consistent with the results from my discrimination studies, even though the method used by Nolan and Kederis involved naming, while in the studies described earlier I used discrimination tests that deliberately avoided naming as a test of perception. In fact, the naming as well as the discrimination studies suggest that difference in the density and number of dots is the most salient factor in recognizing these characters.

The suggestion by Nolan and Kederis (1969) that braille characters were perceived by their outline shape was based on the argument that the patterns which were named in error for a letter resembled the correct stimulus in shape. They illustrated this by connecting the dots in the letters q, p, and f by vertical and horizontal lines. The graphic illustration looks convincing. But the evidence suggests that this is not how the shapes are actually perceived. The findings, considered earlier (Millar, 1985 c), used connecting lines between dots, as suggested by Nolan and Kederis. But far from facilitating recognition of the relevant dot patterns, these outline shapes produced more errors and slowed recognition of the test stimuli.

Nolan and Kederis (1969) also offered the important alternative explanation of the confusions, namely that braille characters lack distinctive features. That is an extremely important point, but it has had much less influence. The very fact that all (64) braille characters derive from a single six dot matrix in which the presence or absence of dot denotes a different character, means that there is a minimum of differentiating features. The sparsity and lack of redundancy in differentiating features is very obvious if you compare braille with print. Print characters are made of a variety of combinations of large and small curves, circles, small and large straight lines, and dots. This means that print letters differ from each other on a number of different features. The lack of redundant spatial features in braille patterns is indeed a reason for not coding the patterns in terms of outline shape. If the patterns are coded spatially by means of connecting lines, some letters could not be distinguished at all from each other (see Figure 2.7).

Two recent studies by Loomis (1993) provide further striking confirmation of the findings. In previous studies, Loomis (e.g. 1981, 1990) reported a number of parallels between tactile and visual pattern perception when visual legibility was reduced to match that of touch, and proposed that pattern perception is functionally the same in touch as in vision. However, two experiments with braille dot patterns and patterns in which the dots were connected by solid lines (as in the Millar, 1985 c studies), showed that visual and tactile recognition was significantly reduced in opposite directions by solid line and dot surrounds, respectively. The dot pattern surround interfered with tactile recognition of braille dot patterns significantly more than the solid line surround. The opposite was the case for visual recognition, even though the legibility of the visual stimuli had been reduced to below that of the tactile stimuli (Loomis, 1993). This is consistent with the explanation (Millar, 1991, 1994) that tactile pattern perception is affected by the composition of the stimuli and informational conditions that are particular to touch.

The findings all suggested that beginners do not first code the patterns by outline shape, and then learn to distinguish the dots. As we shall see, dot density cues are actually easier than global shape cues, and this is even more striking for naive subjects and beginners than for proficient readers (e.g Millar, 1977 a, b, 1978 a, 1985 c). The studies by Nolan and Kederis (1969), Loomis (1993) as well as my experiments (Millar, 1977a, b, 1978 a, 1985 c) suggest that the most salient initial discrimination cue is a difference in the density of constituent dots.

The hypothesis that a difference in the density of dots is the main initial perceptual cue for braille patterns explains the findings for discrimination tests. Perception by touch of what may be termed texture rather than shape seems to underly initial discrimination accuracy. To test this further I compared dot density cues with cues to the location of dots within braille patterns (Millar, 1978 a). The rationale was that if braille letters are coded in terms of spatial features, the time that it takes to decide that two shapes differ should vary with the number of different spatial features between them. Such differences have been reported for visual letters (e.g. Taylor, 1976). By contrast, the number of dots that make up a configuration should be irrelevant for deciding that two shapes are identical. The opposite results would be predicted if texture differences are easier. Pairs of braille letters were, therefore, selected which differed from each other in either one, two, or three locations of the dots (omitting a dot in one location, omitting a dot in one location and adding one in a different location, and omitting dots in two locations and adding one in a different location). The letters were duplicated for judgments of identity. To look for possible changes with proficiency a group of slower readers who took more than 2 seconds to name letters on a pre-test, and a group of faster readers whose average naming latency was less than 1 second, were tested. Naming was not required for the experimental task, which simply depended on discriminating identical and different pairs of stimuli. Discrimination accuracy was again high (3.6 per cent and 1.8 per cent, respectively, for identical and different pairs). The better readers were significantly faster, but they did not judge identical pairs significantly faster than different pairs.

The results were contrary to the prediction that discrimination depended on coding spatial features. The spatial location of dots had no significant effect on judgments of difference, while judging identical shapes depended significantly on the number of dots of which the shapes consisted. This was still more significant for the slower readers. The hypothesis that braille patterns are initially coded by global shape and/or by spatial features predicts precisely the reverse.

8   ORIENTATION, MIRROR IMAGES AND SPATIAL CODING

The effects of the orientation of shapes on perception is another powerful test of the basis of perception. There have been very few studies on stimulus orientation of tactual shapes, and those we have show discrepant findings. Most of the studies compared effects of orientation on touch with vision. Similar effects of orientation were held to show that perception by touch depends on the same mechanisms as vision. Lack of effect or reduced effects were interpreted as evidence for a different mechanism. In fact, both types of results have been found in different studies. There is, therefore, no support for theories which assume either completely identical or completely different mechanisms. On the other hand, the discrepancies are very much what would be expected if the findings are considered in terms of the reference information for spatial coding that is available for different types of shape and experimental conditions.

Shapes are spatially organized patterns. As such, their orientation is sensitive to the coordinate frame in terms of which the features are organized (e.g. Rock, 1973, 1983). In vision, spatial coordinates, based on environmental and on object-centred cues normally coincide with ego-centric coordinates of subjects in upright (sitting or standing) positions. Vertical directions are generally easiest, followed by horizontals, and obliques attract most errors and/or take longer (e.g. Appelle and Countryman, 1986; Howard and Templeton, 1966; Jastrow, 1893; Pufall and Shaw, 1973; Rock, 1973, 1983). On the view taken here, the corollary for touch is that orientation effects depend on the extent to which reference information about environmental frames, object-based coordinates, and ego-centric frames is available and coincides.

A failure to find the same orientation effects in touch as in vision was reported by Pick and Pick (1966). Blind children who had vision earlier in life were better than sighted children when tested without vision, possibly because they were more adept at systematic scanning. The stimuli were small forms resembling greatly simplified print letters. The lack of orientation effect is intelligible because environmental cues were excluded, the forms were too small for the location of features to be determined by reference to body-centred (e.g. midline) frames, and the forms used provided no obvious anchor cues for systematic scanning.

Warm *et al.*, (1970) found significant orientation effects with histograms made up of four-dot and six-dot (solid) matrices that were almost twice the size of the braille matrix. In the upright position these had horizontal (straight line) bases and distinctive features at the top. Rotation by 180 degrees produced figures with the horizontal bases at the top, and the distinctive features pointing down. Under 90 degree and 270 degree reversals the horizontal bases were in the vertical direction and the distinctive features were, respectively, on the right and left of these. The authors considered that these distinctive features were an important factor in the exhaustive scanning which subjects used. Their description suggests that the distinctive features could be used as spatial anchors for systematic scanning. Not surprisingly in view of the additional visuospatial frame cues, the sighted adult subjects performed better in visual than in blind-fold conditions.

The 'oblique effect', well-known in vision since Jastrow (1893), has also been found in touch (Lechelt *et al.*, 1976; Lechelt and Verenka, 1980). Setting straight rods to oblique directions was less accurate than repro-ducing the original direction or rotating to horizontal directions. However, subjects had some visuospatial information of the conditions prior to test. Lechelt and Verenka (1980) eliminated environmental reference cues by encircling subjects with a black curtain with small holes through which they could either feel or see the stimulus rods. The oblique effect was again found in both modalities, although they suggest that it depended on different processes in touch than in vision because errors were much larger in all orientations. However, body-centred reference for the upright 12-inch rods was not excluded in either study for vision or for touch, since the subjects sat midway between the stimuli at an invariant distance. Better performance in vision is most easily explained by the additional environ-mental reference cues which even looking through holes in curtains would afford (Appelle and Gravetter, 1985).

Orientation effects have also been found with braille patterns in condi-tions which afforded knowledge of external reference frames by using visual test stimuli and giving prior verbal information about the tactual shapes and the set of orientations that would be used. Thus, tilted braille patterns show worse results than upright patterns when the patterns have to be matched to visual standards by naive observers who have been given prior verbal information about the shapes and the orientations to be presented (e.g. Heller, 1987, 1992).

Appelle and Countryman (1986) showed that the oblique effect in touch does in fact vary with informational conditions. They used large three-dimensional objects. Oblique effects were largest when subjects were given prior information about orientations, and used one hand to explore and the other to reproduce the orientation of stimuli that were placed either to the right or to the left of their body midline. The oblique effect is eliminated in conditions which combine lack of prior information about orientations and use the same hand to explore and to reproduce the orientation of the stimuli.

Recognition errors by beginning braille readers are often reported as reversal errors and 'mirror image' confusions between left and right sides of a shape coded around a notional vertical axis. The evidence does not support that interpretation in all cases. In the confusion errors documented by Nolan and Kederis (1969), only two out of the fifty-five characters had a mirror image shape among the characters that children named in error for each other. Many more mirror-image confusions would be expected if the patterns were coded by reference to the vertical axis. Millar (experiment 3, 1985 c) found that for congenitally blind beginning readers the main reason for confusing 'mirror image' patterns came from uncertainty about the position of a single dot which differed by only 2 mm from the comparable location in the 'mirror image' pattern. Similarly, when totally congenitally blind readers were asked to draw the outline shape of braille letters, the most common sources of confusion were the spatial position of dots, and in the alignment to the major axes, rather than mirror image reversals. Confusion between patterns depends more on the presence or absence of dots than on their location within a pattern. In braille, reversal errors can depend on a difference of 2 millimetres in the location of one dot for the 'correct' letter and a 'mirror image' pattern (e.g. 'd', 'f', 'h'). By contrast, the findings are entirely consistent with the other (quantitative) findings which show that the majority of errors are accounted for by dot confusions, including by missing dots in the lower half of the matrix (Nolan and Kederis, 1969). Mirror image confusions hardly occur at all when braille readers are asked to reproduce braille patterns on manilla paper which produces raised dots or lines when subjects draw on it with a ballpoint pen (Millar, 1985 c).

In fact, the composition of braille patterns necessarily produces a very high probability that mistakes in identification will be reversals of the pattern, because the characters all derive from the same matrix and differ only in the presence or absence of dots. In terms of rotation of a given cell about a notional vertical axis, all cells (except the six-dot matrix itself and the total blank) are necessarily rotations of some other cell. There is thus a high probability that any cell which is named in error for another will be a reversal. Both the low incidence of mirror-image errors in the drawings of letters (Millar 1985 c), and the comparative lack of reversal errors in the Nolan and Kederis (1969) confusion matrix are more easily explained by the small size combined with the lack of redundancy in the braille system.

However, older retarded readers who have learned to recognize an overall pattern often do make genuine left–right and also up/down reversals (Chapter 7). For instance, when they encounter a letter that contains three dots in the upper portion of the cell, they may name any or all of the letters that have three dots in the upper two rows, or even in the lower two rows of the cell, suggesting that they recognize some global aspects of the letters but still fail to organize the dot locations by external coordinate references which could determine their locations. Exploration is still often poorly organized in these subjects. Retardation in braille reading is discussed more extensively in a later chapter (Chapter 7).

Taken together, the apparent discrepancies of findings on orientation can be explained consistently by the hypothesis that correct shape coding by touch depends on adequate cues which permit systematic scanning and spatial organization. The next section considers the spatial organization of raised dot patterns by comparing symmetry and dot density as discrimination cues.

9   SYMMETRY, DOT DENSITY AND SPATIAL REFERENCE ORGANIZATION

Symmetry seems to be the most economic form of spatial organization of visual shapes (e.g. Royer, 1981). Its effect on touch is, therefore, an important further test of the hypothesis that tactual perception of small tactual dot patterns is not initially organized spatially but depends on dot density cues.

The notion of symmetry entails that features are distributed equally about a spatial axis, and map onto each other precisely when rotated. There is considerable evidence for the advantage of bilateral symmetry in visual shape perception (e.g. Corballis and Roldan, 1975; Fisher, 1982; Locher and Nodine, 1973; Mach, 1897; Julesz, 1971; Palmer, 1991; Pashler, 1990; Rock, 1983). Bilateral symmetry about the vertical axis is usually detected most easily (Corballis and Roldan, 1975; Fisher and Bornstein, 1982; Munsinger and Forsman, 1966; Palmer, 1991; Royer, 1981). Symmetry is sometimes considered a 'higher order' characteristic. A frequent test is to ask adults to judge whether or not shapes are symmetric. In principle, that task cues attention to the concept of symmetry.

There are reasons for regarding symmetry as an encoding property in vision (e.g. Royer, 1981). Although the axis of symmetry need not itself be a visual feature in symmetrical shapes for the advantage to occur, Pashler (1990) found that pre-cuing the relevant spatial axis makes it still easier to detect symmetry. Moreover, the simplest explanation, namely that symmetric shapes require less feature processing, because features around the axis of symmetry are redundant, presupposes that the symmetric spatial organization is detected for the advantage to occur. Royer (1981) suggested that symmetry is the most salient global organizational

PATTERNS

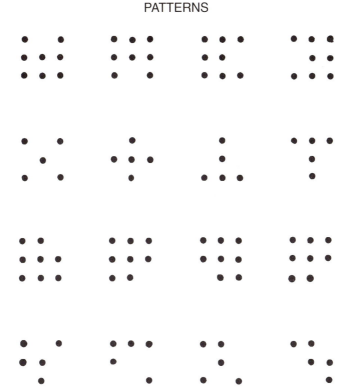

Figure 2.7 Vertically symmetric and asymmetric patterns differing in dot numerosity

aspect of visual shapes. The advantage of symmetric over asymmetric visual shapes is found not only in adults, but also in preschool children (Boswell, 1976; Gaines, 1969; Munsinger and Forsman, 1966), and even in four-month-old babies (Bornstein and Krinsky, 1985; Bornstein *et al.*, 1981; Fisher *et al.*, 1981). Young babies cannot be instructed to judge symmetry. The fact that they detect vertical symmetry nevertheless is more consistent with the assumption that symmetry is part of the spatial organizational structure of visual shape perception, as suggested by Royer (1981).

Braille patterns are not symmetrical about the vertical midaxis. In order to test effects of symmetry against the dot density hypothesis, the basic dot matrix was extended to a three by three (8×8 mm) dot matrix (Millar, 1978 a, experiment 2). This meant that eight-dot and five-dot bilaterally symmetric and asymmetric patterns could be derived, as shown in Figure 2.7.

It was argued that if symmetry is part of the spatial shape organization for tactual patterns, it should be easy to distinguish symmetric and asymmetric shapes by touch. If, on the other hand, dot density is a more salient cue, it should be easier to distinguish patterns with eight dots from patterns containing five dots, whether or not they are symmetric or asymmetric. Symmetry should therefore not be a salient discrimination cue for perceiving small dot patterns that lack redundant features in tactual conditions.

Symmetry was therefore compared with dot density as a discrimination cue in a tactual matching task with six-year-old and nine-year-old sighted children. They were simply asked to judge whether pairs of shapes were the same or different from each other. Neither dot density nor symmetry were mentioned. Environmental reference cues were excluded by blindfolding the subjects. The stimuli were too small for the location of features to be determined by reference to the midline of the body of the seated subject. Self-referent organization of scanning by reference to the body midline was excluded further by using exploration by one finger only. The children were right handed and used the right hand to scan the shapes in pair sequentially from left to right. In one list all shapes consisted of eight dots, but half the pairs differed in symmetry, while the other half were identical pairs in which both shapes in a pair were either symmetric or asymmetric. Identical and different pairs were interspersed randomly. A second list was made up in precisely the same way, except that all symmetric and asymmetric shapes were made up of five-dot patterns. A third list was made up of symmetric shapes in pairs whose members differed in dot density, consisting of one eight-dot and one five-dot pattern, respectively, and these were randomly interspersed with the same number of identical eight- or five-dot symmetric pairs. Another list consisted of pairs of asymmetric stimuli in which both members of the identical pairs were eight or were five-dot patterns, and these were randomly presented with pairs whose members differed in dot number (eight versus five dots). The lists were presented in blocks of counterbalanced trials.

The results were unequivocal. Dot density rather than symmetry determined judgments of identity and judgments of difference. Judgement of identical symmetric and asymmetric shapes did not differ in accuracy. The fact that shapes were symmetric did not, therefore, confer an advantage. Furthermore, identical shapes consisting of five dots were judged significantly more accurately than identical patterns that consisted of eight dots, regardless of whether the pairs were symmetric or asymmetric. Differences in dot density rather than differences in symmetry also determined judgments of difference. Judgments based on dot density differences were significantly more accurate than judgments based on the difference between symmetric and asymmetric stimuli. Similar results were obtained in a third study with blind subjects who had some experience of braille patterns.

The results showed that dot density is a more powerful perceptual cue than symmetry for matching small raised dot patterns by touch, consistent with the hypothesis that shape coding is difficult in conditions that lack reference cues for coding the patterns spatially.

There have been relatively few studies on the effects of symmetry in touch. But what findings there are also suggest that symmetry is not an integral part of shape perception in touch. Walk (1965) found faster association of symmetric shapes with nonsense syllables in vision, but no advantage for symmetry in touch. Locher and Simmons (1978) used one-handed exploration of unfamiliar, solid, large polygon shapes. The task was to detect symmetric shapes. In these conditions symmetric shapes actually took longer and produced more errors than asymmetric shapes. Similar results were found with one-handed exploration for smaller raised line patterns by Ballesteros and her colleagues (Ballesteros *et al.*, 1993) who also used overt judgments of symmetry with one-handed exploration of small raised line patterns. By contrast, judgments of symmetry were better for two-handed exploration of larger three-dimensional stationary objects that were aligned to the body mid-axis, and could be enclosed by the convergence of the two hands about the body mid-axis (Ballesteros *et al.*, in press). The fact that direct judgments of symmetry in touch vary with the size and composition of objects and the means of exploration (Martinez, 1971) is consistent with what may be roughly called the 'reference' hypothesis. Large objects that can be encompassed by both hands provide adequate spatial cues.

A series of studies with one- versus two-handed exploration of symmetric and asymmetric raised line stimuli (Millar *et al.*, 1994) suggested that symmetry effects in touch can be obtained by aligning stimuli to the body mid-axis and using two-handed exploration. But the effect also depended on the configuration of the shapes. The stimuli were somewhat larger than braille and consisted of open-ended raised line configurations or stimuli that contained a closed shape, in order to be able to use an indirect judgment task rather than the explicit detection of symmetry. Only the open configuration showed the symmetry effect with two-handed exploration, and no effects were obtained with one-handed exploration.

The detailed findings were consistent with the explanation that symmetry effects in touch depend on the type and consistency of reference cues that subjects can use (Ballesteros *et al.*, submitted).

10 SUMMARY AND IMPLICATIONS

This chapter has explored the basis of pattern perception by touch, because it is not possible to understand how reading by touch is acquired without some notion of how tactual symbols are perceived.

I assumed that shape perception depends on the reference cues that are available for spatial organization. Shape perception by touch is best described as an intersensory process, because the spatial reference cues depend on the balance of inputs from touch, movement and posture, and that varies with the size and composition of objects. At least six types of shape were shown to differ in the demands they make on the acuity of the touch receptors, on the type and range of exploratory movements or their absence, and the type of reference frames these afford. Behavioural and neurophysiological evidence on receptors and central systems was briefly reviewed, including recent evidence suggesting the enlargement with practice of relevant areas of the brain. Tactual shape perception is, therefore, not necessarily an immediate encoding process prior to experience, nor necessarily identical for tactual forms that differ in composition and size.

The remainder of the chapter reviewed evidence on the perception of small raised dot patterns which form the characters of the braille system. The proposed hypothesis implies that shape coding depends on spatial reference information. Braille patterns lack distinctive features to anchor systematic object-centred scanning, they are too small for individual dots to be located by reference to body-centred frames, and in the absence of vision external reference cues have to be sought or construed. The implication that braille patterns are not initially perceived as global shapes was, therefore, tested against the traditional theory which assumes that braille characters are perceived by their global outline shape.

The findings from a number of converging studies showed that, contrary to the global shape assumption, identity in shape and outline of patterns was no advantage, and pattern recognition did not generalize across size or format. Discrimination accuracy was nevertheless high. But dot density cues were more effective for discriminating unfamiliar small raised dot patterns than either dot location or symmetry. Previous evidence on outline and dot numerosity effects was shown to be completely consistent with these findings.

What was broadly termed the 'reference' hypothesis also explained the discrepancies in findings on the orientation of tactual patterns and in the effects of symmetry. Orientation effects occurred typically with tactual patterns that had distinctive features so that object-centred coding was possible, or in conditions with added external visuospatial cues and/or prior knowledge, and with two-handed scanning that was centred on the body midline.

The findings have practical implications which will be considered in a later chapter (Chapter 8). But they suggest that beginning young readers face a dual task in learning braille. The sounds of the letters of the alphabet have to be learned at the same time as tactual scanning of dot density patterns has to become progressively organized.

Taken together, the experimental findings imply that the perception of braille patterns is best described as constructive processing which starts from the detection of dot density disparities by relatively unsystematic scanning movements. Progressively more systematic scanning involves the spatial organization of inputs from touch and movement with experience and knowledge. Constructive processing is not necessarily deliberate although it suggests interactions with so-called 'higher order' processes from the start. The point is important also in the organization of scanning movements for both the verbal and spatial aspects of reading connected prose, which is the subject matter of the next chapter.

3 Hand-movements in reading: measures, functions and proficiency

I have argued that the processes which underlie shape perception by touch differ with the size and composition of patterns. Even the perception of single braille patterns was found to depend on the nature and type of scanning movements that were made possible by the available reference information and/or prior knowledge. The present chapter looks in more detail at hand and finger movements in fluent reading, and how scanning movements become organized for the spatial and verbal aspects of reading connected prose texts.

The crucial point is that, in touch, the intake of information occurs during scanning (Burklen, 1932; Davidson *et al.*, 1980; Foulke, 1982; Kusajima, 1974). The reverse is the case in visual reading. Visual reading involves left-to-right eye-movements to travel over the text. But the intake of information occurs during the time that the eyes fixate a word, and not during the saccadic eye movements which occur between fixations (e.g. Rayner, 1983; Rayner and Pollatsek, 1987, 1989). The times spent in fixations, rather than movement latencies, are thus the important data in eye-movement studies. For braille reading, by contrast, the important data on the intake and processing of verbal information come from the deployment of the hands in reading and the precise timing of finger-movements over small details as well as over larger portions of text.

An on-line recording and timing device was developed for that reason. It is described first, because it provided data on the precise timing of types of finger movements which are essential for understanding the intake of information in reading by touch. The device is analogous to filming eye-movements in visual reading (e.g. Rayner, 1983). But it video-records hand and finger movements from below transparent surfaces, together with (1/100 s) timing and voice output. The device has the added advantage that people can read texts normally without any physical restraints while the recording provides synchronous timing for each millimetre detail that is being touched during reading. Filming finger movements from below, rather than from above or laterally, improves the precision of the data considerably. It is possible to see directly on the monitor which part of the fingerpad touches any dot of a braille cell of the text and at what point in time. Filming hand-movements from above or laterally obscures the actual locus of text being touched and the part of the finger that is touching. It also difficult to reconstitute millimetre localizations from indirect measures with computerized touch screens. Viewing finger movements in slow motion from below transparent surfaces dispels some common misapprehensions about braille reading. It is not, for instance, the case that proficient braillists keep constant physical contact with the page during return sweeps to the next line. The video-recordings show, on the contrary, that fast readers use one hand as a place marker while the other is in transit to the next line above the text. The apparatus, methods of scoring, data analysis, and the criteria that were used to assess proficiency are described in detail in the first three sections.

The rest of the chapter examines evidence on the functions that the hands perform in reading connected texts. The question whether the right or left hand has an advantage in reading has long been a controversial topic. Reading styles differ between individuals, regardless of their handedness. Findings on advantages for one or other hand are discussed in some detail.

A more promising line of enquiry is to ask how, when and how long the fingers scan any and all parts of a text. Several hypotheses have been put forward about how fluent reading takes place at various times. Among these is the theory considered earlier, that readers recognize words by their global shape (Burklen, 1932), which was not supported for initial levels of reading. But Burklen also suggested that in two-handed reading, the hands actually process two different parts of the text in parallel, and that this simultaneous processing explains the difference in speed between fluent and slow readers. Kusajima (1970) contrasts this theory with a still earlier view that the right and left hands perform different functions: the right hand scans the text for gist in advance of the left hand, while the left hand checks individual words. It has also been suggested that using the two forefingers together on the same line of text, or side by side, 'enlarges the perceptual window', so that more information can be taken in at the same time. One of the most interesting and intriguing hypotheses about fast two-handed reading is that fast readers identify 'temporally extended dynamic patterns' so that timing and rhythm are important cues (Grunewald, 1966). Tests of the various hypotheses are important because the findings lead to models which in turn have implications for the process of learning and for training two-handed skills.

The various hypotheses about the functions of the two hands were tested by analysing the latency measures for precise locations of finger movements in normal and experimentally manipulated texts. Fine-grained timing of the fingers in competent two-handed reading shows how the two hands function in relation to each other, and provides evidence that the hands function to pick up spatial as well as verbal information. One hand reads while the other finds the beginning of the next line, monitors the direction of scanning, or provides a reference location. In competent fast reading the two hands alternate in processing verbal and spatial information. The findings on fluent reading show that simultaneous, or near simultaneous processing depends on sampling information from different domains, rather than from the same domain.

Evidence that good readers actually pick up different perceptual information when reading texts for meaning than they do when searching for specific letters in quasi proof-reading tasks is considered next. There seems to be no single 'unit' of reading in fluent braille. The suggestion that fluent readers process 'temporally extended dynamic patterns' (Grunewald, 1966), which has rarely been taken seriously, is shown to be substantiated for tasks that require lateral scanning in reading for meaning. In letter-search, by contrast, fluent readers typically used systematic circular movements around single characters, indicating search for the shapes of braille characters.

The fact that the physical features which are perceived and processed differ with the task for good readers has implications for the notion that there is an invariant perceptual unit or substrate in reading, which is discussed in the last section and in the final chapter. However, such flexibility of perceptual processing in response to task demands is only established with experience. Beginning and less proficient readers tend not to adapt their hand and finger movements as readily to the demands of different reading tasks.

Not all competent readers use both hands, and many of those who appear to do so, actually use mainly one hand for reading and for checking (regressions), while the other has a mainly guiding and place-keeping role. The criteria for interpreting scanning movements by slower readers, and particularly by readers who use the two forefingers side-by-side for every word are discussed next.

The evidence is summarized in the final section. It is argued that finger movements have more than one function in picking up tactual information, and are progressively adapted to the verbal and spatial demands of the reading tasks. Some implications for the acquisition of tactual reading are considered.

1 VIDEO-RECORDING DEVICE

The recording apparatus is described in some detail, because much of the evidence in this and subsequent chapters depends on the analyses which the device makes possible. The device is also potentially useful for practical purposes of instruction and remediation. The finger movements over the text can be watched on the monitor, as well as analysed in subsequent frame-by-frame replay. It is thus possible for instructors to see exactly what parts of the lay-out or texts produce difficulties and to correct them immediately, or to analyse or display the data subsequently. The details

Figure 3.1 Photograph of the recording apparatus, seen from the subject's side. The experimenter sits on the left, facing the monitor, videotimer and recorder, and the shutters through which the camera and lens can be adjusted if necessary

given here provide information about the construction of replicas for practical purposes or for further research. For the present studies the device has proved crucial in providing accurate data for microanalyses of reading processes.

The device consists of units that can be assembled relatively easily, and is therefore fully transportable (Millar, 1988 b) for testing inside or outside the laboratory. A still photograph of the recording device (Figure 3.1) shows the two interconnecting units which, respectively, house the camera and the reading surface which faces the subject. A videorecorder (Panasonic NV 180), videotimer (GYYR G77) and the monitor are linked into the system, and are placed on the units, facing the experimenter. The monitor displays the text and reading hands on-line. Recording can take place anywhere: in schools, colleges, or in people's homes as well as in the laboratory.

The larger (57 × 66 × 30 cm) of the interconnecting units contains a plate glass (66 × 30 cm) reading surface. It is situated at normal table height (25 cm above the unit base; 76 cm above the floor). Texts are brailled on transparent (drawing Film A/V) sheets with dots darkened from the reverse side. The sheets are secured on the reading surface by slots and taped if necessary. An (45 degree) angled mirror, attached below the reading surface and flanked by two strip lights, reflects the movement of the hands and fingers above the braille texts. The image is picked up by the videocamera (Panasonic Wv-155/B with Computar lens 12.5 mm F 1.3) which is housed in the interconnecting second (43 × 39 × 49 cm) unit. The scan coils of the camera are reversed and the camera is inverted to give a normally oriented picture on the monitor, as indicated in the photograph. The distance between the camera and the mirror, and the fine adjustment of the lens, are important. When the lens and distance between the lens and reflecting mirror are properly adjusted, the definition is extremely good. The units fit onto a (74 cm) square board, supported at the back by a moveable leg, and by a (50 × 38 × 74 cm) kneehole stand at the front.

A small switch on the reading surface is so placed that its tongue rests over the first letter of the text. Touching the first letter to start reading deflects the tongue and starts the videotimer. Cumulative (real) time is recorded simultaneously with the movements of the hands over the braille text. When the videotimer is connected into the system, the cumulative (1/100 s) digital time shows up in the right hand corner above the text in each frame. A microphone, located at the top right hand corner of the first unit on the subject's side, provides voice input. The camera in the second unit can be adjusted as necessary via two shuttered windows. Video (solid state) monitors provide visual and auditory outputs in replay. The total text and hand-movements together with cumulative timing can be displayed on the monitor either continuously, or in slow motion, or in static pictures for frame-by-frame analysis. The movements of the two hands over the braille text can be monitored on-line. Up to fourteen lines of text (thirty-two spaces per line) are visible in each frame on replay. The time that the reading finger(s) take to move over any portion of the text (sentences, words, letters or millimetre constituents of letters) is scored in frame-by-frame replay from the cumulative frame time displayed in each frame.

The important reference point for the frame time is the midpoint on the ball of the reading finger. Pressing a surface, or touching a raised dot produces a slight depression on the skin of the fingerpad. The monitor shows the depression up as a patch ('reading patch') on the fingerpad which is brighter than the surrounding skin. Even a light touch produces the effect. The midpoint of the reading patch is the reference location to which the frame time refers. The reading patch is seen here in a still photograph in which the timer was not connected (Figure 3.2). It shows the right forefinger touching a braille letter. The left forefinger is above the text in transit to the next line at the point of homing in on the start of the next line. The contrast with the right forefinger is obvious from the absence of the reading patch, as well as from the darker colour

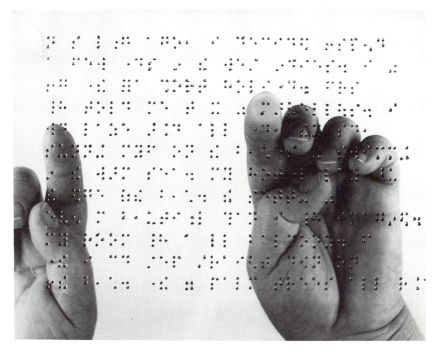

Figure 3.2 Still photograph of the braille text and reading hands from below the transparent reading surface. The right forefinger is touching the first (M) letter of a word, showing the reading patch. The left forefinger is above the text, about to home in on the start of the next line

and smaller apparent size of the left forefinger. Recording from below makes very clear at what points the fingers are actually touching the text and when they are above the text out of touch. The contrast in brightness between the reading patch and the surrounding skin varies with the pressure exerted by the finger on the braille dots. It is much less bright for fluent readers who tend to exert less pressure in reading than for beginners who tend to press harder. But the contrast in brightness even for fluent readers is sufficient to show the reading finger in a still frame as well as in slow and faster motion. When not touching the text, and when moving above it the appearance of the hand and fingers are shadowy (less defined) as well as darker. Hand and finger positions above the text are even more obvious in slow motion replay.

Normal reading can thus take place, while finger positions and movements on the text are timed accurately. Times for each character, word, sentence, or text can be obtained on replay, as required. The device makes it possible to see precisely, not only how the hands are moving in relation to each other, but whether or not they are brushing the text in transit to the next line, or are at a distance from it. Such details would have demanded far more complicated programmes than are feasible with

Figure 3.3 Film of one frame in an ongoing video-recording of silent reading with adjacent forefingers. The cumulative frame-time from the videotimer is seen above the text on the monitor. The left forefinger is touching the space between two words, showing the reading patch. According to the subject, the right forefinger is used only for guidance

computerized touch screens. Subjects were familiarized with the apparatus before starting to read.

2   SCORING AND DATA ANALYSIS

The data are scored in frame-by-frame (40 ms) replay by independent observers who do not know braille. They are given blown-up xerox copies of the braille script as it appears in the frames on the monitor. Their task is to transcribe the cumulative simultaneously recorded (1/100 s) time that appears above the text (Figure 3.3) in each frame (advanced at 40 ms frame-rates) to the precise (mm) location of the corresponding braille dot on the xerox copy of the text which corresponds to the dot that the finger is touching in that frame. The dot or gap at the midpoint of the reading patch on the fingerpad is the important reference location.

The observer transcribes the frame time to the point just below that reference location on the xerox copy for each frame. Observers needed very little experience to transcribe frame times accurately. The transcription is done separately for each hand for two-handed readers. A complete movement path in frame times over the text is thus transcribed for each reading finger, from the beginning to the end of the text being read.

Photographs of the actual transcriptions of frame times for the movements of the left and right hands of a randomly selected subject are shown in Figures 3.4 a and b, respectively. The transcripts show the movement-paths and the amount of text covered (first pass) by each hand quite clearly. The solid lines indicate regression movements. The relevant latencies for regressions are marked in a different colour on the transcripts. The photographs of the transcripts are for a student who uses both fore-fingers, moving side-by-side, except at the beginning and end of lines. The student was a competent reader who had a reading rate of 160 words (168 syllables) per minute on an easy baseline text. The student is here reading a more difficult prose text silently.

The movement paths described by the left hand (Figure 3.4 a) and by the right (Figure 3.4 b) hands are typical for this subject. Like some other two-handed readers, the left and right hands move together and cover almost the whole of every line of text. Nevertheless, the right hand finishes each line of text alone, and the left hand starts on the first few letters before being joined by the right hand, suggesting a slight preference for the right hand.

The timing data that were used in various studies were calculated from the first touch to last touch. First pass scanning (cover) time for a character is the time from first touch of the first dot of a character to the frame time immediately following the last touch on the reference location for the last dot. The time for words is counted in the same way. These times represent scanning (first pass) rather than processing time. Processing time, by contrast, includes all regressions over the relevant word or any character in it. Time spent in regressions away from that word (or character) to other words, or to other parts of the text, is excluded from processing latencies. For instance, if the finger had left the target to go back to an earlier or later word, but returned to the word from the other locations, the additional time actually spent on the target word would be added to the original scanning time for the word. But time spent in transit to other portions of text, or in regression to words other than the target item, are excluded from the processing latencies.

Processing latencies are analogous to 'fixation time' in visual reading. They consist of the time spent literally in the first pass traversing of the characters and the time that the reader is spending in actually processing or attending to the item.

3 READING RATES AS MEASURES OF PROFICIENCY

There are no generally agreed criteria for computing levels of reading proficiency in braille which can be used easily to compare findings for

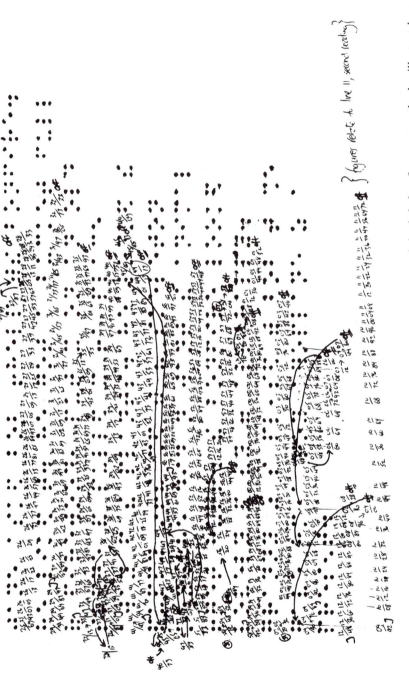

Figure 3.4a Photograph of an actual transcript of frame-times for the movements of the left forefinger over the braille text by a two-handed reader. The movement path in frame times shows that the left forefinger reads most, but not all of every line of text

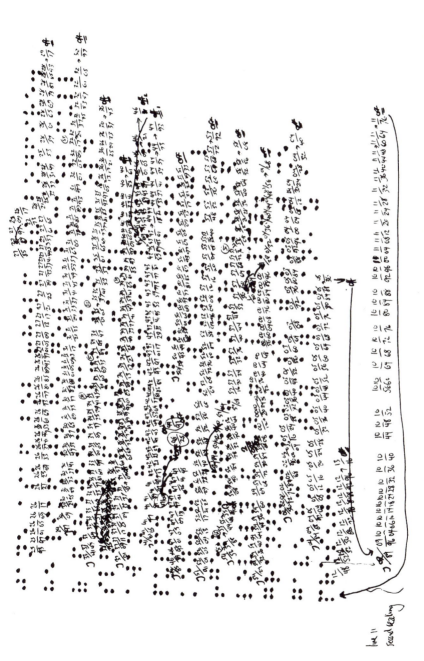

Figure 3.4b Photograph of the actual transcript of frame-times showing the simultaneous movement path over the braille text for the right forefinger. The recurring lines with additional digits indicate regressions

different populations or across different studies. For young children we have a number of useful normative tests. Some measures are based on the number of regular, uncontracted, monosyllabic words a child can read in one minute (e.g. Tooze, 1962). Others provide norms for accuracy, speed and comprehension of a series of specifically selected prose passages (e.g. Lorimer, 1977). Standardized tests have the advantage of having been tested out on representative samples of children at the relevant ages. The disadvantage is that the norms do not apply beyond the early teens or to populations outside the range of the standardization sample.

The traditional 'word per minute' (wpm) measure for adults in both print and braille is calculated in terms of the number of words a person can read in one minute. The disadvantage of wpm rates is that the texts on which they are based can differ greatly in the level of difficulty, and there is little doubt that wpm rates vary considerably with the difficulty of reading materials which are being used. The notion of text difficulty is, of course, itself a complicated issue that depends on many factors. The layout and formats of braille are fairly standard, although too much handling tends to make scripts less legible (Chapter 5). More important differences between baseline texts are levels of difficulty in contents and topics, although it may be assumed that few researchers would deem it sensible to use topics in baseline texts that are likely to be quite unfamiliar to the particular population being tested.

In principle, syllable per minute (spm) rates would be a more useful measure for comparing findings across populations and materials, if the measure were adopted universally. Syllable counts in speech output are equivalent to the monosyllabic words which are used in oral tests for younger children. The measure also does something to equate differences in text difficulty, because there is a very high and consistent correlation between the length of words and their familiarity or frequency (e.g. Zipf, 1935). Difficult (low frequency) words tend to be longer than familiar (high frequency) words, and long words have more syllables and take longer to say than short words with fewer syllables (e.g. Baddeley, 1990). One important difference between easy and difficult texts is the number of unfamiliar, infrequent, long words that the texts contain. Syllable per minute (spm) rather than word per minute (wpm) reading rates could provide a common baseline for comparison with normative tests. I shall be reporting spm measures either in conjunction with, or as an alternative to the wpm score, particularly for difficult texts. Although reading speeds in terms of the number of syllables in any text give reasonable indications of the proficiency level that has been reached, they are not absolute measures of a person's literacy in braille. This applies particularly to experienced older subjects who are capable of reading texts of all levels of difficulty, but are often deliberately cautious and careful, especially in reading aloud. Nevertheless, although neither spm nor wpm measures of speed of reading are ideal, they have advantages over accuracy as a guide to levels of proficiency. Accuracy is easy to ascertain in oral, but not in silent reading. Subsequent measures of comprehension or memory for words measure a somewhat different aspect of reading than accuracy of word recognition, and cannot be used as a baseline across different studies. Comprehension scores are also likely to vary as much, or more, with the intellectual level of readers as with their reading skill as such. The reading rates (wpm and spm) that I am reporting can be taken as a rough guide of proficiency levels of subject. Competence in terms of accuracy and comprehension were also taken into account in assigning readers to levels of proficiency in the actual studies.

It is often assumed that braille reading is limited to about 100 wpm, or at most 150 wpm. However, setting ceilings on possible achievements is misleading. Average rates of 100 or fewer words per minute which are sometimes reported in studies with relatively small populations are not necessarily comparable to those of the University students who seem to form the main subject groups for visual reading rates. Reading rates of 250 to 300 wpm are often assumed for print reading. But it is not always clear whether this is based on university students, or is representative of the general population. Carpenter and Just (1983) report the somewhat lower average rate of 225 wpm for reading *Time* magazine. There is no doubt that the average speed for braille is slower than for print reading. But some individual fluent young braillists in my studies have reached reading speeds of 190 wpm (and over 200 spm) in contracted (Grade 2) braille texts.

The rates go down sharply with difficult texts, and particularly with texts that include long unknown names. In reporting findings from my own studies, the average baseline reading speeds on control texts used in any particular study are given for the group of subjects who took part. In most of the studies, proficiency in terms of baseline reading speeds is a relevant variable. In cases where levels of comprehension do not match reading rates, I have generally adjusted the rates to take account of mistakes or misapprehensions.

4   WHICH HAND IS BEST FOR BRAILLE?

A recurring question in studies on braille has been whether the right or left hand is best for reading. It has partly been a purely practical question whether to encourage beginners to use one hand preferentially. But more often the aim has been to try to deduce underlying processes from hand advantages.

As mentioned earlier (Chapter 2) the cerebral hemispheres function asymmetrically. The right cerebral hemisphere is more specialized for spatial tasks, and the left is more specialized for verbal processes (e.g. De Renzi, 1982; Gazzaniga and Ledoux, 1978; Geschwind, 1972; Milner and Taylor, 1972; Stein, 1992). The majority of fibres from peripheral receptor organs cross over to the contralateral side before reaching the areas of the cerebral cortex which are most concerned in their analysis (Chapter 2). Left hemisphere damage mainly affects the right side of the body and impairs language processes. Right hemisphere damage mainly affects the left side of the body and impairs spatial processing.

However, the reverse inference from hand advantages to hemisphere functioning is more dicey. It only works when the task being performed is already known to involve a particular form of processing. Exploration with the left hand has been found to be superior in a variety of shape and spatial tasks in tactual conditions (e.g. Dodds, 1978; Gazzaniga and Ledoux, 1978; Kumar, 1977; Milner and Taylor, 1972). For touch as for other modalities there is thus broadly a right hemisphere / left side advantage for spatial tasks.

On the assumption that braille depends primarily on shape perception, the apparently obvious corollary is that the left hand must be better for braille. However, it could be argued as easily that the right hand should be superior, on the grounds that reading depends crucially on language skills, and the contralateral left hemisphere is more specialized for language in most people (e.g. Gazzaniga, 1988; Geschwind, 1972; Geschwind and Levitzky, 1968).

In fact, it is not sensible to assume functional representation solely from hand advantages, if only because hand advantages depend also on the type of task, and the relevant factors in task demands are not always obvious. For instance, the right (preferred) hand is better than the left for aimed movements (Roy and Elliott, 1989), although this would seem to be an obvious spatial task. The evidence on hand use in braille can certainly not be interpreted in any simple one-to-one fashion.

The hand people use for braille has little or nothing to do with their general laterality (Ittyerah, 1993). I used a number of handedness tasks with most of my subjects from the start. The tasks included picking up a pencil, peeling a roll of Sellotape, reaching for a bell, kicking a paper ball, as well as answers to questions about the hand they used for brushing their teeth, holding a spoon and cutting with a knife. Most children who were totally blind from birth were predominantly right-handed, as is the rest of the population. Nevertheless, as many of these children use their left hand for reading as those who used their right hand for reading. Most children used both hands, as they were almost invariably taught to do. However, as will become obvious later, two-handed reading does not necessarily mean that both hands are used equally.

Previous reports on hand advantages in braille vary considerably. Some studies have found better performance with the left hand by young braille readers in letter naming tasks (e.g. Hermelin and O'Connor, 1971; Rudel *et al.*, 1977). These findings have been widely used to advocate the use of the left hand by beginning readers. On the other hand, right hand superiority has been found for fluent older braillists (e.g. Fertsch, 1947), while other studies showed either no overall differences between the two hands, or minor advantages for one or other or both hands, depending on task demands (e.g. Bradshaw *et al.*, 1982; Millar, 1977 a, 1984 a).

There are a number of reasons for this variability in findings. Reading depends on several subsidiary skills, and different reading tasks make different demands on these. There is some evidence that tactual acuity for stimulus detection is better for the left hand in right handed people. But detecting that a stimulus is present is not the same as discriminating between two stimuli. Discriminating small raised dot patterns is often quite good even by beginners and by people who are unfamiliar with braille (e.g. Katz, 1925; Millar, 1977 a, b), and can be explained by findings which suggest that discrimination can be based on dot density disparities (Chapter 2) which may not be as decisively lateralized as spatial tasks. Initial dot density coding needs spatial organization of scanning movements or verbal (phonological) recoding for tasks that demand accurate recognition or recall (Chapters 2 and 4). Adequate shape or spatial coding of braille patterns should produce a right hemisphere advantage. But tasks that depend on verbal recoding should produce a left hemisphere advantage. In so far as both spatial and verbal processes are involved in braille reading, these advantages may cancel each other in some tasks. Using the left hand may also have been encouraged in early braille training in the belief that the left hand is better for this. Familiarity, types of coding, as well as task demands are, therefore, relevant considerations in interpreting findings on hand advantages in small groups of subjects.

Stimulus materials and types of task also have to be considered. If the task is to scan single letters, it is usually more efficient to use one finger. The other finger merely gets in the way. For reading lines of text, two-handed reading is usually preferable. Normal reading usually involves scanning words or continuous sentences or prose texts. The most consistent finding in that case is that using both hands is usually better than using either hand alone (e.g. Foulke, 1982; Millar, 1984 a). The reasons for this will become more obvious later (Section 5).

I tested twenty young congenitally totally or near totally blind children (one had minimal light perception), aged between six and twelve years on letter discrimination and on letter-naming tasks. They were predominantly right handed on behavioural tests and described themselves as right handed for a variety of tasks. But individuals varied in whether they preferred the right or the left hand for braille. Moreover, there was no evidence that using either the right or left hand for braille related to reading proficiency (0–98 wpm on three-letter word tests). If anything, hand advantages differed for letter discrimination and naming tasks. Better readers showed a marginal right hand advantage in naming single letters, compared with poorer readers who showed a marginal left hand advantage for discriminating letters. As a further check on the difference between letter discrimination and letter-naming tasks, I tested another eighteen visually handicapped children between the ages of six and four-teen years. They were all right-handed on behavioural tests. On the letter discrimination task, seven of the children made more (29 per cent) errors with the right hand; six made (18 per cent) more errors with the left hand. One subject only used the right hand, and one subject only used the left hand, the remainder showed no difference. The average latencies for correctly discriminated letters by the left hand were faster for fourteen children (921 ms), while the right hand was faster for four children (by 140 ms) . The left hand was therefore marginally faster for the discrimi-nation task. In the recognition task in which they named letters, four children showed more errors when they were using the left hand, and six children showed more errors when they used the right hand. Latencies for correct naming were faster with the right hand for ten children, and four children showed faster correct recognitions with the left hand. The relationship between discrimination and naming was reversed, as in the previous study.

Readers usually develop their own preferences and style. It is unlikely that such preferences are due solely to a single factor. Even braillists who consider themselves two-handed readers do not necessarily cover the same amount of text with both hands. The photographs of the transcripts shown earlier (Figures 3.4 a and b) and below (Figures 3.5 a and b), respectively, are examples of two quite different distributions of the portions of text covered by the two hands by two braillists who both thought of them-selves as two-handed readers. The student in the previous demonstration had used the right hand marginally more than the left. Another example is of two-handed reading by an intelligent adolescent who had a reading rate of 179 words (189 syllables) per minute on a baseline test. Two photographs of the actual frame-by-frame transcripts show the movement-paths in terms of frame times for the left hand (Figure 3.5 a) and for the right hand (Figure 3.5 b), respectively. This is a two-handed reader who typically reads roughly equal proportions of text with the right and left hand, respectively. The left forefinger leaves a line long before the end of that line, and moves to the next line while the right forefinger finishes the previous line. The left forefinger typically starts reading, in the sense of moving to a new letter on the next line, as soon as, or shortly after the right hand has finished the previous line. The left hand is therefore well past the middle of that line when the right hand joins the left. The propor-tion of text in which the two fingers move side by side is thus rather small, in contrast to the previous student. Both subjects (Figures 3.4 a, b and 3.5 a, b) were right handed and used both hands for reading. Nevertheless, one subject used the right hand rather more, and the other used the left hand somewhat more.

The results for ten high school students (see Section 5) who considered themselves two-handed braille readers were similar. On test they were predominantly right handed (83 per cent as a proportion of right laterality

Figure 3.5a Photograph of an actual transcript of frame-times for the left forefinger of a two-handed reader who used the hands alternately for the verbal and spatial aspects in silent reading. The solid lines above the lines of braille text were inserted on the copy as guides to transcribers

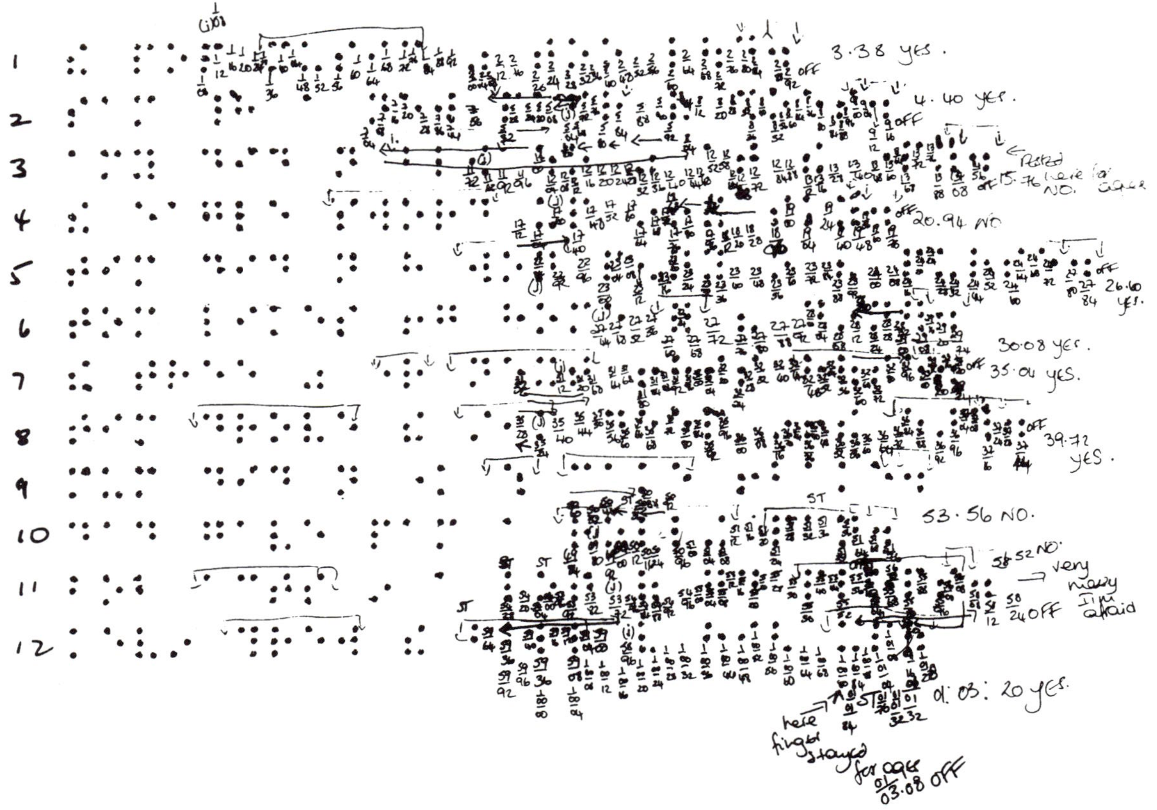

Figure 3.5b Movement path by the right forefinger

on five behavioural tasks). The movement paths described by their reading hands in frame-by-frame transcriptions were analysed separately for the right and left hands of each subject. Five subjects showed less than 5 per cent difference between the coverage of the text by the two hands. Three subjects covered a larger (mean, 32 per cent) proportion of the text by the right than by the left hand, and two subjects covered a larger (mean, 12 per cent) proportion of the text by the left than by the right hand. The difference in the proportion of text covered by the left or right hand by different subjects did not relate significantly to their reading rates, or to the degree to which they were right handed. There are also some braille readers who only use either the right or the left hand exclusively.

The evidence suggests that the notion that one hand, either the left or the right, is necessarily superior for braille is not tenable. There is no good evidence at present that there is a 'best hand' for braille reading, as such, without taking tasks and materials into account. There was no overall balance in favour of either hand for all reading tasks, and no discernible relation of this with reading proficiency, or with blindness. The subjects in the studies which I reported here were all congenitally totally or near totally (a few had minimal, non-functional light perception) blind children, and had learned braille as their only written language. Individuals nevertheless differed quite consistently in which hand they used more for braille or whether they used the two hands fairly equally.

Habits established during the early stages of learning, either because tactual discrimination is more important, or because the use of the left hand is encouraged, may be factors in the development of hand use for braille reading. There seem to be more young people at present with a preference for the left hand, in contrast, for instance, to that for right-handed reading reported earlier (e.g. Fertsch, 1947). In the study of ten young students who all used both hands for reading texts, the average proportion of text covered was 80 per cent for the left hand and 54 per cent by the right hand.

Braille reading depends on a number of subsidiary skills. It is not possible to make direct inferences about the information that is being processed simply from knowing which hand is being used. Further studies of the development of hand use in braille would be of interest, especially with designs that systematically vary stimulus, task and contextual factors at different levels of braille reading.

Evidence on the functions of the hands from detailed analyses of the time relations in scanning is considered next.

5 VERBAL AND SPATIAL FUNCTIONS OF THE TWO HANDS IN FLUENT READING

It has long been observed that fluent braille readers typically show smooth, rhythmic, flowing lateral movements in prose reading (Burklen, 1932;

Grunewald, 1966; Kusajima, 1970). There has been considerable specula-
tion about the functions of the two hands when both are used, and how
these may relate to fluent reading. The hypotheses have varied widely.

The first hypothesis under test here was that the two hands in continuous
fluent reading actually read two different portions of text simultaneously
(Burklen, 1932), and that such parallel processing provides the main difference in speed between fluent and slow readers. The other main hypothesis
was that although the two hands move together, they function differently.
One hand, usually the right, is concerned with gaining a preview of the
meaning or 'gist' by a rapid survey of subsequent sentences in advance
of the left hand, while the left hand follows behind and is concerned with
checking specific features of braille letters or words (Kusajima, 1970).

The hypotheses have important implications both theoretically and for
training two-handed skills, and were therefore tested explicitly. I examined
simultaneous finger positions by fluent braillists during normal prose
reading (Millar, 1987 a). Ten students from a high school for visually
handicapped young people took part. Subjects were selected from twenty
students whom their teachers regarded as fluent braillists, because they
were two-handed readers using both forefingers and were fastest on test.
Their speeds on relatively difficult texts, including passages from Jane
Austen, as mentioned earlier, averaged 111 wpm (142 spm). Braille had
been their only reading medium from the start, and they depended on it
for their academic work, including university entrance examinations.

To test the hypotheses, it is necessary to use a strict criterion of what
types of movements can be assumed to count as reading. I assumed that
to read means to take in information. A minimal requirement to count
as reading, therefore, was that the reading finger should be touching at
least one new letter of text; that is to say, it should touch at least one
letter that had not been touched before.

Touching at least one new letter simultaneously with both hands is a
minimal requirement for being able to infer reading from touch by both
hands. Not all touching can be counted as 'reading' in the sense of taking
in new information. For instance, simultaneously touching a letter and
blank margins, or scanning new text with one hand while repeatedly going
over a previously scanned letter or word cannot not count as simultaneous
reading of two texts. At the same time, the criterion that just one new
letter of different texts has to be touched by the two hands to count as
simultaneously reading, sets a criterion so as to favour the parallel
processing hypothesis.

The hypothesis that the two hands read two different portions of text
simultaneously implies that the two hands simultaneously take in verbal
information from different portions of text. In principle, the parallel
processing hypothesis therefore implies more than simply recognizing
letters. Simultaneous recognition of two new letters is thus a minimal
(lenient) requirement. It predicts that two fingers in two-handed reading

very frequently touch two different new letters in different portions of text at the same time. Two measures of simultaneous reading were used. One was to calculate the frequency with which the two reading fingers touch two letters simultaneously, compared with touching a letter and touching a blank between words or letters. The parallel processing hypothesis predicts that simultaneous touching of two new letters occurs more frequently than simultaneous touching of a letter and a blank between words or letters. Sequential processing would be more consistent with the reverse picture. The second, perhaps more powerful, method was to compare the actual frame times for the locations of the right and left reading fingers during the transitions from one line to the next. The hypothesis that the two hands read different texts at the same time must predict that the reading finger of one hand is still reading new text on one line, at the same time that the finger of the other hand is processing new text on the next line. On the criterion of reading used in the study, the right hand should touch a new letter on the previous line at the same time that the left hand has moved to at least one new (not yet touched) letter on the new line (Millar, 1987 a).

The latency relations for the two hands were quite clear. The first type of analysis showed that when one finger touched a new letter, the other was significantly less likely to touch a new letter at the same time than to rest on a gap between words or between letters. This is contrary to the prediction from the parallel processing hypothesis. The findings showed that when the fingers moved together on the same line they moved to two letters sequentially rather than simultaneously. Thus the least likely combination was that the two fingers touched letters simultaneously. Each of the three other possibilities – touching a space between letters, or between words, or two spaces – was significantly more probable. The findings suggested that the fingers processed letters in words sequentially rather than simultaneously.

More convincing still was the evidence on the time course in transitions from one line to the next. Typically, the right index finger left the last letter of the previous line before the left index finger moved to a new letter on the next line. The time during which the left forefinger moved over new text on the next line coincided with the transit of the right hand from the end of the last line to join the left hand on the new line.

The findings were only made possible by using frame-by-frame analyses of the time course of finger movements in hundredths of a second. To normal observation, either from above or on the monitor, the left forefinger seemed to be scanning the next line while the right forefinger was still reading the end of the previous line. But that was an illusion. The illusion was dispelled by viewing the movements in slow motion. More important, the hypothesis was contradicted by frame-by-frame analysis of cumulative (1/100 s) frame times. Frame times were transcribed (see Sections 1 and 2) separately for the left and right hands for the eleven line changes in the twelve lines of text, for each of the ten subjects. The actual frame times showed that the right forefinger touched the last letter of the previous line (significantly) over a second earlier than the left forefinger touched a new letter on the next line of test. The right forefinger also came off the last line of text significantly ($p < 0.01$) earlier (by 204 ms) than the left forefinger touched a new letter on the next line. Thus the left hand started reading the new line after the right hand has stopped reading the previous line. The left hand went on reading the new line alone until the right hand joined it on the new line, on average about 440 ms ($p < 0.05$) after the left hand had started reading the new line. All ten readers employed the two hands alternately. Although individuals differed in how much of the text was covered by either hand, on average each hand covered nearly half of each line independently, with a minimum of overlap when one hand took over from the other. Typically, after the right hand joined the left hand on a line, the two hands move together for a short time. The right hand then takes over and reads to the end of the line, while the left hand moves to the start of the next line. That movement by the left hand was frequently in a diagonally downwards direction. As soon as it touched text on the next line the finger moved sharply further leftwards beyond the first letter to the blank margin and then back to the first letter of the new line. The finger then remained stationary on the first letter, sometimes with small circular motions over it, until the right forefinger moved beyond the last letter of the previous line. At that point, the left hand started to move to a new letter on the next line. The left hand did not start to read the new line until the right hand had finished reading the previous line.

   It is worth looking at the exact time course of the left and right index fingers of a fluent reader whose reading rate was 188 wpm on difficult materials. Few braille readers achieve higher wpm reading rates than that. The graphs show the line changes from the end of the first line to the second line (Figure 3.6 a), from line 3 to 4 (Figure 3.6 b) and from line 8 to line 9 (Figure 3.6 c). The cumulative frame times from the start of the passage are shown in ascending order on the Y axes. The locations for each finger for the last letter touched and for touching the new letter are indicated on the X axes. The connecting lines in each case indicate the type of movement (stationary or regressive, in transit above the text, or reading new letters). During the change from line 1 to line 2 (Figure 3.6 a), the left hand of the subject joins line 2 (975 ms) after the right hand has stopped reading the last letter of line 1, and (118 ms) after joining line 2. During that time the right hand first moves to the blank margin beyond line 1, and is then in transit to join the left hand on line 2. The time courses for the line change between lines 3 and 4 (Figure 3.6 b) are similar. Interestingly enough, the later transits between line 8 and line 9, further into the text, are much shallower, showing that reading has speeded up. But the relations between the movements of the two

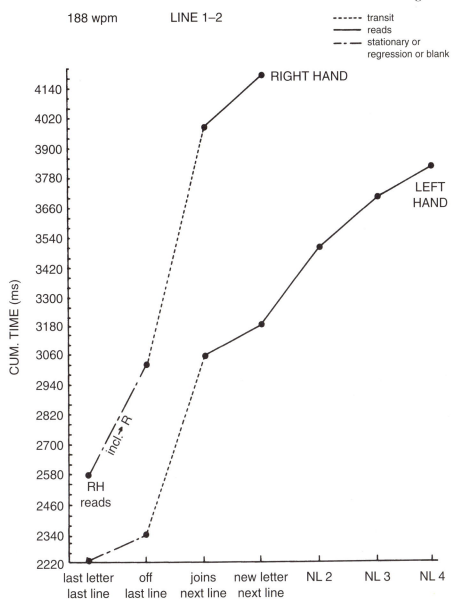

Figure 3.6a Cumulative frame-times (Y-axis) for the right and left forefingers of a competent reader's hands during the transit by the left hand from line 1 to the start of line 2 in silent reading of a continuous text. The solid lines show reading (moving to at least one new letter). The broken lines indicate transit movements above the text. The longer broken lines show that the finger is stationary or makes repetitive small local movements on the spot. The subscripts NL (new letter) on the X-axis show movements to successive new letters

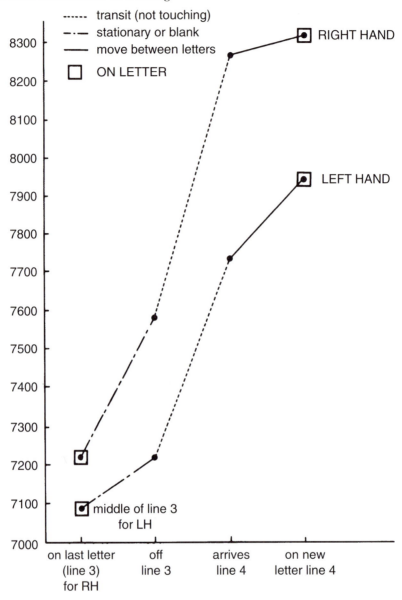

Figure 3.6b Simultaneous movement paths by the forefingers in frame-times for the transition from line 3 to line 4

hands remain similar. The left hand leaves line 8 (450 ms) before the right hand touches the last letter of the line, and reads a new letter on line 9 during the time that the right hand is in transit (480 ms) to join line 9. The right hand starts on a new letter on line 9 (440 ms) well after the

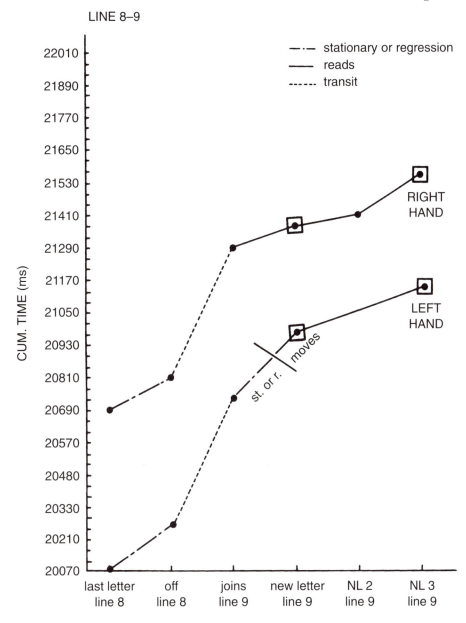

Figure 3.6c Simultaneous movement paths in frame-times for the transition from line 8 to line 9

left hand has read more than three new letters on line 9. As the graphed times show, the two fingers quite often moved at the same time, but they never moved over new letters of text on two lines at the same time.

The example of the time-relations shown here is typical of the time-relations shown by every subject in every single line change for the eleven transitions between the twelve lines of text. One exception was found for one out of eleven transitions by one of the slower of the ten readers. In that transition, the left forefinger moved to a new letter before (by less than one second) the right forefinger had left the final letter of the preceding line. On the strict criterion of reading adopted here, this was counted as 'reading', although it referred to only one new letter. As we shall see later (Chapter 5), the last letter of a word on a line of text is sometimes scanned more quickly, suggesting that it has been predicted. Even this single transition is therefore unlikely to be an exception to the general picture for competent two-handed readers, namely that they use the two hands independently and interchangeably for reading and the spatial (finding and moving to the next line) aspects of the task.

The findings are not consistent with the hypothesis that fast readers use the two hands to process different portions of verbal information in parallel. The two hands certainly moved over separate locations in parallel. But they were processing information from different domains in parallel; not from the same (i.e. verbal) domain. Further, the hypothesis that the two hands are engaged in different verbal tasks – one concerned with advance information about gist and the other in lexical checking – was also disconfirmed. When the right hand read the last section of one line, the left hand was engaged in finding the start of the next line; when the left hand was reading new text, the right hand moved to join it. The division of labour was thus between verbal and spatial domains, rather than between different aspects in the same, verbal, domain. That is the situation in normal fluent reading. The functions of the two hands in regressions or when difficulties occur will be considered presently.

In fluent reading, the advantage of two-handed reading thus seems to lie in the division of labour between the hands for verbal and spatial processing domains (Millar, 1987 a). Either hand can function in pro-cessing verbal or spatial information, as and when such functioning saves time or is physically more convenient. It seems to be the division of labour which is achieved by alternating hand use between the spatial and verbal information domains that makes reading faster. The findings reported by Davidson *et al.*, (1992) in cell-by-cell analyses of two-handed reading show similarly that the advantage of using two hands arises from simultaneously executing different functions.

I want to emphasize that, observed from above, or on the monitor in real time, the finger movements look as if they were simultaneously reading quite different portions of text. It was only the actual time differ-ence in hundredths of a second that ruled out the hypothesis that the two hands read two different sections of text simultaneously, or that one hand read the text ahead while the other was simultaneously checking previous lexical details. The video-recording device described earlier (Section 1) was ideal for obtaining these data. Because touching a dot produces a light round patch on the ball of the finger the monitor shows quite clearly which specific dot in a letter is being touched in a given frame, and at what time finger touches a gap between letters or between word patterns. It is also clearly visible at what point in time the finger leaves a line and is in transit to the next line.

Similarly, it has sometimes been suggested that the reading fingers of braillists are always in contact with the text (e.g. Bertelson *et al.*, 1985). However, that this was not the case for most of the fluent readers tested here was obvious from the recording and displaying of movements from below transparent surfaces. The monitor shows clearly that when the right hand of most fluent readers was in transit from the end of one line to join the left hand on the next line, it was above the text and not in contact with any portion of it until just before joining the left hand on the next line. Some competent but slow readers do stay in constant contact with the text when moving back to the start of the next line. But fluent readers move quickly above the text in transit to the next line before homing in on the start of the new line.

Regressive movements have to be considered separately because in fluent reading they occur mainly for uncommon words. Regressions which indicate checking processes will be considered specifically later (Chapter 5). They are relevant here only because there are some instances in which the timing of regressive movements of the hands overlaps. By definition, regressions over a letter, word or other portion of text necessarily repeat an earlier touch, and do not represent moves to at least one new character. Regressions therefore do not conform to the minimal criterion by which scanning can be interpreted as reading, in the sense of taking in new verbal information. On occasion, even during fluent reading, one finger, usually of the less 'dominant' hand, moves repetitively over a particular letter or word while the other hand is reading a new portion of text. Two-handed checking of different letters in a single word also occurs in regressions when the subsequent text shows the reader that the previous word had been misconstrued, and either one or both hands return to that word from subsequent text. It occurred, for instance, in reading sentences with ambiguous homophone words which will be discussed later (Chapter 4). But such checking differs from reading in the sense of taking in new verbal information. For instance, when the less dominant finger repeatedly touches a letter, apparently in order to check it out graphemically, the finger reading new text is likely to pause during that time.

I recently found an example of a regression which looked like two-handed reading of different portions of text. This occurred in the script of a highly competent braillist when reading one of fourteen sentences which appeared on different lines of text. The normal reading style of this subject was to read the left hand portion of any line with the left hand and the right hand portion with the right hand. But on that occasion, the left hand, after having moved to the start of the new line, regressed to a contraction (ER) in a word on the previous line (ST/ER/IING) that had been read by the right hand, while the right hand scanned a new word (silvER) that contained the same contraction. This clearly was an example of checking a character due to the advance information from the right hand, rather than reading in the sense of taking in new information. On returning to the new line, the left hand went back to the start of the new sentence and proceeded to read while the right hand moved to the new line, as usual.

In the type of two-handed reading that was just discussed, the right hand mainly reads the right hand portions of lines and the left hand mainly reads the left hand portions of a line. There is relatively little time when the two index fingers move side by side on a single line before the left hand moves to the next line. Even during the time that the two forefingers move together, they rarely touch different letters at the same time. When the midpoint of one forefinger is touching a letter, the other is most frequently either on a blank between words or between letters. Deliberate simultaneous touching by the two forefingers of two different characters, as in the previous example, occurs principally as a means of comparison or matching when the reader is in some doubt. I have not seen it on tape during continuous reading by fast competent braillists.

The two-handed reading style that was mainly shown by the fluent readers described in this section is by no means the only style of reading adopted even by fluent readers. As was noted earlier, even those fluent readers who use the two hands alternately for reading do not necessarily use the two hands to read equal proportions of the text.

Much less frequently used by fast readers is reading with one hand alone with little or no assistance from the other hand. But it does occur. Some fluent readers use only the right hand or only the left hand for reading the whole text. The 'free' hand is then often used solely for place-keeping. In left-handed reading, the right hand is free but takes over from the left hand at the end of the line and moves one line down while the left hand is in transit to the next line. In right-handed reading, the left typically stays on the first letter of a line, and moves down to the first letter of the next line during the time that the left hand is reading, and remains stationary until the right hand takes over on the next line. In this style of reading, the tasks of reading and place-keeping and place-finding are divided between the two hands. One hand is solely concerned with language processing, and the other is only used for place-keeping. The reading hand in this style of reading typically comes off the text and moves above it during transit.

Purely one-handed reading occurs also. In this style of reading one hand performs both the language processing and the place-keeping and place-finding tasks. Two main strategies seem to be adopted. The reading finger finds the first line, moves along it, and then either goes back to the start of the line and then moves down to the next line, or moves down to the next line and moves back on that line to the beginning before starting to read. In both cases, the finger remains in contact with the text during the backward movement in transit to the next line. This style of reading tends to be associated with slower reading rates, even if the readers are competent in the sense of understanding complex texts. But the association is not invariable. One fast two-handed reader was noted to use the right hand in a fast backward motion, but in contact with the text of the new line until meeting up with the left hand, and then continuing with left-to-right reading. The braillist said that the backward movement was used as a guiding motion and specifically denied ever using the backward scan for recognizing letters or words.

Attention to the spatial layout and fast intake of spatial information is clearly one factor in fast reading and in movements above rather than in contact with the text during transitions. Almost all fluent readers make sure that they have a good idea of the layout of the text, by fast exploring movements over the top and sides of the text before they start to read. They can be seen to move their hands rapidly over the top, bottom and edges of the text, thus scanning the physical layout, even when they are asked to wait for a signal to start reading. Moreover, these readers usually have little difficulty in regressing to the correct region of text when that becomes necessary. It is clear that most fluent readers have developed a very good idea of the spatial layout of the braille text. The initial scanning of the layout of texts is rarely if ever seen in slow or young beginning readers. But it does seem to be associated with using the two hands as spatial anchors for each other.

One of the most intriguing reading styles which is characteristic of many 'middle rank' readers is to read all lines of text with the two forefingers side by side. It is this style of reading which has mainly given rise to the notion that, used together, the two forefingers 'enlarge the perceptual window' by touch. This does happen occasionally in competent two-handed reading in which both hands are used for reading, as shown by the fact that either hand can read some letters or words alone, and occurs principally when difficult words produce regressive movements (Chapter 5).

Two-handed reading in which the forefingers move side-by-side throughout the text is relatively rare for fast readers. But fluent reading also differs in the type of perceptual information that is picked up in different reading tasks. Evidence on this is presented next, before considering the implications of two-handed reading styles for beginning and slower readers (Section 7).

6 IS THERE A 'PERCEPTUAL UNIT' IN BRAILLE READING? EFFECTS OF VERBAL TASKS ON PERCEPTION

The preceding section shows that fluent reading is mediated by the flexible and economic use of finger movements for processing the necessary spatial information as well as for decoding the verbal information that is the object in reading texts for meaning. Data on finger movements are also relevant to questions about the 'perceptual unit' in reading braille. The main difference between theories of braille lies in their assumption about the physical features that are sampled in fluent braille. The hypotheses which are examined here concern the actual perception of the tactual input during reading. Evidence on this point is also important for the related question to what extent cognitive factors influence the pick-up of tactual information. The studies investigated alternative predictions about finger movements in the pick up of tactual information with experience and in different tasks.

The letter-by-letter theory of reading which assumes that the unit of reading is the global letter shape has been examined extensively in Chapter 2, where it was shown that braille patterns are initially coded in terms of dot density or what may be called 'texture' features. However, the findings related mainly to perception by inexperienced subjects. They leave open the question how braille patterns are coded by experienced readers. The findings on hand-movements that were considered in the preceding sections showed that with growing experience hand-movements are used for spatial reference, both in keeping to lines of text, finding the start of new lines and in obtaining spatial information about the general layout of the text. In principle, therefore, reference cues from finger move-ments should also facilitate spatial coding of individual letters as global shapes. The hypothesis that letter shapes are the units of reading in braille, at least after the initial period of learning, and form the unit of reading with greater fluency, was thus perfectly feasible, in principle. The hypoth-esis that fast reading depends on sequential but fast detection of global letter shapes thus had to be considered further.

The most interesting alternative view, proposed by Grunewald (1966), that fast readers identify 'temporally extended dynamic patterns', suggests that timing and rhythm are important cues. The view had considerable prima facie plausibility from the many observations of smooth lateral scanning movements by fast braillists. But it had never been considered very seriously or tested. It was not actually obvious initially precisely what perceptual features could be involved, or how such dynamic processing could be demonstrated experimentally, if it did indeed underlie fluent reading.

The methods that I finally adopted were suggested by the findings that dot-density cues are relatively easy to discriminate (Chapter 2). It seemed possible, therefore, that the physical features underlying the 'extended dynamic patterns' perceived by fluent braillists were dot-gap density patterns sampled in fast lateral scanning. Scanning lines of braille text from left to right with the reading finger held in a more or less upright orien-tation means that the characters produce a lateral shear pattern across the ball of the reading finger. Lateral dot-density shear patterns would thus instantiate what Grunewald called 'temporally extended dynamic' patterns.

To test the alternative hypotheses I compared a condition which disrupts the perception of lateral shear patterns with one that does not. The effects should differ if perception in reading for meaning is based on lateral shear patterns, but should not affect reading differently if readers code the inputs by the global shape of letters. The studies have been published (Millar, 1987 b). But since the evidence has important consequences for models of braille and in practical teaching, the methods which showed the effect will be described in some detail. In all conditions the texts were rotated by 90 degrees so that the lines of text ran from near to far, instead of left to right. Such rotation was expected to produce lower (wpm) reading rates than for normally oriented texts, as it does in visual reading.

The absolute orientation of the texts was, therefore, unfamiliar in all conditions. But the condition of interest was the orientation of the reading finger. In one condition the reading finger was held in the usual familiar, vertical orientation. In the other condition, the hand and reading finger were inverted laterally. The point was that the vertical finger orientation retains the familiar finger-to-body orientation and normal posture, but disrupts the lateral dot-density shear patterns on the reading finger in scanning the rotated texts orthogonally. By contrast, holding the finger horizontally is physically awkward in posture and disrupts the familiar finger-to-body-orientation. But it retains the lateral scan and the lateral orientation of the finger to the script, so that near-to-far scanning produces the normal shear pattern on the ball of the finger. Two further conditions dissociated the hypotheses. One depended on using two different tasks; the other related to proficiency levels. The shape hypothesis predicts faster speeds with increased fluency, but effects of finger position should not differ with proficiency, or with the type of reading task. The lateral shear pattern hypothesis, by contrast, predicts that performance by fluent readers is significantly worse when the finger is oriented vertically rather than laterally with respect to the text, and specifically more so in reading prose for comprehension. It also suggests that this will occur more with greater reading proficiency. I used reading for comprehension as one of the tasks, and a quasi-proof-reading task which required searching the same prose texts for specific letters. The texts were, of course, counter-balanced over subjects and conditions.

The results supported the Grunewald (1966) hypothesis that fluent readers depend on dynamic lateral (dot-gap density) scanning rather than on letter shapes in reading texts for meaning. Findings for the letter-search tasks, by contrast, were consistent with the letter-shape hypothesis. As expected for rotations, all wpm scores were lower than in normal reading (Figure 3.7). The important finding was that vertical (orthogonal to the text) finger orientations produced significantly lower ($p < 0.001$) reading rates than orienting the finger laterally to the text. Moreover, the results also showed that this was the case only for competent readers, and not for beginners ($p < 0.01$), and also occurred significantly more ($p < 0.05$)

Finger orientation   p < 0.001
Group × orientation   p < 0.01
Task × orientation   p < 0.05

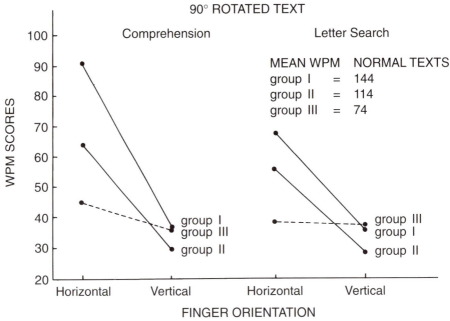

Figure 3.7 Mean wpm rates in reading for comprehension and letter search, respectively in lateral scan (finger inclined horizontally) and vertical (finger positioned normally) relative to the rotated text, conditions. The mean baseline wpm rates for the three proficiency groups are shown in the top right hand corner

in reading for comprehension than in letter-search tasks. Beginning readers showed no significant differences between tasks or finger orientations. There was also a considerably greater loss of comprehension on subsequent tests for the prose-reading task under vertical than with lateral finger orientations. But finger orientation had no significant effect on letter search.

Observations of the finger movements were, if anything, even more interesting. With vertical finger orientations, scanning by some of the best readers veered from lines of text on occasion. This occurs rarely if ever, in normal fluent reading. It was not shown in lateral scanning conditions, despite the more awkward posture, suggesting that finger orientation relative to the text rather than finger orientation relative to the body posture provided the spatial reference frame.

There was clearly no support for the hypothesis that the unit in braille reading is the letter shape at all levels of reading and for all reading tasks. Letter shapes are coded, however, when task conditions demand this. Circular motions over letter shapes were observed even by fluent readers in letter search tasks. They also occurred with the vertical finger orientation. These observations further supported the statistical findings. They were also consistent with the earlier findings which showed that flexibility in using different component reading skills and strategies is a major characteristic of reading fluency.

Although the results were very clear, it was of interest to test the hypotheses also by a convergent method that did not use rotated texts. Texts were used in which a single dot was depressed in very few (eight) randomly dispersed letters throughout a script, so that their presence could not be predicted. The degraded dots would still be felt by circular or up/down finger movements over the shape of the letter in which they occurred. They should therefore not disrupt reading rates which depend on coding letter-shapes. But the dots were sufficiently degraded to disrupt lateral scanning if subjects used a strategy of lateral scanning of expected extended dot-gap density patterns. The hypothesis that reading for meaning depends on shear patterns in lateral scanning, therefore, predicts that degraded dots would have larger detrimental effects in reading for comprehension than in letter search for fluent readers. The results from this very different method supported the previous findings. The reading rates of fluent readers were significantly worse in degraded conditions ($p < 0.01$), and significantly more so in reading for comprehension than in letter search ($p < 0.05$). Slow readers showed no significant differences between tasks or text conditions (Figure 3.8).

The findings from the two experiments are rather strong evidence that the physical tactual features which form the perceptual basis of reading change with reading proficiency. They also show that the tactual features which are perceived differ with the type of reading task. These results have several implications for models of braille reading, which are briefly considered first. They also raise important practical questions which will be examined in greater detail later (Chapter 8).

Perhaps the first thing that needs to be said is that the findings cast considerable doubt on the concept of an immutable 'unit' of reading, at least for braille. There is evidently not only a change in the perceptual information that people gain with experience, but the perceptual features on which reading is based also differ with the task. It seems unlikely that these changes can be described solely in terms of greater automation of a single form of perceptual information. Fluent readers use lateral dot-density (shear) scanning patterns in reading for comprehension, but code letter shapes in tasks that demand attention to single letters. It does not seem to be the case that there is only one single perceptual form which determines the perceptual unit of braille reading.

An important theoretical implication of the findings of the last two studies concerns the relation between perceptual processing of the physical tactual stimulation and the demands of the tasks. The findings show that differences in such 'high level' task demands, as reading for meaning

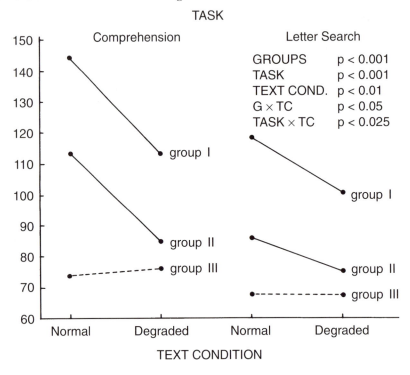

Figure 3.8 Mean wpm rates for the same three groups in reading for comprehension and letter search tasks with normal texts and randomly degraded dots (see text)

versus letter search, produced clear differences in the 'low level' perceptual pick-up of information. This implies clear 'top-down' effects on perceptual processing, at whatever level of awareness or decision that takes place.

An interesting further point is that the disruption of the shear patterns which was produced by the relative orientation of the finger to the text not only reduced reading speeds, but also led to a considerable loss of comprehension. The result had been predicted by the hypothesis that competent braillists implicitly expect lateral shear patterns in reading for meaning, and fail to make the relevant connection when the perceptual pick-up fails to fit the expected word. The result suggests that, in normal conditions, there is a continual interaction between the perceptual, linguistic and cognitive skills that are involved in reading.

Similarly, the finding that a few randomly dispersed degraded dots disrupted reading for comprehension by competent readers suggests that the perceptual intake depended also on cognitively primed contributions, possibly expectations from prior semantic or word contexts. I shall return to that question later (Chapter 5).

The evidence that lateral dot-density shear patterns mediate fluent reading for meaning raises the further question whether these patterns could also constitute what, in the print literature, are sometimes called 'transgraphemic features' (e.g. Henderson, 1982). These are letter clusters that are processed together to access meaning. The question will be considered further in the next two chapters. But the possibility also needs to be checked out further.

The major developmental factor in the pick-up of perceptual information with increased competence is thus not merely an increase in speed. The evidence suggests that there is also a greater differentiation between the forms of scanning and information pick-up, and a greater flexibility in using them. Possible ways in which this may be speeded up during acquisition, and the practical implications for teaching of findings showing that there is more than one means of coding braille patterns, will be considered in Chapter 8.

The answer about the 'perceptual unit' in braille reading seems to be that there is no single unit, independent of the task to be performed. The perceptual features that are picked up in braille depend crucially on the proficiency of readers, and the ease with which they adapt their perceptual pick-up to the demands of the reading task.

The detailed observations as well as the main experimental findings can only be explained by assuming that there is considerable 'cross-talk' between cognitive and perceptual processes. The fact that the type of task determines what perceptual information is processed is not consistent with strictly sequential hierarchical processing models in either direction.

7 READING STYLES AND FINGER MOVEMENTS BY SLOWER AND BEGINNING READERS

Most of the fluent two-handed readers in my population samples used the reading style discussed earlier (Section 5) in which scanning is divided between the two hands, alternating between verbal and spatial functions. The proportion of text covered by each hand differed between individuals even in that population. But two-handed reading in which the two forefingers move together adjacently over most of the text occurred more frequently in slower reading. The function of the two forefingers in these cases cannot be gauged by observing the movements from above, or necessarily even by counting contact frequencies. Video-recording the fingers and text from below shows that in a surprising number of cases when both hands are in contact with the text for most of the time, only one hand actually 'reads' while the other only performs guiding functions.

There are a number of criteria by which, singly and in combination, reading functions can be construed from video-recordings of movements seen from below transparent surfaces with simultaneous timing. One is the relative brightness of the reading patch (Section 1) on the pad of the fingers that are touching braille. The contrast in brightness of the reading patch relative to the surrounding skin is typically greater for beginning and slower readers, because they tend to exert more pressure with the reading finger. Contrast differences in brightness between two adjacent fingers that are apparently reading side by side are often striking. Another indication is the posture of each hand, and in relation to each other. The orientations of the adjacent fingers relative to the text are further indications of their functions. In conjunction, such clues make it quite clear whether both fingers, or only one of them is actually concerned with decoding the verbal information. Additional criteria come from the amounts of text over which the pad of the finger passes. One is whether the finger is ever used alone for a new letter or word, without re-scanning by the dominant hand. Another is to test whether the second hand is ever recruited to re-scan letters during regressions, or remains stationary on a character until the leading hand has completed the regression.

Detailed analyses using these criteria showed that in many instances of apparently two-handed reading in which the adjacent forefingers covered most of the text together, one hand was actually reading, while the other hand was mainly or solely used for guiding and place-keeping.

Three examples of two-handed reading with adjacent forefingers are particularly instructive, because all three readers actually only used the left hand for reading. Two of these occurred at the two ends of the age scale. One was a very competent, very experienced although relatively slow older braillist who used both forefingers side by side for reading. In fact, only the left hand scanned all of the text, including beginning words, while the right hand never scanned any letter alone. It was further confirmed by the typical brightness difference between the reading patches on the pads of the left and right forefingers, and frequently also by the posture of the right hand which made it impossible for the forefinger to be used for reading during much of the apparently two-handed reading. This braillist was actually fully aware of only using the left hand for reading, and volunteered the information that the right hand was merely used for guidance along the lines of text, and for keeping the place while the left hand moved to the next line of text (Figure 3.3).

The other example was a very intelligent six-year-old who had been totally blind since the age of three years. Her reading rates were well above the norms for her age. Polly (not her real name) used the index finger of the left hand to scan the text laterally for the whole of every line of text, as shown by the brighter patch of the ball of the left fore-finger. The right hand was closed almost to a fist, with the forefinger and thumb tightly pressed together so that they formed a downward pointing ridge which she ran along the line of text just in front of the left fore-finger. Neither the pad of the right forefinger nor that of the right thumb ever touched the dots. The guiding was done by the fingernails of the forefinger and thumb which formed an extremely useful ridge along the line of letters in front of the left forefinger.

The particular method that this very bright little girl used was unique, as far as I know. I have never seen it before or since. It was clearly invented by herself. However, styles of reading which look like two-handed reading from above, but which actually use only one hand for reading, while the other performs a spatial guiding function, are quite common. The strategy is useful, because the tendency for the reading finger to stray from the line in moving across the text from left to right is a serious difficulty for beginning young readers. Using one hand as a guide prevents that.

When Polly later took part in a new experiment at the age of nine years and seven months, she had a reading rate of 88 wpm (102 spm) on quite difficult texts. Viewed from above, her reading was still apparently two-handed, but her two forefingers now diverged in movements most of the time. Watching her hands on the monitor showed that it was still only the left forefinger that was actually engaged in reading. The left finger scanned the whole of every line of text, showing the white reading patch on the fingerpad above the darkened braille dots along all lines of text. The right forefinger was used entirely for guidance as before, but now also had place-keeping functions. The right finger typically stayed stationary on or beyond the last letter of a line when the left hand was in transit to the next line, and moved down to find the end of the next line as soon as the left hand had reached the beginning of the next line. The right forefinger stayed at this point until the left hand reached that letter. Whenever the right forefinger scanned a letter, the letter was always re-scanned by the left forefinger. The reverse never occurred. The strategy was very successful, both for keeping to the line of text, and for keeping the place while the reading hand was in transit to the next line. Polly also occasionally still used the forefinger and thumb of the right hand pressed together to form a guiding ridge. This occurred particularly when trying to gauge the (lower) location of a character, especially a full stop. It also sometimes occurred during regressions when the left finger encountered an uncommon or unfamiliar word and repeatedly re-scanned the word, or regressed back to other words, before reading on. But the two hands no longer moved together all the time. Polly had clearly mastered not only keeping to the line at which she was good even at the age of six years, but also now used the guiding hand as an anchor or reference location when the other hand moved to a new line. Such place-keeping for spatial reference is another essential skill for reading continuous braille texts.

The third example of apparently two-handed reading with adjacent fore-fingers on every line of text also showed purely left-handed reading and only guiding functions for the right forefinger. The example also illustrated the fact that keeping to the line of text, and keeping the place while the reading hand is in transit to the next line, are two separate spatial tasks. Braille readers have to master both. The girl, whom I shall call Jill (not her real name), was a congenitally totally blind child, aged eleven and a half years at the time of testing. She achieved reading rates of 119 wpm (148 spm) on a text which included difficult names. However, that rate excluded portions of text when she lost the place at the end of a line by lifting off one hand when the other hand was in transition to the next line. These errors occurred occasionally. Her reading rate reached 164 wpm (198 spm) when difficult names were excluded from the count and she had not lost her way. Jill, like Polly, was a left-handed reader although she used both hands. The monitor showed that it was only her left forefinger which showed the brighter patch above the braille dots as the finger moved across the text. The right forefinger generally presented a more uniform, somewhat darker silhouette, and rested very slightly on the edge of the left forefinger, moving slightly above and in advance of the left forefinger, but in contact with it during almost all scanning of the text. The exceptions occurred when the left hand regressed to an earlier portion of the text. At these times the right forefinger rested on the last letter that had been touched by the left hand before regressing, and remained stationary (as shown by the white reading patch) on that letter during the total regression time until the left returned to it. The example again shows two-handed reading in which only the left hand was actually engaged in the verbal aspects of reading while the right hand was only used for place-keeping. However, the place-keeping function of the right hand was confined to single lines. In this case, the separation of the verbal and spatial functions of the two hands had not yet been fully established. Jill lost her place, because she tended to take both forefingers off the text simultaneously at the end of lines. She thus failed to keep the place of the earlier line during transit to the next line of text.

Jill had a strategy for transitions which served her quite well on most occasions, but which was liable to error. What she did to get to the next line was as follows: She lifted both fingers off at the end of a line, moved both hands back in a relatively straight course above (not in contact with) the line of text, and touched down with both forefingers near the beginning of the same line. She then scanned the next word, evidently to see whether she had read it before, before moving down to the next line. Both the direction and distance of her backward movements were usually quite well judged, and the word she scanned before moving down to the next line of text was normally sufficient to tell her whether or not she had read that line before. The strategy thus worked well a lot of the time, but it explained why such a reasonably good reader was not faster and occasionally lost her way in the text. Such use of semantic strategies will be discussed further in a later chapter.

Polly and Jill were part of a new study which was mainly designed to compare braille readers who had learned braille from the start with younger and older braille readers who had previously read print. The data were based on direct scoring of scanning movements in reading normal sentences or texts for meaning, rather than by using experimentally manipulated texts and conditions, unlike the studies reported in the previous section. Fifteen young high school students, including Polly and Jill, were tested. None had taken part in the earlier study. Five had learned braille for between one and seven years after previously reading print. They ranged in age from twelve to nineteen years. The other ten subjects had learnt braille from the start and were considered competent braille readers by their school. Apart from Polly and an eleven-year-old, they ranged in age from nearly twelve to nearly twenty years, thus spanning roughly the same age range as the five newly blind youngsters. All ten subjects who had learned braille from the start used both hands for scanning; three, including Jill, used adjacent forefingers for most of the text. The others used divergent hand-movements. By the criteria mentioned earlier, four subjects, including Jill and Polly, actually mainly or only used the left hand for reading and the right hand for guidance, while two subjects only or mainly used the right hand for reading and the left hand for guidance.

Forward scanning movements for each word on a line were scored as lateral scans if the finger did not diverge from a straight left–right direction. The other four categories were up/down strokes, diagonal strokes, circular forward movements, and continuous zigzags (diagonal) on any word, and were calculated as a proportion of the number of words on that line. These categories excluded regressions, which were scored separately.

New braillists scored a higher percentage (55 per cent) of movements in zigzag, up/down, diagonal and circular directions than for lateral scanning (39 per cent), without counting regressions over letters or words. The readers who had learned braille from the beginning showed the opposite trend. Their average percentage for lateral scans (89 per cent) was higher than for any other type of scan.

The comparison group of people who had learned braille from the start thus showed the same kind of lateral scanning movements in reading for meaning that were found for a different group of competent readers in the earlier study with experimental texts (Millar, 1987 b). Interestingly enough, even Polly used mainly lateral scanning (81 per cent) movements, although she was quite young, suggesting that lateral scanning strategies in reading for meaning have little to do with age, as such.

Two points are worth considering further. The two children whose reading styles I used as examples were both good readers for their age in speed and in comprehension. Both not only showed lateral finger scanning (96 per cent for Jill), but also some division between processing the spatial and verbal information between the two hands. However, unlike the experienced braillists, Jill had not yet established a smooth and effective division of functions between the two hands.

The case for people who had learned braille after reading print was different. They used lateral scanning much less. At the same time, none of the new readers whom I saw veered from the lines of text, and all had consistent strategies for place-keeping in transitions from one line to the next, although these differed between individuals. One eighteen-year-old intelligent high school student who had learned braille for just two years used a systematic right-handed zigzag strategy for all words on every line of text. The left hand was used only for keeping the place. It remained stationary at the beginning of lines, systematically going down one line when necessary when the right hand had finished a line of text. The zigzag scanning movements were slow. But there were no regressive movements at all in any of the test passages. In scanning any word, this reader performed regular diagonal up and down strokes for each letter, which seemed to cover the whole of the letter. The method suggested that this was a letter-by-letter reader who had perfected a useful method of scanning the global shape of each character in turn.

Not surprisingly, the other new readers were less systematic in exploring letters and words, using lateral as well as up/down and circular movements to scan words and characters. Unsystematic exploration of words, as well as a high percentage of regressions is typical also of beginning young readers who have never read any other script. But few, if any, congenitally young blind readers spontaneously use hand-movements systematically for directional guidance to keep to the line of text, or to provide reference cues for keeping the place during transitions to the next line of text without direction or supervision. Straying from the line of text is common, while it almost never happens to fluent readers, even with rotated texts, provided the finger-position permits lateral scanning (Section 6).

The movement slant which produces the loss of lateral orientation in scanning from left to right by young beginning blind readers is usually in a downward direction, towards the body. This is intelligible because the lower arm and hand normally performs a pivotal movement about the body which is roughly equidistant from it. However, the lines of braille script, like lines of print, are at right angles to the vertical (mid-transverse) sides of the book or sheet and parallel to its horizontal base and the mid-transverse direction of the body.

An important part of acquiring straight-line lateral hand-movements in relation to the upright body posture is the use of one hand as a reference location for moving between lines of text. Some of the brighter children also use the semantic and lexical context in reading as a help in knowing where they are in the text, as in the example of Jill who tested the position of the new line by re-reading a word near the beginning of the previous line. Such strategies will be considered further in later chapters (Chapters 7 and 8).

8   SUMMARY AND IMPLICATIONS

We are beginning to know something about the functions of hand and finger movements which mediate the intake of information in braille reading.

Fast readers tend to alternate the two hands for both the verbal and spatial aspects of reading. The data on the timing of finger movements, hand postures, and text locations show simultaneous sampling of information from different domains. Both hands read and both hands take in spatial information, although individuals vary in the hand they use most. But parallel (or very fast alternate) processing depended on dividing the functions of different domains alternately and flexibly between the two hands.

Another important finding was that the perceptual features which are picked up differ with the type of task in fluent reading. Proficient readers use lateral scanning movements and depend on shear patterns in reading for meaning, very like the description of 'temporally extended dynamic processing' suggested by Grunewald (1966). For quasi proof-reading tasks which depend on the accurate perception of individual letters, by contrast, proficient readers use systematic circular or zigzag movements around the characters, clearly concerned with the shape of the characters, as suggested by Nolan and Kederis (1969).

The findings have several interesting implications. Two apparently irreconcilable theories about the basis of fluent braille perception both apply. But they apply in different tasks. Further, we tend to think of the given perceptual information as an unchanging substrate 'out there' in the physical features which impose absolute limits on tactual perception. Instead, task factors as well as experience determine what information is picked up and used, although the 'objective' stimulation remains invariant. There is thus no single 'perceptual unit' for braille which solely and definitively determines the physical characteristics that are perceived.

The findings also show that cognitive factors influence perception at what must belong to a very 'low level' in the perceptual intake. Finally, the results suggest that the lateral dynamic or time-based shear patterns which fluent readers use in reading for meaning may provide some perceptual basis for the notion that transgraphemic features mediate fluent reading.

Styles of reading in which the forefingers move adjacently also give some credence to yet another theoretical model which suggests that two-handed reading produces an 'enlargement of the perceptual view'. The data showed that such two-handed reading quite often depends on using one hand solely for reading and the other for place-keeping. But there is also two-handed reading in which the forefingers move together, often taking over from each other, as shown by the brightness of the reading patches and relative positions on the text (e.g. Millar, 1987 a). In these styles, the forefingers sometimes touch two separate letters simultaneously during regressions. When this happens for the same word, it certainly suggests that readers process more than a single letter. The conditions under which such 'enlargement of the perceptual window' occurs, and evidence on whether one hand processes the gist of sentences while the other checks on perceptual features will be examined in more detail in the chapter which looks at lexical and semantic processes in braille reading (Chapter 5).

Another point concerns developmental factors. The fact that beginning young braille readers have problems with place-keeping and in keeping to the line is well known. In fact, active hand-movements may be confusing rather than helpful at first. This is partly because the roving finger loses track of dot positions with new patterns. The methods that are used to establish straight lateral hand-movements, such as pre-reading exercises in scanning lines of dots, and the use of double spacing of lines will be considered later (Chapter 8). Most teachers of braille are also aware of the importance of body posture in establishing lateral scanning. However, the relation of hand position to the upright body posture is not itself sufficiently accurate as a reference cue for coding single patterns spatially (Chapter 2). Establishing the lateral direction of hand-movements across the body makes it possible to keep track of finger positions. But how these movements become differentiated from scanning single patterns is by no means clear as yet. The connection between practising lateral (across the body) movement directions, pre-reading practice, and double spacing, and training methods which combine lateral scanning with semantic information and the gradual introduction of contractions will be discussed later (Chapter 8).

The main ingredients of later reading styles seem to be established relatively early, regardless of handedness. The extent to which such patterns become habitual with experience, and the conditions that make them efficient or inefficient need to be explored further. The question of individual differences in developing line-keeping and place-keeping skills, and the extent to which this depends on general cognitive efficiency, motivation, the spatial sophistication and the verbal skills of individual children will be considered later (Chapter 7).

What may not be obvious is that the systematic division of spatial and verbal functions is less well established at lower levels of proficiency, and that there is less differentiation of scanning movements for different reading tasks, and in the pick-up of perceptual information for the different aspects of reading tasks. These differences in the functions of scanning seem to develop rather more slowly than the preference for one or other hand in reading, but the dual nature of the reading task has implications in association with developmental factors that are considered further in later chapters (Chapters 7 and 8).

Taken together, the findings imply that the perceptual and spatial aspects of tactual reading are not acquired in isolation from their verbal functions. The sounds which are represented by the patterns of braille, and the lexical and semantic information which reading materials are designed to convey, are not acquired by processes which are subsequent to the spatial organization of lateral movements. It will not have escaped the careful reader that Jill used her memory for the meaning of the initial word on the line of text that she had just read to help her to find the next line of text. Polly, who rarely lost lines of text at that level of reading, had used semantic strategies earlier to find a word that she had missed out because her reading finger had failed to home in on the first word on the next line of text. The gist she had construed so far gave her the clue to that spatial mistake. Even at the beginning of learning to recognize braille patterns, verbal strategies, such as naming the sequence of dots that make up a character, are often necessary aids (Chapter 2). The developmental findings again imply that the acquisition of braille reading demands the concurrent acquisition of spatial as well as verbal skills. The fact that verbal and spatial skills have to be developed concurrently also has developmental implications which will be considered further in Chapter 7.

Cognitive factors seem to be crucially involved in so-called 'low-level' perceptual processing, although in fluent reading these have clearly become streamlined. Competent readers are probably quite unaware of them most of the time. There is no evidence that fluent readers have to 'think about' using different movement strategies in reading for meaning in contrast to letter search. Fluent readers seem to use the complementary touch, kinaesthetic and movement information automatically in a spatially organized manner. But establishing these processes is by no means an automatic process initially. The following chapters reverse the focus, and centre on how the phonological, lexical and semantic aspects of processing relate to encoding and decoding in reading.

4 Sound and touch in memory and in braille reading

The previous two chapters showed that perceptual and spatial processes cannot be ignored in describing the decoding of verbal information which is the purpose of tactual reading. The focus in this chapter is on the verbal and particularly the phonological aspects of reading and the connection between these and tactual coding during the process of acquisition.

Reading depends on memory from the start. Beginners have to learn the physical tactual patterns while associating them with the heard and spoken equivalents in the language, and to remember the patterns and the associations. Reading therefore involves longer-term memory for stored associations. It also depends on temporary memory for retrieving the associations from longer-term memory and keeping them in mind during the process of decoding the meaning of the symbols in the written script. In the initial stages of teaching braille, there are no flash-cards with pictures of objects that children can immediately recognize and name. Beginning readers have to associate the tactual pattern with the heard name or label. To understand the process of acquisition, therefore, it is necessary to know how the tactual patterns and heard names are coded in short-term memory.

There has long been ample evidence that the most efficient way to remember lists of serial items for short (seconds) periods is to name them and to rehearse the names mentally (e.g. Atkinson and Shiffrin, 1968). For instance, telephone numbers that have just been looked up are remembered better by name than visually. A powerful method, pioneered by Conrad (1964, 1971), made it quite clear that it is the phonological (sound) aspect of naming which mediates better short-term memory. It is much more difficult to remember series of pictures, letters or words that have similar sounding names (e.g. B V D G P T C; mat rat hat bat cat) than lists of letters, words or pictures that have dissimilar sounding names, even if the lists are presented visually rather than by name. Recoding stimuli from other modalities into speech sounds is probably the most efficient means of maintaining them in memory over the short term. The 'working memory' model (Baddeley, 1986) uses the notion of an 'articulatory loop' to describe phonological coding and rehearsal. Short-term memory which involves phonological recoding is importantly involved in learning the names of letters and characters used in reading, and in retrieving them to decode the symbols in the process of reading (Conrad, 1972 a,b).

Temporary memory was originally considered as purely verbally mediated (e.g. Atkinson and Shiffrin, 1968). But there is good evidence that young sighted children can remember shapes by a visual or visuospatial code, even when they cannot as yet name the items well enough to use them for recall (Hitch and Halliday, 1983; Hitch *et al.*, 1988, 1989; Millar, 1972 b). Indeed, developmental theories of visual reading often assume that children initially recognize written words by their global shape or shape features (e.g. Barron, 1980, 1986; Barron and Baron, 1977; Frith, 1985; Marsh *et al.*, 1981). The current model uses the metaphor of an ancillary 'visuospatial scratch-pad' to incorporate the evidence for temporary memory for visual shapes which has been found for adults as well as for children (Baddeley, 1990). The model has no comparable metaphor for coding by touch. The first section shows that this is required in addition to phonological recoding.

The first section discusses findings which show the importance of phonological recoding for short-term memory of braille patterns. They also show that the tactual features by which braille patterns are discriminated (Chapter 2) are coded in short-term memory. Tactual coding and phonological coding relate in almost opposite directions to the size of the memory span. Memory spans for tactual features tend to be small, consistent with the evidence on the difficulty of organizing braille patterns spatially (Chapters 2 and 3). Fast phonological recoding, by contrast, is associated with progressively larger recall spans for tactual items. Coding by sound certainly occurs and is important in braille reading (Millar, 1975 b, 1990a; Pring, 1982). The question how such coding relates to tactual perception is a central question in the present chapter.

The 'word superiority effect' indicates that print words are recognized more easily than the letters of which they are composed. It was originally supposed to be mediated by the apprehension of the global shape of words, and was one of the reasons for teaching methods based on word shape, in braille as well as in print. Subsequently, it was thought that the word superiority effect does not occur in braille. In fact, there is evidence for a word superiority effect in braille also. But it is highly unlikely that the effect is due to detecting braille words as global shapes. The second section shows that children actually find it easier to recognize braille words by their sound and meaning than by their overall shape. Moreover, beginners also show word length effects which are usually taken to indicate letter-by-letter processing. The apparent contradiction between word superiority and word length effects is resolved by taking findings on short-term tactual and phonological memory into account.

Phonological coding is more often regarded as central to reading because written English depends on the alphabetic principle, rather than because recoding facilitates short-term memory. In an ideal alphabetic script each physical character is associated with a specific speech sound (phoneme). English orthography, of course, conforms only very imperfectly to the alphabetic ideal of perfect grapheme–phoneme correspondence (Treiman, 1993; Venezky, 1967). There are many alphabetically 'irregular' words. Nevertheless, the sound of words does have to be segmented (Liberman, 1973) into phonemes in order to learn to read. Phonological coding has been regarded for some time as the crucial step in learning to read print (e.g. Barron, 1980, 1986; Barron and Baron, 1977; Bradley and Bryant, 1983; Brady *et al.*, 1983; Bryant and Bradley, 1985; Frith, 1985; Gleitman and Rozin, 1973, 1977; Liberman, 1973; Liberman *et al.*, 1974; Liberman *et al.*, 1977; Mann *et al.*, 1980; Marsh *et al.*, 1981; Shankweiler and Crain, 1986). Some models propose that there are stages in learning to read print. Coding depends first on the recognition of the shape of words and then progresses to phonological recoding, usually in terms of grapheme–phoneme correspondence in order to make out new words that have not yet been encountered as shapes (Frith, 1985; Marsh *et al.*, 1981). It is a moot point whether the stages that have been proposed for the acquisition of visual reading are necessarily developmentally triggered states. Stages are probably best thought of as convenient ways of classifying forms of coding that children actually use for a variety of reasons, including the fact that methods of teaching may highlight different aspects of scripts. Thus evidence that young children recognize words initially by their shape or by distinctive visual features is often attributed to the 'whole word' teaching method in which children learn to associate pictures of objects with their written names.

That initial step cannot be assumed in beginning braille. If anything, coding by sound is more important in learning braille. 'Phonic' methods are commonly used from the start. The sounds of characters are learned first, and words are built up from the assembled sounds, and these are blended together so that the child recognizes the meaning of the word. The notion of 'assembled phonology' assumes that reading takes place by recoding each physical character (grapheme) into its corresponding sound, and assembling and blending the constituent sounds. The blended sound of the word is used to access its meaning in longer-term memory. The 'letter-by-letter' theory of braille does not specify these processes in detail. But the assumptions are similar.

There is ample evidence for phonological recoding of print words by sighted adults. For instance, it takes longer to decide that a meaningless nonword (e.g. brane) which sounds like a real word (brain) is not a word than to reject meaningless nonwords that have no meaningful homophones, or are not pronounceable. Phonological recoding prior to understanding words, or prelexical ('assembled') phonological coding is assumed in some theories to be an obligatory process before the meaning of words can be accessed, and remains obligatory even in proficient reading, although the recoding becomes automatic (e.g. McCutchen *et al.*, 1991; Perfetti, 1992; Perfetti and Bell, 1991; Perfetti, Bell and Delaney, 1988; Spoehr, 1981; Spoehr and Smith, 1975; Van Orden, 1987; Van Orden *et al.*, 1990). The model is closest to the traditional letter-by-letter theory for braille reading, although it is not clear that the notion of obligatory phonological recoding in models of adult visual reading necessarily implies letter-by-letter reading.

Not all visual reading models assume pre-lexical phonological recoding. Words and nonword-homophones often share letters and are orthographically similar. The opposite position is that all phonological recoding is post-lexical (e.g. Humphreys and Evett, 1985). The meaning of words is accessed directly from the graphemic and orthographic forms, and phonological recoding occurs subsequently for reading aloud, or to the extent that the task makes demands on short-term memory. The 'two-route' model of Coltheart (1978) proposed that the meaning of words can be recognized both directly from the visual (graphemic) information, as well as indirectly via phonological recoding. Recoding the written form (grapheme) of each letter into its corresponding phoneme is most intelligible for alphabetically spelt 'regular' words. But phonological recoding can also occur for irregular words. Irregular new words, or even nonwords, which contain letter clusters that also occur in known words (e.g. lough/cough) can be pronounced in analogy with the pronunciation of the known letter cluster (Glushko, 1979). Goswami (1988) found that even very young children can use analogies of this kind in reading new words.

The question whether pre-lexical phonological recoding is automatic and obligatory or occurs only after the meaning of words has been decoded was not the main issue here. It is not clear that it is necessary to assume that phonological coding is either solely pre-lexical or solely post-lexical (e.g. Gathercole, 1987). However, the models, methods and findings which are designed to address that question are relevant to questions about coding processes in braille.

The more immediate question for braille turned on the role of phonological and tactual coding of braille words in reading texts for meaning, and whether or how this changes with increased proficiency. The subsequent sections look at different forms or functions of phonological coding in reading for meaning.

Coding heuristics were found to vary with levels of proficiency, task conditions, and the semantic structure of the script. The final section discusses some of the conditions under which different forms of phonological processes occur.

1 CODING BY TOUCH AND BY SOUND

Evidence on short-term memory for tactual features is of some importance for understanding the processes in reading acquisition and in fluent

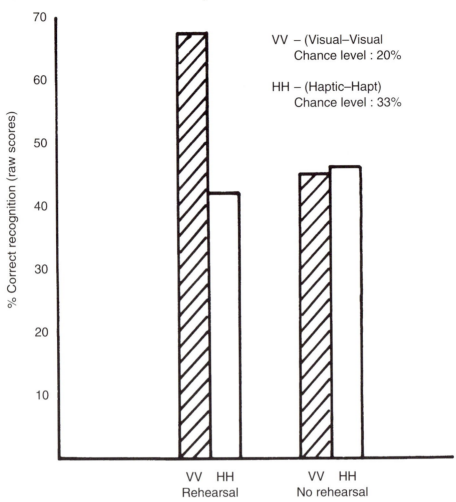

Figure 4.1 Percentages of correct recognition scores by young sighted children for small three-dimensional forms under Rehearsal and No Rehearsal conditions with visual presentation and test (VV), and with haptic presentation and test (HH)

reading, since temporary memory is involved in the process of acquiring and decoding written materials. Memory for tactual shapes other than braille has often been found to be much poorer than memory for the same shapes presented visually (e.g. Gilson and Baddeley, 1969; Goodnow, 1971; Millar, 1971). An early study (Millar, 1972 b) showed that instructing young children to visualize or see shapes 'in your head' improves visual recognition across short delays, suggesting that short-term memory for visual shapes is subject to attentional control. By contrast, instructing young children to mentally rehearse or to concentrate on the feel of the same three-dimensional shapes did not improve recognition (Figure 4.1).

Findings suggesting that tactual inputs may be coded in short-term memory (Watkins and Watkins, 1974) thus need checking.

To test more directly whether the tactual features of braille are coded in short-term memory, and how this relates to recoding phonological coding, I used a tactual analogue of Conrad's (1964, 1971) method. Lists of tactually confusable braille letters were compared with lists of phonologically confusable letters. A serial list of letters that were neither similar in name nor tactually similar was used as the control condition. The letters were embossed on separate small plaques, placed in a left to right series. Probed recall was used as a test. This meant that as soon as the child had felt the letters in a given set the plaques were turned over to the blank side. The child had to place a (duplicate) test letter on the position which that letter had occupied in the memory set.

The results were quite clear (Millar, 1975 b). Tactual as well as phonological features of braille letters are coded in short-term memory. But these codes differ. They relate in opposite directions to the size of the memory set. Children who were able to discriminate letters on pre-test, but could not yet name them, achieved recall spans of two to three letters on the control series. These children were significantly worse on tactually confusable, but not on phonologically confusable series. By contrast, children who had been fast on pre-test letter-naming achieved recall spans of six or more letters on control sets. These children were significantly impaired on phonologically confusable sets, but not by tactually confusable series. Subjects who had named the letters accurately, but more slowly than the fastest group on pre-test achieved recall spans of four or five items in control conditions. They were significantly impaired on both tactually confusable and phonologically confusable series. The significant interactions between memory set size and scores for tactual and phonological confusable series respectively are graphed in Figure 4.2.

Furthermore, the speed of naming letters which had been ascertained previously on pre-test related significantly ($p < 0.01$) to the size of the control spans. The finding is important because it suggests that naming speed, or rather the time it takes to retrieve the name of an item, is a significant factor in phonological recoding.

The fact that naming speed can predict phonological recoding suggested that the relation between set size and type of coding was not confined to blind children. A further study confirmed this. Blindfolded sighted as well as blind children were tested with the same method, but using sets of small objects instead of braille letters. Precisely the same pattern of results was found for both blindfolded sighted and for blind children (Millar, 1975 c).

Evidence that tactual coding occurs and that it differs from verbal coding was confirmed by using a number of different methods that converged on the same question. I used the Posner (Posner *et al.*, 1969) paradigm to test for tactual coding (Millar, 1977 b). Posner and his

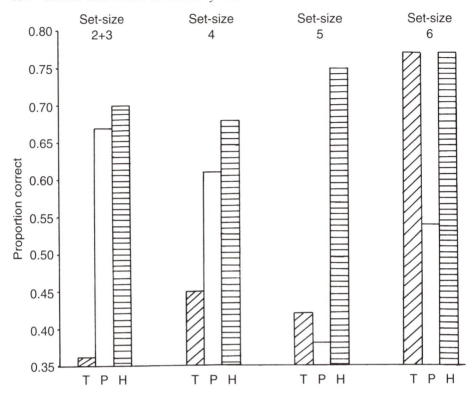

Figure 4.2 The size of recall spans in control (H) conditions, and proportions of correct responses for tactually similar (T), phonologically similar (P), and dissimilar (H) serial lists of braille letters by blind children. First published in the *British Journal of Psychology*, 1977, *68*, 377–387

colleagues showed that it takes longer to judge the same letters as identical if they differ visually (Aa) than if they are visually identical as well as identical in name, showing that the visual features were coded in memory. Braille has no capital letters. I therefore created differences (exp. 3) in physical format by brailling one set of letters with a stylus that produced more pointed raised dots and slightly increased the gap between adjacent dots than in the normal format, and another set of letters with a stylus that produced slightly broader dots which slightly reduced the space between dots compared with the normal format. Both sets were thus of the same overall size and shape as braille, but differed in 'texture' from the conventional format and from each other. Matching two identical letters by name was better when the letters were also identical in tactual format than when they differed in physical format, although they were identical in name and letter shape (Millar, 1977 b). The finding showed that the physical tactual 'texture' characteristics are coded in memory, as well as the name or sound of the letters (Figure 4.3).

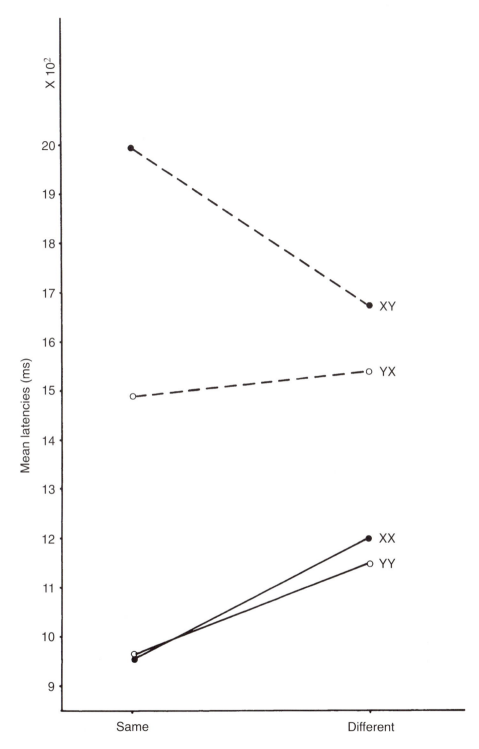

Figure 4.3 Mean latencies (ms) for Same (identical shape and name) and Different (different shapes and names) letters in the same (XX or YY) format and in different (XY or YX) formats. First published in the *British Journal of Psychology*, 1977, *68*, 377–387

A further study on the different characteristics of tactual and phono-logical codes in short-term memory used the fact that grouping items at input facilitates the recall of nameable items (e.g. Miller, 1956). For subjects who could name braille letters easily, grouping them did indeed improve probed recall. The same children not only scored much lower recall spans with tactual nonsense shapes that could not be named, grouping tactual nonsense shapes actually had adverse effects on recall (Millar, 1978 b). The difference between tactual and phonological coding was, therefore, not entirely a matter of individual differences with age, but depended on facility in naming. The findings further supported the hypothesis that tactual features of two to three tactual items can be coded in short-term memory. But, unlike nameable shapes, recall deteriorates more quickly if the items are spaced. Coded tactual features, or 'feels' consisting of more than two or three items are not easy to maintain actively in memory, in contrast to speech sounds.

Taken together, the findings are evidence that tactual features of braille are indeed coded in short-term memory, but that the number of items that can be remembered by 'feel' seems to be restricted to two or three. There is a developmental dimension to this finding. The span of short-term memory increases more or less linearly with age in children (Chi, 1977). The size of short-term recall spans is associated with increased phonological coding in sighted and also in blind children (Conrad, 1971; Millar 1975 b).

As mentioned earlier, the increase in recall span with phonological recoding related significantly to the speed with which subjects could name the characters on pre-test. The pre-test, in which children simply had to name each letter as fast as possible, had merely been carried out as a control exercise to see which letters subjects could actually name, and how fast they named them. However, the fact that there was a significant interaction between the speed of pre-test naming and the size of recall set which was associated with phonological recoding in the span test suggested that the speed of retrieving names from longer-term memory is important in the increase in memory span with age. The fact that the familiarity of items significantly reduces the age difference in the size of children's immediate recall spans provides evidence for the involvement of longer-term memory (Henry and Millar, 1991, 1993; Hulme *et al.*, 1991). The findings imply that decoding the braille script in reading makes demands on short-term memory and its long-term component (Watkins, 1977). The issue will be considered further in relation to developmental factors in learning (Chapter 7).

The point here is that braille readers can call on tactual as well as on phonological coding to some extent. Although short-term memory for tactual features is rather poor unless they are quickly recoded phonolog-ically, the finding nevertheless suggests that learning to read by touch parallels learning to read print in that the physical features of the characters (graphemes) can be coded in temporary memory. At the same time, the relation between tactual and phonological coding during acquisition is not entirely the same for braille as that reported for visual word reading by beginners. This is shown in the next section.

2 BRAILLE WORDS AND NONWORDS: WORD SHAPE AND PHONEMIC RECODING

The fact that words are read more quickly than the letters of which they consist (Cattell, 1886; Huey, 1908), known as the 'word superiority' effect, is one of the main questions that models of visual reading were originally intended to explain. The question is important for understanding how braille reading develops and should be taught. In braille, the word superiority effect has had a more checkered career than in print reading. Nolan and Kederis (1969) found increased word reading time with increased numbers of constituent letters. Such increase in time with word length is often taken to indicate letter-by-letter reading. This seems to preclude word superiority effects. However, word superiority effects have also been reported in braille (Krueger, 1982 b; Pring, 1982).

The apparent difference in findings by Nolan and Kederis (1969) and Krueger (1982 b) is probably due to differences in method. Nolan and Kederis (1969) found that braille words took longer to read than letters, and argued against the view that the words are coded as global shapes for that reason. However, the finding was based on threshold latencies in a tachistotactometer. This is a device which exposes characters serially to passive touch for controlled periods and provides important information about threshold values for the recognition of letters. But the informational conditions are not precisely the same as in normal reading. The reader does not have the same control over the speed of exposure in passive as in active reading. More important, the flow of information about the braille cell is reversed when it is encountered by the stationary compared to the moving finger. When the braille cells pass from left to right under the stationary finger, the right hand dots (4 5 6) are encountered before the left hand (1 2 3) dots. In active reading the finger moves from left to right and therefore encounters the left hand (1 2 3) dots before the right hand (4 5 6) dots. It seems likely that this makes a difference to proficient readers (Chapter 3), and to the process of coding.

Krueger (1982 b) found a word superiority effect in braille by adult readers in a letter search task. His subjects searched for a target letter through lists of six-letter (legally uncontractable) braille words or nonwords. Nonwords are meaningless letter strings that follow the spelling rules which apply to 'regular' English words, and the strings can be pronounced. Krueger showed that adults search significantly faster through braille words than nonwords, and the difference increased later in the word lists.

The question whether words are also recognized more quickly than meaningless letter-strings or nonwords seemed worth investigating further in order to understand whether the effect changes with proficiency in braille. A study was set up to look at word and nonword reading and letter naming (unpublished talk, Princeton, 1984). Three groups of five children of average ability whose average reading rates for three-letter braille words were 28, 41 and 78 wpm, respectively, took part. Lists of legally uncontracted monosyllabic words and nonwords containing three, four, or five letters were brailled on separate lines. In addition, lists of letters, brailled in random clusters of three and five letters to correspond to the appearance of lines composed of three- and five-letter words or nonwords were also brailled on separate lines. Each list of three-letter words, nonwords and letter clusters (ten per line) and each list of five-letter words, nonwords and letter clusters (six per line) contained exactly thirty letters. The lines were presented in random order. Each line was timed manually from first to last touch, or voice-onset for the last item, whichever was earlier. Instructions to read the lines of words and nonwords aloud, or to name the letters in the letter lists were given before the start of each list.

A highly significant word effect was found, showing that words were processed faster than nonwords ($F = 13.86$, df $= 1/12$, $p < 0.006$). Nevertheless, reading time for each word and nonword increased significantly with the number of constituent letters ($F = 49.09$, df $= 2/24$, $p < 0.001$). As would be expected, the three proficiency groups differed significantly in speed ($F = 34.35$, df $= 2/12$, $p < 0.001$). More important, that difference related significantly to increased latencies with increased letters ($F = 7.6$, df $= 4/24$, $p < 0.01$). As can be seen from the graphed speeds (Figure 4.4), the letter length effect was largest for the slowest group, while the best group showed hardly any effect from increased numbers of constituent letters.

The word superiority effect was significant also when the total reading time for each line of words, nonwords and letter clusters was calculated, although each line consisted of the same number (thirty) of letters. Lines consisting of words were significantly faster than lines consisting of either nonwords or letters ($F = 15.06$, df $= 2/24$, $p < 0.001$). On the assumption that letter-by-letter reading means recoding each letter phonemically, and then blending the sound before accessing the meaning of words, lines of letters should have been faster than lines of words, because reading letters does not require any additional process of blending sounds into words. In fact, the difference was significantly in the opposite direction. Letter naming was significantly slower than word naming ($p < 0.01$ on post hoc tests), despite the fact that letter-naming and word-naming lists contained equal numbers of letters. Moreover, reading speeds for lines of letters did not differ significantly from that for lines of nonwords, suggesting that the actual speech output (i.e. pronouncing the items) was not the major factor in the word superiority effect.

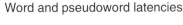

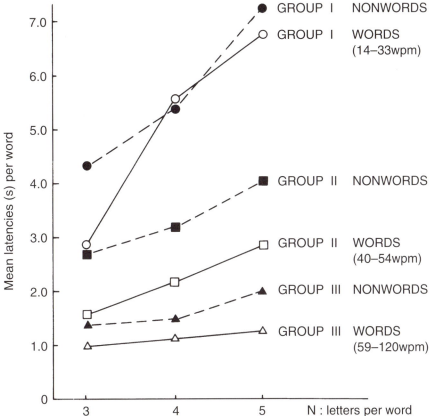

Figure 4.4 Word and pseudoword recognition latencies (s) for three groups of young braille readers

On the face of it, the results seem to support contradictory theories. Reading time increased with the number of constituent letters, but words were nevertheless faster than nonwords. The interaction with letter length makes it impossible to reconcile the two views by assuming that words and nonwords are processed alike initially and that the difference is due to lexical decisions. The notion of assembled phonology assumes that the reader recodes each letter into its phoneme, and the sounds are blended prior to searching for their meaning in the internal lexicon. It takes longer to decide that a nonword has no meaning than to find a word.

However, the assumption that the word superiority effect occurs after word sounds have been assembled does not explain why the letter length effects occurred mainly in the slowest readers, or why the data (Figure 4.4) suggest that these subjects showed the word superiority effect only for three-letter words. The possibility that the word superiority effect might depend on processing larger perceptual 'units' with increased proficiency could, therefore, not be ruled out.

Considering the evidence that even single braille characters are difficult to code as global shapes initially (Chapter 2), it seemed unlikely that young braille readers code words which consist of more than one letter in terms of their overall global shape. But the possibility needed to be tested directly, because the growing ability to use hand-movements in reading for spatial reference (Chapter 3) should make shape coding, including whole word shapes, easier. The next question was, therefore, whether word shape was used with increased proficiency as the basis of word recognition.

Another experiment tested more directly whether young children use the overall shape of braille words, and how this compares with the detection of phonological and semantic aspects of words, and to physical features such as dot numerosity (Millar, 1984 b). Comparing effects of dot numerosity with coding by sound, sense, or shape was of interest for several reasons. There was evidence that proficient readers use lateral dot-gap density (lateral shear) patterns in reading for meaning (Chapter 3). Differences in dot numerosity were used here to establish whether the physical length of words is used as a cue, and how this compares with the use of the global shape of words.

Five lists, each consisting of three familiar braille words were prepared. Subjects were asked to choose the word that they considered to be the odd one out of the three. In each list, there were always two possible bases for the choice: (a) one of the three words differed from the other two semantically, another word differed from the others in overall braille shape (e.g. bell, ball, kick); (b) one word differed from the other two semantically, another differed in dot numerosity (ride, roadway, rice) from the other two; (c) one differed in sound, another differed in braille shape (coal, coat, sole); (d) one word differed in sound, the other in length and dot number (e.g. lays, keys, appletrees); (e) the choice was between a difference in meaning versus a difference in sound (e.g. girl, curl, lady). Fifteen young braillists (aged 6-10 to 11-10 years) took part. They were divided into three reading groups by their reading speed (from 3 to 96 wpm) on Tooze's (1962) test.

The evidence was based on the proportions of choices for each of the coding strategies. Choices differed significantly ($p < 0.05$), and this was because shape was chosen least frequently. There was also a significant interaction of choices with reading groups ($p < 0.05$), suggesting that the slowest group mostly based their choice on dot numerosity cues, the middle group made more phonological choices, and the faster group chose equally often on the basis of meaning and sound. The choices were associated with (tested) mental age. Reading rates alone, when mental age was partialled out statistically, did not interact with choices. More important, even when mental age was partialled out, the more proficient readers in this group based their choices on word meaning or sound rather than on shape. This suggests strongly that average young braille readers are unlikely to use the global shape of words to access word meaning.

The second experiment in that study Millar (1984 b) was run to see how accurately these average young readers could use shape, sound, meaning and dot numerosity as a basis of coding if they were trained to use a given dimension, and were instructed to use it without being given a choice. Four new lists of nine three-word series were used. In each series of three items only one word differed from the other two. The lists differed in whether the 'odd' word differed from the other two words on the basis of shape, sound, meaning, or dot numerosity. The coding strategy relevant to a list was explained and practised with different examples before tests on the appropriate list.

Under direct instruction to detect global shape, accuracy was surprisingly high, at least for the fastest readers (80 per cent) who were significantly more accurate on all tasks (p < 0.001). Beginners were at chance level on coding shape, but above chance level on the other forms of coding. The fact that coding strategies differed significantly (p < 0.001) was due solely to significantly less accurate detection by shape than by sound, meaning or dot numerosity (p < 0.01) for all three reading groups (Figure 4.5). The accuracy for coding by sound, meaning and dot numerosity did not differ.

The findings left no doubt that the shape of braille words is chosen less frequently as a basis for coding, and is more difficult to code even with training and instruction, than coding by the meaning or sound of words. By contrast, dot numerosity or length was chosen quite frequently as a basis for coding, and was detected as easily as meaning and/or sound under instruction. This finding suggests, incidentally, that dot numerosity or word length is a useful additional cue, for instance in reading continuous prose. It is not, of course, sufficient to make out the meaning of single words. But it is, in fact, used by competent braillists as an additional clue when other clues to meaning are difficult (Chapter 5).

The findings show incidentally that coding the global shape of braille words indeed improves with longer-term experience. At the same time, both strategy choices and levels of accuracy under instruction demonstrated clearly that the overall shape of braille words is the least likely clue to be used to find either the sound or the meaning of braille words.

For braille, the notion that the word superiority effect depends on detecting the global shape of braille words can therefore be ruled out. On the other hand, the alternative hypothesis that word recognition depends on letter-by-letter reading does not quite fit all the data either. In principle, the hypothesis that each letter is recoded phonemically, and the sounds are blended before accessing the meaning of the word, could explain the word superiority effect by assuming that it takes less time to find the word that corresponds to the blended sound than to decide that it has no

Proportion correct under instruction

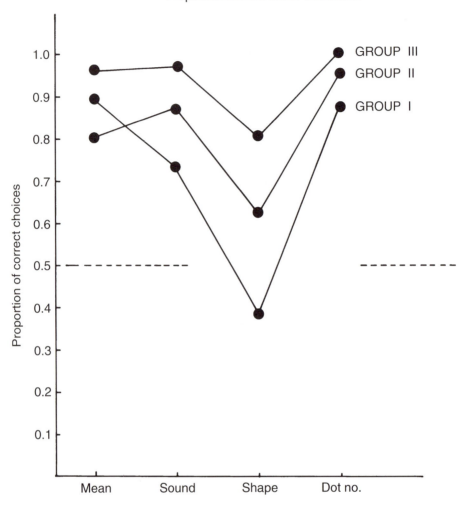

Figure 4.5 Mean proportions of correct choices by children at three reading levels, based on meaning (Mean.), sound, global shape, and dot numerosity (Dot No.)

meaning. But that account does not explain the interaction between reading proficiency and word length in the word superiority effect (see earlier). Beginners had shown the word superiority effect only for three-letter words, and their reading time increased with every additional letter, unlike the better readers whose word superiority effect did not differ between shorter and longer words. Additional assumptions are needed to explain the interaction. The longer words may have been less familiar to the young beginners and therefore took longer to process, while three-letter words were more familiar and/or recognition was easier because the words do not exceed the memory span for serial tactual features (Section 2).

In either case, the additional assumption involves some 'top-down' effects from verbal knowledge. Interestingly enough, this fits very precisely with the description given by Krueger's (1982 b) adult braillists. The reason they gave for finding target letters more quickly in words than in nonwords was that the words allowed them to anticipate the target letter. In other words, they were 'looking up' the meaning of words long before they had processed all the constituent letters. It suggests a picture of continual interaction between perceptual and cognitive processes rather than the purely peripheral to central ('bottom-up') processing implied by the usual description of letter-by-letter reading.

This explanation of the word superiority effect in braille suggests that semantic processes are involved at a relatively early stage. That issue will be examined more fully later (Chapter 5).

3   PHONOLOGICAL CODING AND PROFICIENCY IN READING FOR COMPREHENSION

So far I have considered the role of phonological and tactual coding in recognizing single braille patterns and isolated words. However, the main purpose of reading is to understand connected prose rather than single letters or isolated nouns. The next question is, therefore, how phonological recoding affects processes in reading connected text for comprehension, and whether the effects operate in the same manner at all levels of proficiency.

At least three functions of phonological coding must be considered in investigating reading for meaning. The most obvious is in reading aloud. Speech processes in oral reading must be assumed, although they could occur after the reader has decoded the meaning of words. In order to be able to translate the written text into speech sounds the reader needs to know how written words are pronounced both individually and in conjunction with each other. The output requires the planning, retrieval and execution of speech gestures and the modulation of the voice output to say the words aloud with the stress and prosody that is appropriate to the meaning or gist of the text. Prima facie, none of these output processes are needed for silent prose reading, although it is sometimes suggested that silent reading is based on 'inner speech'.

Phonological coding in silent reading for meaning could also occur because it makes demands on short-term memory. Short-term memory may be needed in order to integrate words into the gist of text, or to remember them for comprehension tests. Such temporary memory involves phonological coding (Section 1). It has been suggested that all phonological recoding occurs via motor programs for speech output, including recoding in silent reading (e.g. Allport, 1979). Working memory is disturbed if the speech system is occupied by mouthing an irrelevant (e.g. subvocal 'blah, blah, blah') sound (Baddeley, 1986). The phenomenon, known as articulatory suppression, disrupts the comprehension of difficult texts by fluent adult print readers (e.g. Baddeley, 1979, 1986, 1990; Baddeley *et al.*, 1975; Besner, 1987; Hardyk and Petrinovitch, 1970). The main idea of the working memory model is that verbally recoded inputs are kept accessible in temporary memory by the articulatory (rehearsal) loop.

A third function has been mentioned already in connection with the hypothesis of an 'assembled' phonology or phonemic recoding. It is assumed to operate at the point of encoding. It makes most sense for learning a strictly alphabetic language in which all words follow the rule that every letter represents a single speech sound, and conversely that every speech sound is represented by a single letter. If so, reading would be acquired most easily by learning the speech sound for each written letter (grapheme), and to read by recoding each grapheme into its corresponding phoneme. English is not a purely alphabetic language. It contains a great many irregular words, and also has exception words that are spelt the same as regular words but are pronounced differently (e.g. the past tense of read). In principle, the sound of such words could be learned independently. But readers can decode new irregular words also by analogy with letter clusters that they have mastered already (Glushko, 1979; Goswami, 1988). In English braille (grade 2) the acquisition process is further complicated by contracted forms which deviate still further from the ideal alphabetic concept of one-to-one correspondence between graphemes and phonemes. Indeed, there are also logographic forms in which a single character represents a whole word. Some of the issues this raises for reading, writing and spelling are considered in a later chapter (Chapter 6).

The notion of phonological encoding at input has been disputed on two grounds. It has been argued that all phonological effects are due to processes which occur after word meaning has been decoded (e.g. Humphreys and Evett, 1985) and that there is no phonological recoding at input. The other suggestion is that at least two phonological codes have to be assumed. One occurs in conditions which require speech output processes or covert articulation, while phonological effects at encoding are based on coding phonological input (e.g. Besner, 1987; Besner and Davelaar, 1982). In fact, some form of phonological input coding without covert articulation has to be assumed, if only because short-term memory and phonological coding have been demonstrated in people who are congenitally unable to speak (e.g. Bishop, 1985; Bishop and Robson, 1989; Vallar and Cappa, 1987).

In principle, therefore, phonological coding can refer to speech-based processes that occur only in oral reading or possibly also as inner subvocal speech in silent reading. It can also refer to phonological coding in order to sustain short-term memory during reading for comprehension. The third form of phonological coding is grapheme–phoneme recoding and assumes coding in terms of alphabetically defined phonemes (e.g. Gleitman and Rozin, 1973).

The basis of phonological coding during acquisition of braille was thus by no means obvious from the print literature. Daneman (1988) found that comprehension scores in braille correlated with short-term memory scores for two groups of adult braille readers. The fact that the braillists were relatively slow (73 wpm and 40 wpm, respectively) suggests that the reading matter may have been difficult for them. However, direct evidence on articulatory coding in silent braille reading was needed, particularly in checking out how such coding relates to reading proficiency and speed (Millar, 1990 a).

Two studies were conducted to test whether articulatory coding in braille could be demonstrated in reading texts for comprehension, and if so, whether and how it differs with reading proficiency. Two results were of interest. One was whether articulatory phonological coding in silent reading only has a maintenance function for comprehension. Findings which show phonological effects in reading difficult texts for comprehension would suggest that articulatory coding is needed to maintain and integrate words. The other was whether speech-based encoding or processing in terms of assembled phonology at input actually occurs at all in reading braille silently for comprehension (Millar, 1990 a). The experiments used the articulatory suppression technique. Mouthing an irrelevant syllable (e.g. saying 'blah, blah, blah' aloud) occupies the speech mechanism during silent reading, and suppresses speech-based phonological coding. That was compared with control conditions in which subjects simply read the stories silently or aloud. Two further controls were used to establish whether any type of interference during reading would have the same effect as articulatory suppression. In the control conditions, subjects had to tap their feet throughout either silent or oral reading. The question of interest for braille was first of all whether assembled phonology, in the sense of phonemic recoding, occurs at all, and if so, whether it occurs at all levels of proficiency in braille, as suggested by a strict letter-by-letter theory.

The first study used a relatively difficult text with braillists whose average wpm rates differed at three levels (145, 70 and 28 wpm) of proficiency. The findings showed that non-speech movements had no significant effects. By contrast, articulatory suppression severely impaired comprehension compared to the other conditions (p < 0.001). Memory and comprehension was thus impaired when phonological (subvocal) coding was made impossible, but other movements had no effect. It replicated previous findings with visual reading that articulatory suppression has strong effects on memory and comprehension (e.g. Baddeley, 1986; Hardyk and Petrinovitch, 1970). But it also suggested that slow readers were more affected. Two of the slowest readers were found to have great difficulties in making words at all under articulatory suppression.

A second study was therefore conducted with much easier stories which contained a higher proportion of high frequency words. That also made it possible to test more beginning (slow) readers. The experimental

conditions interacted significantly with proficiency for accuracy of comprehension ($p < 0.001$), and also in reading rates ($p < 0.01$). Beginners were
proportionately much more severely impaired than more proficient
readers both in comprehension ($p < 0.001$) and in reading rates ($p < 0.01$)
under articulatory suppression. In fact, only one of the beginners was
actually able to make out any words at all. By contrast, the best group
(212.6 spm) showed no significant differences in reading rate or in comprehension between articulatory suppression and any of the other conditions
with the easy stories.

Replay of the videotapes showed that the other beginners were quite
unable to even start reading an easy text silently when they were required
to mouth a meaningless sound ('blah blah') repeatedly at the same time.
The suppression of articulation by having to mouth the sound clearly interfered even with making out letters, let alone words. No such interference
was found when they had to tap their feet while reading, and they achieved
reasonable reading rates (mean = 19.6 spm) in reading texts for comprehension without interference. Proficient readers showed little difference
between different reading conditions.

The findings have several implications. They show that pre-lexical
phonological coding certainly occurs in braille. They also show that it is
based on speech output. Articulatory suppression, but none of the other
interference conditions, disrupted encoding of initial letters of words by
beginners, as well making reading virtually impossible for them. Further,
such pre-lexical articulatory coding was confined to beginners who were
still at very early stages of learning although they could read simple stories.
It was not shown by fluent readers. The findings also imply that normal
silent reading by fluent readers can involve speech-based phonological
coding, but significantly so only with relatively difficult text.

Speech-based phonological coding, therefore, has at least two functions
in braille prose reading. Phonological coding in reading for meaning by
proficient braillists clearly depended on the memory/comprehension
demands of the text, because articulatory suppression disrupted comprehension by fluent readers only with difficult materials. It was not found
with easy texts and had little or no effect on their reading speed. That
suggests a change in processing due to task difficulty rather than to reading
proficiency as such. Beginners, on the other hand, showed speech-based
phonological or phonemic encoding of the input, and there was no
evidence that this was the case for fluent readers (Millar, 1990 a).

Fluent readers can evidently read and remember simple texts which
contain mainly high frequency words even under articulatory suppression.
This raised further questions about the basis of coding by proficient
braillists.

Print readers have another potential resource for coding items in
memory. They could, in principle, encode code familiar words in terms of
visuospatial or shape characteristics, and access word meaning directly

(e.g. Coltheart, 1978), and/or rely on some form of visual memory as envisaged by the metaphor of a 'visuospatial scratch-pad' (Baddeley, 1990) when necessary. It does not have to be assumed that the potential basis of such an alternative coding strategy necessarily depends on coding global word shapes. In fact, word shape is unlikely to be a necessary prerequisite even for fluent visual reading (e.g. Henderson, 1982). For instance, disrupting word shape by alternating upper and lower case letters does not preclude word recognition (Henderson, 1982), although it does have some effects. Nevertheless, fluent print readers often overlook incorrect letters that are graphemically similar to the correct ones in the text (Ehri, 1980; Healy, 1980). There is a good deal of other evidence that adult print readers can use shape as a useful cue in reading (e.g. Broadbent and Broadbent, 1980; Ehri, 1980; Haber and Haber, 1981; Haber *et al.*, 1983).

The question was, therefore, whether similar nonverbal codes may help to mediate short-term memory for tactual inputs. The fact that short-term memory for modality-specific tactual inputs occurs, but produces only small recall spans was consistent with the evidence on the initial basis of perception for braille patterns.

However, the findings on scanning movements (Chapter 3) also suggested that scanning movements became progressively more spatially organized with experience, including the pick-up of shape cues and of lateral shear patterns in different reading tasks. Organized movements can be rehearsed mentally (Millar and Ittyerah, 1991). In principle, such organized movements could provide a basis for a more extended nonverbal memory (Millar, 1985 b, 1991, 1994).

Studies which probed the relation between phonological and tactual coding in reading with increased proficiency are therefore considered next.

4   SOUND, SENSE AND TOUCH IN READING FOR MEANING

As in the case of fluent print readers, the most cogent explanation of the articulatory effects for proficient braille readers is that articulatory codes are used more, or more overtly, when the text imposes a greater memory load because the words are less familiar, or text construction is more complex, or both. By contrast, young beginners showed the immediate articulatory recoding of inputs that indicates assembled phonological processes. The changes with proficiency raise further questions particularly about the relation between tactual and phonological processing in continuous reading which are considered in this section.

The models of adult visual word recognition, mentioned earlier, differ in whether they assume that phonological encoding is an obligatory, automatic process before the meaning of words can be accessed in proficient reading by adults (e.g. McCutchen *et al.*, 1991; Perfetti and Bell, 1991; Van Orden, 1987; Van Orden *et al.*, 1990), or that word meaning is decoded directly from the physical features of the script and/or the orthographic knowledge of the reader and phonological coding occurs only subsequently (e.g. Humphreys and Evett, 1985). The developmental path by which adult reading is achieved is not specified. However, Veronica Coltheart and her colleagues (1988) suggested that processing may change from assembled phonology by young print readers to direct access to word meaning from graphemic/orthographic information. There is ample evidence that meaningless visual letter strings that sound like words are often wrongly accepted as words also by adults in tasks which demand lexical (word/nonword) decisions or semantic judgments (e.g. Van Orden, 1987; Van Orden *et al.*, 1988; Jared and Seidenberg, 1991). The Coltheart study used sentences that contained nonword homophones which differed graphemically from the appropriate word. The findings showed that young children accepted significantly more sentences with nonwords that sounded correct than adult readers.

Braille has a nice methodological advantage for testing graphemic versus phonological effects, because it contains some mandatory contractions that represent whole words. Moreover, these sometimes have homophones that are uncontracted or less contracted longer words which differ quite drastically in tactual features as well as in meaning, but are nevertheless legally (in braille) spelt words. The role of contractions as such will be discussed later (Chapter 6). I used pairs of contracted and uncontracted, or less contracted, homophone words, because they also have other advantages in testing for tactual and phonological effects. Using legal homophone words rather than nonwords as foils avoids the possibility that the very presence of meaningless letter-strings actually elicits phonological coding in the attempt to make them out (e.g. Balota and Chumbley, 1984). Moreover, young children may find nonwords more confusing precisely because they do not make sense. There was also a further advantage. The contracted words and their longer homophones can be matched for word frequency. Long words are known to occur less frequently in written materials and tend to be more difficult and less familiar than short words (Zipf, 1935). That need not apply to length effects that are due to contractions. Less contracted words can be as familiar as the contracted homophone, and both are necessarily more familiar than nonwords. The fact that contracted and longer homophone pairs differ from each other in length, in appearance and in orthography also eliminates the possibility that they are mistaken for each other because they are graphemically rather than phonologically similar. The difference in appearance also makes it possible to test for graphemic effects. Finally, single characters (with or without a pre-posed dot) cannot be decomposed phonemically. Effects of phonological coding of these words must be attributed to coding words rather than phonemes by sound.

The study (Millar, 1995) looked at graphemic and phonological coding at different levels of reading. Homophone word pairs were used, one of which was always a mandatorily highly contracted word, while the (legal braille) spelling of the other homophone produced a graphemically quite different, longer form. Each word was embedded in a sentence in which it made sense, and in a sentence in which it made nonsense although it sounded correct. I shall refer to the graphemic differences as 'length' for convenience. The target word pairs were monosyllabic words. A further constraint on the selection of target word pairs was that the long and short words should not differ in familiarity, as instanced by word frequency counts (Carroll *et al.* 1971; Thorndike and Lorge, 1959). Ten homophone word pairs were found which conformed to these criteria.

Braille contractions are usually transcribed into print as sequences of capital letters, and I shall follow that convention from now on. Each sequence of consecutive capital letters represents the single character that is the braille contraction for that particular letter sequence. Examples of highly contracted words and their shorter homophone pair are WHICH/witCH (one character / four characters), RIGHT/write (one character preceded by a dot versus a five-letter word; THROUGH/Threw (one character preceded by one dot versus four characters); FOR/fOUr (one character / three characters). Of the ten word pairs, seven of the highly contracted words consisted of a single character or a single character preceded by a dot while the homophone pair consisted of three to five characters. In three pairs the highly contracted word consisted of three or four characters while the homophone pairs consisted respectively of four or five characters. Each word in a homophone pair was embedded in a semantically appropriate sentence, and in a semantically inappropriate sentence which was compatible with its graphemically different homophone (e.g. 'People stood on the write to let him pass' and 'She went off to RIGHT to granny'). The sentences were brailled in random order on several transparent sheets (see Chapter 3, Section 1), one sentence to each line, and randomly interspersed with neutral meaningful and meaningless sentences. Only one instance of a given homophone sentence was presented on any one sheet of consecutive sentences. The point was to avoid drawing too much attention to the phonological ambiguities. Subjects were twenty-four braille readers from selective and local authority schools for the visually handicapped. Their reading rates varied from beginners to fluent readers (23–207 spm). Subjects were divided into four groups by reading rate and comprehension scores. The best group were adolescents whose reading rates (155–196 wpm) were considerably faster than the rates (70–100 wpm) usually reported in the literature on braille reading. The beginners were slow (23–60 spm) readers. Subjects were asked to read each sentence silently and to say 'yes' if they judged that the sentence made sense, and 'no' if they judged it to be semantically incorrect. The device described earlier (Chapter 3, Section 1) provided latencies for scanning words and sentences as well as the judgment data.

The hypothesis that braille reading depends on letter-by-letter assembled phonology at all levels was compared with the hypothesis that phonological coding changes with proficiency. The hypotheses make different predictions. The letter-by-letter or assembled phonology hypothesis predicts high rates of failure to reject sentences containing lexically inappropriate homophones and no interaction with reading proficiency. By contrast, the hypothesis that phonological coding changes with proficiency predicts that only beginning readers show a high rate of failures to reject correct-sounding but semantically inappropriate sentences. Fluent readers, on the other hand, should depend more on orthographic/lexical coding, and therefore make relatively few homophone errors.

Further, effects on scanning times were also predicted. Letter-by-letter (grapheme–phoneme) recoding predicts longer latencies by all subjects for scanning longer words than for scanning more contracted words, because each grapheme would need to be scanned and recoded. The hypothesis that phonological coding changes with proficiency, on the other hand, predicts that proficient readers would be less affected by differences in word length if they do not rely on assembled phonology. Any difference in the initial cover time would be masked further in semantically inappropriate sentences, because the target words would be rescanned to make the correct semantic judgments, since the rest of the sentence would render the immediately decoded meaning uncertain. Such additional processing would be expected to mask any differences due to graphemic length (movement time) alone.

Both the predictions were fulfilled. The error results (Figure 4.6) showed that judging sentences with inappropriate homophones was significantly less accurate ($F = 16.87$, df $= 1/20$; $p < 0.001$), and this interacted significantly with proficiency ($F = 6.0$; df $= 3/20$; $p < 0.01$). The least proficient group accepted sentences with inappropriate homophone words differentially more often than more proficient readers (Figure 4.6), consistent with the findings of Coltheart and her colleagues (1988) on print reading.

The latency findings also showed the interaction between proficiency and graphemic length ($F = 4.74$; df $= 3/20$; $p < 0.025$) that was predicted on the hypothesis that phonological coding changes with increased proficiency. Longer scanning of long than more contracted words ($p < 0.025$) was shown significantly only by the least proficient readers. That was predicted by the hypothesis that beginners depend differentially more on phonological recoding of constituents of words than more proficient readers. By contrast, graphemic length was not significant for proficient readers and produced no main effect. Length effects for inappropriate homophones were expected to be masked in the processing times for proficient readers, because of the additional time needed to check on the meaning of lexically inappropriate homophones. Indeed when the analysis of scanning latencies was restricted to homophone targets only from correctly judged sentences, length effects were not significant even for the slowest group, showing that when beginners did judge correctly, they took very long to scan inappropriate homophones (Figure 4.7). These latencies

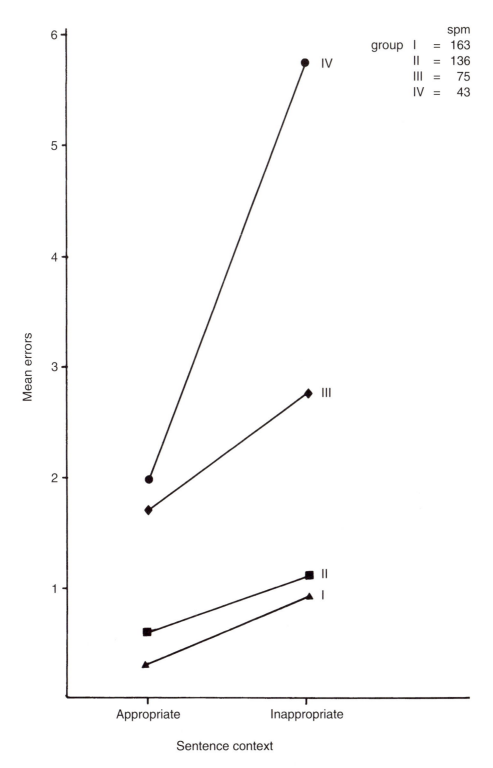

Figure 4.6 Mean errors in semantic judgments of sentences containing appropriate and inappropriate homophone words by braille readers at four levels of proficiency (spm rates)

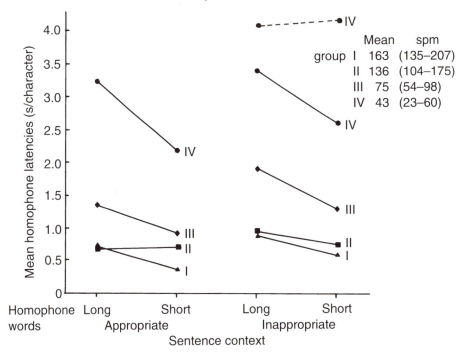

Figure 4.7 Mean (seconds/character) latencies for short (contracted) and long homophone words in appropriate and inappropriate sentence contexts by braille readers at four (spm) proficiency levels. (Broken lines are from correct judgements only)

did not differ with graphemic length, consistent with the assumption that graphemic length differences are masked by lexical checking. In other words, beginners, like fluent readers, had checked on word meaning when they judged correctly. For this to happen, they must have accessed the correct meaning of the inappropriate word initially, although beginners did this relatively rarely.

As expected, target words in inappropriate sentence contexts were scanned significantly longer than the same words in contextually compatible sentences ($F = 7.8$, $df = 1/20$; $p < 0.01$). However, although proficiency was highly significant ($F = 27.91$, $df = 3/20$, $p < 0.001$), as expected, there was no interaction between these two factors. The result implies that all subjects spent more time on inappropriate homophone words, including beginning readers who wrongly accepted far more sentences in which these occurred. It suggests that although beginners based their judgments on sounds, they did perceive that there was something semantically peculiar about these words.

In fact, the data on judgment errors and on scanning latencies for target words were quite coherent. Beginners did indeed judge proportionately more on sound than fluent readers, and were also significantly slower at scanning long (less contracted) words, as predicted for sub-lexical phonemic recoding. The findings were consistent both with the data on articulatory suppression in braille, and with the Coltheart (Coltheart *et al.*, 1988, 1990) finding that young print readers accept homophone sentences significantly more.

At the same time, the fact that all subjects, including beginning braillists, took longer over homophones in incongruous than in congruent contexts showed that even beginners were influenced by the meaning of the wrong homophone, even when they wrongly accepted the sentence. The data thus imply some relation between tactual/graphemic and lexical aspects of the scripts even when phonological effects win out. The results suggest a gradual shift in importance between sub-lexical phonological recoding and lexical coding based to some extent on graphemic/ orthographic information, rather than an abrupt, stage-like shift from one form of coding to another with increased proficiency. The further finding that word length (first-pass time) did not affect latencies for appropriate homophones in correctly judged sentences suggests that the judgement task itself could have drawn attention to the homophone targets, despite filler sentences, because the target words were crucial to the semantic judgments. Corroborative evidence for task effects on phonological coding comes from studies of visual reading. Waters and her colleagues (Waters *et al.*, 1992) found phonological effects in visual reading by adults only for sentences in which a phonologically ambiguous second clause required re-reading the first clause for semantic plausibility. Similarly, a series of sentences in which the semantically important word is phonologically ambiguous is likely to elicit more attention to the target words, even when the series also contains neutral sentences.

But the findings leave no doubt that there is a significant reduction in phonological coding with proficiency in braille as well as in visual reading. For braille, this is not merely a question of greater efficiency by more proficient readers in rejecting sentences with correct-sounding but semantically inappropriate words. The change was also found in the latencies.

The results add to our understanding of what was going on, because beginners who made the vast majority of phonological errors also showed a difference in latencies between inappropriate long and short words in these conditions. Their procedures are consistent with the notion of assembled phonology in which each character is recoded phonologically. However, they must have remembered the word by its sound rather than by its meaning, otherwise they would have realized that it did not fit the sentence. It cannot be assumed that they did not understand the meaning of the words at all. The fact that the same target words took longer in inappropriate than in appropriate sentence contexts even by beginning readers suggests that the discrepancy between the meaning and the semantic context did have some effect on processing. The finding implies that word meaning and the semantic context are integral to reading even at the start, at least for tasks in which the target words are crucial to semantic judgments, and that the ability to resolve that conflict increases with proficiency.

5   SYLLABLES AND TOUCH IN SILENT PROSE READING

It is an intriguing question whether inner speech is a central part of reading for meaning. The findings discussed in the previous section show that at least two forms of phonological coding must be assumed in braille. The question is whether reading braille silently also depends on continuous inner speech.

Introspectively most adults would agree that at least some of their thinking goes on in the form of 'inner speech'. At the same time, the finding that beginners depend on articulatory encoding of letters, and also on word sounds when they have to judge sound/sense ambiguities, whereas fluent readers show phonological recoding only when they are faced with difficult materials, suggest that speech-based coding may be used mainly when there are difficulties. If people are actually using inner speech in silent reading, there is a prima facie case for expecting that syllable effects should be prominent.

There is little doubt that syllables are important in speech perception (Gleitman and Rozin, 1973, 1977; Kelley *et al.*, 1990; Meyer, 1990; Spoehr, 1978, 1981; Treiman *et al.*, 1995; Treiman and Zukowski, 1990; Vennemann, 1988). It is also often assumed that encoding words in terms of syllables is essential to word recognition, and is central to visual reading (e.g. Just and Carpenter, 1980 a, b, 1987; Spoehr, 1978, 1981; Spoehr and Smith, 1975). The assumption that syllables are also central in reading is more controversial.

Phonological coding in terms of syllables is not, of course, the same as grapheme–phoneme recoding. For one thing, children find syllables easier to detect in speech than phonemes (Gleitman and Rozin, 1973, 1977). On the assumption that it is also easier to read scripts if words are coded in terms of syllables, beginners might show this more. On the other hand, the notion that syllabic coding is central to all reading would predict similar effects for proficient readers.

Evidence that syllable length affects visual reading has been found in tasks in which subjects had to parse long words into roots and affixes (Rayner and Pollatsek, 1987, 1989), and in tachistoscopic exposures with supervening masks, and in voice-onset data for naming digits and logographs (Pynte, 1974; Spoehr, 1978; Zhang and Simon, 1985). Word-length in syllables also increases eye-fixation times (including regressions) in visual prose reading (e.g. Just and Carpenter, 1980 a, b).

But the interpretation of findings which suggest obligatory processing of syllables in reading has not been universally accepted. Effects of task conditions cannot always be ruled out. For instance, articulatory coding in tachistoscopic presentations may be due to efforts to remember rather than to normal encoding processes, because items are obliterated by supervening masks too fast to be remembered otherwise. Without fast supervening masks, there is no evidence of obligatory phonological recoding (Spoehr, 1978). Recoding items into 'chunks' of two or three has long been known to improve short-term memory (Miller, 1956). 'Chunking' graphemic letter-clusters into syllables (e.g. Mewhort and Beal, 1977; Spoehr and Smith, 1975) would have advantages for speech-based heuristics. However, it has also been suggested that English has five thousand distinct syllables and that twenty-six letters are really more manageable (Adams, 1979). In naming tasks, syllable-length effects could be due to preparation for speech output for naming, without affecting the process of recognition (Klapp *et al.*, 1973). Similarly, when the task is to parse words, or involves a plethora of multisyllabic words, coding in terms of syllables is a reasonable heuristic. It may not occur to the same extent, or possibly occur at all, in normal prose which does not include many difficult long words. It has been suggested that the relative attention paid to word-stems and affixes in parsing words involves orthographic redundancy as well as speech-based heuristics (e.g. Seidenberg, 1987). It has also been argued that reports of longer fixations for multisyllabic words in prose reading failed to control for letter length and for word frequency effects (Kliegl *et al.*, 1982, 1983). There is a well-known correlation between word length and word frequency (e.g. Zipf, 1935). Kliegl and his colleagues (1982, 1983) found that neither syllable length nor letter length affected eye-fixation time when syllable length, letter length and word frequency were controlled independently.

As against this, Rayner and Pollatsek (1989) pointed out that Kliegl and his colleagues only analysed words which had received a single fixation of not more than 500 msec, and suggested that syllable length effects occur only when processing is slow (Rayner and Polatsek, 1989). The hypothesis that coding syllables is not only easier than phonemic recoding (e.g. Gleitman and Rozin, 1977; Rozin and Gleitman, 1977), but is also central in all reading comprehension would predict large effects of syllables in silent reading, and even more so for braille reading which is slower than print. Since beginners are even slower, they should show syllable effects more. But since the same syllabic strategy is assumed even in fluent reading, syllable length should affect all braille readers.

Speech rates for words with more syllables are lower than for words with fewer syllables (e.g. Baddeley, 1986). This could affect processes in reading aloud even if there is no effect on encoding. There is no prima facie reason why subjects should plan for speech output in silent reading, except when texts are difficult and impose memory loads for text integration and comprehension that can be sustained only by using articulatory recoding and rehearsal strategies, as shown by the study on articulatory suppression (Section 4). The question is whether word length in syllables affects reading even when these conditions of difficulty do not obtain.

It should be possible, in principle, to detect whether braille readers actually pronounce the words they read, if only subvocally or covertly. Words with more syllables should take longer than words that consist of fewer syllables. It is, of course, necessary to control for the fact that longer words usually also contain more letters than short words, and are less frequent and more difficult. But otherwise, it would be expected that multisyllabic words would have the same effect on scanning time in tactual reading that were found for eye-fixation times in visual reading (e.g. Just and Carpenter, 1980 a, b).

The assumption that syllables are central to silent reading constitutes another important test of the relation between phonological coding and graphemic effects in the acquisition of braille. The comparison that was of main interest in trying to understand the relation between graphemic effects and phonological coding in braille was between words that contain the same number of letters, but differ in the number of syllables, and between words that have the same number of syllables, but differ in the number of letters they contain. The next study (Millar, 1995), therefore, tested scanning time for words that were varied independently for length in syllables and length in letters.

In order to ensure that syllable and word length effects were not elicited by the task conditions themselves, the target words were embedded in a neutral prose text that was to be read silently for comprehension. In constructing the prose texts, the intention was that the target words should neither be crucial to the gist, nor conflict with it. This was done to ensure that there would be no special specific difficulties in integrating the target words into the gist which might draw the attention of readers to the target words. The point was to avoid eliciting strategies that readers do not use habitually in normal prose reading. To ensure that subjects were not aware that the target words were in any way 'special', subjects were only told to read the text for comprehension so that they could recount the gist of it subsequently. There was no mention of specific words, and memory for the target words was therefore not tested. The main selection criterion for the target words was that they should differ either in the number of syllables but contain the same number of letters, or differ in the number of letters but with the same syllable counts; in either case, they should not differ in familiarity on average word frequency counts (Carroll *et al.*, 1971; Thorndike and Lorge, 1959), and should conform to syllabification norms (Lima, 1987; Lima and Pollatsek, 1983; Treiman and Zukowski, 1990). The resulting selection (Table 4.1) consisted of five groups of words, each with five samples.

The graphemically short words consisted of five to six letters (mean, 5.8). Five of these were monosyllabic, five had two syllables and five consisted of three syllables. The graphemically long words had seven to ten letters (averaging 8.6 and 8.4) in five two-syllable and five three-syllable words. The words contained at most one mandatory contraction

Table 4.1 Graphemically short (5–6 letter) words that differ in the number of syllables, and graphemically long (7–10 letter) words that differ in the number of syllables

---

1–3 syllable words containing 5–6 letters (graphemically short)
(1 syllable):   piece sleeve scrape sledge plants
(2 syllables): music orange famous granny bucket
(3 syllables): piano banana potato tomato animal

2–3 syllable words containing 7–10 letters (graphemically long)
(2 syllables): bridesmaid blossom football classroom firewood
(3 syllables): chocolates victory bicycles aeroplane skeleton

---

in each of the word groups. Twenty-eight children and young people took part. All, except four subjects, also took part in the homophone judgment study (Section 5), either before or after the present tests. Subjects were divided into four proficiency groups, mainly on the basis of their speed of reading an easy pre-test 'warm-up' story. They ranged from fluent readers to beginners who were able to cope with the relevant prose passages. All subjects were of average or above average intelligence. The video-recording device (Chapter 3) provided the scanning times for target words (from first to last touch, including regressions). The reading rates are shown in Figure 4.8 which graphs the results.

The results were not consistent with the hypothesis that syllables are central to silent braille reading. There was a highly significant effect of word groups ($F = 8.97$; $df = 4/96$; $p < 0.001$), but it was due to word length in letters, and not length in syllables. Two-syllable as well as three-syllable graphemically long (8.6 and 8.4 letters) words took significantly longer ($p < 0.01$ each) than either monosyllabic, two-syllable or three-syllable graphemically short (5.8 letters) words. By contrast, there was no difference in scanning latencies between two- and three-syllable graphemically long words, or between one-syllable, two-syllable and three-syllable graphemically short words. Furthermore, the difference in reading rates between different groups was highly significant ($F = 18.07$, $df = 3/24$; $p < 0.001$) due to the slowest two groups. But syllable effects were marginal even for the least proficient readers. The predicted interaction of proficiency with syllable length was marginal ($F = 1.61$; $df = 12/96$; $p < 0.1 > 0.05$). The least proficient two groups took longer over three syllable than over two-syllable graphemically long words ($p < 0.05$, one-tail t-test). Thus on the most sensitive (for pre-planned comparisons) measure, beginners showed a trend that was consistent with the prediction that beginners would show larger syllable effects. However, the effect was below the level of significance generally considered acceptable. By contrast, there was no doubt at all about the effects of graphemic length on scanning time, and this was shown by all subjects.

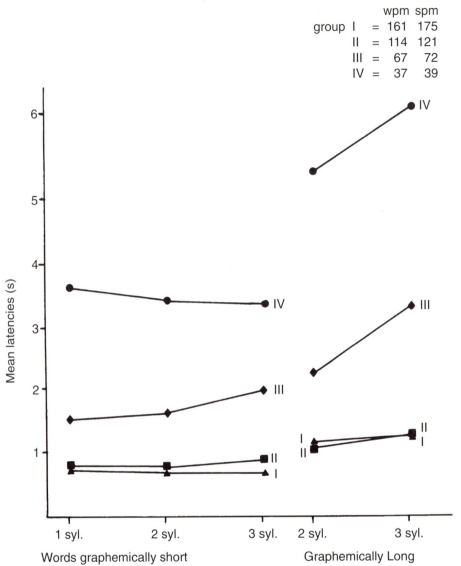

Figure 4.8 Mean scanning latencies (s) for short (5–6 letter) and long (7–10 letter) words, differing in the number of syllables, by braille readers at four (wpm & spm) levels of proficiency

I checked whether syllable effects might have been masked by idio-syncratic responses to individual words in a given group. The relevant analyses did not support that possibility. The least proficient readers produced longer than average responses for one three-syllable (potato) and for two two-syllable (famOUs and orange) short words. But these were not relevant to the lack of syllable differences. The analyses of individual word latencies were completely consistent with the main finding. Word length in syllables had no significant effect on silent reading by reasonably proficient readers when length in letters was controlled. Effects on beginning readers could not be ruled out. But they were marginal.

The apparent discrepancies between syllable effects and phonological effects in the homophone study (Section 5) are of considerable interest in teasing out the processes that underlie braille reading at different levels of proficiency. The same beginning readers who showed considerable homophone effects in sentence judgments (Section 5), produced only marginal evidence for coding in syllables. Phonemic recoding and coding words in syllables are not, of course, identical. However, assembled phonology presumably involves speech-based phonemic recoding not only at encoding, but also in blending phoneme sounds into word sounds, if that is needed to access the meaning of the words in all silent reading. The difference in findings for the same subjects suggests effects of task conditions, as well as underlining the distinction in function between different phonological effects.

In the homophone study, all the target words were monosyllabic. The length effects by beginners showed phonemic recoding. But beginners were misled into accepting the wrong sentence because they relied on the sound of words rather than on their meaning. Phoneme recoding, with or without subvocal pronunciation, would access the meaning of the incorrect target word. At the same time, the sound of the word, rather than its incorrect meaning, must have been kept in mind to produce the confusions which misled beginners into accepting semantically inappropriate sentences. These homophone effects therefore had to do with the demands of the judgment task which required memory for the target words, rather than with the processes of pre-lexical phonemic recoding to access the meaning of the word. That may well also involve pronouncing the word to-be-remembered subvocally. But the fact that the same subject only showed marginal syllable effects in the study with multisyllabic words suggests at least two forms of phonological coding even for beginners.

Considering the homophone and syllable results together thus indicates that in the homophone study beginners used two phonological strategies: one due to (pre-lexical) assembled phonology at encoding; the other due to the use of word sound rather than meaning because the task demanded memory for the target word. There was some evidence that even beginners were influenced by the wrong meaning of the homophone word (see earlier), suggesting that they relied on word sound after accessing the meaning. The syllable task, by contrast, was designed not to make demands on memory for the target words. In principle there was thus no need for phonological coding on account of short-term memory demands. The apparent difference between phonological effects on beginners in the homophone and syllable studies is thus entirely intelligible in terms of the task demands and the semantic structure of the materials in the two studies. In the sentences with homophone words, memory for the target words was crucial to the judgment task. In reading the text for meaning, only the gist of the story had to be remembered, and the text had been so designed that the target words did not bear any crucial relation to the gist.

As noted earlier, findings in the visual literature also show that task variables have to be considered in interpreting homophone ambiguities in reading tasks (Waters *et al.*, 1992). Task conditions can also explain the respective differences in graphemic length effects for proficient readers in the homophone and syllable studies. In the homophone study, the target words were crucial to the sense of the sentences and consequently to the semantic judgments. For proficient readers who relied on the meaning of target words, sound/sense ambiguities would necessarily produce difficulties for semantic integration. Not surprisingly, therefore, the target scanning latencies owed more to processes of checking and semantic integration than to the number of characters that had to be scanned initially. In the syllable study, by contrast, target words were neither ambiguous nor discrepant, nor crucial to the gist of the story. The task was to read the text for comprehension and to recount the gist, and did not require memory for the target words at any point. There was no need to recheck target words since they presented no problems for semantic integration. Scanning time was thus expected to depend entirely on the number of graphemes that had to be scanned, without being masked by additional lexical or semantic processing. The fact that scanning time depended on graphemic length, regardless of syllables or level of proficiency, confirmed that expectation.

It takes longer to move over more than over fewer letters. The notion that graphemic (first pass) length effects, as such, necessarily indicate letter-by-letter, grapheme-to-phoneme pre-lexical recoding is not plausible. All the previous studies which tested for phonological recoding directly found such effects significantly more for beginning and slow readers than for proficient braillists. But there was no evidence at all for any interaction between proficiency and physical (graphemic) word length. All subjects showed this effect. By contrast, the only tendency to an interaction with proficiency which was marginally significant was for length in syllables. On the hypothesis that speech-based pre-lexical recoding of each letter into sounds and blending these into the sound of the word occurs at all levels of proficiency, there should have been longer processing time and thus longer latencies for words with more syllables at all levels of proficiency. That was far from being the case. But first-pass lateral scanning would produce longer latencies for words with more characters when these produce no specific difficulties.

6 ORAL AND SILENT BRAILLE READING

If it is correct to assume that longer scanning latencies for words with more letters do not necessarily imply letter-by-letter reading, differences between oral and silent reading should be found, at least for competent readers.

The findings so far have all suggested that phonemic recoding at input is characteristic only of beginning and slow readers, and that competent braillists use phonological recoding mainly when texts are difficult to comprehend. By contrast, the obvious implication of the letter-by-letter view of braille reading is that oral and silent reading do not differ.

Most good braillists certainly claim that they read far more quickly silently than aloud. The evidence actually bears this out. Competent braille readers do indeed read faster when reading to themselves than when reading aloud. But that is not the case for slow readers. The findings come from a larger study in which subjects read normally-contracted braille texts in a number of counterbalanced conditions (Millar, 1990a) which included oral and silent reading for meaning. The subjects were sixteen adolescent braille readers, aged between thirteen and eighteen years, half of whom had obtained reading rates between 120 and 215 wpm (150–263 spm) in silent reading, while the other half obtained silent reading rates below 100 wpm (55–100 wpm; 92–130 spm). The analysis of (wpm) reading rates showed the obvious advantage of the more proficient readers (F = 36.44, df = 1/14; p < 0.001), and a significant advantage also for silent over oral reading (F = 5.84; df =1/14; p < 0.05). But that was qualified by a significant interaction with proficiency, showing that the advantage of silent over oral reading was due only to the more proficient group (F = 6.31, df = 1/14; p < 0.025). The analysis of reading rates in terms of syllable (spm) rates produced the same results. The significantly faster silent than oral reading rate was due entirely to the fast readers.

It was also possible to test six intelligent young readers, aged between six and a half and eight years who managed to cope with the texts, although their reading rates were very slow (8–38 wpm; 9–44 spm). Their mean rates are shown along with the rates by the older groups (Table 4.2), and did not differ significantly between oral and silent reading.

Table 4.2 Mean word per minute (wpm) and mean syllable per minute (spm) reading rates for silent reading (silent) and oral reading (aloud) for young braillists who achieved reading rates of above or below 100 wpm

Rates	*Silent*		*Aloud*	
	wpm	*spm*	*wpm*	*spm*
Above 100	161	208	122	169
Below 100	80	103	81	102

Clearly, oral reading demands speech output. The fact that for the slow readers there was no difference between reading silently and reading aloud is perfectly consistent with the other evidence which suggested that slow readers depend on speech-based encoding or assembled phonology. Faster silent than oral reading by competent braillists is also consistent with the other evidence that they rely less on inner speech in reading.

A fluent young braillist to whom I explained the reason for using artic-ulatory suppression after she had taken part in that experiment told me spontaneously that she was perfectly able to read stories and to hold a conversation with someone else at the same time. That seemed an extra-ordinary feat. But it is perfectly in line with the common experience of sighted parents who can read well-known stories to their children while planning the next meal or ruminating about quite different events.

The question whether two apparently concomitant activities were actu-ally processed in parallel turns on evidence that they coincide in time very precisely, and were not being performed in very fast sequences or alter-nation, and whether they were performed as accurately, fast and efficiently as either would be on its own. Doing two things at once without their interfering with each other is the hallmark of 'automatic' processing which runs on in parallel without making demands on attentional resources. But the experimental evidence on articulatory suppression cannot be entirely explained in that way. Occupying the speech mechanism by repeating a meaningless syllable at someone else's request is not an 'automatic' activity in any meaningful sense of the term, although it clearly is not difficult to do even for quite young children. Similarly, to read an easy but unfamiliar text sufficiently to report the gist subsequently must require some attention. It is not, of course, necessary to assume that attention is an all-or-none process. Even if two activities are not fully automatic, they may have a see-saw relation either in time, or in the demands they make on the reader's attention, or both.

What is much more difficult to believe is that two activities which depend on precisely the same mechanism operate in parallel. We do not as yet have adequate evidence on whether or how inner speech resem-bles and differs from overt articulation. The distinction between speech-based encoding processes and post-lexical recoding to construe and remember gist was needed for findings under articulatory suppression. The difficulties of beginners under articulatory suppression implied that it interfered with speech-based encoding. But there was little to suggest speech-based phonemic recoding by more competent readers. The fact that articulatory suppression disturbed comprehension of difficult texts by fluent readers, but did not affect scanning latencies, or reading easy texts, does not necessarily imply that the meaning of words had been construed before phonological recoding in difficult texts. But it does imply that phonological coding by competent readers functioned in remembering words or integrating them into gist, rather than as a means of encoding each character to construe the meaning of words. It also implies that phonological coding depends on more than one form of coding.

The elegant solution which attributes all phonological coding to motor programs for speech output (Allport, 1979) runs into the difficulty that people who are without speech from birth show phonological coding (e.g. Bishop, 1985; Vallar and Cappa, 1987). On the other hand, the view that phonological codes are abstract (e.g. Bishop and Robson, 1989) does not specify how they are acquired in the first place. At least two forms of phonological coding need to be distinguished (Besner, 1987; Besner and Davelaar, 1982).

I have argued (Millar, 1981 a, 1990 a, 1994) that by far the simplest explanation is that forms of coding can be derived from more than one input and output modality, and that these normally converge, but do not necessarily operate in precisely the same way. There are a lot of sources of information on which the competent reader can, in principle, call in addition, including lexical and orthographic knowledge, and inferences from prior context (Chapters 5 and 6). But there is a case for supposing that strategies based on speech output are used more, or more overtly when subjects encounter difficulties, whether at encoding or in attempting to construe words or gist (Millar, 1990 a).

7 SUMMARY AND IMPLICATIONS

The focus in the present chapter was on phonological and tactual coding, and how far the relations between these coding processes change with proficiency.

The evidence suggests that phonological recoding is, if anything, more prevalent in braille than in visual reading, especially for beginners. There are several reasons for this. Short-term memory is involved in learning and reading braille. But recall spans are much larger for phonologically recoded than for tactually coded patterns. Memory for sounds is also more important in the initial stages of learning to read braille than print, because in blind conditions braille patterns are associated from the outset with heard sounds rather than mediated via pictures of objects. Attention to sounds, and particularly to speech sounds, is also necessarily more important for blind children than for the sighted (Chapter 7).

There was no doubt at all about phonological coding by beginners. But in assessing phonological coding in relation to levels of proficiency, at least three forms or functions of phonological recoding have to be distinguished. Beginners showed speech-based letter-by-letter phonemic recoding both under articulatory suppression and by the difference between single character words and more 'regularly' spelt homophone words. Neither effect was in evidence for proficient readers. The articulatory suppression results showed that speech-based phonological coding has at least two functions in braille. It serves encoding processes in the very early stages of reading.

But phonological coding also functioned to sustain memory and comprehension, and this differed from phonemic recoding. The distinction is needed because proficient readers only showed effects of articulatory suppression with difficult, not with easy texts. More important, articulatory suppression affected only their comprehension of gist, not the speed of scanning. Longer reading times under suppression would be expected if they used pre-lexical phonological recoding of each input. Moreover, beginners showed not only phonemic recoding, but also relied more on the sound of words than on their meaning in sentences that produced sound/sense ambiguities. Phonological coding in terms of word sounds would help to maintain the words in memory until judgments were needed. What beginners failed to do, unlike proficient readers, was to check on the meaning of words, although their latencies showed that they were affected by lexical ambiguities.

Proficient readers showed no evidence of phonological coding in terms of syllables, or of inner speech during silent reading for comprehension, compared with reading aloud. Oral and silent reading did not differ for beginners, which is sufficiently explained by letter-by-letter reading. However, although they showed significant effects of words in syllables, these were much more marginal than either the effects of articulatory suppression or of homophone ambiguities. The difference suggested that the demands of the reading task and the structure of the verbal materials affect the balance of processes in performance, including the fact that target words were crucial in homophone judgments but not to reading for gist.

An alternative explanation of syllable effects has been that they occur at encoding, rather than at a later (i.e. output) stage of processing (e.g. Spoehr and Smith, 1975). Syllable length effects would therefore not be expected when words are equated for frequency. Effects of syllables on reading are potentially particularly important in braille, because braille contains contracted forms which represent syllables. The possibility that syllable effects occur, but only in so far as the syllables are themselves meaningful morphemes (e.g. Marslen-Wilson *et al.*, 1994), was therefore checked out by looking at scanning latencies for multisyllabic and compound words in normal reading for meaning. Results which show that decomposition into meaningful segments occurs are considered together with other aspects of lexical and semantic influences on processing (Chapter 5). The hypothesis that syllables play a central role in reading presents a problem for braille because contractions that represent familiar words and syllables have to be used within words in which the relevant letter sequences occur. Braille rules try to avoid the use of mandatory contractions when these span normal syllable segmentation. Nevertheless such words occur. The hypothesis was therefore tested directly by comparing latencies for words in which contractions span syllables with words in which contractions enhance syllable boundaries. To anticipate, the main findings may be summed up by the suggestion by Adams (1979, p. 214) that '... syllabification is mediated by the reader's knowledge of orthographic redundancy'. The findings will be considered more fully in conjunction with a more detailed consideration of the effects of contractions in reading, writing and spelling (Chapter 6).

Short-term tactual coding occurs and may play a part in the word superiority effect by beginners in conjunction with lexical knowledge. The fact that for beginners the effect was restricted to familiar three-letter words suggested a possible mediating link between initial tactual (e.g. dot-density feature) coding and familiarity of meaning. Small memory spans are typical of relatively poorly organized inputs (Miller, 1956). Coding the global shape of words was ruled out as a mediating factor in word superiority effects also for more competent readers. However, the progressive spatial organization of inputs by lateral scanning movements produces much more organized haptic inputs. Coding these should produce more stable or extended short-term memory for haptic inputs.

We (Henry and Millar, 1993; Millar, 1990 b, 1994) have argued that one effect of the longer-term memory component in short-term memory is to connect input and output systems more closely. Furthermore, movement information can also be rehearsed mentally (Millar and Ittyerah, 1991). Long-term familiarity of the connection between the haptic, phonological, lexical and orthographic components of the input would make processing both faster and less liable to disruption by the failure of any one of the components.

The main conclusion from the evidence considered so far in this chapter is that braillists code both tactual and phonological aspects of scripts. But speech-based phonemic recoding and undue reliance on phonological coding in memory is characteristic of the early stages of braille learning. Phonological effects in fluent reading occur mainly in conditions of semantic ambiguity and/or text difficulty which make demands on memory and comprehension. The implication is that phonological coding is important in braille both in acquisition and for reading materials that make demands on memory and comprehension. At the same time, beginning young braille readers tend to rely on phonological coding without sufficient lexical checking. The practical implications will be discussed later (Chapter 8).

The results are compatible with a letter-by-letter theory only for beginning and slow readers. A theory which assumes that assembled phonology simply becomes faster with increased proficiency does not adequately account for the findings. Changes in phonological and tactual processing with proficiency in braille cannot be described either by a change from pre-lexical to post-lexical phonological coding. Very young beginners show phonemic recoding and phonological strategies with difficult materials. Proficient readers only showed the latter effect significantly. Phonological but also tactual and lexical factors seem to be operative from the start.

But proficient readers were clearly better at checking on lexical and seman-tic ambiguities. Moreover, phonological effects were clearly not all of the same kind, or followed the same patterns in all conditions. The findings suggested again that task conditions have to be included in any theoreti-cal description.

Findings on phonological and graphemic effects in prose reading, and particularly the evidence on changes with reading proficiency and task conditions cannot be easily accommodated by models which propose a single or even a dual-channel hierarchical process from perception to cognition. The findings are more consistent with models of visual reading which propose more complex interactions between subsidiary skills in reading (e.g. Ferrand and Grainger, 1992; 1994; Jared and Seidenberg, 1991). The theoretical issues will be considered further in the final chapter.

5 Meaning and perception: semantic, lexical and haptic processing

Reading for comprehension in any system necessarily involves perceptual, phonological, semantic and cognitive skills. They include making inferences from the meaning of words and construing the gist of sentences and texts. The findings discussed in the previous chapters showed repeatedly that subsidiary processes do not occur in isolation from each other. The constituent factors relate in a complex, but intelligible, manner which is dictated to varying degrees of proficiency and by task demands and conditions. Even what is usually considered the most peripheral, perceptually 'given' input was found to depend on the progressive organization and differentiation of the functions of scanning movements for spatial guidance and reference, and for the verbal demands of different reading tasks, and these also influenced each other (Chapter 3). Similarly, phonological effects could not be described adequately by a simple hierarchy from touch to sound, except for very young beginners (Chapter 4), although even for beginners phonemic recoding and reliance on the sound of target words had to be distinguished. It seems progressively clear also that effects of word frequency and the precise demands and conditions of the task are important factors in performance. The present chapter focuses on meaning in the relation between lexical, semantic and perceptual factors.

The first two sections discuss issues in whether, and if so how, semantic processes affect the intake of perceptual information in reading for meaning. Factors that may increase legibility are obviously particularly important for braille. Legibility in braille can be thought of as having two main facets. One depends on an objective index of saliency. The other turns on facility of discrimination with experience.

Objective legibility in braille in the conventional format is specified by the height of braille dots, their spacing within patterns and the overall size. It is usual to use the conventional, standard braille format in teaching young children (Chapter 2). The dots are brailled on stiff 'braille' paper or plasticized brailon, and stand out in a relatively durable manner. But legibility also increases with proficiency (Chapters 2 and 3). Patterns that inexperienced people find impossible to identify are distinguished easily by proficient readers. Nevertheless, legibility is a very real practical problem in braille. Too much handling, or use by inexperienced readers who tend to press too hard in scanning, degrades the raised dots and this impairs legibility. Compensating factors are correspondingly important for practical reasons. The problem is also of considerable theoretical interest, because it concerns the question how 'top-down' cognitive processes and 'bottom-up' perceptual processes may be seen to meet. One important question is how far it is possible to use semantic context to improve perception.

Several possible explanations of whether and how prior semantic context may prime or enhance the intake of perceptual information (Meyer *et al.*, 1975) are discussed. The evidence we have from print reading suggests that it is not possible to decide *a priori* on what would be the most likely explanation for braille; nor is it possible to predict the relation between semantic and perceptual processes in braille word recognition with any certainty from findings on visual word recognition. Recognition of physically degraded visual words is better when the words are primed by a prior semantically associated word, but such facilitation depends on the stimuli, on how they are perceptually degraded, and how closely the degraded words are related to the priming context (e.g. Becker, 1985; Becker and Killion, 1977; Levy 1981; Norris 1984). For instance, in print, reducing legibility by superimposing a random pattern does not necessarily have the same effect as reducing contrast, or placing asterisks between letters (Norris, 1987). Context effects have been found in lexical decision tasks, but do not always show up in sentence completion tasks (e.g. Stanovich and West, 1983), although Becker (1985) and Norris (1987) have shown context effects also in sentence completion (choice of word) tasks by instructing subjects to predict the completion word, or by increasing the proportion of validly primed trials, respectively.

The fact that effects of poor legibility differ with the task and with different forms of degrading stimuli in print (e.g. Becker and Killion, 1977; Davis and Forster, 1994; Levy, 1981; Norris, 1984, 1987) made it important to conduct direct tests on processing braille words in normal reading for meaning of continuous texts.

The first section discusses evidence on semantic priming in normal silent reading of easy braille texts in which selected words were physically degraded so that they were difficult to make out. The question of effects of congruent and changed contexts is discussed in relation to proficiency levels (e.g. Stanovich, 1981), word difficulty, and with beginning and experienced adults braille readers. Results on tests in contexts that varied in predictability are described, and the implication that semantic facilitation occurs as and when this is an appropriate strategy is discussed.

The next two sections examine evidence on whether readers actively look for meaning early in processing words, and whether sublexical processing of compound and multisyllabic words occurs habitually in normal reading. Questions arising from the findings on syllable effects discussed previously (Chapter 4) are considered by looking at detailed frame-by-frame scanning latencies for multisyllabic and compound words. Frame-by-frame timing again failed to substantiate the claim that syllables are central in normal reading for meaning. Differences in scanning individual letters in different positions in words show that beginners pay more attention to the beginning characters of multisyllabic words, but on only about fifty per cent of the occasions sampled. Meaningful syllables are a different matter. Competent readers also show evidence of decomposing compound words into meaningful morphemes, but again only for about half the compound words sampled.

In a further section the detailed time courses of scanning movements for regressions and for 'previews' are examined for details of perceptual, lexical and semantic processing during reading. Regressions differ in type. Physically degraded words tend to elicit repetitions over the degraded word, misspelt homophones that create sound/sense ambiguities produce regressions to previous context, and low frequency words tend to start forward as well as backward movements. Lexical as well as perceptual factors mainly produce regressions. But they can also affect first pass latencies, although this varies with local perceptual factors, word frequency, and braille experience.

The findings are summarized and discussed in the final section.

1   SEMANTIC CONTEXT AND PERCEPTUAL CLARITY OF WORDS IN PROSE READING

A theory which is of particular interest for understanding how different subsidiary processes relate in braille is the proposal by Kusajima (1970) that fluent braille depends on cognitive skill, because fluent readers attend to the meaning of sentences rather than to individual words. In one sense it is difficult to see how the reader can construe the gist of sentences in the first place, except by understanding the meaning of the words of which they are composed. However, there is evidence from eye-fixation times (e.g. Carpenter and Just, 1983; Just and Carpenter, 1980 a, b; Rayner and Pollatsek, 1987; Sanford and Garrod, 1981), as well as from everyday experience of reading, that the meaning of difficult words can often be construed from the rest of the context. The findings on homophone sentence judgments (Chapter 4) which showed that subjects spent longer on the same target words in sentence contexts that were inappropriate to them than in congruent sentences is evidence for processes of this kind in braille. The target words were re-scanned because of difficulties with the integration of the target words, rather than because of any perceptual difficulty. Semantic difficulties can also reduce the speed of print reading. Sanford and Garrod (1981) found that print reading is slowed by what they termed 'inconsiderate' discourse; that is to say, text structures that give few or no hints about the words that follow, or actually mislead the reader about the meaning of words that can be expected.

An alternative interpretation of the Kusajima (1970) theory is that skilled braille depends on direct facilitation of the perceptual intake by higher order stored information. As we saw earlier (Millar, 1987 b, experiment 2), fluent readers are much better at detecting local, infrequent dot degradations in reading connected texts than beginning or slow readers. But to support the view proposed by Kusajima (1970) it would have to be assumed that in fluent braille the semantic context influences the intake of perceptual information. The Kusajima theory which assumes that increased reading skill depends on the use of semantic context should predict that fluent braillists would be much better at using prior context or 'top-down' higher order knowledge to compensate for discrimination difficulties than beginning readers.

There are a number of proposals from the visual reading literature on how perceptual cues, word familiarity and prior context relate to each other. The logogen theory of Morton (Morton, 1969, 1979) assumes 'logogens', or word-like meanings are accessed directly by perceptual inputs that can tap into the features of a logogen. Prior context would activate a 'candidate' set of logogens that are related to it. The more information accumulates, the lower is the recognition threshold. Word familiarity and related context act by reducing the amount of evidence required to reach the recognition threshold. But degrading the perceptual input slows the extraction of features that tap into the logogens. However, word frequency and stimulus degradation effects were found to add, rather than to interact, and only interactions between context and stimulus degradation were found (Becker and Killion, 1977; Durunoglu, 1988). Such findings prompted the search and verification models of Becker (Becker, 1976, 1980; Becker and Killion, 1977) and Forster (1976, 1981). These assume that prior context activates a 'candidate' set of words and associated graphemic and/or orthographic cues, and the cues from the candidate set are then verified against inputs from the perceptual scan. Alternatively the reader constructs a representation of the perceptual input and then searches through orthographic, phonological and syntactic/semantic 'files' to access the mental lexicon, and this activates a candidate set of words against which the evidence is tested or verified.

The view proposed by Stanovich and his colleagues (e.g. Stanovich, 1981; Stanovich and West, 1979, 1983; West and Stanovich, 1978) suggests that word recognition in fluent reading is automatic. It is only the beginning readers who depend on facilitation by the context (Stanovich, 1981; Stanovich and West, 1983; West and Stanovich, 1978). The theory assumes that access to word meaning in fluent reading occurs automatically through spreading activation. Beginners, by contrast, use context actively or strategically in order to construe the meaning of constituent words. Facilitation from prior context should, therefore, be shown differentially more by beginners than by fluent readers. The Kusajima and Stanovich hypotheses thus make opposite predictions about the role of semantic context in word recognition in relation to levels of reading proficiency.

Both theories speak to the question whether semantic activation operates directly on the perceptual processes, or whether semantic effects depend on a quasi strategic recruitment of prior information in the case of perceptual difficulties. If Kusajima is right, fluent readers should be more affected by semantic factors than beginning readers. By contrast, the Stanovich interactive compensatory model predicts that subjects actively look for prior context when they encounter perceptual difficulties. Any check on automatic processing could produce more deliberate search (Stanovich *et al.*, 1985).

One question was, therefore, whether misspelling words has the same effect on scanning latencies as perceptual degradation. Misspelt words that sound compatible with the context, should thus increase scanning time.

The experiment which is briefly described below (Millar, 1988 c) was thus designed to answer three main questions: (i) do fluent or slow readers show more effects of semantically 'inconsiderate' discourse; (ii) does interference from changed semantic context affect normally brailled target words, or does it occur significantly only if inputs are perceptually degraded; (iii) are the two effects additive. A further aim was to assess the role of orthographic factors in reading words in compatible and incompatible contexts to test whether misspelling operates in the same way as perceptual degradation. The study tested nine good (mean, 111 wpm, 140 spm) and nine slower (mean, 71 wpm, 99 spm) young braille readers in reading experimentally manipulated and control stories.

In order to test for the effects of degraded words before and after relevant context, and after an abrupt change in context, all stories were designed on the same plan. They were twelve lines long and were constructed around target words. The targets occurred first in a neutral context on the first or third line. They were then repeated on line six after two lines of relevant context, and again on lines nine and eleven, either after further relevant context, or after the context was changed on line eight. Stories were constructed around each of the words in every homophone pair. The target words were selected to be short (four characters or less), familiar (Hofland and Johanssen, 1982; Kucera and Francis, 1967), and to have a legal word as a homophone, such that substituting a minor orthographic change would alter the meaning but not the sound of the word (mail/male; tail/tale; son/sun; waist/waste; bore/boar). In control conditions each text was simply brailled in the normal way. Changed context was produced by altering the story abruptly to one compatible with the homophone of the target word (on line eight of the text). To degrade the target word perceptually, the dots of the target word were depressed evenly with a ruler to near illegibility. In one condition, the degraded word occurred on each relevant line in otherwise compatible contexts. In the dual condition, the target word was perceptually degraded and the context was changed as well. In the condition that was designed to check on orthographic effects, the target word was brailled throughout as the wrongly spelt homophone word. In the dual condition the wrongly spelt homophone was used in the early lines of text, but the context was changed to be compatible with that homophone on line eight. The story plan thus made it possible to assess changes in processing during the course of reading a text.

The results showed that two proficiency groups differed significantly in overall reading speeds, as expected. Context effects occurred also. But there was little support for the notion that semantic effects interact with proficiency level as such. That result supported neither the implication of the Kusajima (1970) view that fast reading depends on using semantic context, nor the assumption that context effects are shown more by poorer readers (e.g. West and Stanovich, 1978). Texts with degraded target words, misspelt targets, changed context, and the combination of changed contest with misspelt or degraded targets, all slowed the overall reading time significantly, compared to the control condition. But this was so for both groups of readers. For the particular subjects in that study, at any rate, there was no evidence that either faster or slower reading showed context effects significantly more.

Latencies for the target words produced the same result. Change in context prior to the target slowed word-scanning time significantly, but this did not differ significantly between the two proficiency groups. In comparing these findings with the results on homophone sentences which were discussed in the previous chapter, it is noteworthy that previous interactions with proficiency related to the phonological aspects of the homophone targets. By contrast, all subjects showed effects of inappropriate semantic context, similar to the context effects in this (Millar, 1988 c) study. Phonological confusions and effects of semantic incompatibility seem to relate differently to reading proficiency. Accepting phonologically inappropriate words seems to be more characteristic of younger or less competent readers. Semantic incompatibility, by contrast, seemed to disturb reading regardless of reading proficiency. The latencies for the target words, therefore, did not support the Kusajima (1974) hypothesis that better braillists use context more, nor yet the implication from the Stanovich (1981) theory that context effects are shown less by proficient readers. However, it could be argued that word recognition was not automatic even for the better braillists. Further evidence on this question will be considered later in relation to highly experienced braille readers (Section 2).

The data of main interest in the Millar (1988 c) study were the latencies for the target words on different lines of text in the various experimental and control conditions. There were indeed highly significant interactions between the position of target words on different lines of text and the experimental conditions as had been expected from the layout of the story plan.

Dealing first with the effects of perceptual legibility, there was no doubt about the importance of intact perceptual stimuli. The fact that perceptual clarity had highly significant effects needs perhaps hardly to be emphasized. Subjects spent a considerable time over trying to make out degraded words on every line of text on which they appeared. That was in complete contrast to misspelt homophone targets in either normal or changed conditions. Although the presence of misspelt targets lengthened the overall reading time (see earlier), the latencies for the misspelt target words themselves did not differ significantly from the controls on any line of text, except marginally immediately after the first mention of relevant context. The pattern thus suggested an effect of orthography on text integration, but not on word recognition. However, the orthographic and graphemic difference between homophone words was here quite small, unlike the homophone target pairs in the sentence judgments discussed earlier (Chapter 4). Orthographic and graphemic differences will be discussed more specifically in detail in the chapter which deals with spelling and contractions (Chapter 6). The point of interest here is that the pattern of latencies for perceptually degraded words was quite different from that for misspelt (homophone) words.

The length of time that subjects took over trying to make out perceptually degraded words is analogous to the findings on eye-fixation times which led Just and Carpenter (1980 a, b) to suggest that readers process individual words immediately as far as possible. That seemed to be the case here also. At the same time, there were additional context effects. In conditions in which the target word was degraded and the context was changed abruptly, the degraded words took still longer than degraded words in coherent contexts, and these latencies did not reduce with repetition but were actually larger on the last line of text. The fact that context change produced worse effects when the stimulus quality was also poor suggested that the semantic and perceptual effects on word processing were additive.

Word repetition had the most consistent effect in lowering target word latencies in the control condition. Scanning time for the target word decreased progressively with repetition on the later lines of text, suggesting that reading became progressive faster, provided the context remained the same. The change of context to the wrong story on the eighth line of text had immediate slowing effects on scanning the normally brailled target word on the following line. Moreover, the effect seemed to be quite specific. With further repetition of the word after the altered context on the next two lines of text, the scanning time for the target word reduced again. There was, therefore, clear evidence that the semantic context influenced the processing of target words.

The influence that context exerted on intact target words seemed to be continuous, but at a distance of about six to seven words, suggesting that meaning is construed in phrases rather than in smaller units, as suggested by Just and Carpenter (1980 a, b) or in larger units at the point of the 'wrap-up' of sentences. Thus the effect of context change was largest on the target word on the line immediately following the change, but target word latencies decreased relatively fast after a new context was established, and the difference was no longer significant at the end of the story. The finding is more consistent with results on pronoun assignments in eye-movement studies of visual reading (Ehrlich and Rayner, 1983). However, from the answers to the comprehension questions at the end of scripts it was clear that subjects also integrate gist over the whole story. Some readers reported the gist of both 'halves' of the changed story. But a surprising number of readers confabulated a totally new story which reconciled the meaning of the two halves.

Taking the different indices of context effects on intact familiar words together, the effects seem to be 'local' and to occur at the level of phrases, rather than in larger or smaller units. By the end of the story there is no effect, probably because the reader is quite sure about the relation of the target word to the gist by that time. However, the story gist is also reviewed as a whole. The attempts to integrate the gist at the beginning of the story with the later changed part of the story was clearly shown by confabulation errors when recounting the gist.

The most obvious semantic context effects shown in the (Millar, 1988 c) study were due to interference from incompatible contexts. Interference in processing an item from incompatible information seems generally to be easier to demonstrate than facilitation for processing that item from compatible information. A number of researchers on visual reading of words have found that inhibition from anomalous context, and facilitation from related context are not symmetrical effects (Antos, 1979; De Groot, 1984, 1985; Fischler and Bloom, 1980; Norris, 1987; Stanovich and West, 1983).

Exactly why interference is more powerful than facilitation is not entirely clear (Antos, 1979, De Groot, 1984,1985; Fischler and Bloom, 1979). One suggestion is that context effects are simply by-products of processes which are designed primarily to resolve lexical or perceptual ambiguity (Norris, 1986). That account would explain the semantic effects which showed up in longer latencies for homophone target words in inappropriate sentence contexts (Chapter 4), as well as for the increase in scanning time for target words after the context was changed (Millar, 1988 c) as by-products of resolving sound/sense ambiguities. The description suggests that poor legibility of a word, combined with an incompatible context, interferes with comprehension processes. The only suggestion that semantic context as well as repetition facilitates the pick-up of intact perceptual information under normal conditions came from the fact that scanning time decreased more for the repeated target word later in the text compared with the initial lines of text.

An experiment was therefore run to test whether compatible prior context facilitates silent reading of normally brailled words, compared with reading the words after neutral context. Both effects were compared also with neutral or compatible prior context when the target words were degraded. The latter condition simulates braille texts in which some words have become illegible. Six target words of medium frequency were used, such that they would not be unknown to readers, but could not be easily guessed from the initial letters. Since the length of words and their frequency in the literature are known to be related (e.g. Zipf, 1935), words that were seven to nine letters long and of medium frequency were selected from a (Thorndike and Lorge, 1959) word frequency count. A further restriction was that the words should contain no letter clusters that, in braille, demand the use of mandatory contractions. That was in order to avoid structural differences between the target words as far as possible, because braille contractions do not all have the same frequency (Lorimer *et al.*, 1982), and are not necessarily all taught at the same time. The words that met these restrictions (factory, hospital, policeman, motorboat, cottonwool, elephant) were embedded in four texts. The positions of the words in the texts were randomized as far as possible without making the passages too artificial. In two of the stories, each target word was preceded by meaningfully related context (from now on called 'PR' stories). For instance, 'elephant' was preceded by a mention of animals, 'policeman' by the mention of patrols in one script and by 'traffic' in another. Words indicating a place of work preceded the word 'factory'. In the other two stories, the same target words were preceded by neutral (semantically unrelated) text (from now on called 'PO stories'). The four texts were each brailled twice: once normally and once in degraded form, so that each of the stories with preceding relevant context (PR) and without preceding (PO) relevant context could be used in both control and degraded formats. Half the subjects received a series in which one of the PR and one of the PO texts was in the experimental condition and the other PR and PO texts were in control conditions. The other half of subjects received the same texts in the opposite conditions. The order of the stories was randomized across subjects. The task was simply to read the stories for comprehension. The students were told beforehand that their reading would be timed, and that they would be asked to recount the gist of each passage after reading it. Care was taken to avoid alerting them to the target words. But if the readers did not mention the target words or synonyms for them in recounting the gist, they were prompted to say more about the story and asked to try to remember as many details as possible.

To check on the relation between levels of proficiency and semantic effects, subjects with a wider range of reading proficiency than in previous studies were tested, although the number of subjects who were very slow but could read the stories and the number of very fast readers was necessarily rather small. Two groups of high school students (Group I, 137–196 wpm, 144–207 spm; Group II, 93–134 wpm, 98–141 spm) took part. A third group of much slower readers from an unselective school for the blind (Group III, 23–71 wpm, 24–77 spm) were young beginners, but included an older child who had started braille relatively late.

The results for word latencies (ms per letter) are graphed in Figure 5.1. All subjects took significantly longer over the perceptually degraded words than over the same words brailled normally (F = 8.76, df = 2/12; p < 0.001). More important, the effects of perceptual clarity interacted significantly with context effects (F = 5.49; df = 2/12; p < 0.05). The interaction meant that the perceptually degraded words were indeed processed significantly faster when they were preceded by related context (PR) than after neutral prose (PO). But target words in the normally brailled PR stories did not differ from the same target words in the normally brailled PO stories. There was thus no evidence that preceding associated semantic context produced faster scanning of intact target words. Reading proficiency was significant (F = 8.76; df = 2/12; p < 0.01), due mainly to the slowest group of readers. But the interaction between proficiency and perceptual clarity was just below the five per cent significance level (F = 3.13; df = 2/12; P < 0.1 > 0.05). This may have been due to the relatively small numbers of subjects. As the graph (Figure 5.1) shows, the third group of readers took nearly twice as long over the degraded words when there was no prior facilitating context than when the same words followed semantically-related context. However, the other groups showed a similar trend.

The task instructions had been deliberately framed to avoid drawing the attention of subjects to the target words. Subjects had consequently not been asked to remember specific words of any kind, but simply to report the gist of the passages. The accuracy of recognizing degraded words could therefore not be tested directly. Nevertheless, it was possible to assess whether target words had been recognized, because almost all subjects commented spontaneously on the faintness of some of the words. Moreover, their attempts to recognize degraded words were usually quite audible. From these, usually audible, attempts, as well as from spontaneous comments, it was possible to estimate failure rates and errors fairly accurately. The slowest group made very few (less than 3 per cent) errors in the two control conditions. But their failure rate for degraded words in neutral (PO) contexts was very high (75 per cent) failure, in contrast to their much lower (18 per cent) failure rate for degraded words when these followed compatible (PR) contexts. The two groups of proficient readers showed surprisingly low failure rates. They recognized most of the perceptually degraded words, with and without relevant prior context (8 per cent and 11 per cent error rate, respectively), and made no errors at

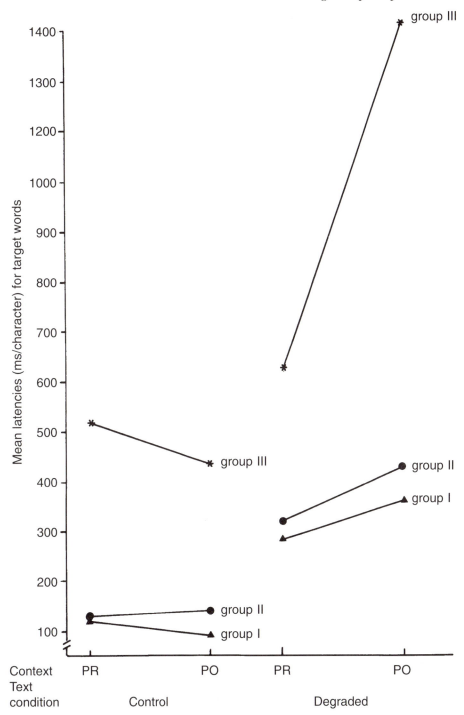

Figure 5.1 Mean latencies (ms per character) for degraded and control target words in texts with prior relevant (PR) semantic contexts and with prior neutral (PO) semantic contexts

all in the normally brailled (PR or PO) stories. The fact that beginners showed substantial failures in recognition as well as longer latencies for degraded words in neutral but not in compatible contexts is consistent with the Stanovich and West (1983) suggestion that word recognition by beginning readers depends to a much larger extent on semantic context than for proficient readers. But for latencies, the interactions with levels of reading proficiency were not robust, and were not found in the earlier (Millar, 1988 c) study. Moreover, similar rather marginal interactions between proficiency and context effects can be found in a (West and Stanovich, 1978) visual reading study. Such results suggest that the inter-active compensatory model (Stanovich, 1981) is not a completely satis-factory explanation of context effects, unless task conditions are taken into account. Thus the earlier study (Millar, 1988 c) which showed no interaction with proficiency used an easier text, and the target words were closely related to the context. Interference from incompatible context was thus a much stronger effect, and so affected proficient and slow readers alike. The degree of semantic association between the prior context and target word may be analogous to the situation in visual print where the proportion of relevant primes is high. Norris (1987) demonstrated that changing the probability of compatible contexts can change the extent to which contextual facilitation of words becomes significant. The texts in the second study, by contrast, were constructed to accommodate a number of randomly distributed target words which were compatible with the context, but by no means crucial to it. The expectation that these words would be preceded by associated terms in some of the texts could, there-fore, hardly have been high. The very fact that context effects differ with differences in the semantic relations between the context and target words suggests that this is an important factor in the relation between perception and context also.

The findings showed no semantic facilitation except for target words that were difficult to perceive. The finding was consistent with the explanation that semantic effects are by-products of attempts to resolve perceptual ambiguity. The fact that compatible semantic context only facilitated perception of degraded words, while incompatible context produced inter-ference with the recognition also of normally brailled words is similar to other evidence that facilitation and interference effects are asymmetric, and suggests that the effect of semantic context on perceptual processing in braille is indirect rather than direct.

The surprising accuracy of proficient readers in recognizing perceptually degraded words suggests that at least one aspect of proficiency is an increase in 'sensitivity' to tactual patterns. A very similar result was found in a previous study (Millar, 1987 b, exp. 2) which showed that fluent readers are quite remarkable in their ability to detect small differences in the height of braille dots. The result is compatible with other findings (Chapters 2 and 3) which show that perceptual experience with braille patterns as such greatly improves recognition, and suggests that the importance of prior context on recognition varies with that factor. The theoretical implication of this effect will be discussed later (Chapter 9).

The possibility raises the question whether slow or less proficient reading is analogous to lack of perceptual clarity, and that facilitation by compatible prior context depends on the probability that such contextual cues will be present. This is tested in the next section.

2   SEMANTIC PRIMING OF SINGLE WORDS AND READING EXPERIENCE

The findings discussed in the last two sections showed both interference from incongruous semantic context and facilitation from congruent prior discourse for word recognition during reading for meaning. Moreover, the results were broadly consistent with the notion that such effects are by-products of processes designed to resolve lexical or perceptual ambiguity. The puzzle was, therefore, why the studies produced so little hard evidence that semantic context effects were associated differentially more with lower levels of reading proficiency, although the gap between proficient and slower young readers was significant.

Both the proposal by Norris (1986) and the view of Stanovich and West (1981) suggest that adult readers use semantic context to compensate for perceptual difficulties. In principle, perceptual difficulties in braille are due to poor legibility of the script, but they could occur also because perception by the reader is poor. It is unlikely that young children who had learned braille from the start, and who were proficient enough to cope with my experimental texts, were lacking in perceptual skill. The possibility that lack of perceptual experience may operate like reduced legibility in texts was therefore checked out with a particularly important group of beginning braillists, namely people who go blind later in life.

It is often assumed that older people are unable to learn braille because their tactual acuity is poor. However, perceptual acuity problems in braille probably have more to do with lack of practice (Pester, 1993), than with absolutely low levels of tactual acuity, as measured by two-point thresholds (Chapter 2). Evidence of increased activity in the sensorimotor cortex with practice (Chapter 2), as well as the differences in perceptual pick-up between beginning and proficient readers (see earlier) suggest that measures of tactual acuity are not the best predictors of useful reading. Even older adults with impaired tactual sensitivity due to diabetes can learn to useful levels (Bernbaum *et al.*, 1989; Harley *et al.*, 1985). The question whether focused and consistent contextual priming facilitate braille word recognition by older recent braillists was of practical as well as theoretical interest, in any case.

I was extremely fortunate in obtaining the help of experienced older braillists and of people who had learned braille later in life. It was possible to match five experienced braillists with five new braille readers on professional status, and years (forty or more) of reading experience in braille and print, respectively. Two of the experienced braillists had read print until early adolescence, the other three had learned only braille from the start. Their average baseline reading rate was 80 wpm (62–158 wpm), and was rather slow. Nevertheless, they were all highly competent readers, in the sense of being able to read even the most difficult texts. The daily use of braille by recent braillists varied from reading labels and some instructions to practising some braille on most days in order to retain literacy. Oral reading a simple story was used to obtain baseline reading rates. Help was given when necessary, and reading rates were adjusted accordingly. The rates were based on the best lines of texts read correctly (without help). The new braillists had an average best speed of 23 wpm (15–37 wpm). Experienced and new braillists were comparable in average and range of chronological age.

On the assumption that tactual acuity is primarily a question of proficiency and/or familiarity, priming effects were predicted for the new braillists only. On the other hand, if tactual sensitivity to braille is primarily a matter of age, related primes should facilitate tactual recognition by highly experienced older braillists in the same way as for the older new braillists.

A further question was whether new braillists would benefit more from priming if the primes are presented consistently. The assumption was that primes are more effective when there is a reasonably high probability that they are associates of the target words. It was therefore predicted that related primes would facilitate word recognition more if they were presented in consistent blocks, than in randomly ordered lists where semantically related word pairs were interspersed unpredictably with word pairs in which the primes were unrelated to the target word, or were associated by sound, or had letters in common with the target.

Three lists of ten (familiar, monosyllabic) word pairs were prepared. Subjects were asked to scan these from left to right without returning to the first word in a pair. The first list consisted of blocks of semantically related pairs (e.g. cat–dog, ham–egg, dry–wet, moon–sun), followed by a list of ten neutral word pairs in which the first word was unrelated to the target word (e.g. six–lot, pop–bet, job–lit, rob–sit). As a further control, a third list of ten word pairs was used in which the prime was graphemically related to the target word. The reason for using this list was twofold. One possibility was that any type of relatedness, not merely a semantic relation, would facilitate recognition. More important, the question was whether repetition of letters in different words would facilitate scanning more than a meaningfully associated term. The word pairs in the lists were therefore constructed by using precisely the same letters but in reversed order (pam–map, pot–top, gum–mug, tar–rat, bat–tab). Subjects always received the semantically related pairs first, followed by the un-

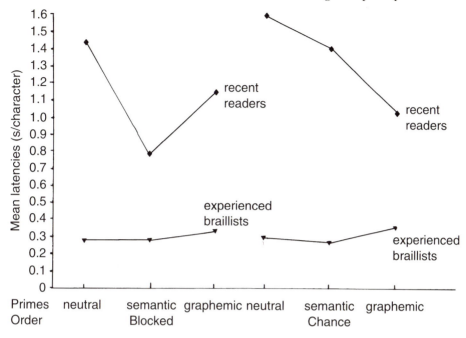

Figure 5.2 Mean latencies (seconds per character) for target words with neutral, semantic and graphemic primes presented in blocked or chance order

related pairs and finally the block of graphemically related pairs. The lists of word pairs were always presented in a fixed order of blocks of semantically related, unrelated and graphemically related pairs.

A second test followed after a rest pause of ten to twenty minutes. The main difference was that word pairs in all priming conditions were interspersed randomly in the presentation, and also included neutral word pairs. In this condition, the proportion of semantically related pairs was thus low (20 per cent).

The mean latencies for target words in neutral, semantic and graphemic priming conditions are shown in Figure 5.2. The scanning times (from the first to last letter of target words) were analysed by types of prime. Experienced and new braillists differed significantly (F = 34.19, df = 1/8; p < 0.001), as expected. The blocked order of presentation also differed significantly from the chance order (F = 13.33, df = 1/8; p < 0.01), but only for new readers (p < 0.01). Semantic primes significantly reduced scanning latencies compared with neutral primes (F = 9.4, df = 1/8; p < 0.025), and that was also true only for the new readers (F = 8.20, df = 1/8; p < 0.025). The interaction between proficiency and type of presentation (ordered or random) was further confirmed by analyses of individual protocols. Every individual new braille reader was significantly faster with semantic than with neutral primes in blocked presentations

(Kolmogorov-Smirnov test, $p < 0.05$ to $p < 0.002$). Random presentations did not produce this advantage. But none of the experienced braillists showed significant effects of semantic primes in either the blocked or in chance presentation.

The hypothesis that prior semantically related words facilitate word recognition by subjects who had learned braille relatively late in life was thus consistent in that respect with the Stanovich and West (1981) theory. Moreover, there was no doubt that semantic priming depended also on the probability with which semantic associations between priming and target words could be expected. No semantic priming was found in conditions in which semantically related word pairs were randomly interspersed with other priming pairs and constituted only a fifth of the presentation pairs. This is clearly consistent with findings in visual reading which show that semantic facilitation of word recognition depends on the probability with which such relations occur in task conditions which either make it obvious to subjects that attending to word associations is likely to help, or in which the proportion of valid primes is very high (e.g. Becker, 1985; Norris, 1987). Adult new braille readers were perfectly aware of trying to 'guess' the next letter, both from the primes, and from preceding letters that they had already construed, and frequently commented on doing so. Errors and longer scanning times occurred when they made the wrong predictions. In other words, they were trying to predict the word from the target prime when they were aware that a connection could be expected.

The assumption that lack of perceptual experience can be regarded as equivalent to degraded or impoverished legibility was supported. The findings thus confirm that the semantic primes facilitate word recognition when there are difficulties in perceptual processing, provided the probability of semantically associated primes is high.

Interestingly enough the findings (Figure 5.2) also suggest that graphemic primes had somewhat different effects. Graphemic primes contained the same letters, but differed from the target word in meaning and the sequential order of the letters. Apart from the expected difference between the two reading groups ($F = 29.36$; df $= 1/8$; $p < 0.001$), graphemic and neutral primes differed significantly ($F = 8.29$; df $= 1/8$; $p < 0.025$), but in opposite directions for the two reading groups ($F = 16.59$; df $= 1/8$; $p < 0.01$). New braillists were faster with graphemic than with neutral primes, while for experienced braillists graphemic primes had negative effects. If anything, these effects were stronger in random than in blocked presentations. For the new braillists, repeating the letters does have facilitating effects, regardless of the proportion of occurrence. This makes good sense, given the other evidence that tactual perception of the characters still presents a difficulty. By contrast, for experienced braillists, the repetition of letters in the wrong sequence interfered with recognition.

The finding suggests that experienced braillists do indeed depend on the association between word meaning and orthography, and presumably also with associated phonology, although that was not tested here. The association with spelling sequences will be considered further in connection with contracted forms and spelling (Chapter 6).

The question whether fluent readers segment words habitually into sub-lexical units or syllables is considered further in the next section.

3   SUB-LEXICAL DECOMPOSITION: SYLLABLES AND MORPHEMES IN MULTISYLLABIC AND COMPOUND WORDS

An important issue that was left over from the findings considered in Chapter 4 was the possible role of sub-lexical decomposition by proficient braillists for recognizing words in reading for meaning. Despite the undoubted influence of phonological input coding, and also of reliance on the sound of words by beginning young readers, there was very little evidence of a central role for syllables in reading normal texts for meaning by more proficient readers.

Two points from earlier discussions are relevant. One is the fact that word superiority effects occur in braille, and are associated with word familiarity and length, particularly for beginning readers who only read three-letter words faster than the constituent letters. The second was the apparent discrepancy in phonological coding and graphemic length effects in semantic judgments of sentences with ambiguous homophone targets, compared with processing unambiguous target words in texts read silently only for gist. I argued that discrepancies were due to differences in tasks and the semantic structure of the materials. In fact, the apparent discrepancies between the two studies are not unlike the differences in semantic priming effects in conditions of high versus low probability of occurrence that were discussed in the previous section.

Evidence on segmenting words, or sub-lexical decomposition, in reading is important for understanding how processing takes place. The previous chapter showed that braille words are processed faster than nonwords or strings of letters, as is the case with print, but also that word length in letters, but not word length in syllables increased word scanning latencies in text reading. The difference between silent and oral reading, as well as the absence of syllable effects suggested that silent reading by proficient braillists does not depend on accompanying covert inner speech. Moreover, since the task was to remember gist rather than the target words there was no need to recode words phonologically in order to retain them in short-term memory. However, the reason for the relatively marginal effect of syllables on the less proficient readers was less clear. If they used strict letter-by-letter processing and speech output to access the meaning of words, syllable effects should be more prominent on the view that such coding precedes decomposition into phonemes (e.g. Spoehr and Smith, 1975). At the same time, the findings on syllable effects do not rule out the possibility that braille readers depend on some form of sub-lexical decomposition, even though this is not necessarily at the level of grapheme–phoneme recoding, except for very young beginners. An alternative possibility is that syllables do have significant effects on words in silent braille reading, but only to the extent that they constitute meaningful entities.

The morpheme is the smallest linguistic unit which carries meaning and cannot be decomposed further into meaningful units. Morphemes may, however, have meaning solely as grammatical markers, such as the 'ed' ending for the past tense of verbs. Articles and prepositions such as 'the' or 'of', or prefixes and suffixes such as 'con' and 'ing' fall into that category. The majority of studies with visual materials have used inflected or derived words of this kind. But morphologically complex words can also be compound words. Compound words are multisyllabic words in which at least one, and preferably more than one of the syllables is a legal English word in its own right. The meaning of such compound words is not necessarily related to either of the constituent words (e.g. 'hatstand', 'buttercup').

In the literature on visual reading the main theoretical interest in morphologically complex words has been to establish whether people's 'internal lexicon' or word knowledge is organized morphologically, and whether such organizations consist of root morphemes and affixes and derivations, or of independent morphemic representation. Taft and Forster (1975) proposed that morphologically complex visual words are automatically decomposed for recognition. Parsing starts with the first letter, so that initial positions are always accessed before final ones. Consistent evidence has come from facilitation of first fixations on compound words by previous parafoveal presentation of the initial but not of the final constituent (e.g. Inhoff, 1987; Lima, 1987; Lima and Pollatsek, 1983). But priming of compound words by a constituent has also been found regardless of its spatial position in the compound in lexical decision tasks (e.g. Monsell, 1987). Moreover, priming is not necessarily automatic. Priming effects vary with the semantic relation between the meaning of the compound word and morphemes or words of which it is composed (e.g. Sandra, 1992; Schriefers *et al.*, 1992; Taft, 1994).

My interest in comparing compound and multisyllabic words here was in the processes that take place in braille reading, without assuming that the results necessarily tap into a universal or permanent inner organization of lexical knowledge. The word superiority effects had shown that familiarity, but also graphemic length, are important factors in braille word superiority effects for monosyllabic words. But the number of syllables in multisyllabic words at best affected only beginners in reading for meaning. This raised the question whether braille readers do habitually decompose multisyllabic words into sub-lexical units in silent reading for meaning, and if so whether the decomposition is into relatively meaningless, albeit pronounceable, syllables or into meaningful morphemes.

Given the evidence that task conditions tend to modulate processing, I wanted to avoid conditions which would elicit decomposition strategies that braillists may not use habitually in normal prose reading otherwise. I consequently analysed frame-by-frame timing data from control texts that happened to contain multisyllabic and compound words, but which had been read silently as control conditions in studies that were designed for other purposes. The test conditions ensured that there had been no means whereby the attention of subjects had been drawn to either multisyllabic or compound words. Normal English prose usually contains far fewer compound than multisyllabic words. Three types of control scripts were therefore used to provide twelve legal English compound words (e.g. firewood, cottonwool, motorboat, bridesmaid, policeman, bonfire, bedside, football, classroom) with a mean syllable count of 2.33 syllables. These were compared with over thirty multisyllabic words which happened to occur in the same scripts, and produced the same average syllable (2.3) count, and did not differ significantly in the average number of contractions they contained (e.g. blossoms, dummy, elephant, hospitals, piano, basket, cautiously, bicycles, luminous, balcony, summer). There was no specific semantically related prior contextual support for either the compound or for multisyllabic words in the texts.

The method used was akin to eye-movement studies, except that the data of interest were derived from frame-by-frame scanning latencies, rather than from fixation times (see Chapter 3). The evidence that I sought was based on the latencies for transition between the letters in each multisyllabic and in each compound word for every subject. The point was to assess latencies for transitions between letters that marked syllable boundaries in multisyllabic words, and latencies between any other two letters in that word. Latencies between the two letters at syllable boundaries that exceeded the latencies (including regressions) for transitions between any other two letters in that word were counted as positive evidence for coding the word by syllables. Similarly, latencies between the two letters that flanked the morphemes of compound words which exceeded the transition latencies between other letters in that word were considered positive evidence that the word had been decomposed into the constituent morphemes. Evidence for lexical decomposition necessarily depended on processing time, and therefore includes time spent in local regressions as well as first-pass time within the compound word. The point was to compare latencies between letters that divide morphemes in compound words with latencies between other letters. The data of interest were thus the proportion of increased transition latencies or 'breaks' in processing between syllables in multisyllabic words and between morphemic components of compound words.

Initially the videorecordings of silent reading of control texts by five fluent high school braillists (mean age, 16–6; mean wpm/spm = 172/181) and by the five most competent younger readers (mean age = 9–4, mean wpm/spm = 62/62) were analysed. It was soon clear that, for the fluent group, the proportion of longer latencies for transitions between component morphemes in compound words was larger (0.57) than the proportion of transitions between syllables in the multisyllabic words (0.24) that exceeded latencies between other letters in the word. In fact, four of the five fluent readers showed no difference between letter transitions for any syllables in multisyllabic words. The younger readers showed similar proportions of longer transition latencies between the components of compound words (0.55) as the fluent readers. But the proportion of longer transition latencies between syllables in multisyllabic words was larger (0.55) than for fluent readers. However, in almost every case, these were for the first syllable in the word. To get a more comprehensive picture transcripts for a total of twenty-two readers were analysed. Half the readers had reading rates above a hundred wpm (113–196 wpm, 119–207 spm). The other half had reading rates below a hundred wpm (30–98 wpm, 31–98 spm). The results are graphed in Figure 5.3. The analysis of the proportions (arcsin transforms) showed that the slower readers produced significantly more exceptional transitions overall than the faster readers ($F = 25.22$, df= 1/20, $p < 0.001$), and this also interacted significantly with the type of transitions ($F = 5.98$, df = 1/20, $p < 0.025$). The faster readers showed effects of syllable transitions on only twenty-five per cent of possible occasions, while slow readers produced as many, or marginally more first syllable breaks as transitions between the components of compound words.

It was clear from the figures that the more proficient readers did not even break up compound words into morphemic components for more than half the time, although this varied between individuals. When they occurred, the longer latencies between the last letter of the first component and the first letter of the last component were produced by regressions to the region either between or near the flanking letters, and so occurred typically in the middle of the compound word. The longer latencies which marked transitions between syllables in multisyllabic words, by contrast, typically occurred for the first syllable only, and therefore near the beginning of the word.

The findings were completely consistent with the results of the previous study on syllables (Chapter 4) which showed that meaningless syllables are not central to the process of prose reading by reasonably proficient braillists. The analysis in terms of increased scanning times at syllabic versus morphological boundaries here suggested instead that morphological decomposition which involves meaningful segments of words does occur, although only on fifty per cent of possible occasions.

The observation that increased latencies at syllable boundaries, though relatively infrequent, tended to occur mainly for the first syllable, was of interest particularly in view of the possibility, already raised by Nolan and Kederis (1969) that fast readers process only the initial letters of words

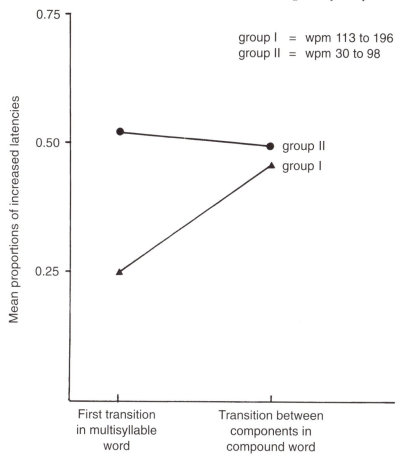

Figure 5.3 Mean proportions of increased latencies (see text) for the first transition between letters or syllables in multisyllabic words and for the transition (see text) between the morphemic components of compound words for two groups of braille readers

and then guess the rest. In so far as breaks in processing of multisyllabic words occurred, these were shown by beginners rather than by fast readers, and mainly for the first syllable of words. The possibility of semantic or lexical guessing at different levels of reading was therefore probed further in the next study.

4 REGULARITIES AND IRREGULARITIES IN SCANNING TIMES BY COMPETENT READERS

The interesting possibility raised by Nolan and Kederis (1969) that fast readers process only the initial letters of words and then guess the end from the previous lexical and/or semantic information has not previously been checked empirically as far as I know. It implies that readers pay more attention to the initial than to the final letter. The possibility that there are actual time differences between scanning the first and last letters of words is in apparent contradiction to the fact that the most commonly reported observation of the hand-movements of proficient braillists is their striking smoothness and apparently effortless, rhythmic fluency (e.g. Grunewald, 1966; Kusajima, 1970, 1974). It is certainly very much the impression anyone has when simply watching the hands of good readers in real time, either from above or below. Nevertheless, the frame-by-frame timing of finger-movements suggested that first-pass latencies across letters even by competent readers are not always evenly distributed.

To explore the guessing hypothesis, therefore, the question was whether the last letter in a word is scanned faster than the first letter during the initial cover (first-pass) time. To get some handle on this, I used randomly selected frame-by-frame transcripts of a text or sentences read silently by each of eight competent young braillists. Their baseline reading (wpm and spm) rates were taken from the mean rate that the subject had scored previously on baseline texts. As the difference between the wpm and spm rates indicate, the texts had been relatively difficult (Table 5.1). To calculate first versus last letter latencies, all legally uncontracted, regular words in the randomly selected transcripts were used for each subject. Words which had been re-scanned or contained regressions were left out of the analyses. The range of words used therefore differed somewhat across subjects, but was roughly in the same frequency range (e.g. milk, room, boys, game, trumpets, football, legs, granny, gave, until, awake, bananas, lamp, boats, orange, bonfires).

The data of interest were latencies for moving across the initial letter and across the final letter of a word. The final letter should take less time if the subject had predicted the word from the initial letters. The mean overall difference between the first and last letter of words for the eight subjects was indeed statistically significant ($t = 3.39$; $df = 6$; $p < 0.02$). However, such facilitation was not shown for every word, nor by every subject. Differences were also calculated separately for every subject as shown in Table 5.1. Moreover, data for differences did not depend only on the words, they occurred more in contexts in which the final 's' of a plural noun could be predicted from the semantic context or from the first three letters of the relevant word (e.g. 'l' in 'until' in the phrase '... wait until').

An illustration (Figure 5.4) of the fact that smooth first-pass scanning depends on the text is of a reader who scored a higher rate on this easy text (163 wpm, 170 spm) than on the previous more difficult text (106 wpm, 132 spm) on which he had shown a significant ($p < 0.05$) advantage for the last letters in some words. The subject used both hands, but read predominantly with the right (87 per cent) and much less with the left (33 per cent) hand. The hands usually overlapped for one to two

Table 5.1 Mean latencies (ms) for first and last letters of regular (legally uncontracted) words from randomly selected scripts for eight competent readers, showing their chronological age (CA), mean wpm and mean spm on control scripts of medium difficulty. Differences that were not significant (NS) and significant differences for each subject are shown in the final column

Subject	Mean		Letter		
CA	wpm	spm	First ms	Last ms	Difference
1 9-7	88	102	168	164	NS
2 11-9	119	147	100	50	$p < 0.01$
3 13-5	116	154	138	99	NS
4 14-8	111	148	140	90	$p < 0.01$
5 15-11	89	139	210	152	NS
6 15-11	120	144	160	98	$p < 0.05$
7 17-4	170	206	97	80	NS
8 19-3	142	201	64	78	NS

words on a line. The example, taken randomly from the frame-by-frame transcript shows the actual cumulative frame times for part of the second line of text ('happy dog. Spot') which includes the end of a sentence and the beginning of the next sentence (Figure 5.4). The frame times from the first to last touch of each letter are shown as connected lines, and the transitions between letters and words are indicated by blanks. The scanning rate for letters here is very regular, although not completely so for the left hand. When the two forefingers scanned two letters at the same time, the left forefinger was on the last letter of a word ('y' of 'happy') while the right forefinger scanned the first letter of the next word ('d' of dog'). It was then rescanned by the left forefinger later, when it coincided with scanning of the last letter of that word by the right forefinger. Except for the full stop, the forefingers otherwise alternate letters and gaps between letters while scanning overlaps.

Nevertheless frame-by-frame timing shows that the first-pass scanning rates even for competent readers are not totally even. Competent readers show slight variations in first-pass scanning rates per space in reading longer versus shorter words (e.g. 107 ms/character or 58 ms/space for 'presENt', versus 80 ms/character or 48 ms/space for 'lot'). It should be noted that smooth lateral scanning which shows little or no variation when processing letters in a word does not imply that semantic factors are irrelevant. On the contrary, it is precisely with texts that are read for comprehension that fast readers show smooth scanning rates. Evidence on lateral scanning in reading for meaning compared to letter search tasks (Millar, 1987 b) was discussed earlier (Chapter 3). Moreover smooth, lateral scanning is shown typically with easy texts. By these are meant texts that contain mainly high frequency words and syntactically and

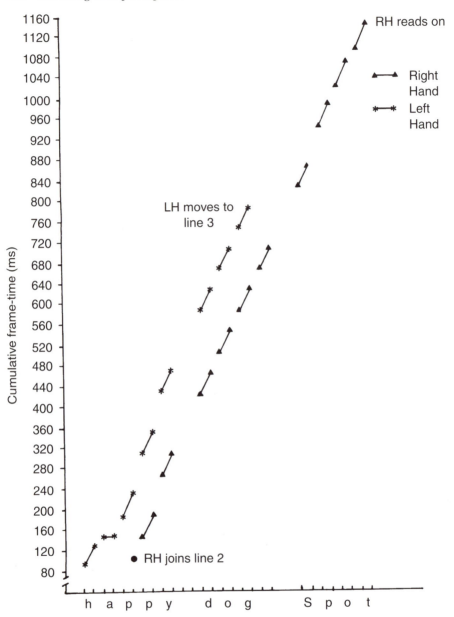

Figure 5.4 Actual (cumulative) frame-times shown by a reader from first to last touch (connected lines) for each character (braille cell). Blanks are shown for transitions between cells and between words. The characters are shown on the X-axis ('happy dog. Spot')

semantically uncomplicated sentence structures. The same readers show a much less even rate with more difficult verbal materials. The example shown here (Figure 5.5) is for a different, right-handed reader (150 wpm, 190 spm) who used his left hand entirely for place-keeping. The graph (Figure 5.5) shows the actual cumulative frame times for each character from first to last touch in connected lines, and movement from one letter to the next, and from one word to the next, by blanks. The example comes from the reading of separate sentences (one on each line of text) and shows the beginning of a sentence ('THE trees WERE'). In measures which sample scanning times over several words and calculate rates by the number of letters or words passed, the scan would look like a straight line. The frame-by-frame (1/100 s) times, however, show that the reader has local control over his scanning movements, although the actual differences in time are very small for competent readers. The contraction WERE which is only a single character takes a relatively long time, for instance, as compared with the contraction for the article (THE) although both occupy the same absolute space laterally.

The fact that detailed time analyses of the apparently smooth rhythmic movements by proficient readers depend on the lexical and semantic ease or difficulty of scripts has several important implications. It clearly means that scanning movements are dictated as much, or more, by cognitive as by perceptual factors. Moreover, the fact that smooth scanning is shown by faster readers and for easy texts indicates that it is a form of streamlining of the relation between perceptual and semantic factors, rather than a limitation imposed by low tactual acuity.

Further evidence for this interpretation was sought by analysing the conditions under which regression movements occur during reading. It is well known that fluent readers make far fewer regressions than beginners (Davidson *et al.*, 1980). Cover-time from first to last touch, including regressions, as well as first-pass scans over the word, may be taken as a reasonable index of processing latencies.

High frequency words take less time and elicit fewer regressions than low frequency words. But the conditions which produce regressions are often informative. The findings are considered in detail in the next section.

5 REGRESSIONS: PROCESSES IN INTEGRATING PERCEPTUAL, LEXICAL AND SEMANTIC INFORMATION

Regressions are not all of the same kind. I shall here concentrate on regressions in reading texts for meaning. I shall, therefore, leave out the category of regressions which include the well-known unsystematic 'rubbing' over individual characters that is typical of very poor readers (Chapters 2, 3 and 7), as well as the systematic exploration of letter contours that was found in a letter search task by fluent readers (Chapter 3). The truncated shape movements often used by previously sighted

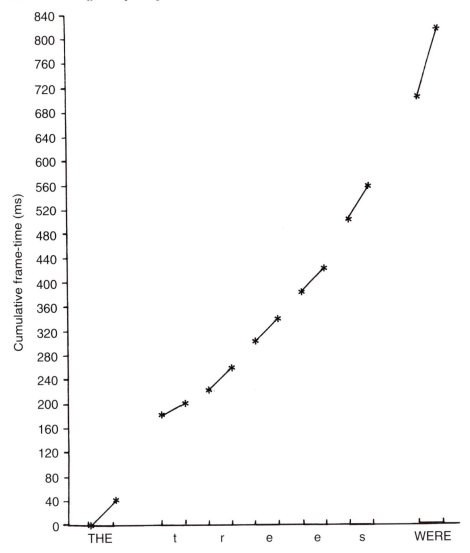

Figure 5.5 Actual (cumulative) frame-times from first to last touch (connected lines) for first-pass scans by a reader for each character, and blanks for spaces between cells and between words. Characters, including single cell contractions, are shown on the X-axis ('THE trees WERE')

braillists will be considered later (Chapter 7). Individuals differ considerably in the total amount of regressive movements they typically use. The point is that types of regression in reading for meaning also differ with the conditions that occasion them.

Regressive movements in reading for meaning fall into several categories which are sometimes, but by no means always, used in combination. The two broadest categories are repeated movements over single words, and discontinuous regressions. In discontinuous regressions readers move to other words before returning to the word from which the regression started. Repeated scanning of single words can occur with or without regressions over particular letters within the word. Discontinuous regressions also need to be divided further into backward movements to prior words that have been scanned previously, sometimes at a distance of several lines, and forward movements to words that had not previously been touched before returning to the word that first occasioned the discontinuous movement. A final category consists of regressions that occur after voice onset in pronouncing the word, that is to say, after the word has been construed and planned for speech output. Such subsequent 'checking' movements may occur over whole phrases, but are more common as very brief (less than 40 ms advances in frame time) touches of a particular character.

Turning first to the studies of texts with physically degraded words in different contexts which were reported in the first section of this chapter, two sorts of internal evidence shed further light on the interpretation of the statistical findings. One line of evidence comes from analysing the type of regression movements that subjects undertook in the different conditions. The other comes from the spontaneous comments, asides and audible attempts by subjects during silent reading which were routinely recorded also.

The study which compared degraded or misspelt and normal homophone words in compatible and altered contexts (Millar, 1988 c) showed differences between types of regression in different experimental conditions. Repeated regressions over the target word alone were more typical for physically degraded targets than for misspelt homophone words, or for normally brailled homophones in compatible contexts. Repeated regressions over a given word also occurred to some extent for normally brailled low frequency words. Nevertheless, by far the most persistent regressions to try to make out constituent letters were typical for the two conditions in which the target words were physically degraded. They constituted attempts to construe the word by accessing perceptual information.

By contrast, normally brailled target words that immediately followed a change in the semantic context typically attracted discontinuous regressions. Discontinuous regressions were also the rule for homophone targets that did not fit into the context semantically, because they were misspelt. Calculated as a percentage of all regressions in a given story, the perceptually degraded target words attracted an average of 34 per cent of all regressions. The average for misspelt homophone words was only about 10 per cent. But the latter attracted more discontinuous regressions.

Typically, a misspelt word did not receive repeated scanning. Instead the reading finger(s) regressed from it to words and phrases on previous lines that had established the prior context. For instance, scanning the misspelt homophone 'sun' after the story had referred to 'mother' typically elicited regressive movements to the disambiguating word 'mother' relatively fast, without many repeated regressions over the misspelt but perceptually intact word. The word 'tail' when preceded on previous lines by the words 'book' and 'library' produced discontinuous regressions to these prior words. Misspelt homophone words also produced regressions to articles and to function words. Readers were therefore also looking for information from the syntactic form class of the ambiguous term and to prepositions that might indicate a semantic link between the two contexts. Similarly, words that continued to be spelt as appropriate to the preceding context, but followed an abrupt change in context which made them inappropriate, attracted regressions to earlier, contextually disambiguating, associated words (e.g. from breed to baker and from mail to apes). They were usually at a remove of five to six previous words.

The observations suggest that continuous repeated regressions within a given word and discontinuous regressions to previous portions in text tend to differ qualitatively between construing perceptually degraded words and construing gist. However, the division also depends on the type of relation that exists between the target words and the gist of the text. Continuous local (word) regressions are more obvious in texts in which the target words are closely tied to the gist of the text as shown in studies with degraded words (Section 1). Words which present sound/sense ambiguities attract additional processing even in control conditions when the semantic ambiguity is spotted (Chapter 4, Section 6). In the second study (Section 1), the perceptually degraded words also attracted local continuous, repeated regressions, but the regressions often included discontinuous regressions to previous words. After scanning the degraded word and/or letters several times, subjects would go back and re-scan previous words before returning to the target, which accounts for the advantage in conditions where the preceding context was relevant. The type of regression, but also the spontaneous comments by subjects, made it quite clear that subjects were attempting to use prior context (e.g. from the degraded word 'elephant' to the prior word 'animal') in order to make out the degraded word. However, in contexts in which the degraded target words are less closely associated with the gist of the story, using relevant prior context also led to mistakes. One subject, for instance, construed the degraded word 'factory' in a text that talked about a toy factory as 'toy-shop' in recalling the story.

The spontaneous comments showed that some subjects also used graphemic length information of the degraded word as an important clue to its meaning. An unexpected voiced aside by a good reader about the poor legibility of the word 'motorboat' included the comment: 'It is motor-something. But it's too long for "motorcar"; I checked'. The fact that she quite deliberately checked on word length means that at least one of the forward movements in a regression was devoted to getting information about the length of the word. Not all regressions over a degraded word can thus be regarded as attempts to make out the individual characters within the word. Explorations of more general graphemic characteristics, such as word length, are reported quite often by proficient braillists. Length information is used in conjunction with other attempts to retrieve likely words that would fit with letters that had been detected. Inferences from the conjunction of perceptual, graphemic and lexical information were thus used to access the meaning of the word.

The notion that readers try to use previews was also substantiated. Such discontinuous 'preview' movements seem to be less frequent than regressions to previously read text. They nevertheless occur, although individuals differ in the extent to which they use previews. The criterion of what counts as a previewing movement is that the finger moves forward to a subsequent word or words, only to return to the word which originated the forward move and rescanning it before finally moving forward more smoothly again to the subsequent words in the sentence.

Unfortunately, the most telling instance of 'preview' movements among regressions was too difficult to depict graphically in the detail that it deserves, because the movements took too long. It is, however, worth describing in some detail. The braillist who was an otherwise competent young adult reader had been given a list of normally brailled separate sentences to read aloud. Among these was the sentence 'The seER FORetold THE future'. The frame-by-frame analysis showed that he first regressed with the left hand from the word 'seER' to the previous article, then moved forward over 'seER' to 'FORet', and back from the 't' to rescan the word 'SeER'. The left hand then remained stationary while the right hand completed the 'old' of 'FORetold' and moved forward to the first three letters of 'future' (42.99 s cumulative time). At that point, the right hand remained stationary while the left hand (at 43.19 s cumulative time) jumped above the text from 'seER' across the text to 'future' (at 43.39 s cumulative time). Scanning continued normally from this point, including saying the sentence aloud with an intonation which showed that the reader had understood it. The fact that the left hand 'jumped' across the intervening text was obvious from viewing the tape and was also attested by the much shorter latency for the intervening ten spaces which included the word 'FORetold'. The average time (20 ms/space) for the 'jump' was much shorter than the normal movement rate of this subject. But it was also quite clear from the video-recording that this forward movement was above the text.

The time course of these scanning movements shows clearly how the reader processed the sentence. The subject did not understand the word 'seER' from the first-pass scan. He went back to the word three times. The article to which he had regressed first evidently told him nothing more, until after he had scanned forward to the next word 'foretold'. The 'FORe' part must have given him some clue, because he went back to 'seer' at that point before having scanned the word fully. But he was not sure of the correct meaning of 'seer' until after he had scanned further forward to 'future'. The first three letters of the word 'future' provided an obvious context for recognizing the meaning of 'seer', and he had no further problem with the sentence after that. The time course thus indicates the processes used in construing the meaning of a low frequency word. A question posed by the experimenter after the reader had completed the sentence (routinely recorded) confirmed that the subject had known the word (seer) only 'vaguely', but had not been sure of the meaning before reading the sentence.

The fact that low frequency and unfamiliar words and words that require more semantic processing take longer to read is, of course, well-known from the literature on eye-fixations in reading for meaning (e.g. Carpenter and Just, 1983; Rayner and Pollatsek, 1989). Word frequency and familiarity also influence the time it takes to recognize single words (e.g. Frederiksen and Kroll, 1976; Garnham, 1985; Monsell *et al.*, 1989). The point of looking at the frame-by-frame time course of finger-scanning over millimetres of braille scripts is the insight it affords into the details of processing. The time course here shows that low frequency words not only take more scanning time, they also produce preview scanning to subsequent words as clues to construe the meaning of an unfamiliar word. Moreover, the initial few letters of the previewed (e.g. 'future') word were clearly quite sufficient to provide the final semantic clue, in addition to what was first gleaned from the next word, to construe the meaning of the unfamiliar word and the gist of the sentence sufficiently to begin saying the sentence with the appropriate intonation.

These data have several implications. Regressions are clearly not all simple repetitions to gain better access to perceptual information either because it is degraded or because the reader is inexperienced. Such regressions differ from scanning movements that are motivated by unfamiliar words or lexical ambiguity. Moreover, the process of construing the meaning of words includes preview scanning for contextual clues. Furthermore, the regression data showed that competent readers look for word meanings from the very start of scanning a word. They do not wait until each word has been scanned completely.

A different strategy which, nevertheless, shows similar processes was used by the other competent reader (152 wpm, 182 spm) mentioned in the previous section. She was a two-handed reader who used her hands divergently and had achieved a much higher reading rate on an earlier easy control text (188 wpm, 224 spm). On such texts she showed relatively even scans and only very occasional very brief regressions. In her reading of the sentence 'The seER FORetold the future' which contained the low frequency word 'seer' that produced difficulties for most readers, there were no regressions at all on the word 'seer' itself. This reader scanned the word 'seER' only once (first pass), although she took twice as long

(80 ms) to scan the ER character than the initial 's', and also took longer than usual to move off from the word across to the next word. The actual regression occurred on the less difficult next word (FORetold), from the 'l' back to the 'e' (Figure 5.6). The girl clearly had no problem whatever with the perception of the (e t o) letters to which she regressed, nor with any other part of 'FORetold'. In fact, the regression coincided with a voice hesitation after pronouncing the first article before 'seer'. Her normal touch–voice span (last touch to voice onset) was at least three words in reading aloud. But her voice onset for 'seer' did not occur until her understanding was complete. The scanning relations and voice onset time thus show that it was the word 'seer' which produced the hesitation and regression on the subsequent word. The regression over the three letters which confirmed the word 'foretold' was evidently sufficient for this reader to construe the preceding word 'seer' correctly. She did not need to rescan it.

Prima facie, the time course in construing low frequency words seems quite different from the smooth movements by the same competent braillists in recognizing high frequency, familiar words. However, that difference is not absolute. As we saw earlier, even familiar words take longer in relatively difficult texts when the latencies for each move are taken into account. Examples showing that a relatively easy word can attract regressions that are motivated by a previous difficulty are a case in point.

Taken together with the fact that familiar words take longer in difficult contexts, the findings on the time course of scanning movements suggest strongly that the importance of context for recognizing low frequency words is merely the upper end of what seems to be a continuous process of integrating information from all sources, not only in word recognition, but also in the semantic integration of words for text comprehension. Recent evidence from eye-fixation times in visual reading (Folk and Morris, 1995) is consistent with this interpretation of the scanning patterns in tactual reading. Folk and Morris (1995) found that context changes which precede ambiguous target words affect their fixation times, in much the same way that scanning times are affected in reading by touch (e.g. Millar 1988 c and Chapter 4).

The tactual scanning data suggest further that the process of integration is actually a forward, predictive process. The detailed findings as well as the fact that familiar words take longer in difficult contexts suggest that readers are not merely processing each word and integrating it with previously construed context as it is being read. They are also forming some idea of what the next word is likely to be. Reading for meaning thus seems to be a mainly predictive process. The semantic process consists not only of integrating the word being scanned with previous words and with the gist construed so far, it also attempts to actively predict what the next word will be.

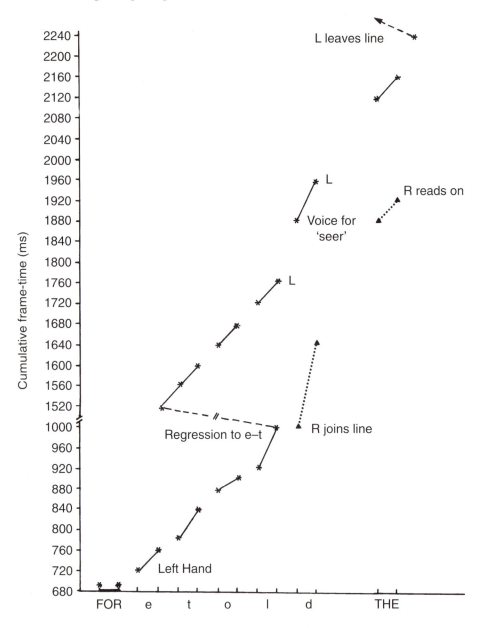

Figure 5.6 Actual (cumulative) frame-times from first to last touch (connected lines) for first-pass scans for the left (L) and right (R) forefingers for each character (cell) by a two-handed reader. Spaces between cells and between words are shown as blank spaces. The words ('FORetold THE') are shown on the X-axis. Regressions are shown by broken lines

Evidence which supports the conclusion that readers do not only process gist to the end of the last word being scanned, but also formulate ideas about what the next word will be, comes from errors of commission in oral reading. These do not consist of misreading words that do occur, but of inserting items that were left out of the text, but might well have occurred. There are a number of examples of such errors by proficient braillists. Typical instances that have come to my notice concerned the insertions of the definite article (THE) when the previous context predicted a noun or noun phrase. An example from a competent (163 wpm) reader was in the sentence 'He was rated as the best in (THE) class'. Another whole class are insertions of the final 's' at the end of singular nouns that might reasonably have been plural in the context of the sentence (e.g. 'the faked picture(s) sold well').

There is a whole literature on the fact that visual readers often fail to process the definite article at all in visual reading for meaning, because they fail to notice misspellings (e.g. Rayner and Pollatsek, 1989). In braille any misspelling for THE is likely to be noticed. The fact that almost all permutations of the braille cell are used for letters, punctuation marks and contractions, means that small differences in pattern are important. As mentioned earlier, competent braille readers are particularly sensitive to slight physical changes in texts (Millar, 1987 b), and notice differences in expected patterns in left–right scans easily for that reason. The fact that readers insert articles and syntactic markers where they may be expected to occur is interesting, because it shows that competent braillists operate in that respect very similarly to competent visual readers, although the empirical findings rely on commission rather than omissions.

The predictive nature of the semantic integration process in reading for meaning is shown by such insertion errors. It would be difficult to explain otherwise why, during the normal course of 'decoding' the meaning of words and integrating them into gist, people read words that are not actually present, but can, quite reasonably, be inferred from the preceding context. The notion that predictive inferences are part of the semantic integration process also explains how facilitation by semantic context occurs.

What I have called the 'predictive' nature of reading for comprehension is exemplified by the almost exhaustive repetitive regressions over unfamiliar proper names. The finding was inadvertent. One of the scripts I had selected from various sources to serve as suitable control scripts for intelligent adolescent readers happened to contain three proper names which, though unusual, did not strike me as particularly difficult when I read them in print ('Cis' for 'Cissy'; 'Thornton' and 'Hetherington'). All, even the fastest readers, showed unusual amounts of local repetitive regressions and/or voice hesitations over these names. The reasons for that difficulty were not immediately obvious. Graphemically the words presented no greater challenge than other words in the same text.

However, the notion that reading for comprehension involves predictions from the gist can explain the difficulty with proper names. Proper names, unlike low frequency or unfamiliar words, cannot be construed from the context. Moreover, English braille has no capital letters so far (that may change soon). Proper names are therefore not 'flagged' by the first letter, and the braille reader cannot infer that the rest of the word cannot be treated as a lexical item. The beginning of a new sentence can be inferred from the preceding full stop. By contrast, there are no means at present in braille of predicting that the next word will be a proper name, unless the context makes that obvious.

6   REGRESSIONS AND VOICE SPANS IN READING FOR MEANING

Further evidence which suggests that construing gist is not merely a process of integrating successive words with each other, but depends on inferences from past context to predict the type or class of a subsequent word or words came from touch-to-voice spans. Sounds, including voice output in oral reading are automatically recorded (Chapter 3) and heard in replaying the tapes. It was quite clear from replaying the tapes that there was a qualitative difference in oral reading between fast and slow readers.

Beginning readers typically pronounced a word as soon as they had ceased scanning it, or while they were still scanning, but before they passed on to scanning the next item. With words they found difficult (i.e. words that attracted several regressions and took longer for that reason) each character was pronounced (overtly or subvocally) as they scanned it. However, the 'assembly' of sounds was by no means necessarily sequential. On the contrary, it was clear from their speech output that the slow subjects constantly attempted to understand the meaning of the word while they were scanning it. Indeed, they usually said that this was indeed what they had been doing.

Competent readers typically do not articulate a word as soon as they cease scanning it, but scan several more words before they start to articulate a phrase containing several words. Touch-to-voice spans were calculated in order to quantify this observation. Scanning time from first to last touch, including regressions over the word, may be taken as a reasonable index of recognition latencies. As mentioned earlier, high frequency words take less time and elicit fewer regressions than low frequency words. The frame which showed the last touch on a word was therefore taken as the end of the recognition process. The data for the last touch on a given word were taken from frame times as usual. The voice onset time for that word was found by slowing down the recorder re-play time until the frame that produced the initial voice onset. The touch-to-voice spans were the number of intervening words between the last touch and the voice onset time.

The average touch-voice spans for two different groups of eight high school students (wpm means of 111 and 120, on different texts) were 2.82 and 2.4 words, respectively, varying from one to four words for different subjects. In other words, the voice onset for articulating a word lagged by about one to four words behind the end of the finger-scan (mean lag time = 1.16 s). The touch–voice lag shown by these braillists is thus not massively less than the eye–voice span of four words (approximately 2 s) reported by Crowder (1982) for visual readers who presumably had much higher reading rates. Slow braille readers (60–100 wpm) who are beyond the initial stage of reading average one word or slightly less in touch–voice spans. This again is similar to an eye–voice span of two words by beginning print readers. The point is that even for slow braille readers, therefore, the voice onset lags behind the word that has been identified already.

Crowder (1982) argued that the delay between seeing and saying a word makes it unlikely that the mechanism which produces the eye–voice span could use the same route that produces access to the meaning of that word. The same argument applies to the touch–voice span in braille reading. At the same time, scanning and voice output are not totally independent. Hesitations in voice onset occur quite frequently when the finger encounters an unknown word while scanning words far in advance of the word to be pronounced. However, we are far from knowing as yet whether the interference arises from the use of the same (i.e. speech output) mechanism, or to the need to allocate all the attention to a local difficulty. In conjunction with other evidence (Chapter 4), the latter seems more likely.

However, competent readers show more than a simple difference in speed between oral and silent reading (Chapter 4). Their stress and intonation patterns in oral reading are clearly tailored not only to a single preceding item, but also to subsequent words, including a descending intonation when the reader is anticipating the end of a phrase or sentence. Obstacles to comprehension, such as low frequency or unknown words were associated not only with increased processing time and pauses in scanning, but also showed in voice hesitations, and contractions in the touch–voice span. Voice spans were typically larger for easy texts which included a high percentage of familiar words of all types (verbs, nouns and function words), but they also showed an intonation pattern that was suitable to the gist of the whole phrase.

It is clear that the written text in English is devoid of information about stress, intonation and the prosodic pattern that is present in oral discourse, and provides the listener with important 'suprasegmental' information about the meaning that is being conveyed. In oral reading, the reader has to provide that information to the listener. Fast readers were more 'expressive' in reading, in that they tailored their intonation to the meaning of the sentence and passages. The gap in time, between the last touch of a word to the initial voice onset in saying it, thus suggests that the construing of gist and planning for articulation, including the 'supra-segmental' (stress and intonation) aspects of expressive speech takes place at these points. The model of Just and Carpenter (1980 a, b, 1987) proposed that the integration of words into gist is an ongoing process and does not lag behind eye-fixations. The time-course of braille reading is partly consistent with that. But it suggests also that the inferences readers make on the basis of what has been read go beyond the actual word being scanned, because the reader reorganizes his phrasing and prosody if the word being scanned tactually fails to fit the gist construed so far. The prosody also ends on an intonation which allows for the next word.

It could be argued that fast silent reading by competent braillists involves inner speech, but that reading aloud is slower because it demands additional planning for articulation in terms of intonation and stress. But whether there is also an 'inner voice' which necessarily operates in reading and is merely faster in silent than overt articulation in competent reading for meaning is open to doubt. Such covert articulation should certainly have produced syllable effects (Chapter 4). The evidence reviewed here makes it quite unlikely that competent braillists spell out every letter or every word to themselves in silent reading for meaning, any more than competent print readers do. Readers certainly have to construe the gist of texts in silent reading. But there is good evidence against the assumption that information is habitually construed or remembered in terms of the literal words that are being read (e.g. Kintsch, 1974). The data on competent braille reading are consistent with that.

7 SUMMARY AND IMPLICATIONS

How then do perceptual and semantic processes relate to each other in braille? The impression that comes through quite inescapably from all the findings so far is what Bartlett long ago (1932) called the 'effort after meaning'. The findings show not only that the semantic context can facilitate the pick-up of perceptual information, but that such facilitation occurs under quite specifiable conditions. As suggested by Norris (1986), a major factor in determining whether semantic facilitation occurs is the probability with which semantic associations between the context or primes and target words can be expected. Both the frequency of such pairings, and the closeness of the semantic association between context and target word, determined the significance of the facilitation. Moreover, the fact that beginning readers show semantic effects more than proficient readers does not require a separate hypothesis. Competent readers are not immune from perceptual difficulties. But they are less likely to encounter them with normal texts, because part of their expertise consists in greater sensitivity to the perceptual information (Chapter 3). They are also likely to have much better-established long-term associations between the perceptual input and lexical knowledge, so that lexical access and retrieval is faster.

The usual asymmetry showing that semantic context facilitates perceptual processes in conditions of low legibility, but not in normal perceptual conditions, was replicated. Nevertheless, findings on sub-lexical processing also suggested lexical 'top-down' effects in segmenting long compound words rather than segmentation in terms of meaningless syllables. There was evidence from the detailed scanning latencies that fluent readers use the semantic context predictively, and do not necessarily scan words fully to construe their meaning. Such predictive processing by fluent readers suggests that fluent perceptual pick-up is also influenced by 'top-down' processes. That is indeed consistent with the findings on 'top-down' effects on the pick-up of tactual features due to task demands (Chapter 3). Semantic context influences the perceptual pick-up by competent readers and by beginners. The difference is one of skill and quasi-automation. Further, in perceptually degraded conditions, competent readers sought information not only from semantic context, but also from longer-term linguistic knowledge, including knowledge about the length of words. It is also relevant that fluent braillists use smooth rhythmic scanning movements, but that the precise timing showed that first-pass rates per character are not completely invariant over small changes in legibility, word frequency and semantic structure.

The suggestion that the process of comprehension in braille reading is essentially predictive is not the same as saying that reading is a 'psycholinguistic guessing game', a view attributed to Goodman (1970) and Smith (1971), and criticized by Rayner and Pollatsek (1989) for considering that readers 'guess' meaning on the basis of all types of linguistic cues equally, instead of stressing the 'alphabetic principle'. Two points need to be made.

First, there is an important difference between predictions based on inference on the one hand, and guessing on the other. The main task in reading for comprehension is to construe the meaning of the written text. According to Kintsch (1974), the reader construes the gist in terms of propositions, rather than by remembering words verbatim. The further implication that readers cannot remember verbatim information has not been sustained. They can, if that is what the task demands (e.g. Crowder, 1982). However, the notion that readers construe a more condensed form of the meaning and make inferences on the basis of these inferences seems a reasonable description of what happens in fluent braille. There is ample evidence for this type of prediction in visual reading, for instance, from 'garden path' sentences which bias the interpretation (e.g. Carpenter and Daneman, 1981; Frazier and Rayner, 1982) so that the next words are unexpected or puzzling until the reader reconstrues the earlier part of the sentence. But Rayner and Pollatsek (1989) suggest that semantic facilitation in print reading may be due to parafoveal visual information that readers extract from the next word before fixating it. There is no analogue of parafoveal information in reading by touch, although readers sometimes try to get a 'preview' of what comes next by a brief touch on the next word, usually when they are uncertain about the currently scanned word. Whether two-handed reading with adjacent fingers provides such 'previews' and checking as a habitual process is doubtful, because there does not seem to be any saving in scanning time in these cases (Chapter 3). But this requires further study. What was quite clear from the studies in which the context was suddenly changed during reading is that braille readers make predictive inferences about target words, because changing the context suddenly in the middle of reading a braille text slowed scanning latencies for a target word that occurred several words later (e.g. Millar 1988 c).

The assumption of the Stanovich hypothesis that proficient reading involves automatic activation of lexical knowledge while beginners use context strategically was not directly addressed by the study here. The comments of some experienced young braillists when they encountered degraded texts, and of most older new braillists in the priming studies, certainly showed that they were aware of using context and other cues strategically.

The view proposed here is that reading depends on a large number of connections, enhanced by learning, between the language and the percep-tual processes. Any reading task activates all the connections to some extent. But the degree of activation also depends on task conditions and the level of proficiency reached through learning. Some tasks would produce differentially higher activation of some connections than of others. Specific task conditions which activate some connections more strongly could arise from poor legibility. Higher order knowledge and skills (semantic knowledge, spelling rules, phonology) would be activated more strongly when the physical features of the text are degraded or unclear. One could suppose either a quasi-automatic redress of the balance of information, or active search strategies involving all the connections. It is not necessary to assume a dichotomy between fully motivated search and quasi-automatic search.

Taken together, the findings suggest strongly that readers attempt to derive the meaning of words as early as possible in the process of scan-ning a word, and use as many sources of prior, past and prospective infor-mation as are available to them when they encounter difficulties.

In braille reading people need to, and do use multiple sources of infor-mation. But the 'cues' are clearly not all equal, nor equally needed in all reading tasks, and some may occur only in certain conditions, as exem-plified by the reader who used word-length as an additional clue to construing a degraded word.

An examination of how readers construe the gist of texts is beyond the present brief. The proposals vary from assuming representation in terms of abstract propositions (Kintsch, 1974), to the construction of scripts (Schank and Abelson, 1977), or mental models (Johnson-Laird, 1983) by using previous knowledge of the subjects matter as a frame for integrating the information that becomes available during reading. It has been suggested that even simply giving the title of a story prior to reading may facilitate braille reading (Hartley *et al.*, 1987). But there is not enough evidence on this topic as yet. One possibility is that the title or the prior context gives the readers a sufficient indication of the subject matter to act as a frame or 'thematic processor' (Rayner *et al.*, 1983) which organizes the text. The proposal implies that what is facilitated is the integration of constituent words into a theme, or possibly the creation of a scenario (e.g. Schank and Abelson, 1977) or mental model (Johnson-Laird, 1983). Precisely how such wider effects of context and of knowledge of the world may work requires a good deal of further study.

However, the more restricted hypothesis that the process of comprehension in braille reading is essentially predictive does not have to assume that people necessarily conjure up the actual spelling of the next word. The prediction by the reader may be much less precise and merely concern the type of word to be expected in terms of its grammatical class (e.g. the likelihood of a noun to follow a definite article), or a word that generally belongs in the domain of discourse. On the other hand, quite precise predictions occur occasionally, as shown by long scanning latencies for initial letters when the wrong word has been predicted. The role of orthographic factors is considered further in the next chapter.

The relations between semantic and perceptual factors suggested by the findings, and the specific conditions under which they can facilitate processing are important in practice. The discussion of the practical issues raised by the implication that readers need to use multiple sources of information without overloading the system will be postponed until later (Chapter 8).

6 Contractions, spelling, writing and output effects

Contractions constitute the most notable orthographic difference between English braille and print. Mandatory contractions pose a number of practical and theoretical questions which relate specifically to braille reading and spelling. But they also have wider implications. They are potentially an extremely useful tool for probing the relation between reading, spelling and speech output processes during development and acquisition. But we know far too little about the effects of contractions as yet. The present chapter explores some of these issues.

The first section briefly describes some of the most common contractions that are learned relatively early, and gives some examples also of infrequently used contracted forms. The scanning latencies for common single character contractions which represent whole words when people are reading texts normally are reported next. Single character contractions that represent whole words when they stand alone are compared with the same contractions when they are used mandatorily to represent the relevant letter sequences within words in normal text reading. The fact that the same contractions take less time to process as single words than as constituents of other words has implications for the early stages of braille reading and spelling, and for the question of sub-lexical decomposition.

Spelling differences between contracted and fully spelt out words are explored in oral spelling and by a matching task with young braille readers who habitually read and write contracted braille, but also learn normal English spelling. Intelligent young braillists took much less time over familiar contracted words than over their fully spelt out equivalent, showing that contractions save time as well as space. But that advantage disappears for contractions in low frequency words. Translating between contracted and fully spelt out braille was no means an automatic process, although accuracy was high. Word knowledge as well as knowledge of the two orthographies seems to be involved.

The next issue is the relation between reading and writing braille by means of the 'Perkins' machine. Beginning readers often find writing braille by means of the 'Perkins' braille machine easier than reading. The advantage seems to be lost later. Reasons for this are discussed in relation to advantages in recruiting kinaesthetic as well as speech output processes to aid recognition. Some effects that using a horizontal keyboard to produce upright characters has on the early stages of learning are described briefly.

The fact that familiar words and syllables are represented by contracted forms that have to be used mandatorily in words in which the relevant letter sequences occur raises further questions about syllable decomposition in braille reading. At the same time, such contracted forms provide another method for testing sub-lexical processes. The findings on the decomposition of multisyllabic and compound words (Chapter 5) suggested that direct tests with contracted forms should produce evidence on encoding processes.

A method was devised which compares common contractions in words in which they represent a compatible syllable with words in which the same contractions disrupt the normal segmentation of the word (Millar, 1995). The method can test whether contractions within words that cut across the usual segmentation of the word present a particular difficulty. The issue has long been debated among practitioners of braille. It also provides a new paradigm for testing whether and how readers segment words in reading, and if so, whether words are decomposed by syllables or by morphemic constituents of the words.

The question of sub-lexical processing was explored first with familiar words that host compatible contractions and familiar words in which the same contractions span the normal segmentation of the host word. The first study tested competent young braillists. The second study compared experienced adult braillists with adults who had learned braille after being fluent in print.

A third study was run with low frequency words that host familiar contractions in positions that either span the normal segmentation of the host word or are incompatible with such segmentation. The importance of long-term orthographic/phonological habits in word processing was shown by the difference in effects for former fluent print readers who had learned braille late, compared to experienced older braillists.

Evidence on crossmodal priming is discussed next. With tactual primes the deleterious effects of incompatible syllabic contractions disappear. Auditory priming reduces the scanning time for target words, but does not reduce the specific effect of incompatible contractions.

It is argued that word processing in braille depends crucially on familiar associated tactual/orthographic/phonological habits and word knowledge, rather than on automatic syllabic decomposition at encoding. Decomposition into orthographic/phonemic segments seems to occur mainly when the new associations run counter to habitual procedures.

1   TYPES OF CONTRACTIONS AND LATENCIES FOR SINGLE CHARACTERS AS WORDS AND WITHIN WORDS

The main point in having contractions in braille at all is to save space and time. Certainly contracted braille makes written communications and books a good deal less bulky and cumbersome. The question whether they also save reading time is more controversial. Investigations which assess the frequency with which contractions occur in a variety of books and written communication have shown that contractions vary very greatly in the frequency in which they occur, and consequently how much they contribute to saving space (Lorimer *et al.*, 1982) have shown that some contractions occur only very rarely in a wide variety of braille books and communications and thus may not save a great deal of space. Nevertheless, experienced braillists seem to prefer these to uncontracted forms.

There are several different types of contractions. Some words and letter clusters are represented as single characters or single characters preceded by one to three dots. Some are abbreviations, more like short-hand, and preserve important letters (e.g. tm = tomorrow, yrvs = yourselves, BEc = because, Bet = between) in relatively common words. Contracted forms that are abbreviations for some low frequency words (e.g. conceiving = CONcvg) occur infrequently, and almost by definition, therefore, save little space (e.g. Lorimer *et al.*, 1982).

As we shall see, the familiarity of contracted forms and how they are embedded in words has important effects on recognition. Intuitively, the linguistic 'transparency' of contractions differs very widely, although we do not know as yet how far that may be a function of their frequency. An important linguistic analysis (Daniels, 1996; Hamp and Caton, 1984) shows that the formal functions of contractions vary widely. This raises a host of issues about the role of particular linguistic structures in reading, their relation to word frequency and sentence structure and to the many mandatory rules and conventions that govern their use and which have to be learned also. Most of the relevant questions have yet to be asked, and it is to be hoped that they will receive thorough investigation in the future. Only a small section of issues are explored in the present chapter and these too perhaps raise more questions than they solve.

Perhaps the most interesting contractions for understanding the process of acquisition are single character contractions that represent whole words. It may come as a surprise to those who are unfamiliar with the system that almost every letter of the braille alphabet also represents a whole word when used alone, flanked only by the usual space between words. Other single patterns, based on the whole braille cell (called 'upper contractions'), and single characters preceded by one or more dots also represent whole words when they stand alone. I made use of some of these in my study on homophones (Chapter 4). Single character words are mainly commonly occurring high frequency words.

Following the usual convention of representing single character contractions by consecutive capitals, the words represented by the letters of the alphabet look like this to the braillist: a = A; b = BUT; c = CAN; d = DO; e = EVERY; f = FROM; g = GO; h = HAVE; I = I; j = JUST; k = KNOWLEDGE; l = LIKE; m = MORE; n = NOT; p = PEOPLE; q = QUITE; r = RATHER; s = SO; t = THAT; u = US; v = VERY; w = WILL; x = IT; y = YOU; z = AS. Other single patterns, based on the whole braille cell (called 'upper contractions') represent further common function words (AND FOR OF THE WITH) when standing alone, and some represent letter combinations within words, but function as whole words on their own (e.g. ST = STILL; WH = WHICH; TH = THIS, CH = CHILD, SH = SHALL; OU = OUT). Single characters preceded by one dot are also mainly frequently occurring familiar words (e.g. DAY FATHER MOTHER EVER HERE KNOW NAME ONE RIGHT TIME WORD WORK THERE YOUNG). Common vowel–consonant combinations (e.g. ER, AR, EN, IN, ED, OW) and other letter combinations for common syllables (e.g. ING) are also represented by single character contractions in the words in which they occur.

Contractions for whole words and familiar syllables constitute an obvious tactual analogue to processing whole words that is sometimes assumed to mediate reading print words (Chapters 4 and 5). In fact, whole word processing in terms of logographs is actually very common in reading English braille, because single character contractions for whole words are some of the most frequently occurring words in English braille. But even single character contractions are not always taught at the beginning of learning to read. It used to be the rule, and still is in many cases, that children first learn uncontracted braille (Grade I) by phonic (letter sound) methods, before learning normally contracted (Grade II) braille. More recently, methods have gained ground in which single character contractions are introduced from the start in conjunction with phonological methods. The issue is still controversial and there are good arguments on both sides. It can be contended that uncontracted (Grade I) braille is more suitable for beginners because they also have to learn that the letters also represent numbers (when preceded by the relevant symbol), so that perceiving them also as words may overload the memory system. The opposing side may point to the perceptual benefits of single characters flanked by blanks (Chapter 2), and the greater motivation of being able to read meaningful sentences that mainly consist of single characters. But punctuation marks and still other contracted forms which make use of dots confined to the lower part of the braille cell also have to be learned, together with rules for their use. The implications of different methods will be considered later (Chapter 8).

We actually know very little about the processing of contractions as yet. Nolan and Kederis (1969) used the tachistometer (Chapter 2) to time final target words in sentences. They found considerable interactions in threshold values for contractions between word frequency, the number of contractions in a word, and context effects. The frequency of contractions is, of course, also related to the frequency of the words in which they occur. The data produced by Lorimer *et al.* (1982) suggest that infrequent contractions are not often encountered in high frequency words. Moreover, low frequency contractions also tend to be taught later. To get some handle on the question whether contractions save time as well as space, I compared the same contractions in different contexts.

The first question of interest here was, therefore, whether familiar contractions that are learnt relatively early take longer to process when they are part of another word than when the same contraction represents an independent word, flanked only by the spaces that normally divide words from each other. Examples of words which contained the familiar contractions (AND THE FOR OF ONE) had been used in a study of oral reading of sentences in which ten high school students (aged from 9–7 to 20 years; mean 129 wpm, 156 spm on a control text) had taken part. Latencies for the contractions when they occurred as independent words, and latencies for the same contractions when they occurred within words were ascertained from the transcripts of frame-by-frame times on each occasion for each subject, for as many examples as there happened to be in the texts. The examples of words in which the contractions occurred were mainly lower in frequency than the contractions themselves (bAND, ANDante, CaTHedral, THEatre, FORgiven, FORk, proOF, OFfer, mONEy, alONE), but only processing time for the contractions themselves (including regressions over the actual contractions, not over the whole word) were calculated.

The results showed that the average processing time for contractions representing independent words was significantly (p < 0.01) lower than for exactly the same contractions when they occurred within words. The fact that single characters that represent words are processed relatively easily has practical implications for the process of learning by beginners. In principle reading matter can be produced which is relatively easy to feel, because single characters are flanked by blank spaces, but the text consists of meaningful materials from the start. Using a mixture of legally uncontracted regular words that have to be decomposed phonologically, as well as single word contractions, in teaching could make the initial stages of braille easier. The implications will be discussed later (Chapter 8).

The findings are consistent with the result by Nolan and Kederis (1969) for low frequency words, and extend them by showing that the slowing of latencies was due not to the contractions themselves, but to the fact that they occurred in low frequency words. This again underlines the importance of lexical knowledge in braille reading. It also provides evidence that familiar whole word contractions on their own do save processing time.

2   CONTRACTIONS AND SPELLING

In principle, the braille system uses the same orthography as print. Apart from contractions, braille spelling is based on the same imperfectly alphabetic principle. Even contractions may be regarded merely as a convenient 'shorthand' for reading and writing, but one which has to be written or spelt out in long-hand eventually. Braille texts are normally in contracted form, and young children learn to write braille almost from the start. But long-hand or uncontracted English spelling is learned also. How do these two forms of writing mesh?

Strictly, the alphabetic principle implies that each letter is associated with a distinctive speech sound (phoneme). The general notion of 'assembled phonology' (e.g. Chapter 4) is that the phonemes are assembled and blended into sounds which are then recognized as words. The advantage is that new, unfamiliar and even nonwords can be 'read' (sounded out) by applying grapheme–phoneme conversions. The process of 'blending' letter sounds is not by any means automatic either but has to be taught, although it can also be inferred from previous experience. Literally pronouncing the sounds of letters before 'blending' them quite often leads to wrong words. For instance, a child who was asked to read 'string' and duly pronounced the sounds of each letter separately thought that the words might be 'stuttering'. The converse problem confronts the child when attempting to spell. Even if the reader is enjoined to 'listen' to the sounds which he or she is producing, they are not necessarily the exact sound that has been associated with a given letter name. Most children begin by spelling 'phonetically' (Treiman, 1993), that is to say, they reproduce what they think that they are uttering, although that is by no means always accurate. Children who mix up the th and f in their speech, for instance, are likely to do so also when writing. If children are asked to 'invent' spellings for words, they typically try to use the sounds that they think the word produces, and make consequential errors. In speaking, sounds are assimilated to their phonological environment, and this can differ quite substantially when spoken in different words (e.g. Treiman, 1993). The problem of segmenting heard speech into letter sequences is therefore quite difficult.

However, notoriously many words in English do not even remotely conform to grapheme–phoneme regularities. Irregular words like 'light', 'taught' 'rough', 'laughter' or 'women' could not be recognized by recoding each letter into its corresponding phoneme. In some words the same letter clusters are pronounced differently in different words, as 'ow' in cow and low, or 'ea' in reading and bread, or as the 'in' sound in mint and pint. Some otherwise identical words are pronounced differently according to their grammatical tense. The past tense of the word 'read' is pronounced differently from the present although it is spelt the same except that an 's' is added in the third person singular in the present but not the past.

Some words that sound alike are spelt differently, such as right and write, see and sea, pail and pale. Homophones and rhyming words as well as irregular and exception words have long been important materials for investigating processes in reading and spelling.

In fact, in English, the links between graphemes and specific sounds are not one-to-one (Treiman, 1984, 1993). At the same time, there are some spelling 'rules' or conventions even though they have exceptions. For instance, the final 'e' in a word lengthens the preceding vowel in regular (e.g. gave) words, albeit there are familiar exceptions (e.g. have). But neither irregular nor exception words are usually wildly idiosyncratic either. Although the letter group 'ough' cannot be decoded by one-to-one sound-to-letter correspondence, the number of ways in which the letter group can be pronounced is strictly limited. Goswami (1988) found that children can use analogies from the sounds they know for an irregular letter sequence to pronounce new words that contain the same letter sequence. The existence of alternative interpretations is likely to complicate processing a specific item. At the same time, the fact that alternative pronunciations of given letter sequences are limited, makes the burden on memory in retrieval manageable, even if it is greater than would be needed for one-to-one correspondence between characters and sounds.

The important work of Treiman (1993) on sighted children's spelling has shown that quite young readers acquire knowledge of much more complex connections between the physical symbols of print and the speech sounds that these represent than those that are described by simple associations between each grapheme and phoneme. Moreover, children use their knowledge to solve the problem of how to pronounce 'irregular' visual letter strings, as well as to translate speech sounds into letter strings in spelling, but this depends on their experience of either. There is every reason to assume that Treiman's findings apply as much to young braille readers as to young print readers.

However, the fact that braille contains contractions adds several further dimensions to spelling as well as to reading braille. As regards output processes in spelling and writing, braille readers learn to write as well as to read words in their contracted form (see Section 6). But they also learn to spell words in their full uncontracted form usually by purely oral methods initially. Such spelling is needed, for instance, in learning to use a print keyboard (typewriter or computer) which is becoming an increasingly useful skill. Nevertheless, learning print spelling as well as contracted braille undoubtedly adds a further complication which increases the amount to be learned, and possibly also constitutes an extra memory load in recall. We do not have any evidence on that as yet. Oral spelling is commonly taught to all young braille readers, and particular emphasis is usually placed on teaching the letters of which contractions are composed.

It is often asked whether braille readers achieve the 'same' levels of spelling as print readers. The question is not actually easy to answer, because normative levels of competence only have meaning in the context of standardized tests. Spelling tests can be extremely useful in practice, especially if the aim is to see what additional help a child may need in learning to spell. However, the scores are less useful for the purpose of comparing different populations. By definition, these are tests that have been standardized on the population for whom the norms are intended. They are not measures of a 'general' or objective norm. It is, therefore, necessary to take care about what is to be concluded from comparing different groups on spelling tests that have age norms for print readers. If braille readers score lower than the norm for print readers, it may mean that they have had to spend more time on other aspects of reading and writing; but it could merely indicate difference in standardization. There are also problems with norms based entirely on visually handicapped children, because they vary not only in the amount of residual vision, but also in a variety of concomitant handicaps, so that the 'norm' may not apply to a child who has no additional handicaps. These reservations are needed in order not to overinterpret data on spelling and reading.

My data on oral spelling by braille readers come from fifteen subjects, who had been tested at chronological ages of eight to thirteen years (mean CA, 9–8), and who were of above-average intelligence at initial testing (mean IQ, 116). Their average spelling age was about a year (mean, 9–1) below their braille reading age (mean, 10–3) on normative tests. But they were not seriously retarded in spelling in relation to their chronological age. I have no data on children of below average intelligence. The spelling data I have on retarded readers (Chapter 7) suggest that they tend to be retarded in oral spelling as much, or more than in reading. But individual young braille readers do not necessarily lag behind print readers in spelling. I have known very young highly gifted children who achieved a spelling age well above their chronological age on any test. Moreover, experienced adult braillists have no problem whatever with spelling.

In advance of much orthographic knowledge, young visual readers tend to rely on the sound of words as they hear and pronounce them (Frith, 1980; Treiman, 1993), and they make mistakes accordingly. In orally taught spelling, children hear the word pronounced by someone else, or pronounce it to themselves, or both. In either case the input is auditory, and spelling mistakes reflect this, in braille as well as in print. The ability to segment the sound of words into phonemic constituents is important for spelling regular words. But the sound of phonemes depends on their phonological environment, and this can explain many spelling mistakes by young children who do not yet have much orthographic knowledge (Treiman, 1993).

Beginning braille readers certainly rely on phonological coding in memory (Chapter 4), and they also seem to use phonological codes for spelling, as suggested by the difference in mistakes for exception and irregular words. Strict phonemic recoding is not likely to produce correct results for irregular and exception words. The fifteen children whose spelling ages I discussed earlier, were also tested on spelling regular and irregular words. The percentage of regular words that were spelt correctly (63 per cent) was significantly ($p < 0.025$) higher than for irregular (49 per cent) words. At the same time, the children were able to spell even irregular words at a reasonable level, although some of the younger children first used the relevant contracted form even when spelling orally. The tendency to rely on phonological coding implies that there is a close connection between the orthographic and phonological mental representation of braille. Such connection is hardly surprising in view of the fact that braille spelling is necessarily conveyed orally in teaching. But it is a significant consideration, both theoretically and in practice.

3   MATCHING CONTRACTED AND UNCONTRACTED FORMS OF SPELLING

Spelling tests typically tap output processes. Asking people to spell a word is a request to them to say or to write the letters of which a word consists in the correct sequence. The process involves recall rather than recognition, particularly for words that cannot be segmented into phonemes but require memory for exceptional letter combinations for given sounds (Waters *et al.*, 1984, 1988). The fact that spelling involves recall whereas reading only requires recognition may be one factor which usually gives reading the edge over spelling. Although there are exceptions when conditions fail to provide sufficient retrieval cues (e.g Tulving and Donaldson, 1972), generally people perform much less well on recall than on recognition tasks (e.g. Lindsay and Norman, 1977).

At the same time, recognition of correct spelling can fail. Proof-reading is actually a rather difficult task for many people. In reading for meaning, print readers often miss spelling errors, particularly in common words and in function words (e.g. Drenowski, 1978; Drenowski and Healy, 1977; Haber and Schindler, 1981; Healy, 1980; Smith and Groat, 1979), and eye-movement studies have shown that people frequently fail to fixate function words (Rayner and Pollatsek, 1987).

Similar effects occur in reading braille for comprehension. In oral reading competent readers sometimes insert function words that they have inferred from prior context but which are not present (e.g. THE, FOR). Moreover, despite the surprisingly even reading rate of fluent readers, not all letters receive equal scanning time (Chapter 5), suggesting that not all characters receive equal attention. At the same time, competent braillists are extremely sensitive to very small physical depressions in the height of individual dots (Millar, 1987 b). The 'oversight' is thus less a question of missing dots than of 'predictive' reading which obviously occurs also in visual reading (e.g. Ehrlich and Rayner, 1981). Since the graphemic basis of such errors clearly differs between print and braille, it is more likely that for braille at least, such errors stem from predictions based on construing gist, or possibly from both perceptual and semantic/syntactic cues. The question is an extremely important one for understanding such errors. But we have very little evidence on it as yet.

It was initially surprising to find that misspelling familiar, short, graphemically similar homophones had very little effect on the scanning latencies for the target words (Millar, 1988 c), although it slowed the overall reading time of the text. Not all readers simply missed the wrong spelling. The regression data (Chapter 5) showed returns from misspelt words to prior disambiguating context, although the regressions were brief, and totally unlike the drastic repetition over perceptually degraded stimuli. The effect of the graphemically similar misspelt words was also in contrast to the long latencies and repetitive regressions for misspelt homophone words in sentence judgments which differed graphemically (contracted length), except by beginning readers who were seduced by the sound of the target words into accepting inappropriately spelt sentences (Chapter 4). The difference in the size of the orthographic effect between the two studies can be explained by the fact that the misspelt homophones which attracted few regressions (Millar, 1988 c) were also graphemically similar to the correct word, while the misspelt homophones, discussed in the previous chapter, which attracted additional processing time were graphemically quite distinct pairs. This has two interesting implications. It shows yet again that the different processes which are involved in reading combine in subtly different ways in different task conditions. It also means that orthographic effects vary considerably with the method that is used to test for them, and that this has to be taken into account in interpretations of findings.

Braillists usually write as well as read contracted braille, but need full spelling to use commercially available typewriter and computer keyboards. To explore the question how easy it is to translate from contracted to full spelling, I used a matching task in which both contracted and uncontracted forms of spelling were available. Matching was chosen, because it depends less on retrieval than does recall, and consequently reduces some of the differences in retrieval time between systems which may have been learned at different times or used to different extents. It also has the advantage over reading for comprehension of eliciting greater attention to spelling without having to use misspelt foils which may themselves differ in the extent to which they disrupt the reading process.

The method used here was to present readers with lists of word pairs in a (same–different) matching task. The target word pairs were always two words, the first hosted an easy mandatory contraction (AR ER IN EN ED AND FOR THE), and the second was the same word spelt in uncontracted (fully written out) form. It was assumed that facility in translating from the contracted to the full orthographic form of a word would show in shorter latencies for the second word (in terms of ms per character), if the contraction predicts the full spelling of the second word. A total of thirty-two target pairs were interspersed fifty-eight 'filler' pairs in which both words were either identical or different contracted words or different words in either contracted or uncontracted form. The fillers were used mainly to ensure that subjects actually scanned both words rather than guessing that the second word was always uncontracted, but also acted as control conditions. Half the target words were either high or medium-high in frequency. Subjects were told how the pairs were designed, so that they could anticipate that in some word pairs the contracted words would be followed by their uncontracted form. I compared the processing speeds (ms per character) for high and low frequency words each in contracted and in fully spelt out form (e.g. hAND with hand, pIN with pin, dENote with denote, abANDon with abandon) by seven competent readers (means, 139 wpm, 150 spm), aged between eleven and nineteen years.

Surprisingly, most subjects found the matching task very difficult. They frequently regressed to the first (contracted) word before judging the identity of the two words. This meant that they achieved unusually (for them) low (character/ms) latencies even for the higher frequency words. Nevertheless, they were significantly ($p < 0.001$, 2-tail) faster on the high frequency contracted words than on the same words in their uncontracted form, although the number of characters in the words had been taken into account. Even competent braille readers evidently did not predict the uncontracted from contracted forms of spelling. By contrast, no significant difference was found between contracted and uncontracted forms for low frequency words.

In addition to the competent readers, three students who had learned braille only very recently after being fluent print readers were also tested. Their data were not included in the analyses, but the latencies for two faster former print readers are also graphed (Figure 6.1). None of the three recent readers showed any difference between contracted and uncontracted high frequency words. They were in fact marginally faster on uncontracted than on contracted low frequency words. The third subject who was too slow to graph together with the others also showed the same advantage for uncontracted words.

There was no doubt that high frequency words containing contractions were read faster than the same words spelt out as in print. For low frequency words the advantage of within-word contractions was often overshadowed by additional processing due to regressions from the fully spelled forms, to check processing by rescanning the contracted forms. Accuracy was almost at ceiling level. It was clear, therefore, that these young students were perfectly able to translate contractions into full spelling. But the latencies showed that the translations were by no means automatic. The number of subjects tested here was, of course, quite small and may therefore not be representative of the general population of

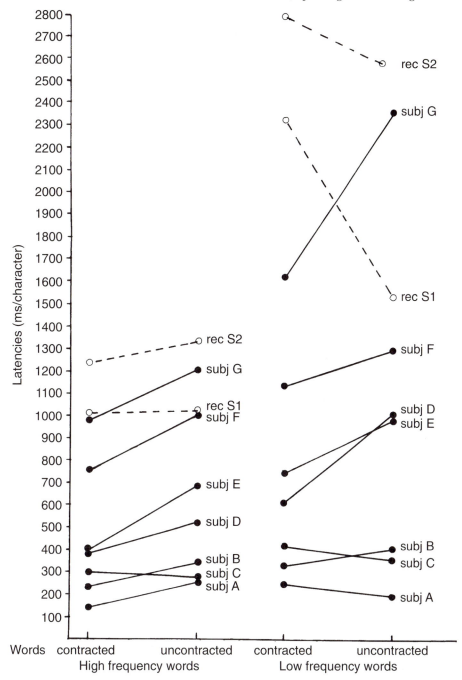

Figure 6.1 Mean latencies (ms per character) by experienced young braillists (subj. A to G), and by two young braille readers who had learned braille recently after reading print (rec S1 & S2), for matching words in contracted and fully spelt-out form

young braillists. On the other hand, they were all intelligent youngsters who were attending selective schools, had no additional handicaps, and had all learned English spelling orally as well as the contracted orthographic forms.

The findings suggest that whatever orthography is used habitually, or is more frequently associated with the relevant script, tends to be faster, or more easily available. Pring (1986) found differences between young adult print and braille readers for auditorily presented words which contained easy contractions in braille, but not in print. Norwegian braille seems to be somewhat less complicated than English braille, but Bruteig (1987) also found that Norwegian braillists identified contracted words faster than uncontracted words. Findings for one of the fastest of the highly experienced adult braillists in my studies showed significantly faster scanning for contracted than for uncontracted forms, despite the fact that the uncontracted spelling followed the contracted form. The difference was in the latency per letter (ms/character). Measures of the total scanning time for the uncontracted forms would simply differ in first-pass time with more letters, in any case. Interestingly enough, the difference for that subject was significant for the low frequency as well as for the high frequency words. Indeed, unlike the competent young braillists, the speeds of that experienced and competent adult did not differ significantly between low frequency and high frequency words. Clearly, the lexical and semantic experience of that intelligent adult was greater than that of the young people.

The findings are relevant to the question whether contractions save time as well as space. The latencies were here analysed in terms of the time (ms) per item, thus controlling for the fact that uncontracted forms contain more characters. The data show that for competent braillists, familiar contractions do save time in high frequency words. For very experienced braillists the advantage of easy contractions seems to extend to low frequency words also.

One further comment is worth making. All subjects found the matching task much more difficult than reading for comprehension. They were also much slower, mainly because of constant regressions from uncontracted to contracted words. The task was, of course, much more like proof-reading than like reading for comprehension. It required attention to individual characters. Even so, word frequency was a significant factor in matching by competent young braillists, suggesting that they used their lexical as well as orthographic knowledge. The one exception was a very experienced older braillist who also had years of print reading and spelling. He literally used character-by-character comparisons. After carefully scanning the first word and using repeated regressions over the contracted character, he went on to scan the second word, keeping the right forefinger on letters that were constituents of the contraction in the first word, and interleaving the scanning of these with regressions by the left forefinger to the contraction in the first word. Systematic character-by-character comparison is, of course, potentially the best strategy in matching tasks. But the majority of subjects evidently relied on their word knowledge rather than on comparisons of single characters. Such individual differences in strategy clearly need to be taken into account in describing the factors that are involved in processing orthographic differences.

From the point of view of understanding how contractions may affect spelling skills, one possibility is that having two orthographic representations for the same letter groups may increase memory load in retrieval. A good deal more work is needed before we understand the relation between the mental representations of the contracted and the full orthography of words. Presumably having two forms that the spelling could take is likely to slow the retrieval process when spelling is required. This is an area of research which has received very little study so far. It is a fascinating topic which has implications for the process of learning and retrieval of information generally. It could usefully be studied by comparing contracted and uncontracted forms of orthographic knowledge by experienced braillists.

4   WRITING AND BEGINNING BRAILLE READING

It is instructive to note that in the early stages, writing braille is actually easier than reading for many young braille readers. Writing is usually done by using the 'Perkins' or similar machine, which produces the raised dots of the braille cell. The advantage of writing was first brought to my notice by the case of a child who could not yet read or recognize braille letters reliably, but was able to write the relevant characters reasonably reliably, and could also write little stories on the Perkins brailler. Her method was to call out the dot numbers required for a given letter and to depress the relevant keys accordingly. However, she evidently had difficulty in associating this conjunction with recognizing the patterns by touch. The case will be discussed in some detail later (Chapter 7). But a similar advantage of writing over reading letters was also found for other congenitally totally blind children, and for some newly blind adults.

A study which confirmed this was conducted with eighteen congenitally blind (sixteen total, two with some light perception) readers from non-selective schools (mean IQ = 105, Williams, 1956) at the time. Subjects were tested on reading, writing and saying the dot numbers of randomly presented braille letters. Errors differed significantly ($F = 6.0$; $df = 2/30$; $p < 0.01$), due to greater accuracy in writing than in reading letters. Saying the dot numbers did not differ in accuracy from writing them, although saying them took longer than either writing or reading ($p < 0.005$). The better readers (aged between 10 and 12-6 years) made very few errors overall, but what errors occurred were in reading rather than in writing letters.

The early advantage of writing over reading letters was initially surprising, because visual recognition is usually easier than production. But that is not, in fact, always the case in touch (Millar, 1990 b, 1991). For instance, producing raised line configurations of the human figure is easier than recognizing them. It is difficult to recognize raised line configurations unless they are very familiar, or subjects are first told what the alternatives are called. The reasons why production is often easier than recognition in tactual conditions are instructive. They have to do with the possibility of recruiting movement and proprioceptive information in addition to touch which were discussed previously (Chapters 2 and 3). The difficulty of recognizing braille patterns because of their small size and lack of redundant distinguishing features was documented at some length, and need not be repeated here. To write braille means to produce the same small, nonredundant patterns. In the past, the main method was to use braille frames. These have lines of (2 × 3) holes for consecutive braille cells. The dots for a character in a cell had to be pricked out with a stylus in reverse (right-to-left) sequence so that they appeared in the correct orientation on the reverse side of the braille paper. There is no doubt that children learned this, and some became quite fast. But such reversals in a system that uses all of the six dot positions, and consequently abounds in many letters that are 'mirror images' of other characters (see Chapter 2), requires a good deal of processing skill. It has to be said that the 'Perkins' machine has some of the same disadvantages, because it has a horizontal keyboard to produce the vertically oriented braille cell. But it has the advantage that beginning readers can depend on a distinctive combination of fingers to depress the relevant keys on the keyboard for each character.

The Perkins keyboard consists of a row of horizontally arrayed keys which produce the braille cell as raised dots on the stiff paper that is inserted as in a typewriter. The keys are depressed in the relevant combination to produce all the characters that are based on the six-dot braille cell. The three keys on the left are depressed respectively by the left forefinger, middle and ring fingers to produce the left (1 2 3) row of dots of the braille cell. The three keys on the right are depressed by the right forefinger, middle and ring fingers to produce the row of dots on the right (4 5 6) of the braille cell. To learn a character, the child has to associate the correct combination of fingers and keys (e.g. 2 4 5) with the sound of the letter (e.g. 'd').

I have described writing by means of the 'Perkins' in some detail because it illustrates how apparently minor features of input and output systems can influence processing, particularly in the early stages of learning. The Perkins is clearly useful, not least because young children can usually operate it. Moreover, the horizontal layout of the keys for producing braille characters is probably the easiest layout for using combinations of fingers to depress the relevant keys. However, the fact that the keyboard is horizontal and differs in spatial orientation from the vertical orientation of the braille character which the keyboard has to produce affects the feedback a child can get from producing a character. It fails to support the mental representation that could be most serviceable. If beginners were to code braille characters by global shape, they would have to perform two mental rotations of ninety degrees to identify the shape on the page with the shape on the keyboard. The set of three keys on the left would have to be rotated by ninety degrees to the left; the set of three keys on the right would have to be rotated by ninety degrees to the right in order to match the shape on the page, and vice versa. There is no doubt that young blind children are, in principle, capable of mental rotation, but also that mental spatial reorganization is not easy for them (Millar, 1994).

What happens in practice is that the mediation in the early stages is through numbering. The left hand column of the braille cell is numbered from one to three and the keys on the left of the keyboard are numbered from one to three, starting with the forefinger. The column of dots on the right of the braille cell are numbered from four to six, and so are the keys on the right of the keyboard starting with the right forefinger. Remembering the dot numbers needed for different characters in reading and writing forms a first strategy for many young children.

The advantage of writing over reading in the early stages is therefore intelligible. Numbering your fingers, and remembering the sequence of number sounds for the combination of fingers associated with the sound of a character presents no spatial confusions. It has the added advantage that mental representations can be based on a combination of speech and finger-movements. The advantages of speech-based phonological recoding for memory are well documented (Chapter 2 and 4). The early use of associating verbal numbering and finger–key combinations which produce characters as mediating factors for character recognition is of particular interest for practical purposes (Chapter 8). It also suggests that linguistic and cognitive factors play a part in braille reading acquisition from the start.

At the same time, the association of verbal number and name tags with the use of finger combinations to press the relevant pattern of keys provides an output process that can, in turn, mediate braille character recognition. There is evidence that producing raised line configurations by drawing is easier than their recognition, as well as evidence for mental rehearsal of movement information (Millar, 1994; Millar and Ittyerah, 1991). Adult print readers often want to see what a word looks like if they are doubtful about its spelling. Mental representation of characters in terms of their verbal associations and fingering provides an alternative means of mental representation in congenital total blindness. It is by no means the only form of mental representation that is available to congenitally totally blind children, but it is a viable alternative form. At least some blind children use that. As one child who had taken part in a braille study said spontaneously "I think with my fingers".

The Perkins machine is not the only means of producing braille. Currently, a number of electronic devices are beginning to be on the market which potentially help the process of writing braille. But they are a long way yet from reaching the majority of young beginning braille readers. Strategies based on dot numbering drop out of consciousness and probably out of the repertoire with skilled reading and writing. Competent readers whom I have asked certainly do not think that dot numbering forms any part in their reading.

The advantage of writing over reading braille was found also with some adult beginners who were learning braille late in life and who had been fluent print readers earlier. For young beginners the advantage of writing over reading disappears as spelling becomes more complicated, although spelling regular three-letter words remains a relatively easy skill for most children. Beyond that, the best readers are also very accurate at writing texts to dictation which they can also read competently.

In the study on reading and writing single letters, the two upper groups of readers were also tested on writing to dictation. The six readers in the best group made less than 8 per cent errors on average in a 200 word text which was at the same level as their reading tests and involved contracted braille. The second group, whose reading was adequate for their age, made more than 30 per cent of errors in the same texts, predominantly because of three children whose knowledge of contractions as well as of low frequency words was poor. This will be discussed further in a later chapter (Chapter 7).

The interesting point, noted in the scripts, was that when the children were in doubt about the spelling, especially with lower frequency words, they tended to spell 'phonetically', as reported for young print readers (e.g. Treiman, 1993). They got the spelling wrong in ways that suggest that they were trying to transliterate what they thought that they had heard, sometimes using the wrong vowels, or leaving out a double consonant, or inserting an additional letter. So 'travellERs' became 'travERls', 'preciOUs' was spelt 'presOUs', 'hoppED' lost a 'p', 'SHoes' was spelt 'SHues' and 'honOUrs' became 'onners'. Some errors could be attributed to slips or mistakes in finger combinations on the Perkins machine. But letter reversals in writing (w for r) were not common.

There were also some errors that must be attributed to confusions produced by braille contraction rules. For instance, the insertion of an additional space within words while using mandatory contractions correctly otherwise (e.g hOW EVER for 'however' and a peAR/ED for 'appeared'), or leaving out a space when it is required suggest confusions about braille spacing. Braille rules prescribe that some separate words are written in conjunction (e.g. IN/TO/THE), but have to be separated in some contexts. Spaces are, of course, meaningful entities even in print (i.e.

they separate words), but they are more easily confused in braille. For instance, in some contracted words (e.g. cITY), a lower (sixth position) dot precedes the upper part of the contraction, thus leaving a space between the first letter and the upper part of the contraction that may initially feel like a space between words. Confusions that were directly due to the use of contractions were shown particularly by subjects who had the highest spelling error rates. One subject, for instance, used a mixture of contracted and uncontracted forms (e.g. 'e' in addition to ED in a word), or used an uncontracted form (st for ST) or contractions for letters that these contractions do not represent. His reading on speed tests for regular words that did not involve contractions was perfectly average for his age and intelligence.

5 CONTRACTIONS AND SUB-LEXICAL SEGMENTATION

The finding that contractions that occur within words take longer to process than the same contractions when standing alone as words (Section 1) raises the issue of sub-lexical segmentation yet again. The contractions within words were all monosyllables. Although the findings on syllable effects in silent braille reading considered so far (Chapters 4 and 5) provided little support for the view that syllabic structure, as such, is central to reading, decomposition of compound words into meaningful components (Chapter 5) occurred about fifty per cent of the time. Moreover, the multisyllabic and compound words studied so far were all legally uncontracted words. The question of sub-lexical decomposition therefore needed to be tested also with words in which syllabic contractions occurred.

The issue relates to the debate among practitioners whether it matters that some mandatory contractions within words disrupt their normal syllabic segmentation. The importance of syllables in speech perception is not in question (e.g. Gleitman and Rozin, 1977; Liberman *et al.*, 1977; Rayner and Pollatsek, 1989; Treiman *et al,* 1995). Perhaps for that reason, the view that syllables are also central to reading has had considerable influence on practitioners of braille in the use of contracted forms within words. The rules for the mandatory use of contractions within words are, as far as possible, framed so as to avoid using contractions in words in which they cut across the usual syllabic segmentation of that word. But there are actually a number of quite frequently occurring words which host common vowel–consonant contractions that are not compatible with the natural sound segmentation of the words.

The question whether contractions that occur as different segments of words pose specific difficulties is clearly an important issue. As far as I know, there is no empirical evidence on this point so far. As I mentioned earlier (Chapters 4 and 5), there is no consensus about the role of syllables in the literature on print reading (Crowder, 1982; Rayner and Pollatsek,

1989) and the evidence is controversial. At least three theories are relevant to the question. Gleitman and Rozin (1977) argued that the alphabetic principle demands the detection of phonemes and that young children have difficulty in detecting phonemes. By contrast, they detect syllables and rhymes easily and could be taught phonemic segmentation by these means. That seems a very reasonable procedure for the process of acquisition. There is good evidence that training in phonological segmentation does indeed facilitate learning to read (Bradley and Bryant, 1983). But the fact that phonological segmentation is important for learning to read does not, as such, necessitate the assumption that syllables are central to the process. The very marginal effect that word length in syllables had on beginning and slow readers when graphemic length was controlled, compared with the large effect of graphemic length when syllable length was controlled (Chapter 4) could not be explained by assuming that subjects recoded the words first into syllables and subsequently also into phonemes.

On the other hand, beginning and slow readers paid more attention to the first few letters of multisyllabic words than to transitions between other letters in the words (Chapter 5). Recoding the first few letters as a syllable might well make it easier to recode subsequent letters phonemically. The fact that greater attention to the first letters occurred less than half the time suggests that such segmentation is a reasonable strategy that children may adopt some of the time, possibly when they find long words difficult, rather than that it is an inevitable first step in all processing.

The more stringent theory that syllabic encoding is an automatic and obligatory initial process in reading by adults, but that the effect dissipates too quickly to be detected by methods other than tachistoscopic exposure of words for milliseconds (e.g. Spoehr and Smith, 1975; Van Orden *et al.*, 1990) is somewhat difficult to test. The failure to find syllable length effects in scanning latencies by fluent readers can be attributed to not testing the effect early enough in processing. But it can also be argued such processing is only found in special conditions. For instance, tachistoscopic exposure with fast superimposed masking may demand phonological recoding in order to keep the items in memory, rather than that it is part of an obligatory initial process.

As a method of dealing with that problem which, at the same time, explores an important potential problem in braille, I used words that host the same contractions at different points in the normal segmentation of the host words. Comparing words which host compatible contractions with words that host contractions that are segmentally incompatible constitutes a natural paradigm for testing theoretical assumptions about decomposition of words into syllables. The practical problem is whether contractions that span syllable boundaries produce difficulties for braille. The method can also test whether syllables are central in encoding processes in reading for meaning. If they are, scanning latencies for words which host compatible contractions that represent compatible syllable segments should be much faster than latencies for words in which the same contraction violates the syllabic segmentation of the host word.

A method was therefore designed which tests for syllable encoding during normal reading by comparing words with compatible and incompatible contraction segments. Encoding syllables in words during normal reading can be tested by using the very contractions that may cause difficulties in braille reading because they occur in words in which they violate the normal segmentation of the host word. Any theory which assumes that syllables are central to reading, and that initial syllables are particularly important in the process must also predict that words which host contractions that cut across their normal segmentation should take longer to process than words with compatible contractions.

My findings with multisyllabic and compound words (Chapter 5) suggested that decomposition into meaningful sub-lexical components occurs as often for the more proficient as for beginning or slow readers. The fact that such sub-lexical decomposition occurred only for less than fifty per cent of the words examined, suggests again that it is not an inevitable processing requirement in word recognition. The second hypothesis which needed to be considered, therefore, was that differences in processing the stems and affixes of words are due to orthographic redundancy rather than to syllabic recoding (Adams, 1979; Seidenberg, 1987). If so the representation of orthographically redundant letter sequences by a contracted form within words should therefore not have seriously deleterious effects on the familiar host words in which they occur, even if the words are read aloud.

A third hypothesis that needed to be considered assumes that syllable effects are due to speech output processes or preparation for speech output, but do not affect the process of encoding or recognition (Klapp *et al.*, 1973). The failure to find syllable effects in the studies considered earlier is therefore to be explained by the use of silent reading. Beginners would still be at a stage where they rely on speech output strategies to sustain encoding, and therefore only they should show syllable effects in silent reading. In oral reading, on the other hand, all subjects would need to plan for speech output. The simplest explanation for syllabic and morphemic decomposition in recognizing multisyllabic and compound words in silent reading is that syllable effects as such occur mainly when articulatory (speech output) strategies are used because there are processing difficulties. These would be expected to occur more for beginning and slow readers.

The first study was designed to explore these alternatives. The aim was to test whether contractions that represent orthographically frequent vowel–consonant sequences produce longer latencies when they cut across the normal segmentation of a familiar host word than in words in which the same contraction is a compatible affix, or represents the sound in the middle of the word. A second question was whether beginning and slow readers show such differences more than proficient readers.

The choice of contractions was determined by a number of considerations. The most important were that they should be frequent, familiar even to readers at a relatively low level of proficiency, and that the same contraction should occur in compatible, incompatible and middle sections of words of equal frequency. To obtain a sufficient number of comparable words in which the same contraction occurred in three different forms, the most frequent contractions which all have the same (vowel–consonant) construction were chosen as the basic contractions for comparison words. The most frequent vowel–consonant contractions (in descending order of frequency of occurrence, respectively, from 2nd to 10th per million, are ER IN ED EN AR. These were similar in their mean frequency values in four different corpora (Lorimer *et al.*, 1982). For each contraction, 10 words were selected in each of three segment categories. These consisted of ten words in which the contraction was inconsistent with the usual segmentation of the word, ten words in which the same contraction preserved the normal sound either in the middle or (in the case of ed) at the end of the word, and ten words in which the same contraction occurred as a stressed syllable segment, usually at the beginning or end of words. Examples in the respective segment categories for each contraction were as follows: For ER: beER, pERson, keepER; for IN: traIN, drINk, INdia; for ED: bleED, likED, fatED; for EN: screEN, presENt, elevEN; for AR: feAR, rEAp, fARe. The middle category for the AR contraction was the EA (another high frequency) contraction, because the AR contraction violates the normal ea sound (as spelt in print) when r follows e, and thus has to be compared with the EA as well as with the AR contractions when this follows a consonant and the contraction segments the sounds in the same way as print orthography. The words in the three segment categories were chosen so that the average word frequency (Thorndike and Lorge, 1959) and word length matched in the three segments for every contraction. In order to obtain a sufficient number of examples, words with intermediate as well as high frequencies were used with the restriction that frequency counts should match across the three segment categories.

The basic material thus consisted of 150 target words. Each word was embedded in a sentence, with the restriction that target words in each category would occur with roughly equal frequency at the beginning, middle and end of the sentences. The main reason was to ensure that the three categories of contracted words had the same probability of being 'guessed' or inferred from the context of the sentence. To check on the extent of contextual facilitation for target words at different locations in the sentences, the sentences were scrambled and submitted in print form to ten independent sighted observers. In the print version, each sentence was presented up to and including the first letter of the target word. The observers were naive as to the purpose of the experiment. They were asked to guess the next (target) word from the portion of sentence context and the first letter given in the print versions of the sentences. The observers produced 14.5 per cent correct guesses of target words in all, with similar proportions in the three segment categories. The sentences were then brailled in random order onto transparent sheets, one sentence on each line, and presented in the video-recording apparatus described earlier (Chapter 3). The task was to read the sentences aloud as fast and as accurately as possible.

The data of main interest were the latencies for the target words, and for the contractions within the target words. The processing time for words included first-pass and regressions over the word. Processing time for the contractions included only first-pass time and regressions over that character. Fourteen able adolescent (mean age, 16-6) students from a selective school for the visually handicapped took part. The seven faster readers had baseline reading rates above 100 wpm (mean, 152 wpm; range 119–188 wpm). They had learned braille from the beginning of their schooling, and had an average of 11 (from 7 to 15) years experience of braille. The slower readers (mean age, 13-10) had baseline reading rates below 100 wpm (mean, 57; range, 15–89 wpm). The group included three older students who had learned braille for less than two years, and four younger children who had less than six years of braille experience. One older subject with eight years of braille experience was an accurate but very slow reader. It should be noted that the slow readers could not be regarded as 'retarded' readers in any meaningful sense of that term. All subjects were using braille daily in their studies. The overall error rate for slow as well as for fast readers was 0.87 per cent, and too low for analysis.

The analyses of latencies showed no significant differences between words in which the contractions were inconsistent or occurred in the middle or at the end of the host word. As expected, the more proficient group was significantly faster than the slower readers on all target words, and also in the analyses of latencies run separately for the five forms of contracted words ($p < 0.05$ to $p < 0.025$). The findings are graphed in Figure 6.2, together with the results of a second study with former print readers and experienced older braillists.

The findings did not support the hypothesis that words with inconsistent vowel–consonant contractions take longer to recognize than words in which the same contractions are compatible. Considered in terms of the three theories of syllabic coding mentioned earlier, the findings are difficult to reconcile with the assumption of automatic initial syllabic recoding. Such initial coding should be slowed for relatively short words with inconsistent contractions, and this should have shown up at least in the scanning latencies for the relevant contractions by the slow reader. The lack of effect is not consistent either with the notion that syllable effects depend on speech output. Oral reading was used so that speech output factors were involved.

Adverse effects of incompatible syllabic segmentation should therefore have shown if that were a major factor in speech output or preparation for pronunciation. But there was no evidence that incompatible segmentation by contractions made a significant difference to scanning latencies.

The findings (Millar, 1995) were more consistent with the suggestion that familiar orthographic redundancies (Adams, 1981; Waters *et al.*, 1984, 1988) are an important factor in word recognition than with either of the other hypotheses. The failure to find segmentation effects could have resulted from constant recent practice of braille, because even the slow readers necessarily had constant daily braille practice. Moreover, with the exception of two recently blind older children, they had not been highly practised print readers previously. Since the vowel–consonant contractions and the words in which they occurred were high in frequency in braille materials, daily use of these could have produced high levels of familiarity for both groups of readers for all the target words.

The absence of segmentation effects for slow readers was more surprising initially. However, inspection of the individual data made it clear that some readers in the slow (below 100 wpm) group often processed contractions as fast as readers in the more fluent (above 100 wpm) group, despite the significant difference in their overall speeds. It suggested that familiarity with the contractions rather than reading speed, as such, could be a deciding factor. Certainly even the slower braillists would be required to use braille in school every day, and would be exposed to much the same materials. The vowel–consonant contractions used here do occur quite frequently as inconsistent segments within words.

There was another indication that processing contractions depends more on familiarity than on other factors. Thirty filler sentences had been randomly interspersed in the lists of target sentences, both as a control and as a means of exploring effects of lower frequency words. The sentences included words in which further contractions did not follow normal segmentation (e.g auTHEntic, phONEy, crEAte), and words in which the (uncontracted) middle sounds consisted of two vowels that are pronounced separately (e.g. biology, riot, geologists), as well as some words with relatively rare but compatible contractions (deITY, seANCE). The results for these disparate items were not suitable for inclusion in the formal analysis. But they were of interest. Responses during reading showed that few young readers knew the meaning of 'seANCE', and all had difficulty with 'deITY' although they knew the meaning once it had been construed. Such findings raise interesting speculations about the relation between access to words that can be recognized but not recalled, and unknown words that can be construed from the context.

It is, of course, difficult to separate frequency effects and familiarity. One means of doing so is to compare subjects whose braille experience is unlikely to overlap. This would be true for experienced braillists compared to people who have learned braille late in life but can read well enough to cope with the contractions and the sentences used here. The effect of contractions on people who had learned braille late in life was, in any case, of special interest in the present studies.

A second study was therefore carried out which used exactly the same materials and procedures to compare older, previously fluent print readers who had learned braille later in life and experienced braillists who had comparable years (forty or more) of braille reading experience. As noted earlier (Chapter 5) the experienced braillists (Group EB) had a mean (averaged over texts) reading rate of 80 wpm (from 62 to 158 wpm), and even the slowest readers in this group were highly competent in terms of comprehension. The late readers (LR group) scored a mean reading rate (averaged over texts) of 23 wpm (15–37 wpm). All except two people used braille only intermittently. Help was given when necessary, but was counted as an error and the item was omitted from latency counts if it concerned a target word.

Responses by former print readers were particularly important for understanding effects of syllabic/orthographic effects on reading. It seemed likely that if such contractions do present special difficulties, they would be shown by people who had learned or were still learning braille late in life after having been fluent in print reading and orthography. The main hypothesis, materials and procedures were precisely the same as in the study with young readers. The further hypothesis was that new braillists who had been fluent print readers previously would be affected more by contractions that violate sound segmentation and orthographically (in print) frequent letter combinations than could braillists who had little or no experience of print. Subjects were tested singly, either in their own homes, or in a testing room in my university department, as they preferred. In the case of slow readers, testing took more than one session. The experienced braillists were accurate (0.55 per cent errors). The overall target word error rate by recent readers (3.07 per cent) was also too low for statistical analysis, although the rates varied somewhat (4.4, 2 and 2 per cent), suggesting that there were more errors for the inconsistent segment words. But the error rate was too low for statistical analysis.

The results on scanning times showed that recent braillists took significantly longer over the same contraction when it occurred in different positions in the host word. None of the experienced braillists was affected by any of these. As expected, recent braillists were significantly slower (F = 26.41, df = 1/8, p < 0.001) on scanning target words. There was also a significant interaction (F = 2.25, df = 8/64, p < 0.05) which showed that for the recent readers, but not for experienced braillists, segment effects differed for different contractions. As expected, recent readers also took longer over the contractions (F = 26.86, df = 1/8, p < 0.001), and this interacted with all the other factors, showing that only the recent braillists were affected by the location of the same contractions in different segments of the host word. Thus, the effects of proficiency interacted significantly with

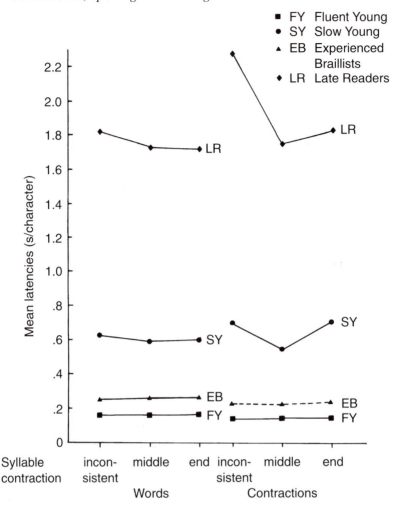

Figure 6.2 Mean latencies (s per character) for words and contractions in which the same contraction disrupts the normal segmentation (inconsistent), or occurs in the middle of the word (middle), or at the end of the word (end)

the type of contraction (F = 12.49, df = 4/32, p < 0.001), and with the segment category in which they occurred (F = 5.79, df = 2/16, p < 0.025). Proficiency also related significantly to the interaction between contractions and segment categories (F = 3.51, df = 8/64, p < 0.01). There were no effects for experienced readers. Mean latencies for correct target words (s/character) and for the contractions (s) are graphed in Figure 6.2, together with the results for the young readers that were discussed earlier in the section.

The results supported the hypothesis that recent braillists show segmentation effects. Experienced readers showed none of these. For recent readers the contractions showed the effect more than the words as a whole, suggesting that they had spent more time over the contractions in the wrong position than over the other parts of the word. However, the strength of the effect was not the same for all types of contractions, as can be seen from the statistical interactions. The further analyses of the interactions for the different types of contractions showed that the inconsistency effect was due mainly to the ER, AR and IN contractions in which the incompatible segment took significantly longer than the middle segment ($p < 0.05$, $p < 0.01$ and $p < 0.05$, respectively on Neuman Keuls test). The incompatible ER and AR sections also took longer than the start or end sections where they acted as an affix ($p < 0.01$, $p < 0.01$, respectively). The start and end section segments for the IN contraction took longer than the middle section ($p < 0.01$). By contrast, the EN (dots 2 and 6), which is formally a mirror image of the IN (dots 3 and 5), contraction took longer to scan as the middle segment than in the inconsistent position, or in final position ($p < 0.01$). Moreover, ED contraction showed no segment effects of any kind.

The fact that consistency effects varied with the specific type of contraction is of considerable interest for teaching purposes and in trying to understand the processes in reading. Several factors, either singly or in conjunction, need to be considered. One is the physical composition of a given contraction in relation to the graphemes that surround it in a given word. Discriminability, as such, was not in question here, because all segment types were tested with the same contraction. The most likely contributory effect comes from the grapheme–phoneme relation between a contraction and the surrounding letters. The segmentation of vowel–consonant combinations is influenced by surrounding phonemes (e.g Treiman and Zukowski, 1990). Equally, surrounding graphemes influence the discriminability of a given contraction (Nolan and Kederis, 1969). But it may also be necessary to consider the syntactic status (Daniels, 1996) of contractions (e.g. the ED ending marks the tense of verbs), not only as word segments, but also in particular semantic contexts. More work is clearly needed to tease out the precise contribution to effects of contractions on word recognition from graphemic factors and syntactic factors, as well as the effects of orthographic and phonological habits. All the contractions here were familiar and occur very often indeed in braille texts. The fact that they nevertheless had differential influences on word processing makes it all the more important to understand how the contributing factors work.

The fact that experience and familiarity reduced all interference from such factors also raised further questions. Inspection of results for the additional, more difficult words which had been included also in the sentences to be read, showed more errors (total of 14.67 per cent) by the recent braillists. Like the young new braillists in experiment I, they had specific difficulties with contractions (BLE, ITY and ANCE) which are normally learned later, even though these were not in positions that violated a syllable segment in the words in which they occurred. Some of the uncontracted double vowel sounds (e.g. lions, geology) also showed some errors and took as long (per character) as some words in which the contraction spanned a syllable or contracted a double sound (e.g. phONEy, europEAn).

Again, none of the experienced braillists showed significant segment category effects in any analyses, even when this was checked additionally with nonparametric tests. Familiarity, both with contractions and with the combination of words and the contractions they host is possibly the most important factor in braille word recognition. The vowel–consonant (ER IN EN ED AR) contractions in the studies that I have just reported were high in frequency in that sense. The average word frequency was the same for the three segments of host words for any given contractions, but individual words varied from high to low frequency words. The fact that the significant segment effects were found for the older new braillists and not at all by experienced older or younger braillists or even by slow and young and beginning readers suggests that the frequency of exposure to the materials or familiarity rather than word frequency in any absolute sense was a factor.

The older previously fluent print readers who took part in the study had all learned the five contractions and knew them reasonably well on their own. Moreover, low frequency words were more familiar to them than to the younger braille readers. However, they differed from the slow young readers in the first study in two important respects: regular and frequent exposure to braille reading materials, and long-standing familiarity with print orthography. For the young students exposure to braille materials was routinely part of the necessary daily intake of information. Almost all their lessons required them to use braille materials. For recent older braillists access to reading materials was greatly restricted, and could be quite cumbersome.

It seemed possible that familiarity, not so much with the contraction itself, but with the contraction in particular word contexts, is an important factor in reading facility. If so, it is likely that inconsistency with the normal orthographic/phonological segmentation of sounds is an additional difficulty even after contractions have been learned, but before subjects are sufficiently familiar with the words in which they must be used, particularly if this cuts across long-standing knowledge of a different orthography. The next study was designed to test that.

6 ORTHOGRAPHIC EXPERIENCE, SUB-LEXICAL PROCESSING AND CROSSMODAL PRIMING

The main aim of the study which is reported in this section (Millar, 1995) was to test further the assumption that orthographically as well as phonologically well-defined familiar morphemes disrupt reading if they violate syllabic segmentation in lower frequency words. It was predicted that recent braillists should show the effect more, since incompatible contractions would violate long-standing orthographic associations of letter clusters with sounds. The problem has obvious practical applications for learning braille later in life.

The related theoretical question concerns the hypothesis that there is a strong link between word sounds and letter shapes for fluent readers (Van Orden, 1987; Van Orden *et al.*, 1990). The hypothesis implies, inter alia, that a strong association between particular syllables and graphemic forms could interfere with recognition.

An important second aim was to see how far such interference effects, if they occurred significantly, could be reduced effectively in the short term, and if so, to what extent this depends on the modality of the priming condition. Exposing the same stimulus prior to its being repeated either after some delay, or after a number of intervening items at a distance of several words is well-known to facilitate recognition (e.g. Scarborough *et al.*, 1977; Schacter, 1990). The interest here was in the quite specific question whether auditory and tactual conditions are equally effective in reducing recognition time, or whether specific tactual experience of the contraction in the context of host words is needed. The practical reason for using crossmodal (auditory–tactual) as well as purely tactual repetition priming was that auditory tapes are now widely used as teaching aids in braille. There is no doubt that this is extremely useful. But the relative effects require further testing since they have clear practical implications about the balance of such materials early in learning.

The comparison of crossmodal and intramodal priming conditions was also of interest for probing recognition processes for braille words further. Models of reading which assume close connections between phonological and orthographic representations of morphemes in long-term memory (e.g Van Orden et al, 1990) should predict that for previously fluent print readers, hearing a word automatically activates the orthographic representation associated with the sound. Auditory primes for words in which the contraction violates the normal syllabic segmentation should produce interference rather than facilitation, while tactual primes should produce repetition effects.

The hypothesis for crossmodal effects was, therefore, that host words in which contractions violate syllable segmentation take longer to recognize than words in which the same contractions are compatible with the spelling–sound segmentation of the word, and that effect is significantly greater for experienced print readers than for experienced braillists. Moreover, prior exposure to the sound of the word would not eliminate the difference. But prior tactual exposure should make the new orthography more familiar, and should, therefore, reduce the difference in effect.

The point of the study was, therefore, to use familiar, high frequency contractions in low frequency words in both tactual and auditory priming conditions. The contractions were chosen to represent orthographically, phonologically and morphemically well-defined syllables which commonly occur in almost any text, but are also used mandatorily within the words in which the relevant letter combinations occur either as legitimate syllables or in segments where they violate the normal segmentation of the word. Contractions for the function words THE, AND, OF, ONE and for the morpheme ING are high in frequency (Lorimer *et al.*, 1982). Sufficient target words were needed in which these morphemes occur as mandatory contractions in positions that were incompatible (IC words) with the normal phonological and orthographic segmentation of the word, and which could be matched for length and frequency (Thorndike and Lorge, 1959) with words in which the same contractions were compatible (C words) with the normal segmentation of the word. Ten lower frequency target words were selected in which the five contractions occurred mandatorily in positions that were not compatible (IC words) with the normal segmentation of the word, and these were matched with ten words in which the same contraction was consistent (C words) with the normal segmentation. A further restriction on the target word selection was that half the words in the IC and in the C target word groups should be comparable with each other in average length and word frequency so that they could be randomly allocated to the two priming conditions. The target words were relatively low in frequency, but they were not unknown by the subjects who were the same older experienced and recent readers that took part in the second study reported in the previous section. It was possible to find ten IC words (THErapy, baTHE, hONE/ST, atONE, wAND/ER, squAND/ER, hoOF, proOF, hINGe, syrINGe) which could be matched with ten segment category C words (diTHEr, anTHEm, hONEy, mONEy, dANDelion, abANDon, OF/fER, prOFile, actING, slING). Each target word was embedded in a sentence, such that the target word was always the second word in the sentence. Filler sentences were randomly interspersed with these. For the filler sentences the priming word was always a semantic associate of the second word in the sentence. This ensured a high probability that subjects would expect the second word in the sentence to be associated with the priming word, without being able to predict the target word or the precise relation between the prime and the target word prior to reading. Half the sentences with IC words and half the sentences with C words were allocated to auditory and half to tactual priming conditions. The sentences were brailled in random order on two transparent sheets for each priming condition. The order of braille sheets was balanced for each subject such that subjects who received an auditory presentation first, received the two tactual conditions next and the other auditory condition last. For subjects who received a tactual condition first, the reverse would apply. With this restriction, the order of presentation was randomized across subjects. For the auditory priming conditions, each sentence on the brailled sheet was preceded by a regular meaningless dot pattern, separated by two spaces from the sentence. In the tactual priming condition, each sentence on the sheet was preceded by the brailled target or filler word, which was separated from the sentence by two spaces.

Experienced braillists and recent braille learners were kind enough to agree to take part. The instructions were to read sentences aloud as fast and as accurately as possible, and that before each sentence they would either feel or hear a single word. Subjects were to start reading the sentence that followed it as soon as they had recognized the word. In the auditory priming condition, the target word, or an associate of the second word in a filler sentence, was spoken by the experimenter. While the experimenter was speaking, the subject kept his/her finger on dots which preceded the sentence by two spaces. They were asked to start reading the sentence aloud as soon as they had heard the priming word. In the tactual priming condition, subjects read the priming word silently, and proceeded to read the sentence aloud as soon as they had recognized the prime. The recording device (Chapter 3) was used, so that it was possible to time reading accurately for all parts of the text, including all start and stopping points.

The results showed that the recent braillists did indeed show the expected difference between words in which the contraction disrupted the orthographic–phonological segmentation that would be habitual to former print readers and words in which the same contractions were compatible with the segmentation expected in print spelling. None of the experienced braillists showed that difference.

Accuracy for primed target words was high. Experienced braillists made two errors in all, one for a target word in the C segment category, and one in the IC category. The recent braillists produced six errors, all for words with inconsistent (IC) contraction segments. The error rate was too low to analyse further. The scanning latencies for contractions and for the target words (s/character) in all conditions are shown in Figure 6.3. In the analysis of latencies for the target words (s/character), proficiency ($F = 11.61$, df $= 1/8$, $p < 0.01$), repetition ($F = 9.37$, df $= 1/8$, $p < 0.025$), and segment category ($F = 11.24$, df $= 1/8$, $p < 0.025$) were all significant, as were the predicted interactions of proficiency with repetition ($F = 8.32$, df $= 1/8$, $p < 0.025$), and with segment category ($F = 8.21$, df $= 1/8$, $p < 0.025$) as well as with the further interaction between these ($F = 6.73$, df $= 1/8$, $p < 0.05$). The interactions meant that the experimental effects were significant only for recent readers. Experienced braillists showed no effects. But recent braillists took significantly longer over the incompatible target words on first presentation, as predicted by the hypothesis that processing would be influenced by long-term associations between spelling and sound patterns.

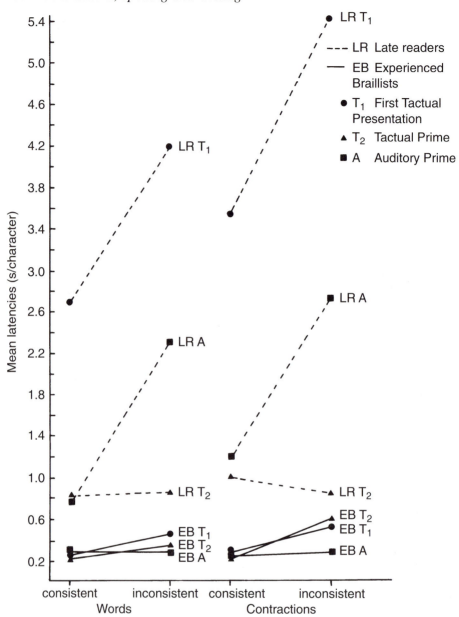

Figure 6.3 Mean latencies (s per character) by experienced braillists (EB) and former print readers (LR) for words in which the same contraction is consistent or inconsistent in segmenting the host word. Latencies for the contractions are shown on the right. The results are for target words and contractions after an auditory prime (A), for target words and contractions on first tactual presentation (T1), and for target words and contractions after a tactual prime (T2)

Separate analyses were run for the contractions. Analysing the repetition effects for the tactual priming conditions showed the usual effect of proficiency (F = 12.96, df = 1/8, p < 0.01). Tactual repetition significantly reduced scanning time (F = 9.81, df = 1/8, p < 0.025) for the recent braillists (F = 10.05, df = 1/8, p < 0.025). The IC contractions took longer to scan (F = 7.31, df = 1/8, p < 0.05). The result was confined to recent braillists on the first presentation of the target word (Newman Keuls test, p < 0.05), and was thus consistent with the hypothesis.

The second analysis focused on the crossmodal priming effects. These were more significant for the target word latencies (s/characters) than for the contractions themselves. This is intelligible, because the priming conditions, especially the auditory primes, would necessarily draw more attention to the word as such than to its constituents. Thus for the contractions themselves, latencies only showed the effect of proficiency significantly (F = 8.36, df = 1/8, p < 0.025), although tendencies to interactions were all in the predicted directions. For the target words (s/character) there were highly significant effects of proficiency (F = 16. 09, df = 1/8, p < 0.005), of priming modality (F = 25.44, df = 1/8, p < 0.001), and of the (C/IC) segment category (F = 10.28, df = 1/8, p < 0.025).

As before, all conditions interacted significantly with levels of proficiency, showing that only recent braillists were affected by the experimental conditions. Scanning latencies by experienced braillists showed no significant differences between conditions. Thus, the proficiency interacted significantly with all factors and with further interactions between these. Thus proficiency interacted with the priming modality (F = 25.55, df = 1/8, p < 0.001), and with IC and C segmentation (F = 6.37, df = 1/8, p < 0.05). The further interaction between priming modality and segmentation (F = 5.66, df = 1/8, p < 0.05) also interacted with proficiency (F = 7.33, df = 1/8, p < 0.05).

The interactions between the auditory and tactual priming modalities with the segmentation conditions were of particular interest. Auditory primes reduced all scanning latencies for the target words significantly. But they did not affect the difference between compatible and incompatible contractions for the recent braillists. Tactual primes, on the other hand, eliminated the difference. In other words, hearing the target word before scanning it made scanning faster for both types of words. But scanning the target words tactually first made it also much easier to recognize words with incompatible contractions to the extent of eliminating the discrepancy.

The results were rather exciting. There was clear evidence that readers with long-standing association between orthographic and phonological and morphemic units were selectively disturbed by words which disrupted these associations. Crossmodal repetition priming had significant effects in reducing processing time. Hearing a word prior to reading it reduced scanning time on the second presentation. Priming was thus not confined to a single modality. At the same time, tactual primes not only reduced scanning time for target words further, they also eliminated the effect of incompatible segmentation. This is important. Both findings have practical and theoretical implications.

Considered in terms of the hypotheses, the findings provide new evidence that long-term habits of combined orthographic–phonological–morphemic associations are indeed a powerful factor in processing words during reading. The stimuli were contractions for orthographically and phonologically well-defined morphemes. The experienced older braillists were by no means ignorant of spelling rules. Indeed they were mostly professional people whose orthographic ability was not in the least in doubt. The main difference between them and the recent readers was a life-time of exposure to contractions within words which often, but by no means always follow segmentation rules. The recent readers, by contrast, had been fluent print readers and had a life-time's exposure solely to the orthographic–phonological conventions of English print, and only these subjects showed significant differences between processing words in which contractions violated these conventions compared with words in which the same contractions followed the usual orthographic–phonological associations.

It had been predicted that people who were previously fluent print readers would show the effect of inconsistent contractions, because they would have strong associations between sounds and graphemic/ orthographic (print) representations (e.g. Van Orden, 1987; Van Orden *et al.*, 1990). The effect showed on the first presentation of the target word. But it also occurred after priming by hearing the word first. The hypothesis was that for former print readers, hearing a word would elicit orthographic representations which interfere with processing new graphemes when these are inconsistent with the previously associated segmentation. The results support that hypothesis.

Word frequency and familiarity clearly influenced the results. Embedding familiar morphemic contractions in low frequency target words produced much more dependable and predictable results than were found for familiar affixes in high frequency target words for the same subjects. It suggests that for low frequency words, sub-lexical, morphemic decomposition is more important.

Two further findings also suggested that familiarity with the material as well as word frequency was a factor. It had been predicted that experienced braillists would show little difference between target words with consistent and inconsistent contractions on the grounds that their long-term orthographic knowledge would include rules for using morphemic contractions and experience of both kinds of segmentation. The almost complete absence of any segmentation effects by these subjects is consistent with that assumption.

Perhaps even more striking was the effect that the relatively short-term exposure to the relevant tactual forms had on processing by recent braillists. This has practical implications (Chapter 8). But it also adds further to the growing evidence that processing in reading does not follow an invariant route in all conditions.

Despite the much larger effect of short-term experience with the tactual forms, it is of considerable interest also that the findings confirmed the importance of using advance information in the auditory modality to facilitate processing. At the same time, experience of the tactual forms is clearly needed. Not all priming conditions are likely to produce precisely the same advantages. As noted earlier (Chapter 4), it is likely that the achievement of fast reduction of segment effects depends on whether subjects expect (whether or not this is explicit) that the advance information is relevant to the subsequent reading task. In the present study, expectation was manipulated by having the target word always as the second word in a sentence, although the word could not be guessed because the second words in the randomly interspersed filler sentences were remote associates of the primes. The manipulation evidently worked because the same conditions were, of course, used also in auditory priming which did not reduce adverse effects of inconsistent contractions. The point is that for tactual repetition priming to be useful in practice, the probability of repetitions may need to be relatively high, at least early in learning.

The finding that tactual priming and repetition reduced recognition time very substantially for words in which contractions violate syllables or previous orthographic representation is also very relevant to learning braille by people who lose sight later in life. Far from being 'too old to learn', which is the usual assumption, it is clear that these subjects can achieve very substantial improvements even with the most difficult aspects of braille.

In considering contractions as a means of probing sub-lexical decomposition processes in reading, as well as their use in practice, further work is clearly indicated. The syllabic violations which I have used so far were contractions for meaningful syllables which disrupted the syllabic segmentation of host words, but not its meaning. The evidence that I reviewed earlier (Chapter 5) showed that sub-lexical decomposition of compound words into their constituent words occurred on at least half of the possible occasions even by competent braillists. A contracted segment that violates not merely the syllabic segmentation of the host word, but also disrupts the decomposition of the compound word into its meaningful constituent words would be likely to disrupt processing. However, the braille rule that contractions should not disrupt syllable boundaries actually applies most consistently when the syllable boundary is also the boundary between lexical components.

From the evidence reviewed so far, I would expect that a dual disruption of sound, meaning and associated orthographic groupings would disrupt processing by competent braillists. But braille rules tend to avoid these in any case.

The main findings here on syllable segmentation again highlight word knowledge, the frequency of exposure, and length of experience as major factors in the acquisition of braille. But they also clearly imply the importance of orthography and particularly the association between orthographic and phonological knowledge. Contractions disrupted processing only in so far as they disrupted long experience of orthographic–phonological associations by readers who did not have sufficient exposure to alternative associations, particularly with low frequency words. The findings suggest that considerable improvements can be achieved over short delays. But they also highlight the role of orthographic experience in reading.

The practical implications of the auditory priming effects found here are specific to the difficulties explored here. Advance information in the auditory modality was effective. What the findings suggest is that considerable improvements can be achieved in a relatively short time. But the tactual exposure was clearly important in reducing the effect of the habitual orthographic–phonological habits of former print readers. It is likely that to achieve fast reduction of segment effects probably also depends on whether subjects expect that the advance information is relevant to subsequent reading.

The crossmodal priming results are important because they show that priming is not confined to a single modality, but also because they show that modalities cannot be considered as purely abstract aspects of processing. Both modalities produced priming effects. But the effects were not entirely the same for both modalities, as would be expected if the effect depended on purely abstract representations. Nor was the difference merely a question of an increased effect by a prime in the same modality.

The relative contribution of tactual and auditory priming needs further study for practical purposes (Chapter 8), and because it can provide important further evidence on the relative importance of orthographic and phonological habits in different conditions. Some theoretical implications are briefly considered below.

7 SUMMARY AND IMPLICATIONS

The findings speak to three main issues: the effect of contractions on braille reading and spelling, the role of input modalities and output processes in reading, spelling and writing, and the evidence that contractions provide about speech-based encoding and the role of orthographic habits.

The question whether contractions save time as well as space does not have a single yes/no answer. Contractions which represent whole words when standing alone do save processing time as well as space. Moreover, familiar words which contain contractions are processed faster in terms of time per character than the same words spelt out in full. The advantage also depends on lexical knowledge. Unlike the young braillists, experienced adult braillists with comparable reading rates showed the advantage of contracted over fully spelt out words for low as well as for high frequency words. Older adults are not always at a disadvantage. A larger vocabulary is an asset in learning braille.

Intelligent young braillists were quite competent at oral spelling of both regular and irregular words, although spelling lagged somewhat behind their competence in reading. They were also able to identify contracted and full forms of spelling. At the same time, the evident difficulty of the matching task, as well as the fact that they were faster with the contracted than with the fully spelt out forms of familiar words, implies that the two orthographic forms were not automatically connected. There was no evidence that contractions generated the grapheme–phoneme (print) representations of the constituent letter sequence automatically.

Two apparently contradictory practical inferences about early processing in reading and spelling can be drawn from the findings. Fast recognition of single character contractions that represent whole words has clear advantages for making the early learning process easier and more meaningful. But contractions may have disadvantages for learning to spell orally. Contractions for whole words constitute an obvious tactual analogue to the processing of whole words that is sometimes assumed to mediate reading print words (Chapters 4 and 5). Contractions are not always taught at the beginning of learning to read. It used to be the rule, and still is in many cases, that children learn uncontracted braille (Grade I) first. More recently, methods have gained ground in which some single character contractions are introduced from the start in conjunction with the learning of letter sounds which is necessary in braille in any case. The issue is still controversial and there are good reasons on both sides which are briefly considered later (Chapter 8).

Many of the spelling errors made in writing braille by young children are similar to the phonetic errors reported for young print readers. However, some of the problems of writing braille turn on the use of contractions. Issues on the feedback from braille writing systems and oral spelling on reading, and vice versa, are discussed in Chapter 8.

The importance of familiarity with the connections between knowledge of words and how they are spelt was shown even more clearly by the studies on words in which contracted syllables were either compatible or incompatible with the segmentation of the host words. Experienced adult braillists showed no difference between processing words with contractions that were inconsistent with the segmentation of the host compared with processing words in which the same contractions were consistent. That was so with vowel–consonant contractions in relatively high frequency words, and also with whole word contractions in low frequency words. That is not to say that contractions in low frequency words were as easy as high frequency contractions even for experienced braillists.

But they did not show the particular difficulty that was caused by the disruption of habitual print spelling patterns.

By contrast, recent braillists who had been fluent print readers previously showed some effects of inconsistent segmentation even for familiar contractions in familiar words. The extent to which consistent and inconsistent vowel–consonant contractions influenced processing familiar words was also modulated by other factors. Among these, the relation between the contraction pattern and the tactual features that flank contractions within words, as well as the syntactic standing of the contraction were considered to need further study. But there was no doubt that contractions for short words and syllables which disrupted long-standing sound/spelling associations in low frequency words had highly significant effects on recent braillists. For former fluent print readers, contractions that cut across habitual sound–spelling segments do constitute a significant difficulty. The results suggest that special attention to contractions is needed in the early stages of learning, especially in conjunction with graphemic and semantic factors that seem to modulate the effect.

The results on tactual priming suggest that specific practice may be needed for syllable contractions in different word contexts. At the same time, the evidence also suggests that inconsistent segmentation does not constitute an over-riding factor even for inexperienced braillists who have learned braille late in life. The findings on auditory priming raise a number of intriguing practical questions that require a good deal of further study, both on the use of auditory aids in braille learning and on how to use inputs in different modalities (Chapter 8).

The finding that people who were previously fluent in print showed significant segmentation effects supports the hypothesis of strong associations between sounds and graphemic–orthographic representations in fluent reading (e.g. Adams, 1981). It also explains the effects of auditory and tactual priming. Hearing a word would elicit representations which interfere with processing new graphemes when these are inconsistent with the previously associated spelling pattern and segmentation. The finding that tactual but not auditory primes reduced scanning time for incompatible compared to compatible contractions in the repeated word provides further support for this hypothesis.

The absence of segmentation effects for skilled adult braillists should not be taken to imply that contractions within words necessarily save time in all cases. Contractions in low frequency or unfamiliar words, or words in which the contraction violates familiar associations may well take more time than uncontracted forms even for experienced braillists. That was not tested directly here. But the findings, taken as a whole, suggest that contractions within words seem to save time in proportion to the familiarity of the contraction and the host word. What the absence of segmentation effects for experienced braillists does show is that knowledge and experience of contractions rules and their application within words is the important factor in reading, rather than syllabic segmentation as such. Scanning by experienced braillists who knew the contraction rules and when they apply did not differ between legally contracted words in which the contraction also constituted the sound of a syllable and one in which it did not.

The findings show that syllable effects are not due to slow reading as such (e.g. Rayner and Pollatsek, 1989). The experienced older braillists were extremely slow by print reading standards, and indeed also by comparison with some younger fluent braillists in my previous experiments (e.g. Millar, 1987 a). The findings suggest that the association between slow reading and syllable effects which has been proposed can be attributed to lack of experience rather than to reading speed as such. The explanation is consistent with the phonological, syllable and morphemic effects reviewed earlier (Chapters 4 and 5), as well as with the inconsistent syllable effects found in print reading (e.g. Rayner and Pollatsek, 1989).

The notion that syllables are part of encoding processes (e.g. Mewhort and Beal, 1977; Spoehr and Smith, 1975), but occur so fast in print that they can only be detected by tachistoscopic exposure was not supported for braille reading, which is notoriously slower than print. The possibility that skilled braillists here encoded contractions so fast as syllables that inconsistencies in sound segmentation could not have affected scanning seems highly unlikely. Their processing times for single character contractions were longer than the sampling time in hundreths of a second (1/100 s) of the apparatus. Recent braillists certainly showed time differences between the same contractions in words in which they followed the normal segmentation, compared with words in which they did not. The fact that experienced braillists showed no such effects even in low frequency words is evidence against the hypothesis that syllables are part of the encoding processes for experienced readers. That is not to say that words which host unfamiliar contractions are necessarily easy. But the difficulty does not seem to come from any disruption of syllabic segmentation.

The most parsimonious explanation of the findings on syllables in the previous as well as the present chapter, is in terms of two factors: long-term lexical knowledge and associated orthographic–phonemic redundancies, and the use of speech-output processes with difficult material and/or insufficient experience. The use of syllables is based on speech output strategies. These seem to be invoked mainly or solely in conditions of difficulty.

The crossmodal findings have further implications. It was quite clear that both auditory and tactual priming had facilitated processing by recent braillists. But they had quite different effects. Prior exposure to the sound of the word produced a significant overall reduction in scanning time by recent braillists. Tactual primes, by contrast, had quite specific effects which eliminated the difference between consistent and inconsistent syllable contractions. A model that would explain these effects may be to assume that hearing a word lowers the 'threshold' for recognizing the meaning of the word, as in Morton's (1979) model, but at the same time primes the association between the habitual spelling and articulation pattern of the word. Recognition would, therefore, be faster overall than without such priming, but without reducing discrepancies between habitual and new orthographic associations. On the other hand, recent exposure to the new orthography together with a condition in which the word needs to be articulated would override that discrepancy.

The assumption and implications will be discussed further in Chapter 9. But the finding speaks to the issue of how modalities relate to each other and whether they are represented together or separately as multiple modality systems (e.g. Schacter, 1990). The findings suggest that neither of these hypotheses is an adequate description. The fact that only the tactual prime eliminated the difference between words with compatible and incompatible segments showed that it also involved some modality-specific effects and is therefore not well explained by the assumption that representations are purely abstract, nor is it compatible with the obvious importance of orthographic–phonological habits in decoding written words. These results are more consistent with the assumption that the modalities provide complimentary and convergent information which overlaps, but does not coincide completely (Millar, 1981 a, 1994). That also applies to the representations of that information. The issue is discussed further in the final chapter.

7 Individual differences and braille learning

The chapter examines three related aspects of individual differences that are relevant to reading by touch: the development of language skills in conditions of visual handicap, retardation in braille reading, and effects of developmental and experiential factors on the process of learning.

Language skills are clearly important in the absence of sight, and, if anything, also more so for learning braille than print. Phonological competence is considered first. Some popular misconceptions and confusions about lexical knowledge and semantic concepts in congenital blindness are examined next.

The subject of specific reading difficulties is too large to be surveyed in detail here, and I shall not attempt it. It embraces problems shown by literate adults who have sustained specific brain damage, developmental dyslexia associated with phonological difficulties and deficiencies in learning to read, and the problems of children whose braille skills are retarded relative to the norms expected for their age and general level of ability for a variety of reasons. The term 'dyslexia' is often used interchangeably with the phrase 'specific reading difficulty'. But retarded reading does not have quite the same connotation in braille as in print. Older children who have learned braille late and lag behind their contemporaries, for instance, fall into the category of retarded readers who require educational help. But it would be inappropriate to consider them dyslexic. For clarity, distinctions between acquired dyslexias, from brain damage in adulthood, degrees of traumatic 'alexia' (linguistic problems) caused by specific brain damage at birth, and genetically (familial) caused or triggered developmental dyslexia are discussed briefly first. The term 'specific reading difficulty' is here used as a neutral umbrella term for children whose reading level is below that expected for their age and intelligence in the absence of known brain damage.

Findings on phonological, semantic and tactual coding of uncontracted familiar braille words by two independent sets of retarded and competent braille readers are discussed next. Two further sets of data on totally congenitally blind young retarded braille readers are presented. Similarities and differences in scanning movements provide further data on the difficulties that are encountered in the early stages of braille.

Developmental and experiential factors are examined by comparing adults who learn braille as a second reading skill after reading print fluently and young children who learn braille as their first written language. Finally the verbal and spatial challenges that learning braille present for literate adults and those that confront the young learner are discussed with reference to development and learning.

1 LANGUAGE SKILLS IN CONGENITAL TOTAL BLINDNESS: SOUND AND SPEECH

As mentioned earlier, in most people (an estimated 95 per cent) the left cerebral hemisphere is more specialized for language than the right, and involves particularly two areas (Chapter 2). The region situated near the premotor area in front of the central fissure (Figure 2.1) is involved in speech output. The other main area, situated in the temporal lobe near primary auditory areas, is important in the perception and comprehension of speech. There is evidence that some lateralization is present from birth (Molfese and Molfese, 1979), but also for modifications due to perinatal and even postnatal events (Galabruda *et al.*, 1987). It has been suggested that lateralization does not seem to change greatly during childhood (Hiscock and Kinsbourne, 1978). But interhemispheric (corpus callosum) functions increase during childhood at least up to the age of ten years (Hatta and Moriya, 1988). There is no reason why this should differ for blind babies. Unless they have suffered brain damage, the potential of blind children for acquiring normal language skills should not differ from that of sighted children, and is not seriously in doubt.

The vibrations of speech surround the baby even in the womb, and there is now some evidence that infants recognize their mother's voice already very shortly after birth (DeCaspar and Fifer, 1980). Speech sounds are discriminated very early (e.g. Eimas, 1975). Moreover, human babies babble spontaneously from the first few weeks of life onwards. Single syllable and then two-syllable babbles are found in much the same way for babies everywhere in the first six months. After the age of six months the babbling of profoundly deaf babies starts to decline. Lack of feedback from hearing their own voices as well as inability to hear the speech of others are considered to be the main factors in that decline. From the age of about six months also the babbling of babies who are not deaf begins to sound progressively more like the language which they hear around them. They begin to imitate the intonation of the person who is speaking to them, including the rise and fall (pitch) of questions (Liberman, 1967; Tonkova-Yampl'skaya, 1969, quoted by De Villiers and De Villiers, 1978). The link between hearing a distinctive sound pattern and trying to produce it becomes noticeable during that time. At the age of nine months, one of my children produced what can only be described as the prosody of an exclamatory English sentence. It occurred in response to seeing the sudden glow of a fire which, by turning round to me and gesturing, the baby clearly wanted me to notice. That was before the child had ever uttered the first word. The babbled 'sentence' contained no intelligible word. But the sound pattern showed implicit knowledge of the sound of an English sentence. No baby surrounded by French speakers would have produced that intonation. Other instances of the kind have been reported in the literature. The distinctive sound patterns of 'motherese', the mother's speech to the infant (Newport, 1976; Fernald and Simon, 1984) and their association with distinctive events (e.g. fondling, taking something away) may give even preverbal infants some inkling of the nature and function of a sentence. Such hunches need confirmation from research that uses responses to 'motherese' rather than to single words. However, there are findings which suggest that the prosody and stress of speech are not the only clues to word recognition that eleven-month-old babies use (Myers *et al.*, 1996). More evidence is needed about the relation in acquisition between speech sounds and syntactic forms that seem to have no specific meaning. French children seem to learn the concordances of gender markers for inanimate objects initially through sounds of word endings (Karmiloff-Smith, 1979). Spontaneous play with the speech sounds of newly acquired words occurs almost as soon as children learn new words. At the age of eighteen months, one of my sons was heard to repeat the word 'lorry' in a variety of enthusiastic intonations while performing head-over-heels gyrations when he was supposed to be asleep. Such play is well documented in the literature (Weir, 1962).

By the time they enter school at the age of five years, children have quite reasonable language skills on average. Young children can detect some syntactic anomalies already by the age of two to three years, produce simple, syntactically correct sentences by the age of about four, have quite a sizeable vocabulary, and can detect and use word play, rhymes and syllables well before they enter school. At the same time, their sentence structure is simpler, their vocabulary is far more restricted, and their general verbal competence as well as their general knowledge is less than that of older children and adults. The phonemic segmentation and blending skills that are needed for learning to associate arbitrary physical letter patterns with the constituent sounds of spoken language, and the orthographic conventions that connect them, have yet to be learned.

There have been few studies of very young blind babies. Some reports suggest that the babbling of blind infants declines in the second half of the first year (e.g. Warren, 1977, 1984). This is similar to the decline in babbling of deaf babies. But, if so, the causes are likely to be different. Deaf babies do not receive auditory feedback from their babbling. That is clearly not the case for blind babies. Reduction in babbling by blind babies has been attributed to lack of environmental stimulation. Unless this is specifically attended to by parents and caretakers, totally blind babies are likely to get less stimulation from the environment, if only because they lack the changing visual inputs which tend to elicit babbling in the sighted. Blind babies tend to be more passive generally (Fraiberg, 1977), unless parents and caretakers provide adequate stimulation (Warren, 1977). It seems doubtful that a reduction in babbling, as such, necessarily leads to poorer language skills later, unless there is a persistent lack of stimulation and insufficient exposure to the speech of other people. In that case, normal language development may be delayed. Blind babies and children are more likely than the generality of babies to experience short periods of hospitalization. These often provide relatively low levels of general stimulation and specific exposure to language. However, these episodes are unlikely to have permanent effects if the child receives sufficient linguistic stimulation otherwise.

There are a number of reports which suggest that blind children have more difficulties in articulation, and require more speech therapy than the sighted (Ellstner, 1983; Hollins, 1989). But the reasons for this are unclear. General surveys of relatively small groups of visually handicapped children are likely to include a larger proportion of children who also have additional handicaps than the general population (e.g. Fielder *et al.*, 1993). The reports on speech problems often fail to distinguish between associated difficulties. Warren (1984) also noted that the criteria that are used for speech problems in different reports are far from uniform. Above all, it is not always clear how many of the blind children who are reported to show speech difficulties have additional handicaps, including slight degrees of peripheral deafness, which would account for these. There is no evidence that blind children without brain damage or additional handicaps differ significantly in articulatory confusions from sighted children of the same age and ability level.

There is one potential phonological discrimination difficulty which is directly relevant to blind conditions. Consonants which are easier to see from the movements of the speaker's lips than to hear from the voice (Miller and Nicely, 1955) may be less easily detected by blind than sighted children. The McGurk (McGurk, 1976) effect shows that perception of heard speech is affected by simultaneous visual inputs from looking at the speaker's mouth (McGurk, 1976; Mills, 1983). Dodd (1979) found that sighted babies, as young as ten to sixteen weeks, responded to the redundancy of simultaneously seeing as well as hearing the same sound being uttered. Some articulatory confusions (e.g. /m/ versus /n/, /θ/ versus /f/ in English) seem to be common among blind children (e.g. Wills, 1978). But it is not clear whether such confusions are generally greater among blind than sighted children. Mills (1983) compared a congenitally totally blind child with good hearing with two sighted children, all aged around two years. All three children made some articulatory errors in their spontaneous speech and in imitating syllables. But the two sighted children apparently made fewer errors on syllables that involved visible articulatory mouth movements, while the reverse seemed to be the case for the blind child. Detection was here tested by spontaneous or elicited (imitated) speech output rather than directly by recognition (e.g. 'same–different') tasks. But sighted children do not attain adult pronunciation of some speech sounds (including th) either until the early school years (De Villiers, and De Villiers, 1978). In any case, more speech sounds are discriminated better by hearing than by vision. Hearing is certainly the more important channel for detecting speech sounds.

It is also important to note that absence of sight can produce advantages for phonological awareness. Attention to sounds, and especially to speech sounds, is far more essential from an early age for blind children than for the sighted. Attention to sound, and especially to what people say, is usually encouraged by parents and teachers. Indeed, while we can discard the notion that blind children produce 'empty verbalisms' (see Section 2), the fact that blind children tend to engage in play with nonsense sounds has been observed (e.g. Ellstner, 1983). It certainly suggests that attention to sounds and phonological skills are by no means lacking in blind children.

Teaching based on letter sounds in conjunction with braille characters (phonics) usually occurs from the start in the acquisition of braille (Chapter 4). Such teaching is likely to produce a further advantage in attention to the sounds of phonemes, alone and in combination. There is some evidence that the need to attend to speech sounds spontaneously produces greater reliance on phonological strategies in short-term memory tasks. That was clear from the initial study on phonological and tactual coding (Millar, 1975 b). Coding braille letters phonologically was far superior in recall to tactual coding. Blind children used phonological coding strategies spontaneously as soon as they were good at naming. The finding that beginning braille readers were clearly attending more to sounds than to the meaning of homophones is further evidence that they tend to rely on phonological strategies (Chapter 4). There is also some evidence that blind braille readers have better short-term memory for digits than partially sighted print readers (Tobin, 1995). The data were based on a longitudinal study in which children were retested at two-yearly intervals between the ages of five and twelve years. The scores reported for blind children between the ages of five and six years seem to match a seven-year level on scales that were standardized on the sighted population. A ten-year level was found for blind braille-reading children at the age of nine and a half years.

Since phonological and articulatory skills are important in short-term memory and reading, the findings we have so far suggest that the phonological skills and preferences of young blind children should make it easier for them to learn the phonemic detection and segmentation skills that are needed for learning braille (Chapter 4). Conversely, early braille learning should also facilitate phonological skills (Mann, 1986).

2 SEMANTIC CONCEPTS AND CONCRETE EXPERIENCE IN BLIND CONDITIONS

Traditionally, the main assumption about the effects of blindness on language development has been that lack of vision produces a lack of knowledge of the meaning of words. Attention to sound and deficits in semantic knowledge and in knowledge of the world was supposed to lead to 'verbalisms' or the use of speech sounds that are empty of meaning. The use of meaningless verbal expressions in play, and games with sounds that are devoid of sense have certainly been reported for by blind children (e.g. Elstner, 1983). But such games can have advantages for phonological coding (see earlier). It does not follow from such play that the talk of blind children is full of empty speech which makes the right sounds but signifies nothing.

The idea, which used to be prevalent, that it is impossible to understand the meaning of words or of concepts in the absence of sight is, of course, obvious nonsense. Vision is by no means the only sensory modality that conveys concrete experience. It is not even the only direct source of knowledge about spatial cues. Spatial information is obtained through touch and movement, hearing and even variations in the intensity of smells, and typically depends on the balance of convergent information from all sources (Millar, 1981 a, 1988 a, 1994), although the absence of a sensory source tends to reduce information (e.g. Hatwell, 1985). But most of our knowledge is derived from indirect sources in any case. The knowledge of sighted adults depends more on indirect descriptions and inferences from the testimony of others than on direct experience of the referents of discourse. Our understanding of terms like 'the Bank of England' or 'taxation' is not limited by the fact that neither can be seen. The word 'ghost' is meaningful not only for people who think that they have seen one; nor is it necessary to believe in the existence of fairies to understand the meaning of the term.

The notion that the speech of congenitally totally blind children necessarily consists of vacuous expressions can be discarded. Fortunately, popular attitudes to what are often lumped together as 'disabilities' have changed. Blindness is no exception to the swing in popular beliefs about the capabilities of handicapped children. However, it has to be said that the swing in popular attitudes from assuming 'inability' to assuming 'ability' is, in practice, often merely a swing from assuming that nothing can be done to assuming that nothing needs to be done.

There is no doubt that language difficulties and restricted vocabularies are reported more often for blind children than for sighted children (e.g. Elstner, 1983; Hollins, 1989). Researchers who compared the vocabularies of blind and sighted children have found the lexical knowledge of blind children more restricted (e.g. Tillman, 1967). Elstner (1983) found that differences between the blind and sighted are largest for knowledge of words, and suggested that blind children achieve the same levels later than sighted children. The vocabulary study by Tobin (1972) comes to a similar conclusion. Clearly, adequate exposure to language and experience has to be provided. But the notion that visual, or even concrete experience at all is necessary to make speech meaningful, and that 'verbalisms' are inevitable in the absence of sight can be discarded (e.g. Landau, 1983; Landau and Gleitman, 1985; Millar, 1983; Tobin, 1992).

Blind conditions do reduce environmental stimulation and information, and these need to be restored through other channels. But it is not sufficient to assume that children who lack sight will necessarily obtain the relevant information if they are simply left to their own devices. They require intelligent help and assisted learning from other people who can link words and concepts explicitly with the relevant experience.

For the preverbal infant, vision provides an important channel of communication. The baby can see the mother's face as well as hear her voice. The mother can establish joint attention to the object or event in the surrounding world to which she is referring by name or in her talk to the baby. Since visual channels of communication – for instance, joint looking, pointing and communicative gestures – are not available to blind babies, considerable ingenuity by parents and caretakers is required to make the links from sounds to experience through the remaining modalities (Landau and Gleitman, 1985; Preissler, 1993; Urwin, 1983).

Absence of sight can certainly give rise to failure to understand the precise implications of a particular scene, unless people realize that explicit information and explanations are needed. One of my subjects habitually listened to football matches with her family and was an ardent football supporter. But she thought that the goalpost was in the middle of the field (Millar, 1994). The point is that such misunderstandings can happen if a subject lacks knowledge for reasons other than lack of vision (Tobin, 1992). In principle, normal blind children whose caretakers provide adequate links between language and haptic experience where these are lacking, should not have specific linguistic difficulties. Schools for the blind are usually aware of the importance not merely of the speech environment and verbal explanations, but also of providing sufficient experience for the child to flesh these out. Given the possible sources of difficulties in acquiring adequate lexical and semantic knowledge in blind conditions, it was actually quite surprising to me that the congenitally totally blind children without additional handicaps whom I knew during the course of some years of research, actually showed remarkably few linguistic impairments. That itself could be a welcome effect of the efficacy of training methods by parents and teachers of the blind who are aware of possible problems and provide extra help (Chapter 8).

Nevertheless, the question how concrete experience relates to semantic knowledge and representation is important. Two sets of distinctions are relevant. The first is about direct versus indirect sources of knowledge. The second is about types and functions of mental representation.

The clearest evidence that understanding does not need to be based on direct experience is the understanding of colour words by congenitally totally blind children. Such children have no sensory experience whatever of colour. But that does not necessarily lead to an 'empty concept'. It does not prevent correct inferences about colour. The evidence comes from an experiment in which I used word pairs consisting of adjective–noun combinations (Millar, 1983). The targets consisted of colour, tactual, auditory, and spatial adjectives. In half the instances the adjectives were paired with nouns for which they were appropriate. In the other half the pairing was inappropriate (barking cat, soft iron, tall dwarf, black snow). The word pairs were presented orally. Subjects had to judge whether the adjective–noun pair was appropriate or not by pressing one of two response bars that were linked to a timer. Timing was activated simultaneously with the start of the oral presentation. Subjects pressed one of the two response bars to indicate whether they judged the pair to be compatible or not, as soon as they had made their decision. Twelve congenitally totally blind children, aged between eight and thirteen years, were paired with sighted children of the same age, sex and socioeconomic status on auditory word and digit spans.

The error rates on both appropriate and inappropriate adjective–noun combinations were low (2 per cent by the sighted, 4 per cent for the blind). The errors by blind children were due to the youngest group who made errors on spatial and visual pairs. The older (above the age of ten) blind did not differ in errors or in response times from the sighted for either appropriate or inappropriate auditory, spatial, or tactual pairs. More important, the older blind were as accurate as the sighted on appropriate and inappropriate colour–noun pairs. But the blind took significantly longer over inappropriate colour–noun pairs than the sighted. In other words, these congenitally totally blind children were not only able to make correct judgments about correct colours for objects that they had never experienced, they also made perfectly correct judgments about inappropriate combinations. They could not have learned these by rote.

The basis on which the blind children made inferences about inappropriate colour terms can only be speculative in advance of further studies. The fact that they took longer over these suggests that they may have based their (correct) inferences on somewhat more complex strategies in the case of colour terms than for other combinations, possibly via analogy with other sensory properties. Blind children use the word 'see' for perceiving something by touch. Reconstructing events by inference and analogy with what the subject knows about the world is part of the process of comprehension, in any case (e.g. Garnham, 1985).

The second point about mental representation is that congenitally blind children can use nonverbal imagery as well as semantic representation. Nonverbal imagery can be derived from sources other than vision (Schlaegel, 1953), without necessarily being identical with semantic representation. Nor are nonverbal representations, for instance those based on movement configurations, necessarily more 'abstract' than visuospatial images (Millar, 1994). But the meaning of words is learned by blind children, as by the sighted, in association with events or contexts from which their meaning derives, and which is refined or changed by subsequent contexts. Traditionally, concrete terms have been considered to be particularly difficult for blind children, because they have less opportunity to link up concrete experience with the sound of words.

However, the fact that blind children made correct inferences not only about colours that they had never experienced, but made correct inferences also about colour–noun combinations that they could not have learned by rote, has implications for text reading and comprehension by blind children. Texts that are primarily designed for the sighted and carry a multitude of pictorial terms may initially require more complex reconstructions of events, and inference from other semantic knowledge, by congenitally totally blind children, but they clearly can and do convey meaning also to children without sight.

3 THE DYSLEXIAS AND RETARDATION IN BRAILLE READING

The term 'dyslexia' is often used for all types of reading difficulties in people who are of average or higher intelligence. However, reading problems that are produced by actual brain damage need to be distinguished from difficulties in learning to read that can be ascribed to genetic predisposition, particularly for phonological skills, and from illiteracy due to poor learning conditions which may include ill-health, lack of linguistic stimulation at home, frequent absence from school, as well as additional, secondary motivational factors.

I shall restrict the term 'acquired dyslexia' to the problems shown by previously literate adults, or older children who have suffered actual (known) brain damage through accident, strokes, or other cerebral insults which have left them with a variety of impairments of their previously acquired reading skills. The fact that reading, whether by touch or vision, crucially involves language means that the cerebral insults are likely to be mainly (not necessarily solely) in the left cerebral hemisphere. There is ample evidence that the left hemisphere, especially particular areas in that hemisphere (Figure 2.1), are the most important association areas for expressive and receptive language skills (e.g Gazzaniga, 1988; Geschwind, 1972; Geschwind and Levitzky, 1968; Kimura and Dunford, 1974) for most righthanded people, although some aspects of language are also processed by the right hemisphere (e.g. Zaidel, 1985). Given the fact that to read means to decode written language, it would be surprising if damage to the left cerebral hemisphere were not associated with acquired dyslexias.

Acquired dyslexias have been further subdivided according to the prevailing reading impairment (Ellis, 1984). In what has been called 'surface' dyslexia, people produce misreadings that can be classified as pronouncing words as if they were alphabetically transparent, either because people apply grapheme–phoneme rules inappropriately (Marshall and Newcombe, 1973; Patterson *et al.*, 1985), or because they use the wrong phonological analogy (Henderson, 1982). People with phonological dyslexia can read familiar words, but fail to read pseudowords or nonwords that have no meaning (Funnel, 1983; Funnel and Davison, 1989). In another syndrome, sometimes designated as 'deep dyslexia' (Coltheart *et al.*, 1980), the difficulties seem to be connected more with lexical, semantic and visual factors. The errors are very striking, because deep dyslexics tend to substitute words that are in the same or related semantic domains as the word to be read (e.g. 'bag' is read as 'basket'; or 'forest' as 'trees'). Misreading function words and some syntactic markers is also often involved. The two-route model (Coltheart, 1978) of word recognition originally offered a neat solution by supposing selective impairments of the direct route from visual analysis to the internal lexicon, and impairment of the indirect route in which lexical recognition is mediated by phonological recoding. However, there are also other specific difficulties with word forms and with letter sequences. The precise relationship between different forms of phonological, orthographic semantic and visual errors and types of brain insults is not clear as yet (Hanley *et al.*, 1992).

I did not include children with known brain damage or severe general learning difficulties in my studies of braille reading, in order not to add to the number of factors that need to be unravelled. As mentioned earlier, it is of course probable that, in any unselected group of handicapped children, a larger proportion of children will have additional and associated handicaps than is found in the general population, and that is the case also for visually handicapped children (e.g. Fielder *et al.*, 1993). Additional handicaps can include brain damage due to birth traumata. If severe, such damage can lead to general learning and cognitive difficulties. Studies on visual reading usually exclude children with general learning difficulties as well as known brain damage, because reading requires cognitive skill. If anything, braille reading requires even more cognitive skill than print (e.g. Nolan and Kederis, 1969). While minimal brain damage at birth to specialized cerebral language areas may go unrecognized, specific left hemisphere damage from birth which leads to severe delay or deficit in the acquisition of language and consequently also in learning to read is probably more appropriately covered by the term 'alexia' rather than dyslexia, although the linguistic deficits are not simply a matter of word knowledge.

Reading and phonological skill are highly correlated in print reading (Barron 1980, 1986; Brady *et al.*, 1983; Liberman *et al.*, 1977; Mann *et al.*, 1980; Shankweiler and Liberman, 1972; Shankweiler and Crain, 1986). Early phonemic segmentation skill is a good predictor of later reading, suggesting that there is a causal link between phonological skill and reading (Bradley and Bryant, 1983). On intelligence tests which give separate scores for verbal and nonverbal problems, retarded print readers tend to score more highly on nonverbal than on verbal problems, while this is reversed for good readers, even when both groups achieve the same overall average ability score.

A significant proportion of children who have severe specific difficulties in learning to read, without being cognitively impaired otherwise, have relatives with similar problems. This strongly suggests a genetic origin which, moreover, seems to be linked primarily to deficits in phonological coding (Pennington, 1989). It is not known as yet whether the genetic link is due to one or more defective genes, or whether people who fall into this category merely constitute the lower end of a combination of normally (binomial) distributed genetic substrates that constitute predispositions for phonological coding and segmentation skills. More evidence is needed also on whether the phonological segmentation problems occur only with language processes, or have to do with more peripheral auditory discrimination deficits (e.g. Tallal and Piercy, 1973). There is also evidence which suggests that some retarded print readers have vergence (fine oculomotor control) problems (Stein and Fowler, 1984, Stein *et al.*, 1987). In so far as this also turns out to be a familial problem it should probably also come under the umbrella of developmental dyslexia. It seems likely that very severe and intractable problems in learning to read are either due to traumatic alexia, or to genetic or familial developmental dyslexia.

There are no *a priori* reasons to suppose that the incidence of genetically determined developmental or phonological dyslexia is proportionately smaller or larger in blind than in sighted populations. Since there are relatively few totally congenitally blind children in this country, the number of blind children who are genetically predisposed to phonological dyslexia should, in principle, be proportionately small also. At the same time, braille is essentially a system for conveying language and speech through another medium. I therefore assume that any child with poor verbal and phonological endowment is likely to have major problems in learning to read braille. Phonological skills are, if anything, even more important for braille, because recoding into sounds is needed from the outset (Chapter 4).

The phrase 'developmental dyslexia' is frequently applied indiscriminately to all children whose reading is retarded relative to their age and intelligence. However, it seems more useful to reserve the term 'developmental dyslexia' for reading difficulties that are due to deficits which are likely to be grounded in genetic or familial predisposition, and to use the more neutral term 'specific reading retardation' as an umbrella term that can also cover retardation in reading for other reasons, and for children for whom we do not have any precise causal history.

It is to be expected that children who are predisposed to phonological deficits, for whatever reason, are as likely, or even more likely, to be retarded in acquiring braille as in learning print reading.

At the same time, phonemic segmentation, recoding and the blending of sounds which is necessary for learning a more or less alphabetic system like English seem to depend to quite a large extent also on early exposure and teaching (Bryant and Bradley, 1985). Training in phonetic segmentation which takes account of the sound contexts that influence the decoding of consonants in spelling (e.g. Treiman, 1993) and in reading is clearly needed also for braille. At the same time, as mentioned earlier, attention to sound is more important for blind children, and there is some evidence that they are actually better at short-term memory tasks that involve phonological coding than their sighted peers.

The more neutral term of specific reading retardation is more useful for braille in any case. Unselected groups of retarded braille readers may include subjects with acquired dyslexias, although cases of severe accidental cerebral injuries after reading is established are likely to be known to teachers and researchers. Unselected groups of retarded braille readers may also include children with some degrees of alexia due to undiagnosed minimal brain damage at birth, and some developmental dyslexics whose difficulties are due either to specific genetic factors or to low level (familial) phonological endowment. But retardation in braille can occur also because some children become blind after they are of school age. Many are still young enough to need special attention if the late start in braille is not to lead to retarded and slow reading later. The picture of reading retardation in braille is more complex than for print also for several other reasons. Even blind children who start braille early are more likely to have interruptions in their early schooling than their sighted peers, because they have to spend some time in hospital and in medical check-ups. Additional difficulties, including minor hearing problems, are also more common than in the general population, and so are minor ailments that may cause absences from school, and/or lower the general level of health and stamina of the child. Disrupted or difficult family backgrounds also seem to be more common among retarded than good readers. More positive reasons are that many visually handicapped children have some residual vision which makes it useful for them to learn systems that involve learning print characters in addition. This can have repercussions on the time that is available for their braille so that they appear (and are) retarded in braille.

The neutral term 'specific reading retardation' covers all of these contributing factors. The next section reviews findings which look at forms of coding by retarded and average braille readers.

4 CODING BY SHAPE AND SOUND BY RETARDED BRAILLE READERS

Reading by touch is a complex skill which makes linguistic but also perceptual demands that involve additional cognitive competence. The relative importance of component processes is thus not necessarily the same at all levels of skill or for all systems. It is clear from the evidence (Chapters 2 and 3) that, for braille, the tactual and spatial aspects of reading are by no means a triviality that can be disregarded. Language skills are, of course, as important, and probably more important, for braille than for print reading. But the fact that phonological deficits tend to produce reading difficulties does not necessarily entail that all reading retardation is due to poor phonological endowment.

The initial case which exemplified this was brought to my attention by the teacher of a congenitally totally blind little girl, then aged about nine years, who was severely retarded in braille. Her main problem turned out to be an exacerbated form of the difficulty of coding braille patterns sufficiently well to identify and remember them that was discussed in earlier chapters (Chapter 2 and 3). When Helen (not her real name) was first brought to my notice as a retarded reader (Millar, 1983), I was inclined to dismiss her problem on the grounds that her intellectual potential was rather too much below the average for it to be surprising that her reading was at a level below her chronological age, especially as braille requires more intellectual skill than learning print. However, her teacher insisted, on the eminently sensible grounds that although Helen had great difficulty in reading, she was able to write letters, words and even little stories on the Perkins braille writer. If she could do that, what was preventing her from reading braille at the same level as writing it?

Helen's teacher was absolutely right. On being tested, it was clear not only that Helen was retarded in reading, but that she hardly recognized any braille letter reliably at all, let alone read any words. She was adept at fooling the unwary by 'reading' a phrase or even a simple story that she had heard previously, by moving her fingers across the braille as if following the script. But the book could be as easily upside down. Indeed when I first tested her reading, Helen had no idea that there was a right and wrong way up for books. That was typical of her performance on most spatial tasks. By contrast, Helen's verbal memory was excellent. She could recognize voices easily, retell stories and would remember for years apparently unimportant details about people that she had only been told about. Helen's verbal skills were actually better than her general cognitive ability (IQ, Williams, 1956) indicated. On formal tests of producing and detecting rhymes and sounds, an important diagnostic indicator of phonological skill (e.g. Bryant and Bradley, 1985), she did not differ from the three more intelligent cohorts with whom she was compared and who were good braille readers. On every spatial test Helen was worse than her blind cohorts, and that applied particularly to recognizing braille patterns as shapes, and coding these sufficiently well to remember them. At the same time, as her teacher had pointed out, on tests of writing, Helen could and did produce letters correctly on the Perkins brailler (see Chapter 6), and was able to write little stories.

Helen's writing of words and stories on the Perkins brailler was not by any means brilliant or even very accurate. The point is that she was able to write braille characters and words at all without being able to recognize letters, let alone words on the page. What Helen in fact used were oral number codes. It will be remembered (Chapter 6) that the Perkins brailler has a horizontal keyboard on which the three keys on the left correspond to the three left-hand dots (1 2 3) of the braille cell, and the three keys on the right correspond to the three right-hand dots (4 5 6) of the braille cell. Helen remembered braille letters by their numbered dot values (e.g. 1 4 5 for D), and associated these with the combination of fingers needed to depress the relevant keys. There was no doubt about the strategy she used, because she called the relevant dot numbers for a letter out aloud – to every one else's discomfiture – while depressing the appropriate keys. The association between the dot numbers for the braille cell for a given letter and the combination of fingers that were needed to depress the correspondingly numbered left and right keys on the keyboard enabled her to write letters, regular words and some contractions.

The case study suggested that Helen's retardation in reading was initially largely due to her neglect of the spatial aspects of reading by touch. Helen was congenitally totally blind due to anopthalmia. There was no reason to suppose that her spatial problems could be attributed to parietal damage. She was evidently quite able to associate hand and finger positions with verbal tags. Her spatial problems were most obvious in tasks that demanded coding shapes and spatial locations by external and object-centred cues. She was perfectly happy to 'read' books upside down.

The fact that vision is not necessary for acquiring spatial concepts and skills should not obscure the fact that absence of vision diminishes the amount of reference information that is available, especially about external frames, and has to be sought actively. Unless adequate spatial experience is provided early, there is a tendency to rely on body-centred frames (Millar, 1994). Spatial coding, even in small scale space, is more difficult without vision because it requires active looking for reference cues. In Helen's case, there was an almost total absence of any desire to actively orient herself in space, or to use object-centred coding of shapes, even to the extent of making sure to turn reading books the right way up by feeling the location of the spine of the book relative to herself. Preference for tasks at which one succeeds, and avoidance of those that show up failure or weakness is common enough. Helen's problems were due to the combination of relying on verbal memory, at which she was good, and avoiding spatial tasks that required looking for and making inferences about external reference cues which was more difficult for her. Lack of motivation is more often a response to failure rather than its cause. But it cannot be ignored as a factor in the vicious circle that can perpetuate and progressively worsen the problem of retardation in whatever area this surfaces.

It took many months of devoted extra work by Helen's blind teacher, who took infinite pains with her, to get Helen finally to recognize letters reliably and to begin to read. The method that we had worked out was to make use of Helen's writing strategies by trying to transfer the association between her verbal knowledge of dot numbers for letters and finger combinations to recognizing these patterns in the raised dot formats of the braille script. Unfortunately, Helen's teacher had to leave soon after that, and progressively tight staffing levels made it impossible for Helen to continue to receive the very special help and attention that she had been getting. Her reading and writing undoubtedly received a set-back. Nevertheless, when I met Helen again as an adolescent, she was now able to read braille. Her reading speed was still half that of another little girl who was similar to Helen in age and intellectual level, but who had always read at a level that was commensurate with her age and ability. The surprise and gratification in Helen's case was that she could read at all, and that she understood what she read at a useful level.

Helen could have been an exceptional case. According to Frith (1985), phonological dyslexics continue to read print logographically after average readers have discarded that form of coding. Although there was little evidence (Chapters 2 and 4) that beginning braille readers code word shape initially, the possibility that retarded braille readers would code by shape rather than phonologically could not be ruled out. I therefore compared retarded with average readers on coding words by shape, by sound, by meaning and by dot numerosity in the study described earlier (Chapter 4). There are no very precise criteria for what is to count as retardation in reading. One criterion is simply to apply standardized tests with age norms and to consider reading skill simply as a function of age. However, there are problems with this criterion, because it does not take account of general cognitive skill which is particularly important for learning braille (Nolan and Kederis, 1969). Children whose intellectual potential is seriously below the average cannot be expected to do as well as their more gifted peers. Conversely, intellectually gifted children whose reading falls below average age levels are not working up to their potential. A generally useful standard, and one that I have mainly used, is that children whose score on standardized reading tests is more than twenty months below the expected norms for their mental age require additional help. For children of average ability, mental age scores coincide (by definition) with chronological age. Children who achieve mental test scores well above the norms for their chronological age also normally achieve above-average levels on braille reading tests. Conversely, children who score below average on general tests of cognitive potential and achieve comparable (low) scores on reading tests cannot be said to be specifically retarded in reading. In the study (Millar, 1984 b), children were considered retarded readers if their combined scores on normative braille word reading, and reading comprehension tests (Lorimer, 1962; 1977; Tooze, 1962) fell seriously below the scores predicted by their Mental Age by an average of twenty-one months. The mean IQ scores for average (104.43) and retarded (104.88) readers did not differ significantly, and the actual range of reading rates for the two groups (6–96 wpm and 3–45 wpm, respectively) overlapped.

The findings showed that retarded young braille readers do not always exhibit the same patterns of difficulties as retarded print readers. When given a choice, detecting the word that differed in shape was always the least preferred option, whether the other alternatives were to choose by sound, meaning or dot numerosity. Coding by shape was the least preferred strategy by retarded as well as by average readers ($p < 0.05$). By contrast, the item that differed on dot numerosity from the other was chosen quite often, particularly by the average readers. More important, the most frequent choice by retarded readers, and the one which produced a significant interaction between strategy choices and groups ($F = 3.08$, df = 3.39, $p < 0.05$) was based on the phonological features of words. This was particularly striking in view of the evidence that phonological coding is the major problem by retarded print readers.

Preference for a given form of coding does not necessarily indicate levels of efficiency. The children were therefore also trained and instructed to select words on the basis of sound, meaning, shape and dot number. When trained and instructed, the retarded as well as the normal readers achieved between 80 and 90 per cent accuracy in detecting all features, except shape. Shape detection was significantly less accurate ($p < 0.01$) than each of the others and accounted for the highly significant overall difference in coding ($F = 13.53$, df = 3/39, $p < 0.001$). Retarded readers were thus as accurate on phonological coding as the normal readers when instructed to use phonological coding. But their detection of shape was very poor.

The picture for this group of retarded congenitally totally blind braille readers was thus similar to that found for Helen. I have mentioned earlier the general consensus that retarded print readers are poor at phonological coding rather than in shape coding, and this is shown particularly in rhyme and phoneme detection tasks (Barron and Baron, 1977; Bryant and Bradley, 1985). Neither Helen (Millar, 1983), nor the retarded braille readers in the later (Millar, 1984 b) study differed significantly from average readers in detecting phonological differences and similarity. The difficult dimension was that of shape for all readers, including the retarded group.

The fact that attention to sound is a necessity for blind children, and is certainly encouraged by the adults around them, and that braille shapes are difficult to code, makes it intelligible that phonological coding may become an easier, and therefore, a preferred strategy.

5   RETARDATION IN BRAILLE AND INDIVIDUAL DIFFERENCES

As we saw earlier (Sections 1 and 3) effects of congenital total blindness on phonological skill can work in two contradictory directions. Phonological skills are needed more in blind conditions in general, and braille requires phonological recoding skills earlier than does print. At the same time, and for the same reasons, any difficulties in discriminating sounds are likely to have more serious consequences. But the braille code itself also presents more difficulties, both because it makes more demands on active spatial coding than does print (Chapters 2 and 3), and because contraction rules have to be learned as well as the rules and exceptions of English orthography (Chapter 6).

In an early (unpublished) study with eight retarded (four boys, four girls) and eight good readers (three boys, five girls), I used a considerable variety of baseline tests that provide data on individual differences. The general population of visually handicapped children from whom the two groups were drawn is, of course, quite small. An even smaller proportion of children are congenitally totally, or nearly totally blind. The two groups were nevertheless well matched on age and IQ, as well as on schooling. The retarded readers differed by over four years on average in Reading Age (p < 0.01). The children, aged between nine and thirteen years, had all learned braille from the start. Seven of the eight retarded readers were congenitally totally blind. One boy was blinded at the age of three and had minimal light perception. The competent readers were congenitally blind, but three had minimal residual light perception and one girl could distinguish hand-movements (not shapes). The children were all tested on intelligence tests. The mean IQ (Williams, 1956) scores for both groups were above average, and ranged from low average to superior for the retarded subjects (89–139) and also for the competent readers (89–130). Their reading ages were based on a test which uses only legally uncontracted short words (Tooze, 1962), and were also checked on another scale (Lorimer, 1977). Three forms of phonological tests were prepared, similar to those that have been found to predict reading skill. An oral rhyme (yes/no) recognition task was scored in terms of percentage correct. Subjects had to detect whether word pairs sounded alike. Another phonological task was to produce as many rhyming words as possible in one minute, respectively, to five orally presented words, and was scored in terms of the average number of rhymes each child produced for each. The third phonological test was to select the word that differed in sound either at the start or at the end of words from four others. The children were also tested on tactual (same/different) discrimination, letter

Table 7.1 Scores on intelligence test (IQ), chronological age (CA), mental age (MA), reading age (RA), mean rhyme production score (RHP), and percentage scores on rhyme recognition (RHR), sound detection (SDT), letter recognition (LR), recognition of contracted words (CTR), tactual discrimination (TD) and spelling by competent (Group I) and retarded (Group II) readers

Group	Normative scores				Tests						
	IQ	MA	CA	RA	RHR %	SDT %	RHP	TD %	LR %	CTR %	SP %
I	106	11-9	11-1	11-7	99	73	4.2	97	94	75	78
II	107	11-4	10-7	7-5	96	71	3.5	94	82	57	82

recognition, recognition of contractions (Lorimer, 1962), and on a brief oral spelling test, all scored in terms of percentages of correct performance. The results for the two groups are shown in Table 7.1.

The retarded children scored consistently below the competent readers on all except the spelling test. But none of the differences was statistically significant. The profile of scores is instructive. The retarded readers were somewhat lower on all three phonological tests, but also on tactual discrimination tests that did not involve reading, as well as on letter recognition, and on recognizing contracted forms. But despite the quite large difference in reading age, none of the test scores differed significantly between good and retarded readers. On spelling regular words the retarded children did not lag behind the average readers at all, as was the case with Helen (see also Chapter 6 on writing). The profile of scores thus suggests a generally lower level of functioning on tactual as well as phonological aspects of reading by the retarded children, rather than a single difficulty.

Another set of data comes from younger retarded and competent readers from different 'vintages', whom I saw at different times soon after they had begun to read braille, either because they were reading well enough to take part in my braille studies on text reading, or because they seemed to have difficulties in the early stages of reading. I was also able to follow some of these children over a period of some years. The data originally focused mainly, although not solely, on congenitally blind children with little or no light perception, rather than on children with sufficient sight to be able to use large print in addition. Several other blind children who were reading at levels seriously below what would be expected for their age and intelligence had sufficient residual sight to see large print in favourable conditions. Some were taught print alongside braille, because there was some uncertainty which system they would need to adopt later. It was not always obvious whether these children had actually spent enough time on braille to be compared with children for whom braille was the only written language that they were learning at that time. Issues in learning more than one system of reading will be discussed in the next chapter. Learning two systems is not necessarily detrimental in the long run. But it may become so when there are other difficulties already.

The second set of data thus concerned two different sets of younger children. Scores for readers who were retarded in braille relative to their mental ages when first tested were compared with the data for young competent readers who were similar in age (six to nine years) range when first tested. The visual impairment of all but one child in each group dated from birth, and all had been taught braille from the start. Two of the seven retarded children had minimal light perception. Among the eight competent readers, four had residual light perception, and in two cases this was useful for spatial orientation and large scale shapes. Although both groups were above average in intelligence, they could not be matched exactly on IQ scores. The competent readers scored more highly (mean IQ = 122, from 100 to 150) than the retarded readers (mean IQ = 109, from 98 to 128).

The reading tests showed that the good readers were already reading at levels more commensurate with their higher mental age, above their chronological age, even at the age of six years (mean RA, 8-4; from 7-3 to 10-10 RA). The retarded readers already showed signs of reading retardation by the age of six years, and were not achieving appropriate reading levels. An example was an intelligent little girl (IQ 128) who was not yet able to read or even to recognize letters reliably at the age of six years, and remained retarded until early adolescence. By contrast, a boy of six and a half (IQ 109) who read above the level of a seven-year-old also remained a competent reader until early adolescence. The data indicate that retardation in braille can be picked up quite early on, especially if reading levels are assessed relative to children's potential ability, rather than relative to their chronological age alone.

Retarded readers ranged from not being able to score (assuming a notional RA of 5-0) to a reading age of 7 (mean RA= 6-5). The results on phonological and tactual discrimination tests were similar to the previous set of data. The retarded children scored less on phonological and tactual tests (67 per cent and 78 per cent) than competent readers (75 per cent and 90 per cent). But, as before, the range of scores overlapped. Some children among the competent readers showed poor phonological discrimination; and some of the retarded readers achieved good scores on rhymes and on sound discrimination.

Consideration of some of the individual data strengthened the impression that retarded braille reading is typically associated with a variety of factors that may, or may not, be secondary. The first example is of a congenitally totally blind boy with a family history of psychiatric illness that could (possibly) have links with dyslexia. He was unable to recognize tactual letters at the age of six years, despite IQ scores in the average range, and good vocabulary. He scored poorly on phonological and on tactual discrimination tests, but was able to write letters (characters) to dictation on the Perkins braille machine, although he could not recognize them by touch. He was a highly anxious child, and was absent from school with minor ailments very frequently indeed over a period of some years. His reading was still somewhat retarded in early adolescence, but much less in reading comprehension than in speed tests. Another retarded reader of low average intelligence wore a hearing aid and received speech therapy. Deafness is, of course, known to be associated with poor speech and reading (Conrad, 1972b, 1979). The child showed both phonological and tactual confusions at the age of six years, but made reasonable progress over a period of two years, although her reading age was still slightly lower than her mental age at that point. Another retarded, very intelligent, reader also had some, much slighter, hearing loss, not severe enough to affect speech and which was treated (by grommets) in late childhood. At the age of six the child showed both phonological and tactual confusion errors, and continued to have difficulties in using the two hands in conjunction with each other in early adolescence. This student was still not reading at an appropriate speed at that point, but was writing original stories for pleasure. Another retarded reader of average intelligence who had equally poor sound discrimination at the age of six caught up in reading within a year of being tested, although still showing phonological confusion errors. Finally, two very bright children in the competent reading group had mild hearing loss and showed considerable phonological confusions at the age of six, but excellent tactual discrimination skills. One of these children gained two years in reading age over a twelve month period. The other child made similar progress and both read at levels well above their chronological age.

The most severe retardation in braille was shown in a case that did not fit the criteria of retarded reading despite normal intelligence. Bob (not his real name) scored poorly on general ability, especially, though not solely, on verbal tests (IQ = 75). The case is nevertheless instructive. At the age of six, Bob was very poor on phonological tests, tests of vocabulary, and on tests of small-scale spatial skills, despite relatively good large-scale geographical spatial orientation. He also had attentional deficits. Not surprisingly, Bob greatly disliked having to read at all. His braille remained at the level of a six-year-old even in early adolescence. At that point his mental age, even on purely verbal tests, was well above his reading level. His auditory discrimination, though not perfect (83 per cent) had improved, but his scanning movements were still quite chaotic. Very poor general and verbal ability, combined with attentional deficit, and an undoubtedly secondary, but potent, dislike of reading at all, probably accounts for the failure to make any progress. The point is that the factors in retardation, as well as in progress, seem to combine in a multiplicative fashion in negative and positive directions, respectively.

By definition, 'normal' progress in reading on standardized tests for children is in terms of calendar months and chronological age. Some longitudinal data on annual progress in braille on such tests were made available to me by courtesy of the principals and teachers of the schools in which I was conducting the research. In addition, I had data from control tasks for some of the children over a period of years. The longitudinal data suggest, not surprisingly, that average and good readers progress at fairly steady yearly rates from the age of about six to early adolescence. But that was not invariant. One competent reader, for instance, developed a stammer in adolescence. Curiously enough, this seemed to be associated not with speed, but with the reading comprehension score that had not improved from the previous year. Progress by children whose reading lagged behind their age and intelligence from the start was much more variable as well as proportionally slower than for good readers.

The picture that emerges from the data suggests that specific retardation in braille reading seems to be associated with a combination of factors, and particularly with the conjunction of phonological and haptic/spatial problems.

6   COMPREHENSION AND PLACE-KEEPING: THE DUAL TASK FOR YOUNG AND OLDER BEGINNERS AND RETARDED READERS

The findings discussed in earlier chapters showed that the pick-up of perceptual information and scanning movements changed with proficiency, the type of reading task, and with the lexical and semantic difficulty of the reading materials (Chapters 3 and 5). There was no evidence that scanning movements dictate the pace or adequacy of braille reading. On the contrary, scanning movements were clearly dictated by the reading task and the proficiency of the reader. The movements and regressions indicated the types of processing that readers were using in decoding the scripts (Chapter 5).

At the same time, tactual scanning movements in braille have to serve dual verbal and spatial functions. The findings described earlier (Chapter 3) showed that fluent readers use their hands efficiently for the spatial functions of place-keeping, gauging the length of words and finding the next line, at the same time as performing the main task of decoding of the verbal information. Indeed in blind conditions the intake of information in reading depends on deploying the hands adequately. The problem hardly arises in visual reading, although a subsection of developmental dyslexic print readers have been found to have vergence (eye-coordination) problems (Stein and Fowler, 1984, Stein *et al.*, 1987). The issue in braille is not one of hand-movement coordination as such. Such coordination is established long before normal blind children start to learn braille. However, there are reports of adult dyslexics with deficits in tactile-motor coordination and inefficient transfer between the cerebral hemispheres (Moore *et al.*, 1995). These subjects apparently had no defects in rhyme fluency tasks, which are a frequent diagnostic sign of impaired phonological skills in dyslexics. I know of no reports so far of impaired interhemispheric processing in cases of reading retardation in braille.

The problems of deploying the hands flexibly for the spatial and verbal aspects of reading are more analogous to dual task conditions. The issue is how to combine attention to decoding the meaning of the script, which is the main object of reading, with the spatial aspects of reading which involve keeping track of the line, keeping the place at the end of a line while finding the next line, and keeping track of the locations in the layout of the script in order to be able to regress to previous text when that becomes helpful or essential, and the like. Fluent readers evidently solved the problem of the dual task of spatial monitoring and at the same time understanding the verbal message, by allocating the hands alternately to the two domains (Chapter 3). The data suggested that improvements in reading were characterized by the progressive differentiation of the dual role of verbal decoding and spatial tracking.

Observation of the discrimination and scanning movements of retarded readers raised the further question whether poor scanning is entirely the result of the level of reading that has been attained, or differs from that of competent young readers who have similar reading levels. The rather chaotic scanning movements of some of the retarded readers could, of course, simply have resulted from their poor reading levels. If so, younger children who have the same reading levels, although their reading is adequate for their age, should show recursive and chaotic movements similar to those of the retarded readers.

A study was therefore undertaken to analyse the scanning movements of six retarded readers who had been tested earlier but were now older (mean CA = 10-2) and were operating at a comparable level of reading proficiency (mean RA = 8-1) to the competent young readers described earlier (Section 4). The design took the form of various baseline and story reading tests, and a second series of tests about a year later. Video-recording was used as usual so that oral reading as well as hand-movement data were available for analysis. Two types of script were prepared to provide materials for letter search and for continuous reading. For the letter search task 'scripts' consisted of lines of full braille cells in which a letter was interspersed at random intervals. The task was to scan the rows of cells silently, but to name the letter aloud as it was encountered. The reading texts were very simple stories, constructed to include mainly high frequency words and only the most common contractions. They consisted of simple sentences with constant repetitions of the main sentence structures and words throughout the story, in the manner of texts used for young beginners.

Five of the retarded readers, as well as Bob (see earlier), were seen a number of times for short sessions at (for practical reasons) very irregular intervals of some weeks during that twelve-month period. The reading materials used in the sessions were mainly similar to the baseline scripts. The main aim of these sessions was to assess their 'best hand' and the types of mistakes and regressions they produced with materials that had the same layout as braille but only required letter search and no reading. The children also received feedback on mistakes in oral reading, and on their scanning movements and in place-keeping when moving to subsequent lines of text. The sessions were neither sufficiently regular nor numerous to be considered remedial training. Nevertheless, during that period one boy who had been less seriously retarded than the others caught up in reading with his peers, despite still noticeable difficulties in the discrimination of sounds. Another child, who had not learned contractions previously, still confused these shapes and improved only at about the same rate as previously. Bob made no progress whatever in the sessions. Three of the other children progressed at faster (nearly twice) the rate than hitherto. The hand-movements, scanning and place-keeping data are of interest.

The method used to compare scanning movements by retarded readers (not including Bob) with those of the competent younger children who had similar reading scores was the same as in the study on intelligent recent and experienced adolescent braillists (Chapter 3), except that the reading materials were much simpler and more repetitive. The hand-movements of retarded readers are best described as chaotic. They tended to rub unsystematically over the same letters over and over again, and produce so many regressions that frame-by-frame scoring becomes extremely slow and laborious. Regressions over particular words also occur when phonological strategies have gone awry, particularly in trying to 'sound out' a word and failing to blend the constituent sounds correctly. That occurs also in visual reading where a retarded reader may produce the regular sounds for the first three letters of the word 'university' and on that basis read it as 'anniversary'. But retarded braille readers also usually fail to develop strategies for keeping the place. They neither move back systematically in contact with a line of text, nor use one hand for place-keeping or finding, but take off both hands and lose their place. They may omit words and whole lines of text without noticing that they have done so.

The scanning picture for retarded readers suggests that the verbal and spatial tasks interfere with each other. This is in contrast to fluent reading where place-keeping and finding sustain and are sustained by verbal processing (Chapters 3 and 5). That seems to be the case also in using two rather than one hand for reading. Unlike the regressions of competent readers who tend to look for prior context that can disambiguate a difficult word, the regressions by these children tend to consist in rubbing repetitively over particular characters or words. One problem seemed to be that using the forefingers to converge on a pattern from opposite directions could give conflicting information. The lateral shear patterns on the two fingers are likely to interfere with each other in coding the location of dots, thus producing reversal errors. Trying to avoid these was, in fact, the reason given to me by one bright little retarded reader for only using one hand to read. The possibility is among the issues in haptic perception that need to be investigated further.

The young beginners whose reading was commensurate with their age and ability also showed regressions, circular and up/down movements and fewer lateral scan movements than older fluent readers. Nevertheless, the competent young readers produced an average 78 per cent of lateral scanning movements, and only 22 per cent of up/down or regression movements. The older retarded readers whose reading was at the same level as the young competent readers scored an average of 46 per cent on lateral scanning movements. In other words, 54 per cent of all their reading movements were spent in regressive circular and up/down movements over words or characters. A similar difference was shown in place-keeping, especially in transitions to the next line of text. A five-point scale was used to assess place-keeping, from excellent (+2) to very poor (–2). The young readers, although not perfect, mainly obtained positive scores (mean, +0.9). The retarded older children whose reading was at the same level or even slightly higher than that of the beginners mainly obtained negative scores (mean, –0.5).

The scanning movements of the retarded readers thus differed not merely from those of more proficient readers. More important, they also differed from those of children who read at the same 'absolute' level of proficiency, but were not retarded in reading relative to their age and intelligence. The main difference seemed be qualitative. The younger competent readers typically used their verbal and semantic skills to repair omissions due to faulty hand-movements, as well as using systematic place-keeping strategies to keep their semantic processes on line. A typical example was that of an intelligent six-year-old who failed to track back to the beginning of the next line when her left forefinger landed on the second word before starting to read that line. But as soon as she had read two further words aloud, she realized from the gist that she must have left a word out and regressed to the start. In other words, she used her verbal skills to repair a spatial error. Equally, her reading strategy consisted of very careful tracking (not reading) of the line by the right hand in advance of reading by the left, thus using a spatial back-up for the verbal task. Retarded readers, by contrast, almost never used semantic strategies to repair faulty place-keeping, nor systematic spatial strategies to guide the verbal aspect of reading. The worst instances showed processing that seemed to be locked into the local difficulty. If a character was difficult to perceive, the gist construed so far was forgotten instead of being used to help to decode it. The problem seemed to be due to failing to construe the gist rather than to grapheme–phoneme recoding. Some subjects even failed to notice when faulty place-keeping landed them in the wrong part of the text. But the precise relation between their strategies in recoding words and construing gist also needs further study.

The difference in scanning between retarded and good readers at the same level of proficiency is instructive. The faulty place-keeping of the retarded was not occasioned by their reading level; nor was their poor reading level due to faulty hand-movements. The difference seemed to be that the good readers recruited spatial skills to aid the reading process, as well as recruiting verbal skills to aid the spatial aspects of reading. Poor readers, by contrast, not only fail to recruit information from one domain to help the other; the spatial and verbal aspects of the task seem to interfere with each other. This may be because retarded braille readers tend to have more than one difficulty. Two weak systems may produce interference rather than facilitation when used in conjunction.

It may also be the case that retarded braille readers have difficulties in coordinating verbal and spatial aspects of texts, either because both their phonological and shape coding skills are poor, or because they have difficulties in integrating the two domains, or both. But that remains speculative at present. The evidence that verbal and spatial aspects of braille may interfere with each other in acquisition by retarded children is largely circumstantial so far. The hypothesis requires a good deal more work. But the possibility needs to be borne in mind in practice.

7 AGE, EXPERIENCE AND LEARNING BRAILLE

It is a common assumption that adults who learn braille later in life must be at a disadvantage compared to young learners. On average, older adults have higher tactual (two-point) acuity thresholds (Stevens, 1992; Stevens *et al.*, 1996). Older adults are also assumed to have greater difficulties generally in learning new skills, to be slower in the uptake of information, quicker to forget, and to be slower in all aspects of movement and performance. Many newly blind adults are discouraged from learning braille for reasons of this kind. In my view such discouragement is very largely unjustified.

The older former print readers had all learned to read braille later in life. They had the advantage over young beginners in the important linguistic and knowledge aspects of reading. Their phonological skills could not be in doubt, whether for phonemic recoding, morphological segmentation, or homophone ambiguities. Compared with young beginners the adults had a much larger vocabulary for both frequent and infrequent words, well-established orthographic habits to bring to bear on decoding new scripts, and a much wider knowledge of the world for understanding the scenarios of stories and texts. These advantages were not all in one direction. Highly skilled orthographic–phonological habits can work against learning a different combination, as in words in which contracted forms violate prior associations (Chapter 6). But even that interference was evidently relatively easy to remove, at least in the short term.

The division of cognitive skills into linguistic competence and general knowledge, which do not change with advancing age, and skills in processing new information fast, which deteriorate from middle to old age, has some justification (Birren *et al.*, 1980; Salthouse, 1991; Waugh and Barr, 1980). But the dichotomy is too simplistic. Even the ubiquitous assumption that short-term memory is impaired in old age rests more on anecdotal testimony than on experimental findings, and may have more to do with slowing of perceptuo-motor than decision or rehearsal processes (e.g. Fozard, 1980). Both the so-called 'crystallized' and 'fluid' aspects of intelligence (e.g. Horn and Cattell, 1967) are involved in most complex tasks. It requires ability to acquire the knowledge that a task requires, and also skill and/or speed in retrieving that knowledge, and in knowing how and when to apply it, and movement speed in the execution of responses. Individual differences in cognitive efficiency, but also task complexity, and differences in the degree and extent of prior practice, all affect the relation between performance speed and age (Rabbitt, 1993; Rabbitt and Goward, 1994). Information processing speeds in choice reaction time tasks, as in pressing the correct key in response to one of four letters, correlate significantly, though not highly, with timed tests of cognitive ability. But high and low scores on timed IQ (e.g. AH4) tests relate differently to processing speeds at the beginning and end of extended practice, and in speed–error trade-off (Rabbitt, 1993; Rabbitt and Goward, 1994). The relation between processing speed, intelligence and age thus depends on more than one factor. The fact that the relevant factors include the amount of practice that has been expended on a task is extremely important for the practical purpose of learning braille.

The findings are relevant to the interpretation of performance by older recent and experienced braillists reported earlier (Chapters 3–6) in two respects. First, they are consistent with the fact that average wpm scores of highly experienced older braillists were slower than for adolescent braillists. But experienced older braillists who had learned braille from the start, and were using it consistently, were as fast as most competent young readers. The findings are also consistent with the fact that adult readers who learnt braille late coped better with low frequency words which some competent young braille readers could not construe at all (Chapters 5 and 6).

More important for understanding the reading speeds of adult braillists is the considerable effect of extended practice on processing speeds. A study of 200 blind people, aged between ten and eighty-nine years, who learned braille after having started with print, found important effects of the time allotted to braille instruction and the frequency of instruction

(Pester, 1993). As mentioned earlier, newly blind adults, who learn braille in order to retain their literacy, receive very much less instruction and practice than young students who have learned braille recently but use it necessarily in their daily studies. The findings suggest that with sufficiently extended practice in braille, intelligent newly blind adults do not necessarily have to lag behind younger students.

There is evidence that tactual acuity of the fingertip, as measured by two-point thresholds (see Chapter 2), deteriorates with age and the performance becomes slower (Birren *et al.*, 1980). But this does not allow direct inferences about learning braille either. There is no doubt about the typical findings. A report on eighty people, aged from eighteen to ninety-one years, showed that the two-point threshold increases from an average of 1.95 mm between the ages of eighteen to thirty-three years, to 2.68 mm for people aged between forty-one to sixty-three years, while people aged between sixty-six and ninety-one years show a further rise in threshold to 5.03 mm (Stevens, 1992). However, the perception of braille patterns does not depend on distinguishing two passively felt adjacent raised dots, but on scanning them actively. The problem is rather how to organize the dots spatially (Chapter 2). The intervals between words in a conventional braille text are nearly twice the threshold at which even the oldest group could tell two points apart. Nevertheless, even for younger beginners the intervals between words in normal format scripts only become obvious with practice. Diabetes can reduce the acuity of peripheral receptors, including tactual acuity (e.g. Bernbaum *et al.*, 1989; Harley *et al.*, 1985). But even diabetics with impaired tactual acuity can learn to discriminate braille well enough to be useful in daily life (e.g. Harley *et al.*, 1985). There is therefore no reason, in principle, why such learning could not be extended further (Chapter 8). However, by no means all diabetics are worse at discriminating standard or enlarged braille patterns than non-diabetic cohorts, in any case (e.g. Harley *et al.*, 1985).

Finally, a striking difference in scanning pattern was found between people who had learned braille after reading print and braillists who had never used print. Older former print readers used what can only be described as systematic 'zigzag' or up/down strokes over each letter in first-pass scanning of lines of text from left to right. These strokes differed from the circular repetitive regressions over difficult characters that are common also for slow readers who have learned braille from the start. Circular regressions over letters tend to be repetitive and unsystematic. By contrast, the zigzag and up/down scanning motions are executed on every character. They are regular, almost rhythmic in time and extent, and follow each letter without regression.

These smooth, regular zigzag or up/down strokes are not shown at the very start of learning. They seemed to be the result of extended practice by the most competent of former print readers. Indeed, two extremely experienced and competent older braillists who had read braille for over forty years after reading print in their youth showed just such patterns of scanning. The pattern was also shown by a young student with six years of braille experience after reading print until early adolescence. This type of scan could not be explained by the level of reading speed as such. The scanning patterns of a highly intelligent and literate lady who had learned braille in middle age and was a very competent though relatively slow reader was compared with that of a highly intelligent seven-year-old who had learned braille from the start and had attained the same wpm speed. The young reader showed the typical lateral scan in reading easy texts for meaning, even in regressions, although these sometimes elicited circular motions. The former print reader scanned the text throughout by using smooth, rhythmic zigzag motions over every successive letter. When regressions did occur, the movements showed systematic explorations of the letter shapes.

The regular zigzag and up/down motions in scanning from left to right by former print readers gave the impression of gaining information about the shape of successive individual characters, though the exploring movements had been attenuated, with extended practice, to systematic small sweeps. It seemed convincing evidence, not only of true letter-by-letter reading, but of letter-by-letter reading that was indeed based on shape.

An obvious explanation is that people whose visual experience had accustomed them to think of letter patterns in terms of global shape were using that coding strategy also for braille. While vision is by no means necessary for perceiving shape (Millar, 1988 a, 1994), even braille patterns are much more easily perceived as global forms by vision than by touch (e.g. Millar 1977 a). There is no reason to assume that shape strategies are used inevitably by people with visual experience. Reading styles by recently blind young students who were learning braille at school also included some lateral scanning, though much less than by students who had learned braille from the start (Chapter 3). But we know little about the long-term effects of different forms of instruction as yet.

There are inevitable methodological problems in assessing effects of aging on any form of new learning by population averages, because individuals differ considerably on a wide range of contributing factors. The interesting point about the systematic, rhythmic zigzag and up/down scanning by recent braillists was that it was evidently due to the kind of streamlining which occurs with practice (e.g. Rabbitt and Goward, 1994; Shiffrin and Schneider, 1977). The scanning patterns of the more practised recent braillists looked like more streamlined versions of full-scale scanning of individual shapes. It seemed to be an attenuation with practice of full-scale shape coding rather than a stage in changing to lateral scanning, because the method was also used by very experienced older braillists who had read print in their youth. Changes in scanning with practice require further investigation.

8 DEVELOPMENT AND LEARNING

At the other end of the age scale, it is perfectly obvious that younger children are less familiar with most events, have less knowledge in any subject, and are less practised at almost every skill than older children or adults. Maturational processes are also by no means complete at the time children enter school. We are very far as yet from being able to disentangle the complex interactions between the many genetic and external factors that operate in development from the start. But it is pertinent to ask how development with age affects the child's ability to 'take in' and cope with new information.

Questions about the invariance, or otherwise, of cognitive efficiency with increased age are not as problematic with regard to children, simply because standardized test scores control for age. On average, the overall scores for performance on the variety of standardized problem-solving tasks that we use for one age-group predict later scores on similar tasks by older children very well. We assume, therefore, that potential cognitive efficiency remains relatively stable over age. Scores on tests of cognitive efficiency correlate relatively highly with braille learning (Nolan and Kederis, 1969). It is the strength of such tests for practical purposes that the scores are based on a wide variety of problems in each case. But such catch-all tests do not tell us why older children can solve more difficult problems.

The fact that the short-term memory span increases in a linear fashion with age and mental age in children is one of the best-established findings in developmental psychology (Chi, 1976, 1977). Moreover, the memory span is an item in most intelligence tests. The amount of information people can 'hold in mind' at any one time is limited (Miller, 1956). The question whether increase with age in the size of the memory span is due to an increase in absolute 'capacity', or to the way in which the items are coded or 'chunked', or to both, is not completely settled as yet. The memory span of adults involves more than one factor (Watkins, 1977). It has been suggested that the increase in span with age is due largely to an increase in the speed of information processing (e.g. Howard and Polich, 1985). But the increase in span with age has also been explained as resulting from an increase in speed in identifying items (Case *et al.*, 1982), and by the rate of covert articulation which limits the speed of mental rehearsal of the items (Baddeley, 1986; Baddeley, 1990). However, as we saw earlier (Chapter 4), the memory span for braille letters varies with modes of coding. The span was larger with fast phonological recoding which relates to fast naming (Conrad, 1971), than for tactually coded items (Millar, 1975 b). However, that is not the whole story. We (Henry and Millar, 1991, 1993) equated the speed of identifying items, as well as the rate of articulation for items in span tests between younger and older children, but still found significant differences in the size of spans at different ages. The factor that related significantly to age was the familiarity of the items in span tests. The difference in span between older and young children depended significantly on the familiarity of words (Henry and Millar, 1991). Other studies (e.g. Hulme *et al.*, 1991) have reported similar effects. The point is that this implicates longer-term knowledge of words in the increase in short-term memory span with age.

Speed of identification, speed of subvocal rehearsal, as well as the familiarity of the items related to the size of spans, although age differences in span related significantly only to the familiarity of items. Increased span with age could be due to the speed of retrieval from long-term stores. More items are lost and subvocal rehearsal is also slower. The point is that information processing speed is not independent of familiarity and the effects of practice (see earlier). Theoretical issues in the combination of variables that determine processing speed will be discussed later (Chapter 9). But the variables clearly affect the question how much new information we can expect young children to process at any one time.

Several consequences follow. The very fact that familiarity with words influences age differences in immediate verbal memory means that young children will be proportionately less able to deal with new information and require more extended practice and more redundancy in the inputs they receive from all sources (Millar, 1994). I am using 'redundancy' here as a portmanteau term to include familiarity and long-term knowledge, but also knowledge of procedures. 'Knowing how' as well as 'knowing that' increases with age.

In learning braille, however, the new information applies not only to the new, alphabetically defined sounds that have to be learned, and to phonological segmentation skills, but also to the progressive organization of scanning skills to recognize and code the tactual information (Chapter 3). The finding that tactual short-term memory spans are very small (Millar, 1975 b) referred to early stages in processing the patterns. Mental coding of movements has been demonstrated (Millar, and Ittyerah, 1991; Smyth and Scholey, 1996). It seems likely that memory spans for tactual scanning movement may also increase in size or capacity as relatively unorganized tactual input codes become progressively organized in terms of movement output (Millar, 1985 b, 1990 b, 1994). Auditory inputs seem to 'fade' relatively rapidly unless they are linked to output mechanisms (Baddeley, 1990). The progressive link between input and output systems explains some of the developmental findings on verbal rehearsal in very young children (Henry and Millar, 1993).

The explanation implies that, early in learning, the immediate spans for the verbal and the haptic information are likely to be small. We know relatively little as yet about how that would affect what amounts to processing two streams of information at the same time. Performing two tasks at once is easiest when at least one of them has become 'automatic'. The fact that braille makes attentional demands on the spatial as well as on verbal processes raises the question how far it is possible to use the inputs redundantly to reinforce each other. The question is taken up in the next chapter.

9 SUMMARY AND IMPLICATIONS

The main conclusion that emerges from the brief survey of language development is that total lack of sight has two effects on phonological processing that seem to work in opposite directions. On the one hand, some auditory discriminations are more difficult without the redundant input from looking at mouth movements, though these are relatively few and hearing is more important. At the same time there is greater attention to sounds, including speech sounds, and a preference for playing with sounds and coding in terms of sound in blind conditions. There seems to be a reciprocal relation between phonological skills and reading, at least in fluent braille. Phonological skills are needed in learning to read, and reading and spelling itself also fosters phonological skills. Learning to read braille involves phonological recoding from the start, and could have larger effects on reading for that reason. Certainly, the received wisdom suggests that blind children are more skilled in using the sounds of language. There was some evidence also that there are beneficial effects on the short-term verbal memory of blind children. Phonological coding seems to be better in blind conditions. That is important, but needs a good deal of further study.

The evidence on lexical and semantic processing showed that the traditional notion that blindness leads to 'empty verbalisms' can be discarded. Totally congenitally blind children can make sensible inferences about the meaning even of concrete experiences that they do not have. Nevertheless, congenitally totally blind children require help in acquiring the lexical and semantic information that is reduced in the absence of sight.

Reading retardation in braille was distinguished from acquired and developmental dyslexia, and was used as a neutral overall term. It was assumed that poor phonological skills and poor verbal skills generally would retard reading in any symbol system, including braille. Results for retarded and competent braille readers, and detailed assessments of individual readers with average or higher ability levels were presented. Preference for phonological coding and relative neglect of systematic spatial organization of touch-movement inputs which characterized some retarded braillists were explained by the combination of greater attention to sound in the absence of sight generally, and in braille learning specifically, and the haptic and spatial demands of the braille system. The evidence so far suggests that, with the exception of children with severe verbal deficits, phonological difficulties were not the only problem for retarded braillists, but occurred typically in combination with other problems, including difficulty in coding haptic inputs spatially. The findings make good sense in terms of the informational demands of blind conditions and the braille system. But they raise further questions about the effects of having to combine inputs from different domains with diminished information.

The final two sections examined effects of increasing age in adulthood and in development. The assumption that higher tactual acuity thresholds and limitations in processing speed in older adults prevent them from being able to learn braille is shown to be misconceived. The notion fails to take effects of practice, motivation and previous linguistic knowledge into account. At the other end of the age scale, the change with age in the amount of information that can be processed is shown to depend on a combination of factors including the familiarity of the information. This raises both practical and theoretical questions about the interactions between the spatial and verbal demands of braille which will be discussed further in the next two chapters.

8 Practical implications and additional systems

The aim of this chapter is to clarify what implications particular findings have for practical problems in learning to read. There is no royal road to reading. The description of processing which is discussed in the next chapter is a tentative model that needs testing. But the findings we have so far on how the processes in reading by touch link together also raise questions about practical procedures. The application of findings to individual situations, and how they are best implemented, are matters that can only be gauged by the readers themselves and the teachers that help them to learn.

It will have been evident throughout that though the empirical studies necessarily focused on particular processes in reading, these processes do not occur in isolation. On the contrary, they depend to a very large extent on each other. The ability to use tactual information to represent language requires the combination of phonological and semantic skills with convergent inputs from touch, movement and reference cues. Tactual coding can be useful, but memory spans are larger for items that were sufficiently familiar to be recoded quickly into phonological form. Beginning readers depended on phonemic recoding and memory for the sound of words. But they were also influenced by the familiarity of words. Well-practised lateral scanning and spatial organization as well as language and orthographic skills were involved in reading continuous texts for meaning. But errors in scanning or place-keeping were also repaired by knowing the gist of the sentence or passage in which the error occurred. Experience and familiarity of orthographic–phonological habits were also important in processing contracted forms.

In important respects, therefore, the practical implications turn on the issue how the multiple verbal and spatial demands of braille reading can be integrated during acquisition without producing mental 'overload'. Young children particularly require more redundancy of information and more assistance than adults or older children, if only because they know less about any aspect of complex tasks, and are less experienced and less practised in all the subsidiary skills that these require. Additional information is needed also to restore the informational redundancy that is lost in the absence of any sensory source, as well as the more specific loss of visuospatial cues which need to be substituted in blind conditions. The number of subsidiary skills that need to be enlisted include body posture, finger position, and lateral scanning movements, as well as phonological segmentation and blending, word and orthographic knowledge, and skill in semantic integration. As I see it, the performance of dual or multiple aspects of complex tasks raises crucial issues which deserve far more study than they have received in developmental psychology so far.

The dual task issue is especially acute for braille because the patterns themselves lack redundancy. The results of studies on tactual pattern perception suggested that coding the shape of small raised dot patterns depends on constructive processes. Although processing becomes smooth and automatic with practice and experience, progressively constructive perceptual processes are initially an integral part of learning the sounds and meanings that the patterns represent.

The implication that the development of tactual perception is an integral part of learning braille will not come as a surprise to practitioners of braille who use a variety of methods to help the perceptual process with young children. Methods vary from numbering the dots of the braille cell and getting children to remember the number sequences, to teaching beginners to explore enlarged patterns systematically, or using sequences of meaningful characters to encourage lateral scanning. The point is that children have to learn to recognize the braille patterns in order to associate names with them. What the present findings suggest is not that there is one particular method which achieves that better than any other, but that different methods tap into different linguistic and spatial demands of reading by touch.

A second aim of the present chapter is to highlight the further questions about the interrelation between different aspects of processing that are raised by the proposed model. At least two forms of input have to be assumed. An important question is about the conditions which facilitate rather than interfere with processing more than one input. The findings suggested that complementary information from different sources can actually be an advantage in the acquisition of braille reading. But the means by which inputs from different sources can be used to provide informational redundancy need to be tested in practice.

Implications of findings for the initial learning of braille patterns are considered first in the context of types of teaching methods, and then in relation to the demands of different reading tasks. The issue of facilitating versus interfering effects of information from different sources is then discussed in conjunction first with visual information when that is available, and then with additional information from hearing.

Similar issues arise in learning to use the optacon as an additional aid and as a substitute reading system. Processes in reading raised line maps, line diagrams and graphs as additional informational aids are briefly considered also in relation to the use of computers and electronic devices in blind conditions.

1 BEGINNING READING BY TOUCH

Evidence that braille patterns are not initially perceived as global outline shapes was discussed in great detail, because it goes directly against the traditional view. However, if the traditional view were correct, children would not need to learn how to recognize braille shapes in order to learn their sounds. Few practitioners doubt that such learning is needed. A variety of pre-reading and instructional devices are available to help this process (Gill *et al.*, 1996). Practical discussions centre on how braille pattern recognition is best learned so that patterns can be associated with the correct sounds; not whether such learning is required.

The fact that braille patterns are difficult to code as global shapes does not, of course, mean that they cannot be coded as shapes; nor does it imply that there is only one method of teaching braille reading. On the contrary, the findings show that braille patterns are processed in a variety of different ways by different people and in different conditions. Perhaps even more important are the implications of the finding that fluent readers pick up different forms of tactual information in different reading tasks.

I shall consider the findings first in relation to four main types of method in braille teaching, although they by no means exhaust all the methods that are actually being developed and used. The hypothesis that fluent understanding of words and sentences 'occurs ... through the apprehension of word forms' (Burklen, 1932) is now rarely held by braille practitioners. There is actually very good evidence against the notion that relying on the shape of braille words facilitates the recognition of the sound or sense of words; nor is it a preferred strategy (Chapter 4). On the contrary, although the more experienced braille readers were able to detect word forms quite accurately when instructed to do so, such detection was inferior to the detection of words by sound and meaning.

Moreover, letter shapes are not good discriminators in braille. All methods for young children necessarily include teaching the sounds of letters as well as the sounds of words and syllables for the relevant contractions. There is no other means of conveying these. However, although all the methods I shall mention teach the sounds that braille patterns represent, they differ in their implication for pattern recognition. Each of the methods that I am considering has its advocates and detractors, and for good reasons. The point is that each is most effective for a slightly different purpose, and these are not necessarily mutually exclusive.

Consider the method of getting a child to recognize a braille character by keeping his finger still which I mentioned briefly in the second chapter before looking at the perception of single braille characters in detail. The method had puzzled me initially, because of the known general superiority of active touch. The reason why and how a passive method might work became clear to me only in the course of finding that coding the patterns as spatial shapes requires reference cues, or advance information, for systematic exploration of new inputs to take place. In keeping the finger stationary on a pattern, the top and sides of the fingertip can, in principle, be regarded as a spatial frame in relation to which the dot positions in the pattern can be determined. Such a frame would be particularly useful when all reference has been lost by undue 'scrubbing' with the finger. At the same time, stationary passive contact of the finger with a pattern would have to be light, and above all, brief. Sensation is lost altogether with prolonged, unvarying touch and undue pressure. Moreover, using the fingertip momentarily as a spatial frame is not necessarily an obvious strategy for children, before they know something about the composition of braille patterns. Active movement is necessarily involved. But the point of the exercise is to facilitate fast recoding of the pattern into the phoneme or into the word-sound that the character symbolizes. Prior information about the composition of the pattern in association with the sound it represents is likely to be useful also.

Most other methods which focus on recognizing single characters are based on active scanning. As we saw earlier, spontaneous systematic scanning of outlines is difficult because the patterns lack salient features which could act as spatial anchors for systematic exploration. Active scanning is not necessarily helpful, because several different letters have the same outlines. The problem for establishing systematic exploration is therefore how to anchor scanning movements, given the small size, format and lack of salient features of the patterns. Moreover, systematic scanning involves cognitive skills. It is easier for older than for younger children even in visual tasks (e.g. Vurpillot, 1968). In braille, the problems of systematic scanning are usually solved more quickly by cognitively able children. Scanning by the less able child tends to result in the repetitive, unsystematic rubbing over the same letter, and losing lines of text, which is very familiar to braille teachers.

One way to circumvent the initial tactual difficulties in finding how to anchor movements for systematic exploration is to use enlarged or 'jumbo' braille patterns. A method which combines jumbo braille with auditory information (Section 4) has been very successful with newly blind adults (Tobin, 1988; Tobin *et al.*, 1986). Learning jumbo-sized letters before relearning them in conventional format was found to be better than starting with the conventional format for adult beginners (Tobin, 1987). The point of using enlarged forms is that it is much more possible to plan and execute systematic movements in vertical, horizontal and circular directions. Moreover, the use of enlarged forms takes care of initial acuity problems which are likely to be more important for older people, although there is evidence that these can largely be overcome with sufficient practice (see Chapter 7). Once systematic exploration of the characters has been established, the format is reduced to the conventional dimensions (Pester *et al.*, 1994). From personal reports it seems that newly blind adults can use their knowledge of shapes and can envisage the directional lines that produce the set of possible shapes. It may be that prior knowledge of braille patterns as shapes facilitates the generalization of scanning movements to the small, conventional format. That needs to be tested.

There has been some controversy over the use of an enlarged braille format for young children (e.g. Tobin, 1971) who learn braille as their first reading system. The debate exemplifies the complex relations that exist between specific empirical findings and their use in practice. There is evidence that getting children to scan larger arrays systematically produces better shape recognition by young children (Berla and Butterfield, 1977; Berla *et al.*, 1976; Newman *et al.*, 1984). The main reason for not continuing to use enlarged patterns for teaching young children was that the eventual change-over to the conventional small format would require a whole process of re-learning the sounds of characters, and it would take as long or longer to relearn the characters in the conventional format as learning the letters in the conventional format from the start.

The findings show that both arguments are based on quite real concerns. Two factors need to be considered quite explicitly in using enlarged formats with young congenitally totally blind children. One is the active use of spatial reference cues. The other is the fact that the spaces between dots in braille patterns carry meaning. The fact is that external reference cues for spatial coding are not salient in blind conditions, and have to be sought or produced. But the notion of actively looking for spatial reference cues, or actually providing reference anchors when exploring, is not a spontaneous strategy for any young child, and that includes young congenitally totally blind children, unless they have had a good deal of prior experience and help. There are, for instance, well-known instances of arithmetic errors by blind children which are due solely to the fact that the children have failed to use reference cues actively in order to check the spatial position of numbers in units, tens and hundreds in the sums that are set out in vertical format on the page. In conventional format the need for children to provide reference cues themselves for place-keeping becomes clear mainly in starting to read continuous texts (Chapter 3). It may not be as obvious that children also need to know how to use reference frames actively to anchor systematic directional scanning when using enlarged braille formats. Unless they have sufficient residual vision for external reference cues to be obvious, the attention of young children needs to be drawn specifically and repeatedly to looking for and using reference anchors (e.g. the finger-tip, the side of the page, using one hand as a marker or reference point for the other). In principle, using enlarged forms can make it easier to teach scanning in the major (vertical and horizontal) directions, in much the same way that mobility training uses body movements in orthogonal directions for path finding (Millar, 1994).

In practice, the extent to which such explicit training is needed is likely to vary widely between individual children.

The second factor that has to be taken into account explicitly in changing formats is the fact that the size of spaces between dots in braille characters is an important clue to the phonemic identity of the characters. To give but one instance, a large space between two vertically oriented dots indicates the letter 'k'. A space that is half that size between the upper two rows indicates a different letter ('b'). There is good evidence that changing braille formats does involve re-learning (Chapter 2). That may well be more important for beginning young braillists than for adults who are former print readers and habitually attend to outline shape more. The findings showed that, for young blind beginners, even generalizing pattern information from the conventional smaller to larger formats of the same letters was not automatic, and this was the case although the change was from the more difficult small format to the potentially easier larger format which should produce less discrimination problems. The change from large to small formats may require learning a restricted set of letters initially, or possibly a more gradual reduction in physical size. But the practicality of doing either can only be decided in the field.

The fact that changes in the size or format of braille affect pattern recognition does not necessarily imply that changes in pattern size cannot or should not be used with children. But such findings do suggest that the reasons why changes in format can produce difficulties need to be carefully taken into account when using that method. For instance, generalizing a pattern to a replica that differs only in size is easiest when the original pattern has been coded as a global shape. For readers who use global shape as a coding strategy, therefore, changing to the conventional small format should not present a major difficulty. But the fact that the size of spaces between dots in a character is meaningful in braille needs to be considered carefully in effecting a change-over between formats, particularly with young children. It is necessary to know how the child codes the patterns. To the extent that a child uses dot–gap density coding for recognition, the transition to a smaller format is likely to involve a good deal of relearning. A crucial factor in the change-over between braille formats is thus the extent to which the reader uses global shape as a cue, or is able to gauge spaces between the dots in the patterns proportionally. Younger and/or less cognitively able children may require a more extended period of specific teaching to establish the change-over from enlarged formats. But discrimination even of conventional braille patterns improves with practice (e.g. Berla, 1982). The feasibility of either using enlarged forms and changing, or starting with conventional formats and using extended practice or means of importing redundancy into the system cannot be established *a priori* for all braille learners.

What I have called the 'numbering' method is probably used most commonly as an additional aid in teaching young beginners to recognize single braille shapes (Chapter 6). The dots of the braille cell are labelled by numbers, and the child learns the pattern of numbers that constitutes a particular character, in association with the sound and meaning of the linguistic symbol (letter or contraction) that the sequence represents. It works quite well initially, particularly for otherwise poor braille learners (Chapter 7). As was pointed out earlier, the numbering system in association with the sound of the letter can form a useful connecting link between reading the upright patterns and writing them by means of the horizontal keyboard of the Perkins brailler (Chapter 6). The dot-numbering method has the advantage that it harnesses an additional verbal system to mediate the identification of dot locations with key positions on the brailler. The sound pattern that is represented by the sequence of dot numbers can then be associated with the letter sound that the character is to represent, as well as with the tactual dot pattern in recognition, and the finger-movement combination in writing. For blind children who tend to be good at remembering sounds, that dual association of letter sounds and numbers with the tactual pattern can be an advantage (Chapter 7).

The numbering method also has its critics. The main charge is that it fails to concentrate attention specifically on the global outline shape of braille patterns. That this may indeed be so is shown by the very fact that the numbering system can mediate between reading and writing braille without having to use complicated forms of mental spatial rotation (Chapter 6). The fact that fluent young braille readers consider that the numbering method is fit only for 'babies', suggests that this initial aid tends to drop out later in any case. Recognizing individual braille patterns is, of course, crucial. But concentrating on global shapes is probably not the most useful strategy initially, because global outlines are shared by several letters, in any case, and can be therefore be confusing for that reason (Chapter 2).

Nevertheless, the numbering system alone does not deal adequately with confusions between characters that have dot positions in common, and are typically 'mirror image' patterns or rotations of each other (Chapter 2). The fact that they have positions in common also means that they have numbers in common (e.g. 1 2 4; 1 2 5; 1 4 5; 2 4 5). If numbering is used, therefore, the young child has to be alerted to the importance of the sequence in saying the numbers. Traditionally, characters occupying the upper two rows of the matrix, including the examples given above (f d h j) were taught first. The justification for doing so is that lower dots in cells are more easily missed. There is good evidence for that assumption (e.g. Nolan and Kederis, 1969), and for the fact that, individually, the ten first letters of the alphabet (a to j), which consist of one to four dots in the upper two rows are easier than subsequent letters which use all three rows of the braille cell and consist of two to five dots (Newman *et al.*, 1984). Nevertheless, patterns that are identical when rotated are highly confusable with each other, precisely because they differ minimally from each other because they have equal numbers of dots, equal dot density, similar number tags, and differ by less than 2 mm in the location of the absent dot.

The problem of confusability applies to some extent to all braille characters, because they lack the redundancy of print characters, and consequently the salient features that redundant dimensions produce. Means of importing redundancy without changing the system are very limited. Findings from a study which used dot density and outline shape redundantly (Millar, 1986) are relevant to three practical concerns. Redundant cues did improve the discrimination of different adjacent characters significantly. The most effective 'imported' redundant (systematically correlated) cues were large differences in dot density between adjacent patterns. Even preschool children below the age of five years were able to use these, and they were clearly easier than either size or shape outlines. There is no way of altering the conventional braille format to produce concomitant variations of this kind consistently. But it is possible to introduce young children initially to characters which show maximal contrasts in dot density or dot numerosity. An instance is the word 'we' in which a four-dot letter precedes a letter that only contains two upper dots. It is not, of course, feasible to produce whole teaching schemes in that vein. However, schemes that embody the principle of using successive characters that differ not merely in the position of dots but also in terms of dot numerosity are likely to be easier for young beginners.

It may also be worth going back to that principle with readers who are prone to confusing characters, provided the basis of the confusion is not purely phonological. It depends on creating texts in which the words consist of letters which differ maximally in dot-density contrast, and also in the sounds of the letters. Confusion errors are less likely to arise when confusable braille patterns are introduced separately, as far apart in time, and in as widely different phonological contexts as possible. Once a child has become prone to such errors, remediation depends on ensuring that the child's particular weakness is recognized. If scanning is unsystematic, the reader is likely to need help with establishing systematic reference to the external spatial layout and to his body position, as well as paying attention to the direction of the movements. Systematic, unidirectional scanning from left to right may be useful to identify the sequential sounds of tactually confusable patterns. Contextual cues were found to be important (Chapter 5). That could help to establish distinctive lateral shear patterns for different letter sounds in regular words. But such methods require further study. It may be necessary to return to enlarged forms to ensure systematic scanning, especially for tasks that demand the recognition of single patterns.

Smooth versus rough textures that were produced in dot patterns by using round versus pointed raised dots were found to be more difficult to discriminate by young children than dot density differences. However, correlating these textures redundantly with different outline (square versus rectangular) shapes of dot patterns facilitated discrimination, especially for older blind children. Whether introducing texture differences of this kind could make braille pattern recognition easier for younger or for retarded readers is more doubtful. Textures produced by differences in dot size may not benefit subjects who press too hard to feel that texture difference easily. A pilot study in which I used such texture differences to emphasize the difference between letters did not succeed. Another problem in adding a texture dimension is that it may interfere with discrimination if the reader perceives it as irrelevant to the task or the strategy being used. The added dimension could then act as an orthogonal confusing dimension rather than as a redundant cue that makes the relevant dimension more salient. But such texture differences may be more important in reading tactual maps and diagrams where they occupy a larger expanse (see later).

There are disadvantages in starting with isolated letters alone. It presents the beginner initially with a meaningless, rather monotonous task that bears little obvious relation to reading. In braille it means having to learn to associate a number of meaningless phonemes that are difficult to detect in either the words they hear or in their own speech with equally difficult, meaningless tactual patterns. Two difficult discriminations have to be combined. The very fact that both are difficult means that both need assisted learning. There are various means of overcoming the monotony as well as the difficulty by combining different approaches. Learning how to build up and to decode short regular words into their constituents is one way, provided the constituent letters differ as much as possible both tactually and phonologically.

An important practical question is raised by the findings which showed that fluent readers use different forms of scanning, and extract different perceptual features in reading for meaning than in identifying individual letters (Chapter 3). The difference in perceptual pick-up in different reading tasks is important. The majority of research on braille seems to have been conducted with individual braille patterns, on the tacit assumption that letters need to be coded as global outline shapes. But the tactual basis of identifying a letter is by no means necessarily the global outline shape of that pattern (Chapter 2). The problem is whether we should start by emphasizing the shape of individual letters, and can assume that lateral scanning will develop spontaneously; or whether we should start with lateral scanning, and can assume that individual characters are picked up by lateral scans. Alternatively, it may be possible to lay the foundations for both forms of scanning from the beginning. The point is that, in a very real sense, the main effect of the lack of redundancy and salient features of braille characters is on reading sequential characters in words. Lateral scans that pick up information about the succession of dot–gap patterns seem to be used by fluent readers in connected texts (Chapter 3). Whether this develops in any case, or can be encouraged in the early stages by using left–right scans in conjunction with sound blending requires further study.

Beginners clearly have to learn the sounds of letters, and they must also learn to blend the sounds into word sounds. The findings here suggest that by starting with familiar regular words that consist of two to three easily differentiated letters, the child can associate discriminable dot-density patterns that he can remember with two to three successive new sounds, and can retrieve the familiar word at the earliest opportunity to mediate and consolidate that association. Most experienced braille teachers also ensure that children write the same words that they read. That provides further redundancy for the segmentation and blending skills to be learned in conjunction with each other so that they facilitate each other. Such conjunctions would have to be tested in the field. The proposed explanation here predicts that these conjunctions might take longer to acquire initially, but that they would facilitate memory, and therefore reading, more in the long run than learning each skill in isolation.

The connection between reading and writing is particularly important in braille (Chapter 6). It may also be worthwhile to separate the different types of reading tasks that demand the recognition of single sounds from single patterns, from tasks that demand lateral scanning of continuous regular words. In principle, that should encourage lateral scanning in connection with phonemic decoding and blending, compared with tasks that require attention to single patterns. It may help the process of tactual differentiation to make use of the fact that the optimal pick-up of perceptual information in reading for meaning occurs in lateral scanning, and that the optimal cues to be picked up are not the same as in tasks that demand the recognition of individual shapes.

Logographic processing is actually an integral part of English braille, because single character contractions represent some of the most familiar nouns but also useful function words (articles, conjunctions, prepositions) and syntactic markers (e.g. word endings). The fact that nearly all braille letters represent not only the letters of the alphabet, but are also contractions for familiar whole words can be turned to good account. It makes it possible, in principle, to introduce the children early to the notion of contractions and the decomposition of sounds that is necessary for regular words, as well as giving them a quite explicit understanding of what to expect in the braille system.

The reasons for beginning with an association of letters and sounds differ from the reasons for introducing letters also as contractions for whole word sounds. The former is the most usual method in braille. Beginners learn uncontracted (Grade 1) braille letters first, before the gradual introduction of (Grade 2) braille contractions and the rules for their use. Teaching letter sounds is necessary both for decoding words that are heard and in associating the sounds with characters (Chapters 4 and 6). Once phonemes are attached to single characters, beginners can start to assemble the sounds of letter sequences, and these can be 'blended' into word sounds. The same principle can then be used to make out regular new words. But the fact that almost all braille letters are also contractions for useful words when they stand alone can also be used to advantage early in learning.

There are different arguments for and against introducing letters and the other single characters as contracted words from the start. The main objection is that introducing characters as contracted words, as well as phonemes for letters, may confuse the child. That depends, of course, on how it is done. On the interpretation here there are a number of advantages to doing so. The words which single letters or characters represent are usually familiar to the child by sound and meaning, unlike letter-sounds which children often find difficult. Associating the familiar word-sound of the contracted character with the sound of the first letter ('g' for 'GO'), is likely to make the letter easier to remember. As a contracted word, the character is flanked by spaces as words are, and is therefore easier to discriminate. From the evidence it is also clear that readers have far fewer problems with very familiar contractions, presumably because they were learned earlier.

Nevertheless, the method requires care. Teaching a letter as the first phoneme of the contracted word can be used to draw the attention of the young learner to the fact that the first sound of a word can be isolated in speech. But the contracted words that letters represent are not all regular words. Using contracted words can be a help for segmenting sounds, but it is clearly not a substitute for teaching the combination of letters that build up regular words. The main point of teaching phonemes early is precisely the same as for teaching contractions early. It is because phonemes are difficult that their detection, segmentation and blending needs to be familiarized as early as possible if the child is to learn to perform these operations reliably and smoothly later.

An impressive reading scheme that I saw in action was devised by a group of infant teachers in schools for the blind. It combined the sentence method with teaching letter sounds and the gradual, though early, introduction of characters which on their own represented contractions for familiar words. It introduced letters, but also some contracted words early, and made use of the fact that regular words contained letters that differed maximally from each other in dot density. Additional interest was introduced by using relevant materials (e.g. a bell when that word appeared). I gained the impression that the infants for whom the scheme was devised not only learned braille rather fast, but also used lateral scanning earlier.

By introducing some letters that are also contractions for familiar words early, the young child can start by reading simple, short but meaningful sentences at the same time, or soon after learning a sequence of phonemes that produce short regular (uncontracted) words. Such methods clearly need to combine word sound with phoneme detection in regular words, building word sounds up from letter-by-letter recoding and blending these into words. The child has to learn both.

However, the success of any scheme that combines different skills and sources of information to guide the mastery of a complex task depends crucially on fine-tuning by those operating the scheme. The fine-tuning in reading schemes centres on ensuring that the different sources of information are combined to reinforce each other redundantly, and do not produce interference. For able children, or children who have already received assisted learning, the order in which letter sounds and the words they represent are learnt is probably irrelevant. For younger children and retarded readers the question whether learning letters and words simultaneously is more beneficial than using a strictly ordered sequence needs to be tested out individually. On the hypothesis that I am proposing, I would expect that a child who finds phonemic distinctions difficult would learn them more easily if the new sound were linked to a familiar word sound ('d' for DO) that is also meaningful. In other words, I would expect less able children to cope better with associating an unknown sound with a difficult tactual discrimination, by connecting it with a well-known word which the letter represents also, provided the pace of learning is slowed. Similarly, procedures which combine building words up from individual sounds with procedures which segment words into their constituent sounds should produce better results than using either procedure alone or in strict sequence. Such methods would probably take longer for learning to take place in the first instance, but should facilitate reading once it has been established. Again, such predictions need to be checked out in practice. Their feasibility will depend on the particular weaknesses that are shown by individual children.

The question whether subsidiary skills should be taught separately in sequence or in conjunction with one another is also relevant to the problem of lateral scanning. Active hand-movements are actually often confusing rather than helpful at first. This is partly because the roving finger loses track of dot positions with new patterns. Training and experience are needed to use active movements properly. Lateral hand- and arm-movements in relation to upright body posture are particularly important in prose reading for keeping to the line and other spatial aspects of text reading. Fluent readers, by contrast, seem to use the complementary touch, kinaesthetic and movement information automatically. The typical differences in scanning patterns found between former print readers and young beginners who learned braille from the start (Chapter 7) suggest that scanning patterns are driven by the strategies individuals use, rather than the other way round. The typical zigzag scanning shown by the more fluent of the former print readers was most easily explained by their use of a letter-shape strategy which had been streamlined with experience into a regular scan that exposed the whole of each character by diagonal strokes that also led smoothly to the next characters. Repairs were also typically executed by up/down or circular scans that encompassed the character. In contrast, competent young readers tended to use lateral scanning not only in reading across lines of texts, but also increasingly in repairs during regressions by using right–left/left–right scans for individual letters, suggesting that they were picking up lateral (dot–gap density) shear patterns rather than outline shapes.

We do not know as yet whether, or to what extent, early methods of training, or differences in coding of braille patterns as visuospatial shapes rather than in terms of habitual tactual shear patterns, contribute to such differences in scanning. Practice in scanning lines of dot patterns before they have acquired meaning is, for instance, often used as a part of pre-reading exercises for pre-schoolers. Some of these exercises look rather boring to the naive observer, though lateral scanning could also be practised by devising finding games (e.g. an individual letter in a line of cells).

There is no hard evidence as yet on how scanning practice relates to later reading styles or to speed, or whether hand-movements can be taught in isolation. Rayner and Pollatsek (1989) report that attempts to train the eye-movements of retarded print readers in scanning visual print failed to improve their reading. That does not necessarily mean that the same would be true of tactual scanning. Eye-movements seem to have guiding rather than processing functions in visual reading, while tactual scanning is crucial to the pick-up of information in reading by touch. Nevertheless, merely practising lateral movements may be less useful than combining instruction and practice in systematic lateral movements and place-keeping with the verbal functions of reading.

The fact that beginning young readers use their knowledge of the gist that they have decoded in order to repair omissions due to faulty scanning is a case in point. Such meaning-driven repair of scanning movements is not necessarily an inferior means of learning to scan the full extent of lines, nor one that should be discouraged. The fact that failure in place-keeping and lateral scanning produces nonsense gives the child important feedback that the scanning requires repair. But in general, assistance is needed for the child to learn to produce scanning movements that are orthogonal to the vertical edge of the text, and to maintain a constant distance from the horizontal base and top edges of the paper. These movements do need to be established early. Hand-movements from left to right by beginning young blind readers tend to veer downwards at a constant distance from the body rather than in relation to external layout of the text, and so lose the line of text.

The fact that fluent readers divide scanning functions systematically but flexibly between the two hands has implications not so much for types or styles of hand-movements, as for the use of the two hands for two different functions at the same time. For slower readers particularly, the implication concerns the role of the two hands in the pick-up and processing of verbal as well as spatial information. The findings tell against rather vague instructions to children to "use both hands", unless it is made clear how that two-handed reading can help. Quite specific instructions about the use of reference cues may be needed for functions such as keeping to the line, and keeping the place when moving to the next line, especially for less able children. A reader who does not know a word is unlikely to understand it better by scanning it faster. But a fast regression or forward movement to context words that can give clues to meaning may well pay off.

The practical question is how to effect that. Programmes which are designed to increase reading speeds by readers who are already fluent tend to use quite specific instructions in the use of the two hands (e.g. McBride, 1974). Specific instructions about different strategies of coding hand-movements spatially can be used with quite young children (Millar, 1985 b), provided they are demonstrated first.

The implication of the explanations proposed here is that the main problem with younger and less able children is how to help them to attend to both the spatial and verbal aspects of reading simultaneously. The fact that the flexible division and alternation of the spatial and verbal aspects of reading between the two hands (Chapter 3) was very significantly related to levels of reading proficiency suggests that such flexibility in processing information from two different domains depends on high levels of practice. The spatial layouts of conventional braille texts are fairly standard and consequently relatively invariant. The fact that fluent readers seem to use complementary information from touch, kinaesthetic and movement information 'automatically' may mean that the quasi-automation of place-keeping and return sweeps in moving to the next line occurs with long practice. However, if the present hypothesis is correct, movement practice alone will not achieve that as easily as will combining verbal redundancies in the text with invariant spatial cues. For the young and less able child, the verbal and spatial aspects of reading constitute a dual task which is particularly difficult. However, how redundancy in both spatial and verbal aspects can be achieved in practice constitutes a considerable practical problem that would need to be tested out in practice.

Automatic movement habits can also lead to errors. For instance, the change from the (very necessary) double spacing of lines in texts for beginners to the single spacing in conventional texts tends to produce omissions of lines initially because the extent of the downward movement that is needed to hit the next line has become habitual. At the same time, such habits are important in increasing reading speeds. Individual differences in systematic scanning and the use of reference cues, as well as the length of practice and the verbal demands of the reading task have to be taken into account (Chapter 7).

Nevertheless, the value of reading speed, as such, should not be over-estimated. Fast reading is useful, especially in skimming texts for a particular point of information. But it was clear from regressive movements and pauses when words were difficult, or the context had been changed (Chapter 5), that the timing of movements was an effect rather than a cause of fluency. Familiarity with words and acquaintance with the topic is at least as important as scanning speed in reading braille texts for comprehension.

2   SOUNDS, SENSE, CONTRACTIONS AND SPELLING

The importance of establishing attention to sounds and discrimination between sounds is, of course, obvious in blind conditions for purposes of spatial orientation. But it is also more important for blind than for sighted children to attend to speech sounds in any case. Teachers of the blind are usually well aware of the detrimental effects that even slight hearing loss can have, and take steps to have these remediated. Nursery games with rhymes and word play are common in getting blind pre-school children to attend to language sounds. But quite specific attention to the possibility of sound confusions (Chapter 7) may be needed in addition. As most teachers of reading know well, the process of blending individual phonemes into sound clusters is by no means automatic. It often requires a good deal of teaching, especially when the child pronounces the individual sounds of consonants in letter clusters.

Perhaps it can now be recognized also that the apparently meaningless play with sounds that is commonly reported for blind children (Chapter 7) can actually be put to good use in learning the somewhat difficult discrimination between phonemes, and the sounds of the letters in different phonological environments. The fact that games with word sounds and nonsense sounds are more common for blind children is to be encouraged rather than regretted. Nevertheless, attention to the meaning of words and the concepts they represent is clearly also more important for braille learning by blind children. Games that use both, but clearly separate nonsense from sense by using different contexts (e.g. in creating rhyming verse) could be useful.

The fact that reading by adults as well as by children was clearly influenced enormously by familiarity with the meaning of words and the gist that had been construed so far was so obvious that it hardly seems worth stating, except that the traditional focus in braille has been on problems of tactual acuity in the perception of single letters, and the more recent findings on visual reading have centred on letter sounds. There is no doubt about the importance of both these factors for braille. Indeed, if anything, coding by sound is more crucial for braille initially, and far from deprecating play with meaningless sounds, such play can actually be turned to good account in learning to read. Nevertheless, it will not do to play down the importance of meaning in written language any more than in spoken language. Phonological recoding was crucial for beginning young braille readers. But they also made significantly more errors because they relied on sound more than on meaning when confronted with semantically ambiguous homophone words (Chapter 4). The practical problem is how to balance attention to sound and meaning early in learning.

Trying to 'guess' the meaning of words from initial letters, or from prior context, is often discouraged to make sure that the child attends to the tactual information. Adult beginners also use such 'guessing', and tend to apologize for doing so, especially when it happens to fail. However, apparent 'guessing' of words from initial letters and from prior context was never simply due to random choices (Chapter 5). The actual mistakes could be traced to inferences from attempts to understand difficult information by using contextual as well as the tactual cues to decode the script. When looked at in detail, attempts to use meaning to decode scripts are, in fact, mostly 'benign' mistakes which follow from a basically sound strategy. But that will work only if mistakes are promptly corrected so that the child gets adequate feedback.

Priming word recognition by prior context was strongest when the context was relevant to the meaning of the target word, and the reader could expect there to be a connection. To make use of priming for practical purposes, priming of characters or words that a child finds difficult probably has to be more frequent and more sharply focused than is likely to occur in continuous story texts, unless these are constructed for the purpose. Even for adults who learn braille as a second reading skill, prior knowledge of the context and of the range of words that are likely to come up in the text facilitates the recognition of characters and words (e.g. Tobin, 1988). Such initial facilitation is likely to speed the acquisition of fluent reading rather than to retard it. Proficient readers evidently used such predictions successfully, as shown by the findings on regressions, for instance. Younger or slower readers may need more initial prodding to test their 'guesses', and to change their hypothesis about the next word or character when necessary. The teacher probably needs to ensure that they receive relevant feedback for the kind of prediction that 'guessing' implies. As implied above, it is not possible to learn quickly without the feedback that only prompt correction of errors can give.

Taking account of contexts is important in braille, in any case. For instance, prior signs can completely change the meaning of the patterns that follow. A prior number sign changes the patterns that follow from letters to numbers (the first ten letters of the alphabet). Recent adjustments which are designed to harmonize braille in all English-speaking countries provide signs for upper case letters where these would normally occur in print. In print, such differences in meaning are usually signalled by alterations in shape (e.g. arabic numerals versus print letters, and upper case versus lower case letter shapes).

The types of mistake that are made are usually good clues to the strategy that is being used, and the kind of difficulty (tactual, spatial, phonological, lexical, orthographic or in the integration of gist) that has led to an error. Simply correcting such mistakes may not be enough. Repetition as well as feedback from hearing, saying as well as re-scanning a character or word may be needed, and the word may need to be spelt as well as repeated. In principle, writing contractions by means of the Perkins keyboard in combination with reading very early in learning (Chapter 6) could also be combined with oral repetition of the characters as well as of the word as a whole. The extent to which this may benefit spelling uncontracted words as well as word recognition is probably worth testing in braille.

English braille is undoubtedly complicated by the need to learn contraction rules for relatively infrequent words, as well as the rules which govern the use of the more frequent contractions within words (e.g. Lorimer *et al.*, 1982). However, we know far too little as yet about the variables that affect contractions in reading connected texts. The experiments that I reported on the segmentation of phonological boundaries by contractions within words showed that syllabic segmentation as such was not a major problem for young or older experienced braillists who were familiar with braille rules and orthography. But it was a problem for adult former print readers whose orthographic–phonological habits interfered with reading words in which contractions violated these boundaries. The habitual strategies and spelling habits of former print readers need far more study if we are to understand how the process of learning may be accelerated. At the same time, the fact that these readers adapted surprisingly rapidly with a relatively short experience of repetition priming is yet another indication that learning braille as a second written language in adulthood is much more feasible than is often supposed.

However, we need further studies on the effects of the frequency and invariance of contracted forms that have more than one pronunciation (e.g. ONE versus phONE and mONEy), especially in relation to practice effects. The dual task of having to learn contractions, rules for their use, and the role of fully spelt-out forms of contractions in processing written texts raises a number of issues about which we know little as yet.

The findings on contractions (Chapter 6) raise a number of further questions both for practical purposes but also for understanding the processes in reading by any system. The fact that contractions were read more quickly when they stood alone as words than when they occurred within words could be due to more than one factor. One is simply that discrimination is better when characters are flanked by word spaces than when they succeed each other. But it may also be a function of the relative recency of learning single character contractions and using these within low frequency words. The early (gradual) introduction of contracted forms is a relatively new method with young children, and is also now more common with late learners (e.g. Tobin, 1987). In principle, such schemes should increase the familiarity of contractions within words, and consequently decrease recognition time. But whether the greater ease of recognizing single-character contractions as words than within words is due to the spacing, or to the fact that the rules for their use within words have to be remembered, needs further study. Incidental findings also suggested that spacing can be a problem for contractions that occur at the end of words if the contraction consists of a letter preceded by a lower dot. When these contractions occur at the end of a word the size of space between the last letter and the contraction may feel like the type of blank space that normally separates words. It is not clear as yet whether these are genuine spacing problems in the sense that the reader mistakenly thinks that a new word follows next, or whether the difficulty occurs mainly in children who tend to ignore lower dots more in any case. The remedy would differ. The first interpretation implies that what may be needed is familiarization with words that end in contractions which produce quasi word spacing. It is also possible that such mistakes occur more if readers postpone the integration of words until the end of sentences, or have difficulties when the context fails to predict the syntactic category of the next word before touching it. If so, readers who do update the gist as they are reading the sentence should not make that type of error. Alternatively, the difficulty may be part of a general habit of missing lower dots. In that case, remediation of scanning style rather word practice or practice in text integration is needed.

Contractions are usually seen as detrimental to learning to spell words in their orthographic (print) form. Knowledge of English orthography is desirable for a number of reasons, but as noted above, it means that the child has to learn two divergent orthographies for contracted forms, and may know the contracted forms better if they have been mastered earlier. At the same time, spelling skills can contribute to reading proficiency. Treiman (1993) showed that reading and spelling skills can alter children's awareness of phonemes. In the present studies on braille, it was found that the incorrect spelling even of similar sounding (homophone) words was registered in comprehending the gist of texts by proficient readers (Chapter 4). Learning to spell, including learning the rules and exceptions of English orthography, can be used to make braille reading easier, especially by young readers who use letter-by-letter phonological recoding and have little orthographic knowledge. For instance, sequential scanning with assembled phonology creates difficulties particularly for words in which the ending alters the sound of an earlier vowel (e.g. the 'magic e').

The rules that govern such vowel changes are not always taught explicitly to young blind children, either because it is thought that they cannot absorb or apply them, or that regularities are best picked up incidentally rather than by direct instruction. It is an extremely interesting question to pursue further, because it involves the relation between implicit and explicit knowledge (or knowing 'how' and knowing 'that') during the process of acquisition. The hypothesis that young children need informational redundancy predicts that a judicious combination of explicit instruction in the rules and exceptions, in conjunction with practice in reading materials in which these occur maximally, should produce better results than either method alone.

The findings on the effects of differences in graphemic–orthographic–phonological habits between former print readers and experienced braillists certainly suggest that familiarity with the connections between the different aspects of a script is a major factor in processing.

3 COMPLEMENTARY INFORMATION FROM VISION

I have assumed throughout that braille is used principally by people who cannot obtain sufficiently fine-grained spatial information through vision to see braille shapes, and have therefore concentrated throughout on decoding language through touch, movement and the spatial reference information that these complementary inputs afford. The topic of partial sight, and of residual vision which is sufficient to cope with visual print in physically or artificially (e.g. computer-assisted) enlarged formats is extremely important. Some crucial educational issues are about the early encouragement and use of residual vision both alone and in combination with touch and sound (e.g. Chapman *et al.*, 1977). Visual aids for people with residual vision are becoming increasingly more sophisticated. But the topic is beyond the brief of the present book.

One question, however, needs to be considered briefly. Should people who can still see quite well, but who are likely to lose their sight in the foreseeable future, learn braille by vision, or by touch, or both? As far as I can see, there is no conclusive evidence at present on which one could base a considered judgment about the use of vision in braille learning in all cases. We have a large number of experimental studies on crossmodal shape perception by touch and vision (e.g. Millar, 1981 a; Walk and Pick, 1981; Warren and Rossano, 1991), and although texture judgments can be more accurate by touch than by vision, shape is usually perceived better by vision (e.g., Heller, 1982, 1989; Warren and Rossano, 1991). As noted earlier, tactual performance differs with tasks, size and shape conditions (Chapter 2). Although it is not possible to make any direct inferences from larger and from three-dimensional shapes that are most commonly used in crossmodal studies, children also recognize braille patterns more easily by vision than by touch (Millar, 1977 a). Vision is also superior to the combination vision and touch, for learning auditorily presented names (Newman *et al.*, 1990). There is no evidence that sighted children or adults translate tactual braille patterns accurately into visual shapes if they have not seen them before (Millar, 1977 a, 1985 b). Added vision facilitated braille pattern identification when individual stimuli were tested by indicating the visual form (Heller, 1987). But low lighting was evidently better than normal illumination for identifying two-letter (uncontracted) words or word-like sequences, and blind braillists were far superior to the sighted in either case, suggesting that visual information interferes in some conditions (Heller, 1993). The findings suggest that this is the case particularly for braille words that contain consecutive letters rather than for single patterns.

The difference in the dual effects highlights some of the conditions in which added information from another modality does not produce facilitation, and can interfere with learning. One is the relative efficiency of the two modalities that are to be added (e.g. Millar, 1986). Shape perception is generally better by vision than by touch. Adding visual to tactual presentations adds cues that improve shape perception over tactual cues alone, but the reverse is not the case (e.g. Millar, 1971). The fact that shape information is better from vision than from touch means that the added tactual information is irrelevant and tends to be ignored. The hypothesis that shape perception in touch depends on the balance of intersensory inputs from all sources (Chapter 2) implies that when there is an imbalance of information, perception will depend more on the more 'dominant' information. The hypothesis explains the well-known fact, for instance, that sighted people, including experienced braille teachers, tend to read by vision if there is a chance of doing so. However, that may merely mean that when good vision is present, people pay little attention to tactual information. If the aim is to learn to read by touch, therefore, vision is probably best excluded. But, for the same reason, the results are also likely to differ with the visual status of beginners. Touch seems to provide little extra shape information unless the visual conditions are poor. However, the answer may differ as vision deteriorates and the relative efficiency of the two modalities for shape perception changes. If the Heller (1989, 1993) lighting conditions are analogous to reduced vision, the hypothesis predicts that with equally moderate levels of efficiency in the two modalities, the dual condition should produce cue redundancy. For people with reduced sight, using both vision and touch should facilitate learning. But such predictions clearly need to be tested out in practice.

However, a second factor may need to be considered also. To produce redundant information, inputs from different sources are assumed to be complementary and to converge. If the basis of coding inputs from two dimensions differs unpredictably, they are more likely to interfere than to facilitate each other (Millar, 1986). It cannot be taken for granted that the initial basis of coding braille patterns by touch and vision is identical. On the contrary, the evidence suggested that the initial tactual coding of braille patterns relies on dot–gap density cues rather than on global outlines. In vision, by contrast, the outline shape is salient and tends to be coded. If the aim is to get people to code the outline shape by touch, vision can be used to 'educate' touch. But visual conditions which facilitate coding outline shape cues would provide different cues than the tactual shear pattern cues derived from lateral scanning. The inputs from the two modalities could thus vary unpredictably rather than be mutually redundant. In such discrepant coding conditions, therefore, adding visual shape information could be expected to interfere rather than to facilitate reading. Heller's interesting (1993) results suggest that this may indeed be the case when the material consists of words, i.e. successive letters that need to be scanned laterally.

The precise conditions in which two inputs provide facilitation rather than interference require a good deal of further study. But it is clear already that, in deciding when residual sight should be used or eschewed in learning braille by people whose sight is deteriorating, or for children who cannot see print but have useful residual vision, more than one factor needs to be considered, including the relative efficiency of sight and touch, and the fact that tactual coding may differ from visual coding in some task conditions.

4   COMPLEMENTARY AUDITORY AND MULTIMEDIA INFORMATION

The fact that auditory information is important in conditions of visual handicap hardly needs stressing. But its main use is often on its own, as a substitute modality, rather than in deliberate conjunction with information from other sources, and particularly in combination with touch and movement.

An evidently successful method combines information from multiple sources in teaching braille to newly blind adolescents and adults (Tobin, 1987, 1988). Auditory instruction is provided on tape giving information about the jumbo-sized braille patterns that are then later relearned in conventional format. It also introduces single character contractions for words early so that people can read meaningful sentences, controls carefully for word frequency, and maximizes dot density differences between sequential letters in the regular words that are being introduced. Beginners thus not only get prior information about the words that they can expect to feel, and encouragement to scan them systematically, they can also then get auditory feedback from the tapes about their success or failure in reading the words. The fact that the scheme is largely based on self-instruction makes it particularly suitable for adults. However, newly blind adults may also need opportunity and encouragement to practise braille further to the degree that is considered a matter of course for young students.

Similar schemes for young blind beginners (Section 1) have to rely on teachers for the necessary one-to-one auditory feedback. It is not yet clear how far very young children could also use auditory feedback from tapes for the materials they use. But purely verbal inputs are unlikely to be enough, in any case. Frequent one-to-one contact with teachers is needed for explanations and expansions of meaning that tap into the child's current knowledge, and ensure the compatibility of different simultaneous inputs from different sources.

The practical importance of ensuring compatibility between inputs added from the same, or from different, modalities and the reading strategies readers use was highlighted also by the effects of priming words by prior auditory and tactual information (Chapter 6). Auditory primes, not surprisingly, tended to elicit the orthographic–phonological print associations in former print readers, and although even purely auditory primes made processing faster, repetition alone did not eliminate the disadvantage for former print readers who evidently construed the heard target word in terms of print orthography. That discrepancy was eliminated better with tactual primes which also primed the new orthography. The findings underline the importance of repeated exposure to tactual information in producing improvements. They also suggest that the usefulness of additional auditory priming is probably enhanced when the orthographic–phonological associations match the tactual inputs.

Auditory inputs from talking books and tapes are, of course, widely used by blind people. However, it is often assumed that it is the only form of information that is suitable for adults who have lost their sight. The findings here suggest that getting older and losing sight need be no bar to retaining literacy. Auditory tapes can also be used in conjunction with braille to facilitate learning (e.g. Tobin, 1988). A judicious combination of listening and reading by touch could combine the greater ease of listening, with the greater control over the material, including the pace or rate of taking in information, and the ease of re-reading a given passage that is provided by braille. A very competent tactual braille reader who instructed newly blind people in braille found that it was useful for learning to read braille initially to play auditory tapes of the text prior to reading it in braille.

5 THE OPTACON, AND COMPUTERS AS AIDS AND SUBSTITUTES

The optacon device which was briefly described earlier (Chapter 2) has been used extremely successfully by blind people (Sherrick, 1991). The fact that the optacon translates visual print letters into vibrotactile stimulation may make it particularly suitable for recently blind people who formerly read print. But it can also be a useful additional aid for people whose main script is braille. Most good braillists also learn the shapes of print letters and uncontracted spelling at some stage after having learned braille.

However, parameters relating to tactual acuity, including threshold measures, are important for devices that use passive touch with vibratory stimuli. There are excellent reviews of studies on the factors that are crucial in discriminating vibrotactile stimuli (Sherrick, 1991; Sherrick and Craig, 1982). Very briefly, acuity in vibrotactile stimulation has been found to depend crucially on the time interval that is needed between the pulses of two vibrators for these to be detected as separate impulses, as well as on the distance between vibrators (density) in an array. The parameters which produce good discrimination have long been established for the optacon. The use of the optacon thus raises questions about the effects of diminished tactual acuity by older subjects, and by diabetics who have reduced acuity levels (Chapter 7), although it should be stressed that reduced tactual acuity is not necessarily a bar to learning the optacon any more than to braille (e.g. Pester *et al.*, 1994).

Initial letter recognition with the optacon can be rather poor (e.g. Epstein *et al.*, 1989). Two possibilities for enhancing the recognition of print letters via the pattern of vibration that is delivered to the fingerpad are briefly considered here, but both need further study. The array of vibrators forms a rectangular shape under the fingerpad. In principle that makes the layout into a potentially usable coordinate reference frame to which the patterns of vibrations can be related initially. For me, for instance, the pattern of stimulation for the print letter 'S' was difficult to recognize at first, until I realized that it consisted of a tickle in the top right area of my fingerpad, followed by a tickle in the lower left portion of my fingerpad. Initial responses are, no doubt, idiosyncratic. There is no empirical evidence so far whether using the finger and rectangular array as a spatial frame could facilitate recognizing the shape of the pattern of vibrations. But the possibility is worth testing especially for beginning optacon users.

It has also been suggested that although vibrotactile stimulation is normally passive, moving the finger actively over vibrotactile stimulation may enhance perception initially. Shorter identification times have been reported, for instance, for Hebrew letters when vibratory and temporal characteristics coincided (Zakay and Shilo, 1985). Some advantage of being allowed to actively palpate digits produced by an array of vibratory stimuli has been found for adult subjects without previous experience of the optacon (Heller *et al.*, 1990). But it is not clear that the advantage of such activity persists over trials.

Because the optacon depends on stimulating the pad of the finger which rests on the array of benders, only one character pattern can be sensed at a time. As such, the device seems to be particularly useful for scanning of single characters (e.g. labels or numbers), for instance in leafing through documents to find a particular text quickly. However, people seem to be able to read continuous texts by means of the optacon at speeds of thirty to sixty words per minute on average (Sherrick, 1991), and at least two highly practised individuals have been shown to achieve much higher rates (Craig, 1977). For people who know braille well, the optacon is probably most useful as an additional aid. It may be most useful in searching through documents by the page number, detecting a printed label, or in conjunction with computer displays, rather than as the sole means of reading continuous texts. Learning the optacon system is not likely to interfere with well-established braille skills. But because the physical patterns and some of the orthography differs, it is probably better to learn the two systems in sequence, rather than at the same time.

Parameters relating to thresholds are important also in the design of vibrator arrays for touch reception keyboards as interfaces with computers for blind users (Schiff and Foulke, 1982). Some devices have touch reception keyboards that are designed to display more than one letter or word. This can be done by means of electronically controlled 'pins' that are raised or pop up when activated. Some devices are rather difficult to handle if the pins are not securely locked into the system. Keyboards that use lines of vibrators combine passive stimulation of the fingerpad with active lateral (left–right) scanning. There seems to be little information as yet about the parameters that govern the combination of passive vibratory stimulation and active scanning. Passive stimulation by vibrators under the ball of the finger could interfere with gaining information by active lateral scanning of the message. Not all the design problems that are likely to bother the blind user have yet been solved.

However, there is now an increasing number of devices that make computers accessible to blind users (Gill *et al.*, 1996). Some do so by using speech input facilities and synthesized speech outputs (e.g. Kessler, 1984), and these are becoming more sophisticated. Computer displays which use tones to indicate positions are also being developed. Carefully positioned tones can give accurate information also about small scale spaces (Juurmaa and Suonia, 1975; Wanet and Veraart, 1985). Early problems in translating between braille and print are also beginning to be solved. Such translation devices should make it much easier for the blind braillists to communicate without difficulty with print readers, and vice versa.

Even newer and more splendidly futuristic technological aids (e.g. 'soundscapes' to simulate spaces) seem within reach (Probert *et al.*, 1996). At the same time, the proportion of blind people who actually use even any of the simplest devices that are currently available as aids is apparently extremely small (Probert *et al.*, 1996). It is not clear why this should be so. It has been suggested that the designs pay insufficient attention to the actual needs of the average blind user, or that older blind people or people who are multiply handicapped do not adapt to new computing devices. It is equally possible that it is considered too expensive to provide adequate training, information and backup services, even when the devices are affordable.

The role of extended practice, for instance in cases where acuity is diminished, was discussed in relation to braille. But it applies also to learning to use the optacon, or computing devices. A balance does, of course, have to be struck between the benefits of extended practice and the fact that difficult tasks require more effort and are both more tiring and more discouraging than undemanding tasks that ensure early success. Only the people concerned can decide whether the effort is worth it for them.

But it also has to be recognized that the discouraging stereotypes about what the old, the young, or the blind 'cannot' do or learn about braille or computers or both, are often poorly grounded in empirical fact.

6   READING MAPS, GRAPHS, ICONS AND USING NONVISUAL IMAGERY

There has long been ample evidence that raised line drawings, maps, and other small scale spatial layouts can be used effectively by congenitally totally blind children, although prior information and cognitive inference is involved to a greater extent than in vision (e.g. Berla, 1982; Berla and Butterfield, 1977; Berla *et al.*, 1976; Heller, 1989; Herman *et al.*, 1983; Kennedy, 1980, 1993; Leonard and Newman, 1967, 1970; Millar, 1975 d, 1985 b, 1991, 1994; Pring and Rusted, 1985; Spencer and Travis, 1985). It is high time to quietly forget the outdated notion that vision is crucial to spatial representation, or that maps cannot be used by blind people, without substituting the equally simplistic idea that map reading is unlearned, or that perceptual information is irrelevant. It is by no means irrelevant to ask what medium best substitutes for visual representations.

In assessing the benefits and costs of nonvisual analogues of visual representations for blind users, two distinctions are essential. First, the term 'visual representation' is often used misleadingly for what are, in fact, presentations of events on film, television, or radio. The point of electronic and radio transmissions of events is to make the presentation as like the perceptual experience of watching and listening of a bystander as possible. Like the actual experience, 'virtual' or near virtual presentations usually contain more raw information than verbal (or other) descriptions of the same events. By contrast, visual representation in maps, graphs or icons refer to symbol systems which contract information. Symbol systems save time and effort in proportion to the amount of knowledge that each symbol represents, and the fewer the number of symbols that have to be learned or remembered. Maps are symbol systems in that sense (Liben and Downs, 1989, 1992; Millar, 1991), as are drawings, graphs and 'icons' on computers (Millar, 1975 c, 1985 a, 1994). That is important. Map symbols and their uses have to be learned, and this requires knowledge of the subject matter, knowledge of the symbols, and cognitive skill in deploying the symbols by sighted children (e.g. Liben and Downs, 1989, 1992) as well by children without sight.

The second distinction is between arbitrary and non-arbitrary symbols. It is here that the perceptual modality of the representation becomes relevant. The sounds of words, the shapes of print letters, and the dot patterns of braille derive from arbitrary associations between the symbol and its referent. By contrast, onomatopoeic sounds and two-dimensional visual drawings 'resemble', in very simplified or 'abstracted' form, the attribute that is to be represented. Modality is relevant to the extent that symbols 'resemble' the attributes they represent. The resemblance makes it easier to learn and remember these symbols than arbitrary associations. Imperfect imitations of sounds made by dogs ('bow-wow', 'wow-wow') are more easily used as symbols for the animal by infants than the arbitrary name. No head is a flat circle. But children draw circles to represent heads as the simplest two-dimensional shape that exemplifies a very general characteristic of the three-dimensional object (Millar, 1975 d, 1991).

Maps represent three-dimensional spaces by two-dimensional lines and shapes. It is no accident that visual symbols are used, because the two-dimensional and three-dimensional shape data in vision have important features in common, and are both spatially organized by external frame cues. The lines, curves, turns and even 'blobs' on the two-dimensional page provide some of the same cues as outlines of three-dimensional configurations (e.g. Gibson, 1971). A line seen on the flat page has some similarity to lines made by a road that is seen stretching into the distance. Although that is rarely stressed, miniaturization is part of our visual information, for instance from the perception of distant objects and scenes. Some visual illusions can be recreated on the flat page. The similarity in perceptual 'affordances', and the tacit knowledge that shape is invariant over size, makes it easy to 'recognize' a flat outline drawing as the three-dimensional object that it represents. Two-dimensional shapes are therefore more 'transparent' as symbols for three-dimensional shapes and spatial arrays than is the case for touch.

Map symbols are less 'transparent' than drawings, because the symbols have to be decoded strictly in terms of distances and directions, relative to an invariant vertical–horizontal coordinate frame. Such decoding, even by adults, rarely rests on Euclidean calculations, but is influenced by the context in which the perceptual information is presented (e.g. Tversky, 1981). Maps differ in the detail and complexity of representation, as well as in the type of information and the precise meaning of symbols (contour, political, geographic) they represent. The essential similarity between maps and the spaces they represent is that the symbols are organized with regard to the same reference frame. If the map is used for pathfinding, the coordinates in maps have to be aligned correctly to coordinates in external, large scale space to be read correctly. Correct alignments are often difficult (e.g. Rossano and Warren, 1989). Aligning map coordinates with geographic positions requires the explicit use of coordinate reference frames which are normally merely implicit in the spatially organized visual information we receive when moving through space. Alternatively, mental rotation of the information is needed. Map reading thus requires general knowledge, cognitive skill, knowledge about geographical space, and some explicit use as well as implicit knowledge of the alignment of the coordinates of spaces which is acquired gradually (e.g. Liben and Downs, 1991, 1992, 1993). But sighted children have easier access to perceptual knowledge about the relation between external planes, and do not need to learn to use external reference cues to update their movements in either large scale or small scale space. Moreover, map symbols that represent three-dimensional landmarks and routes are, in important respects, as for instance in the relative length of lines and size of angular turns, similar to their referents.

All these aspects of knowledge can also be acquired by young blind children, provided the relevant information is supplied by other means. But since more than one factor is involved in map reading, there is also more than one reason why map reading can be much more difficult in the total absence of visual experience (Ungar *et al.*, 1995). These factors have to be examined in detail if map reading is to become easy and useful in practice. An increase in the relevant general knowledge is only one factor, and is probably most easily supplied. More important, complete absence of visual information has the quite specific effect of reducing information about the external frame cues which determine the relative location of objects and surfaces to each other and to the viewer, and which normally overlap with complementary inputs from body-centred cues and from auditory and other sources (Chapter 2). The lack of reliable information about external reference frames, and about their usefulness for determining locations and directions, tends to produce a bias towards coding in terms of movements and body-centred frames. Unless corrected by knowledge of updating rules, such coding makes it more difficult to align different reference frames when these are 'out of synch' with body-centred frames, or rotated with respect to each other (Millar, 1981 b, 1985 a, 1994). Familiarization with geographical spaces and attention to auditory, tactile, movement and other cues is needed for orientation and provides relevant knowledge (e.g. Cratty, 1971). But quite explicit information about how external planes relate to each other, and to body-centred reference frames and to movement information, may be needed to provide adequate knowledge about the use of external spatial frames and relations in geographical space (Millar, 1994).

There is a further factor which relates directly to the difference in initial perceptual information between touch and vision. The fact that haptic information differs with the size and depth of configurations (Chapter 2) means that small two-dimensional raised line configurations are not immediately recognized as having essential features in common with the three-dimensional spaces that they are intended to represent. It is for that reason that pre-cuing and training in systematic exploration is necessary, for instance, for students to understand the contours in small scale tactual political maps (e.g. Berla and Butterfield, 1977). The finding that congenitally totally blind young children were actually better at producing raised line drawings of the three-dimensional human figure than at recognizing raised line drawings of the figure (Millar, 1985 b, 1991) underlines this further. By contrast, production lags far behind the recognition of line drawings by sighted children (Maccoby and Bee, 1965). Successful recognition of tactual replicas of two-dimensional drawings usually involves some inference from prior knowledge of what the alternatives in the set are likely to be (e.g. Heller, 1989; Pring and Rusted, 1985). But by the age of about ten years congenitally totally blind children are quite good, for instance, at producing (2-D) raised line drawings which symbolize the human figure by much the same types of schemas as their sighted peers.

Raised line maps, graphs and drawings are larger than braille patterns so that the main information comes from scanning movements. Recognizing these as similar to the movements required to recognize the object in question provides nonvisual similarities that can be used for mapping. Taken together, the evidence suggested that productive movements and their organization by small scale reference cues can form an important basis for nonvisual spatial representation (Millar, 1985 b, 1991). Blind children have to organize movements in small scale space by actively seeking and providing reference cues (Millar, 1994). Able children understand this quite early with experience, for instance, with the layout of braille (Chapter 3). We have also shown that congenitally totally blind and sighted children can mentally represent movement information, because a merely imagined movement extent alters the performance of a subsequent movement, and this does not happen if they do nothing in that interval or perform a verbal task (Millar and Ittyerah, 1991).

I have argued that mental representation of active movements in producing, and getting tactual feedback from tracing, raised lines, is one perceptual basis for deriving nonvisual imagery or representations of shape and spatial information (Millar, 1991, 1994). In principle, organized movement information can be used symbolically. Blind children do not spontaneously represent a movement turn in large scale (geographic) space by reproducing the turn in a raised line drawing on manilla paper. Naive blind children produce a straight raised line when asked to draw the (square) space around which they have just walked, even though they know that they have turned several times, and can tell you so. But simply telling them to show the turns in their drawing of the space is sufficient. They can then infer that a particular hand-movement can be used to represent a similar body-movement in large scale space, and use that information to draw a square or closed figure with turns. No lengthy associative learning is needed. Attention does need to be drawn to the possibility of representing one by the other for recognition of the symbolic likeness of small scale hand-movements and large scale body movements to occur. Using the same name (e.g. turn) could be sufficient (e.g. Pring and Rusted, 1989).

There is more than one means of representing spatially organized information for blind as well as for sighted people. It is possible, for instance, to calculate geometric relations by inference from Euclidean principles. However, tests of mental spatial representations with sighted adults show that they tend to use visuospatial strategies instead (e.g. Kosslyn, 1980). Movement-based representations provide a nonvisual, nonverbal analogue which could make it easier for blind children to enjoy using maps and other tactual spatial displays (Millar, 1994).

The implication that tactual maps may be learned best by initially using active, spatially organized drawing movements which produce feedback in small scale space, in conjunction with actual movements and feedback in geographic space, needs to be tested further in practice, not only in relation to maps, but also with other tactual displays. There is some evidence that such training can be useful (e.g. James, 1982). In principle, raised line displays could also be used for clarifying a variety of spatial notions that are less easily available to young blind children (Millar, 1975 d, 1985 b; Pring and Rusted, 1985), as well as in making braille books more interesting (e.g. Schiff, 1982). Kennedy (1980, 1993) has used a series of raised line drawings which subjects produce and identify to illustrate stories, and has shown the devices blind children can use to depict depth and movement. Raised line diagrams for biology students (Hinton and Ayres, 1987), and geometric figures for teaching mathematics are important additions to purely verbal information. But the fact that two-dimensional tactual representations of three-dimensional objects are less 'transparent' as symbols than they are in vision, and therefore require more initial translation and inference, does have to be recognized if they are to be useful.

The main alternatives to tactual maps have been 'auditory' maps or tapes which give spoken directions. They may be easier for newly blind adults because they do not require special learning (James, 1982). But the combination of spoken information and tactual maps which allow the information to be followed and aligned with reference to actual orientations is likely to be more useful. Aligning or rotating the coordinates of an actual map is certainly easier than using mental rotation alone. An exciting new portable computer device is being developed to give people information about their position and how and where they need to proceed. It links the user to auditory information via satellites, and incorporates a hand held compass and electronic map for directional guidance, and the user can also follow the directions on a tactual map (Gill *et al.*, 1996).

A good deal of research has focused on the discriminability of symbols, using a variety of textures which can be used for different symbols (e.g. James, 1982; Gill, 1974). Legibility may also be improved if shape and texture cues are used redundantly so that symbols differ on both counts. Another important limitation is the tactual 'clutter' that occurs when too many symbols are used in small format diagrams. Problems can also arise because symbols are not standardized and are unfamiliar to users (e.g. Schiff, 1982). Curiously enough, some tactile maps fail to provide unequivocal reference information about the important coordinates without which landmarks cannot be located and the direction of routes becomes equivocal.

The standardization as well as the clarity of symbols is also important for tactual graphic displays that are used as illustrations for subjects like biology, statistics and the principles of geometry. But reading such illustrations by touch involves a number of factors, including knowledge of the subject matter, previous exposure to the system, and a degree of practice in decoding the symbols. Simple comparisons of performance by blind and sighted people cannot disambiguate these factors, whether the groups differ or perform equally. The question which modality is better, or whether two are better than one to represent spatial information in blind conditions, needs checking with regard to each of the factors. Auditory maps are not always easy to use (James, 1982), while the symbols in tactual maps may not be sufficiently familiar to the user (Berla, 1982; Schiff, 1982). In such conditions, two sources of information are likely to be better than one. But that requires further study.

It is also relevant to ask whether the physical symbols in the displays are as 'transparent' or non-arbitrary in touch as in vision. The point is that small scale shapes that in vision resemble their larger or three-dimensional referents in essential characteristics, do not necessarily have the same transparency in touch, because that is likely to differ with the size and composition of the symbols (Chapter 2). Arbitrary symbols can be equally useful, provided they compress a good deal of information. But the symbols that lack transparency initially probably require more learning or experience, and that is relevant to assessing their usefulness in facilitating comprehension rather than interfering with it.

7   SUMMARY

I have been mainly concerned with the further questions that some of the practical implications of the findings raise. If there is an overall suggestion, it is for further work on the interactions between the different forms of information that the reader needs to process.

For braille, I have suggested several points that need testing in the field. One is that the relative ease of dot–gap density detection by beginners could be harnessed to produce a faster transition to lateral scanning in reading for meaning, while methods that facilitate shape detection could be used in the context of recognition tasks, or in games for which shape is the important perceptual cue. It is possible, of course, that the differentiation between tasks and the perceptual cues that are needed for them is only achieved with experience. But it is probably worth testing. Feasibility studies would also be useful to test further the effects of encouraging rather than deprecating the use of context to aid phonological and tactual decoding of inputs.

There is little doubt that a good deal of further work is needed to ascertain effects of added visual and auditory information. The close relation between different sources of information and the processing these elicit is nowhere more obvious than in reading. It seems to me that the question is not whether such additions are useful, but under what conditions the added information facilitates or interferes with learning and comprehension. Learning a different system, such as the optacon, or computer keyboards raises similar questions. My final point was about encouraging the use of memory for active movements in small scale space as nonverbal representations in mapping tasks.

Educators will be aware that I have totally left out the emotional and social context in which learning takes place. But it is paramount. Reading by touch presents greater challenges even than reading by vision. But it can certainly be achieved by more people than is often believed, although it needs even more individual attention than learning to read print, both in terms of error correction and feedback and for encouragement. The motivation for the effort, and the resources in manpower that are allocated to it depend on the value that individuals and society place on literacy in any medium.

9 Towards a theory of reading by touch

In asking what kind of model best fits the findings on reading by touch, three main factors have to be considered: perceptual processes, knowledge of the language, and knowledge of the orthographic rules and conventions which govern the translation between the sounds of language and the perception of the tactual patterns which symbolize them. The model must also be able to account for maturation and development, and specify how learning takes place.

The working model of reading by touch that I am proposing uses the overall metaphor of 'converging active processing in interrelated networks' (CAPIN for short) for human information processing (Millar, 1994). It stresses the inherent activity of the system which incoming patterns of impulses modify, and which also influences incoming patterns of activation. The notion of converging processes is needed to describe the intersensory nature of perception by touch. I used the description originally to account for the spatial organization of intersensory cues from touch, movement and posture in the absence of current external frame cues (Millar, 1981 a, 1994). The description applies to the initial perception of braille patterns, and the progressive spatial organization of scanning movements found here (Chapters 2 and 3). The metaphor of networks of interconnections also accounts for the variables involved in language acquisition. The connections between heard sounds, speech output, semantic and linguistic inputs become progressively more organized in converging networks. Incoming information that activates part of the system will activate other connections to some extent also.

I am also making assumptions about developmental processes. We know that the central nervous system is innately biased towards accepting and organizing some inputs more than others. The patterns of connections that serve hearing, speech and language must be assumed to have stronger connections with each other originally than with the patterns that serve the connections between touch and movement. At the same time, even 'dedicated' parts of the network have connections or potential connections with other parts of the network. There is increasing evidence that even inherently dedicated connections in the actual neural network can be altered not only by lack of activation, but also by new incoming patterns of activation, especially, though not solely, during initial periods of plasticity (Chapter 2). Longer-term knowledge is distributed over most of the network.

As a general framework, the metaphor of interrelated networks belongs to the class of connectionist models (e.g. Hinton, 1989; McClelland, 1987, 1989; Rumelhart and McLelland, 1986; Rumelhart *et al.*, 1986; Seidenberg and McClelland, 1989). The advantage of connectionist or neural network models is that they are, in principle, intended to be compatible both with descriptions of how the actual neuronal connections function in the human central nervous system, and with psychological descriptions of how human information processing takes place, based on empirical findings.

The main objection to connectionist models has been that learning is assumed to take place incrementally. That seems to be at variance with the empirical evidence that learning can take place in a single trial, that learning by rule and learning by rote differ, that people make inferences, use symbols, and represent information in a variety of ways that affect performance. McClelland (1989) suggests that it is, in principle, possible to redescribe these phenomena in terms of network connections. With that proviso, I am assuming that learning takes place by incoming patterns of impulses which strengthen or change patterns of activity by spreading activation to larger areas, or by facilitating connections in existing pathways. But incoming patterns in learning are also influenced by existing patterns.

The additional developmental assumptions which I am proposing imply that familiarity, or the strength of prior connections, influences the amount of redundancy that is needed to activate the connections by incoming patterns of impulses, and the extent to which the activation spreads to other parts of the network. Connections become increasingly stronger and more resistant to divergence with invariant repetition. But they also converge increasingly with connections to other networks, depending on the amount and type of variation in the incoming impulses that reactivate the whole or part of the previous pattern of connections. The implication is that a combination of lack of maturation and lack of knowledge produces conditions of informational uncertainty. More redundancy is, therefore, needed in the incoming patterns of information, and more overlap with existing knowledge, by young children and early in learning than later in learning and when children are older. That has obvious implications in practice (Chapter 8), and for formal (computational) descriptions of the learning process.

Learning braille by young beginners is thus explained by the progressive patterning of connections between networks that underlie increasing language skills, and networks that have to do with the constructive spatial patterning of scanning skills. The development of braille reading involves increasingly stronger patterns of connections between the two patterns of networks. But the findings also suggest an increasing specialization of connections with different reading tasks. There is no single developmental path from greater generality to greater specificity, or from restricted connections to wider ones. The important assumption is that development occurs in both directions.

The next section gives some reasons why the findings on reading by touch are better served by a general description in terms of active developments in the patterning of haptic and language processes, than by more traditional assumptions.

1   SOME REASONS FOR THE CAPIN METAPHOR

The metaphors that scientific descriptions use can lead to useful predictions, but they tend to colour our practical expectations. The traditional metaphor that describes how we process information is that of an architectural structure with levels which house particular stores of knowledge and procedural skills. The lowest level is the intake area, and houses receptor processes and perceptual analysers. The highest levels contain a lexicon or dictionaries, and libraries which store semantic, syntactic and general knowledge. Intermediate levels receive outputs from the intake areas, and automatically change or recode them into a more suitable form to get access to the top level, or organize them sufficiently by means of some collaterals to get a direct match without an intermediate change. The metaphor is plausible, because it can also be used to describe relevant anatomical facts and physiological processes, albeit not in a one-to-one fashion. For instance, peripheral receptors pass impulses along neurones via a number of subcortical relay stations to specifically dedicated areas of the brain and surrounding association areas. Theories of how reading takes place are usually classified as 'bottom-up', 'top-down' and 'interactive', according to the direction in which the information is assumed to flow through the system.

However, metaphors which have the flavour of static stores or repositories, such as a lexicon or libraries for words and concepts, fail to indicate that the system is never static. For instance, the very act of trying to 'look up' the meaning of a word mentally must change its representation, if only by leaving it more accessible next time. The point is important for describing development. New phonological and graphemic inputs, or inferences drawn from new semantic contexts, can change knowledge and representations, either by extending the meaning or associations of a word, or by associating new sounds, or all of these. For the beginning young reader, phonemes are initially new sounds, as well as new segmentations of familiar word sounds. But they also have to learn new tactual patterns and to associate them with the sounds. Taken too literally, the 'look-up lexicon' metaphor needs a homonculus who is constantly overwriting entries and changing the footnotes that link them to other entries. In principle, the metaphor of active interrelated processes that converge in a variety of combinations does that job more neatly. The difference is important in practice, because it influences what we do and expect in practice, as well as predictions about the outcome of different procedures.

Most theories of adult visual reading assume some form of interaction between higher level cognitive and linguistic processes (e.g. Coltheart, 1978; Coltheart *et al.*, 1993; Just and Carpenter, 1980 a, b, 1987; Rayner and Pollatsek, 1989; Rumelhart and McClelland, 1986; Seidenberg and McClelland, 1989, 1990), although immediate obligatory, automatic phonological recoding is assumed in some theories (e.g. Van Orden *et al.*, 1990). The advantage of the metaphor of divergent but interrelated networks is that it can accommodate the evidence that exists, for instance, for phonological coding both before and after words have been recognized (Coltheart *et al.*, 1993), without having to assume two quite separate routes to meaning. Some network models also assume that higher order semantic, lexical, syntactic and orthographic knowledge influences the synthesis of letter features into word patterns in parallel (Paap *et al.*, 1982, 1984). It should, therefore, be possible to include convergence of processing with still 'lower levels' than spatially organized perceptions. That is needed to account for the development of tactual scanning, and 'top-down' effects in acquisition and in proficient reading.

Developmental models of visual reading tend to imply that acquisition proceeds by sequences of processes, from the recognition of words by shape or shape features, to learning the means of phonemic recoding via phonological segmentation (e.g. Barron, 1980, 1986; Barron and Baron, 1977; Frith, 1985; Marsh *et al.*, 1981). Theories differ in the number of subsidiary stages they describe, and whether these stages are assumed to be determined by maturational factors. It is not clear that there is any empirical basis for the assumption of developmental stages in learning to read. It is likely that the sequence of processes in acquisition is largely determined by the sequence and flexibility of teaching methods, and by what has already been learned. For instance, using 'whole-word' methods of matching pictures of objects with pictures of their written names, without any instruction in phonics, is likely to delay the ability to construe alphabetically regular new words. Similarly, exclusively phonic methods that pay little or no attention to the meaning of words, or to ensuring comprehension, are likely to encourage 'barking at print'.

The model here assumes that maturational and experiential factors interact in a complex fashion from the start. To some extent at least, they can be specified. For instance, the linear increase in short-term memory span with age (Chapter 7) has clear implications for learning braille by young children. But the increase depends on a number of variables which include modes of coding, processing speeds, longer-term familiarity with naming and speech-output connections. It seems clear therefore, that the variables in increased short-term memory spans with age are not completely independent of each other. The notion of convergent processes in interrelated networks seems a good overall description, especially as some of the contributing processes are beginning to be teased out. The idea of spreading activation and interactions (e.g. Stanovich, 1981) fit into that picture, although developmental as well as experiential biases need to be included.

Theories of braille have not specified sequential processes very precisely. Letter-by-letter theories assume that letters in a word are identified sequentially. The implication is that processing simply gets faster with proficiency. The closest visual model is that of 'bottom-up processing' (Gough, 1972). There was indeed good evidence that the description actually applies to beginning braille readers. However, young beginners also relied on memory for word sounds more than older readers (Chapter 4). The strong version of a letter-by-letter processing theory could not account for that without additional assumptions. Nor could it explain easily why graphemic length effects related differently to phonological coding in homophone judgments than to syllable length in prose reading, nor why silent reading by competent readers is faster than their oral reading (Chapter 4). Some 'top-down' effects of orthographic habits or their conjunction with word sound also have to be assumed to explain the findings on contractions that violate syllable boundaries for former print readers compared to slow but experienced braillists (Chapter 6).

Purely 'top-down' theories are clearly not viable either. The hypothesis that meaning is accessed by the global shape of braille words (Burklen, 1932) was not supported. Instead, there was evidence that lateral (probably temporally extended) shear patterns develop with experience in text reading. 'Top-down' lexical and context effects were found in processing perceptually-degraded stimuli, and by adult beginners who used informed 'guessing' from context quite consciously to recognize words whenever possible. Moreover, younger braille readers spent more time on initial letters of longer words, suggesting that they were trying to construe meaning from initial letters as soon as possible, though this was the case for only about half the number of words sampled. Competent readers did so much less. But compatible context facilitated the recognition of perceptually degraded words also by proficient braillists.

The findings thus showed no invariable pay-off between reading proficiency and the use of context. Better readers were simply more successful with such strategies, and needed them less. The hypothesis that context effects are often a by-product of processes which are designed primarily to resolve lexical or perceptual ambiguity (Norris, 1986) was supported by a number of results, in contrast to the notion (Kusajima, 1974) that semantic context facilitates fast rather than slow reading. At the same time, and interpreted differently, the Kusajima hypothesis was supported by findings which showed that competent readers used predictions about the next word, based on gist and the use of syntactic markers (Chapter

5). Competent readers sometimes also scanned predictable endings of words faster. It is a moot point whether that counts as 'guessing', or merely indicates that less redundancy is needed with experience. Further evidence for cognitive modulation of perceptual intake processes was also found in the results on reading for meaning compared with letter search by competent readers. The conclusion must be that 'top-down' effects are not all of the same kind.

Interestingly enough, a similar point applies to the perception of tactual features. It is often tacitly assumed that tactual perception is based on invariant physical features. Poor acuity limits reading speed and constrains letter-by-letter processing, but does not enter into interactions beyond that. In fact, the basis of tactual perception was not invariant. Tactual perception based on dot density disparities, shape features, and on temporally extended dynamic patterns as suggested by Grunewald (1966), are not mutually exclusive descriptions. Both occur, but in different task conditions. The findings make sense by assuming progressive perceptual organizations that are cognitively modulated by the verbal and spatial functions of the reading task.

Taken together, therefore, the findings show that processing tactual, phonological, lexical and semantic/syntactic information in braille reading follows a much less tidy course than would be predicted by a notion of invariant sequential progression in any single direction. The findings, perhaps rather disconcertingly, suggest that almost all the phenomena that have been proposed as central to reading by different braille theories are in fact found. The point is that the demands of the task, and the information it provides must be included in theoretical descriptions of how reading takes place.

We do not yet know by any means how all the connections work. But the findings suggest that some of the combinations and the conditions in which they occur can be specified. These are detailed next, together with some of the predictions that follow from the hypotheses about the functional conditions.

2 INTERRELATIONS BETWEEN HAPTIC AND VERBAL PROCESSING IN ACQUISITION

The primary task in braille learning by young beginners is to associate the sounds of language with the feels of braille patterns. The aim of the learning process is to understand the gist of written texts. This section summarizes the evidence on how this comes about, and the processes and connections that need to be included in an adequate description of braille learning.

Taking the evidence on perceptual processes first, the perception of braille patterns seems to develop progressively from detecting dot density disparities to coding organized shape features on the one hand, and temporally extended dot–gap density (shear) patterns, on the other. Scanning sequences of characters or lines of text became spatially organized with experience and training by reference to body-centred frames, and projected and coordinated with the spatial outlay of scripts. With experience there was a progressive streamlining of movement scanning patterns on the one hand, but also a progressive differentiation of the spatial place-keeping and verbal decoding functions of the hands in scanning, on the other. Movements became systematic for line-keeping, place-keeping and regressions. The findings thus suggest that, without prior knowledge, perceiving small raised dot patterns as shapes is a constructive process. The 'ingredients' depend on the shear pattern that is encountered by the forefinger pad in moving laterally across the dot density patterns. A different type of movement produces global shape patterns. The important cues are from joint movements that provide reference anchors for organizing the dots in the patterns spatially. The construction involves cognitive processes from the start, and is also finally governed by the demands of the reading task.

But though the findings were consistent with the reference hypothesis, they could not be explained solely by the progressive spatial organization of scanning movements. The findings also implied that the perception of individual braille patterns was facilitated initially by associated verbal and movement output strategies. New letter sounds were associated more easily with finger combinations in writing via known number sequences, and these were used to mediate systematic scanning of the single tactual patterns (Chapters 2, 6 and 7). Adequate short-term memory for letter sequences depended on immediate phonological recoding. Large recall spans were associated with phonological recoding and depended on fast naming (Chapter 4). Once phonemic coding was established, word recognition was mediated by speech-based sequential decoding by beginning readers. Phonological and letter length effects differed with task difficulty, task demands, and with the semantic structure of the materials. Word familiarity also played a part in letter-by-letter processing, shown by what has been called 'guessing' from initial letters.

Semantic factors in construing gist also influenced the spatial organization of scanning movements. The effect was thought to be due largely to feedback from the detection of semantic errors which triggered repair functions. Failures to make sense of the text also elicited the attention of subjects to using the two hands to provide references cues for each other. Familiarity had large effects on word recognition, and on perception. Patterns that beginners find it almost impossible to identify are recognized easily with extended practice. Acuity in this sense is thus a highly relative term. But more surprising, the verbal task also determines scanning movements and the perceptual information that is picked up. Thus the fact that in fluent reading, different perceptual information is picked up for different reading tasks was not merely a question of improved scanning with greater familiarity, but was directly associated with the verbal task.

These findings suggest that convergent inputs from phonological, semantic and lexical processes affect the organization of hand-movements. In turn, the systematic spatial organization of hand-movements is necessary for the pick-up of perceptual information that is needed for decoding the verbal information in letter and word recognition and in construing gist quickly.

Three further points are relevant to the specification of interrelations between processes. The first two are about the distinctions that are needed for phonological processes, and the distinctions within semantic effects. The third concerns the learning and functioning of orthographic rules and conventions of contracted forms as well as of English spelling.

Phonological coding must be regarded as a portmanteau term for different forms of coding that involve speech sounds. They are related, but do not all have the same patterns of connection with the processes that govern the perceptual pick-up of tactual features, and do not exhibit the same time course of learning and experience. Phonemic coding at input, sub-lexical morphemic/phonic segmentation in decoding, coding words as sounds, 'inner speech' in construing gist, and the intonation and prosody of continuous speech in oral reading call on different combinations of processes. The point is that not all phonological effects seem to be subject to precisely the same developmental or time-course. We need far more information about this. But the present findings are relevant to some of the conditions that differentiate these forms of coding, and are summarized in the remainder of this section.

The sounds children hear and produce when they first learn the sounds of letters are 'all-purpose' sounds. They are not actually precisely the same sounds that a child hears in all word contexts. Detecting and producing such alphabetically defined phonemes in association with the pick-up of new tactual information is an integral part of the initial stages in learning to read braille for young readers. Phoneme detection and production have to be learned or trained in young readers. The fact that the same letter sounds different when it occurs in a different word context is something the child has to learn in addition. Blending constituent sounds into word sounds is important initially because the speech sound that is produced for consonants often ends in an additional vowel which has to be suppressed in linking the letters so that the reconstituted sound can be recognized as a familiar word. Phonemic segmentation, recoding and blending thus have to be learned in terms of speech output for decoding regular words. What is clear is that the association of heard letter sounds, speech output and character recognition evidently becomes so close that silent reading was impossible for some beginners under articulatory suppression (Chapter 4). Phoneme detection is learned. But input coding of heard sounds tends to fade relatively quickly without support from speech output or articulation. Speech based phonological coding seems to form the initial basis for the association between the sounds of phonemes and the felt dot density pattern. Such decoding requires longer first-pass scanning for longer words. In fluent reading, speech-based assembled phonology which involves phoneme coding and blending is either greatly attenuated or drops out. It is certainly no longer discernible in normal reading by proficient braillists. Whether such phonemic recoding simply drops out of the processing sequence with practice, or is merely attenuated but recurs in special conditions, or whether the special conditions reactivate or produce such coding is part of the much larger question about the automation of any action sequence with practice (Section 3).

The model here predicts that strategies, once learned, remain available in proportion to their age of acquisition and the recency with which they have been reactivated. Even letter-by-letter processing returns when experienced braillists – and probably fluent print readers also – encounter long words for which they have no long-standing orthographic–phonological associations. However, letter-to-sound connections are not necessarily activated fully or contribute as much in reading familiar words or orthographically and phonologically familiar segments (Chapter 6).

Coding familiar whole words phonologically is a much more habitual skill for young blind children than coding phonemes or letter sounds. Coding words by sound, and phonological recoding of items in memory, is not a taught procedure. Phonological recoding strategies of that kind seem to arise spontaneously. They are associated with fast naming and familiarity. The preference for relying on word sounds rather than on meaning shown by beginners and by some retarded braille readers is most simply explained in terms of compensatory effects. When one pattern of connection is weak, more strongly connected patterns get activated first, or faster. Such effects seem to be cumulative. In terms of connectionist assumptions, the networks that serve phonological coding of words are acquired early, and are therefore activated easily when there is a failure of other parts of the system. Phonological recoding seems to be used specifically, even by proficient readers, to sustain memory when processing or recall is difficult. Phonological coding skills increase rather than decrease with age and efficiency, as shown by increased memory spans. But proficient readers need to use such strategies less because they encounter fewer difficulties.

The notion of phonological coding as continuous inner speech differs both from phonemic recoding in assembled phonology, and also from phonological recoding to remember and/or integrate word meanings. Oral reading requires not only phonological recoding, but also output planning to execute speech gestures. If inner or covert speech is a necessary part of silent reading it should not differ from overt speech output. Beginning and slow readers do indeed show no difference in speed or comprehension between oral and silent reading, although even for beginning readers the effects of word length in syllables was only marginal in silent reading.

In terms of network connections it is possible to explain the different forms of phonological coding without having to assume either that they belong to quite different routes to meaning, nor that they are identical. One solution is to assume that different forms of coding by sound have some, but not all patterns of connections in common. In principle, they can, therefore be activated by different task conditions. There was no evidence, for instance, for phonemic recoding by fluent readers. But such coding would be predicted even for fluent readers for unknown or difficult long words for which there are no network connections of meaning to orthographic or phonological codes that could be activated by the incoming patterns. That does not require the assumption that all silent reading necessarily depends on obligatory phonological recoding prior to lexical access.

Fluent readers showed no effects of word length in syllables at all in silent reading. Moreover, their silent reading was faster, and their comprehension was as accurate or better than in oral reading. The fact that word length in letters again becomes a significant effect in fluent silent reading (Chapter 4) was better explained by fast, possibly automatic pick-up of lateral shear pattern information in first-pass lateral scanning, than by letter-by-letter phonemic recoding. The description again makes use of the notion of 'streamlining' of connections between different processes with experience. Lateral scanning became increasingly smooth and regular as well as faster, suggesting a progressive 'automization' of the network organization with learning and experience.

If we now turn to word meaning and contextual, semantic/syntactic processes, these did not always relate in the same way either to the pick-up of tactual inputs, or to proficiency levels, or to phonological strategies. The word superiority effect is a case in point. It occurred at all levels of proficiency. But for young readers it was significant only for three-letter words. The effect thus depended significantly on word length and familiarity, and on reading proficiency. As suggested by Morton (1969, 1979) the familiarity of words may facilitate word recognition by lowering the 'threshold' of activation. In terms of the metaphor here, repeated exposure facilitates activation of the connecting paths. For the younger children only familiar three-letter words may have reached a level of activation that produced early recognition. However, at least two other factors need to be taken into account. The tendency for young beginners to 'guess' the meaning of words as early as possible from initial letters has been mentioned. Such a strategy may benefit familiar short words, since up to three items can be coded tactually in memory (Chapter 4). The meaning of three-letter words is thus assumed to be available earlier than that of words that require sequential phonological recoding. The hypothesis that requires testing is that the combination of tactual, phonological and lexical familiarity produces a rise in activation levels, so that the combination of the associated sources and task demands activates early search for meaning in conjunction with phonemic recoding. But the prediction requires specific experimental test also with single word contractions.

Semantic context effects were of at least two different kinds. The findings supported the notion that readers compensate for perceptual difficulties by using meaning and gist, and that less competent readers compensate for their inexperience in the same way. The effects on the perceptual pick-up of such 'top-down' effects can be specified quite precisely in individual cases. One obvious mechanism by which interrogation of prior or subsequent context can facilitate the perceptual pick-up is by restricting the number of possible alternatives. Consider the case when the previous word was an article so that a noun was to be expected, the prior context included a reference to animals and suggested moreover that the animal was likely to be familiar, and scanning the degraded word showed that the perceptually degraded word was long. That information excluded all animals with short names. Even the presence of a fragmentary tactual feature of the letters or 'e' or 'l' makes it possible in that case to generate a restricted number of alternatives which can be checked out as being more or less probable (e.g. Becker and Killion, 1977). Such 'epigraphic' detection clearly went on (Chapter 5), and can be explained by compensating for perceptual or lexical difficulties (Norris, 1986; Stanovich, 1981). But that is not the whole story. Proficient adult braillists are less adversely affected by poor legibility than are slow readers. But like experienced epigraphists, they are also more likely to solve the problem. Proficient braillists have more efficient tactual scanning strategies, more experience of the tactual input, and can detect small tactual differences that elude the beginner, but they also have more lexical and orthographic knowledge and greater facilities in using phonological strategies than young beginning readers. The influence goes in both directions.

The point is that semantic effects were not confined to compensatory strategies. Good readers use lexical, contextual and perceptual cues also predictively in fast reading. That was evident from mistakes in oral reading which are very quickly remedied and checked out by regressions, often by a single, very brief touch of a single letter. Predictions also occur in slow braille reading, but are not confined to braille. On the contrary, errors due to unfulfilled semantic/syntactic predictions occur also in fast print reading (Just and Carpenter, 1987). In braille, the predictions need to based additionally on knowledge of the contracted tactual form that should be encountered if the next word is predicted to be a plural noun.

The fact that English braille contains mandatory contractions has received far too little study as yet. Potentially, such forms are particularly interesting clues to reading processes. Contractions, even more than the irregularities in English orthography, limit the potential usefulness of strategies based strictly on graphemic–phonemic decomposition. Although young children are usually taught to decode regular words first, learning single character contractions for whole words means learning that sound–touch pattern associations do not all require phoneme detection and letter recoding. We do not yet know what effect whole word contractions have, except that they were easier than the same contractions as used within words.

The model explains this by assuming that the meanings and sounds of single-character contracted words are usually already very familiar to children. Consequently only the tactual pattern has to be coded sufficiently well to be associated with the known word meaning and sound. By contrast, the rules for using contractions within words have to be taught quite explicitly. Some rules are cognitively or morphemically more transparent than others. As for irregular and exception words, their recognition depends largely, though not solely, on the frequency with which the reader is exposed to them. But frequency of exposure to the actual contraction is not enough. Contractions also have to be experienced tactually as constituents of other words (Chapter 6). The prediction from the assumptions about how these effects combine includes the relative familiarity with the contractions and relative familiarity with the mandatory rules as major factors.

Again, we are confronted with the problem how rules that are learned explicitly are employed apparently 'automatically' in fluent reading. Single character contractions, either with or without one to three pre-posed dots, range over a whole gamut of syntactic forms (Daniels, 1996). They include function words (e.g. THE AND FOR FROM), verbs (e.g. CAN DO GO LIKE WILL), nouns that cannot be spelt phonetically when uncontracted (e.g. KNOWLEDGE PEOPLE MOTHER FATHER), and grammatical morphemes (e.g. ING ED ER). But although they are not predictable by grammatical form overall, proficient readers do spend less time on contracted grammatical morphemes (e.g. ED) when these can be predicted from the context and the word form (i.e. verb in the past tense). The whole question of coding whole word contractions, and the familiarity of contraction rules needs a good deal of further study. The predictions here again include interactions between the absolute familiarity of contractions as words and within words, and with the extent to which the lateral shear patterns can be predicted from a given context.

The fact that contractions within words take longer to process than the same contractions standing alone as words (Chapter 6) needs to be investigated further in relation to other factors, such as the retrieval of rules that have not yet become automatic, the greater clarity of tactual patterns when flanked by spaces, or to the decomposition and blending of the sounds of the constituent contractions with the remaining letter sounds into word sound and meaning, either singly or in combinations. The fact that word frequency as well as the frequency of contractions within words affected recognition latencies also needs to be tested in relation to the hypothesis that spelling, sound and meaning are closely associated connections, but that the degree of activation depends on a combination of the age of the connections and the recency with which they have been activated.

The learning course of former fluent print readers differs. They do not need to learn to detect alphabetically-defined phonemes in addition to learning to scan braille patterns systematically. But the present model implies that habitual associations of phonemes with print letter shapes would interfere with learning new shapes for known letter sounds. We have no evidence on that as yet, and it requires testing.

Even competent braillists find it difficult to recognize low frequency words that also contain low frequency contractions. In these cases readers often to resort to character-by-character decoding, and this becomes difficult if the words require an additional vowel change in the contracted syllable, even though that does not affect syllable boundaries in the host word. Good knowledge of the relevant contraction rule is essential in these cases. The evidence from experienced readers and former print readers suggested that the latter process depends very largely on long-term habitual phonological–orthographic habits (Chapter 6). Here again, the model predicts that the 'age' of phonological–orthographic habits, and the familiarity of graphemic-to-phonological connections determine whether contractions within words facilitate or interfere with processing. That also requires specific further testing.

The present findings show the complicated processing that competent braillists accomplish in decoding contractions that violate syllable boundaries when the contracted word or syllable within the host word is familiar. That, and the relative difficulty of former fluent print readers, strongly suggest that habitual orthographic–phonological connections influence processing in reading for meaning. A great deal more work is needed in order to specify the contribution of these factors to the recognition of contractions in braille reading. The findings raise practical questions (Chapter 8), but also address issues that potentially have wider implications for understanding the relation between lexical and sub-lexical processes and orthographic knowledge in fast processing.

Clearly, fluent fast reading cannot depend on deliberate 'epigraphic' detective work in which the epigraphist calls on all aspects of available knowledge of the spoken language and the conventions by which these are translated into the physical symbols that can be detected. Even if the speeds of fluent braillists (150–200 wpm) are less than for fast print readers, some of the processes must have become more or less automatic.

The constituents and connections that are needed in a working model of learning braille are listed below, together with some assumptions and predictions about their relative effects in acquisition, and the chances of some connections 'dropping out' or becoming attenuated in fluent reading.

3 INGREDIENTS FOR A WORKING MODEL OF BRAILLE READING

To answer the developmental question, it is necessary first of all to specify the initial state of the networks. A 'tabula rasa' is not a reasonable supposition even for neonates, let alone for five- to six-year-olds before the start of braille learning. There is no need to do so. It can be assumed that the cognitive potential of blind children who have no other handicaps is the same, on average, as for their sighted peers. It is also possible to specify an approximate starting level in language skills for average five- to six-year-old blind children who are not otherwise deprived. They can be expected to have a working knowledge of the major syntactic categories and connectives, and to understand and to produce syntactically-correct sentences. Estimates of a vocabulary of about twelve thousand to fifteen thousand words have been suggested. Another important developmental ingredient is the immediate memory span (Chapters 4 and 7), which is certainly not less than for sighted children. The rate of identifying heard words, as well as the rate of speech output, is slower for younger than for older children. Speech-rate is connected with span size. But familiarity with the items, speed of retrieving their names or name-sounds from longer-term memory, and the link between phonological input and speech-output are at least as important in the difference of span-size with age (e.g. Henry and Millar, 1991, 1993; Millar, 1975 b). The limits on the number of items that can be maintained actively in temporary memory make it more difficult for younger children to be able to cope with more than one task at a time. To take account of these factors in a connectionist model of braille learning, differential weightings would be needed for at least the following connections before the start of learning:

1 A relatively small but useful, mainly high frequency vocabulary in which heard sound and meaning are highly associated, and are linked also to speech production.

2. Working knowledge of the major syntactic categories and connectives, linked to word and semantic knowledge. They are assumed to be activated in understanding heard speech, and in producing syntactically correct and meaningful sentences, including some compound constructions.

3 Skilled detection of the sounds of familiar words in the stream of heard speech. Some skill in detecting syllables and rhymes in words, and in producing them in play.

4 Little or no skill, before attention is drawn to it, in detecting alphabetically defined phonemes. The connections between these and previously familiar word meanings and sounds they hear and pronounce are assumed to be weak or absent.

5 Little or no knowledge, prior to learning, of the orthographic conventions and regularities that connect the pick-up of haptic information

with the sounds of language. That also applies to the rules for contractions.

6 An immediate memory span of slightly above four, but below five, familiar serial items (e.g. digits), linked to longer-term memory and speech output systems. Spans of less than two serial items are assumed for tactually coded dot density features that cannot be named. Some, but relatively weak, links between touch and movement inputs are assumed for these.

7 Good hand coordination for movements within personal space, but unsystematic use of the hands for exploration, place-keeping and lateral scanning.

8 Detection of gross dot density disparities in small braille patterns by relatively unsystematic repetitive local scanning.

We also have to assume that the language, memory and haptic skills, and the connections between them, are constantly expanding and changing the processes which enter into braille acquisition, and are also increased or fine-tuned by learning to read braille. The initial weights attached to each of these would thus change constantly in response to the patterned inputs specific to braille learning.

I list below some of the skills and knowledge which young blind children lack prior to learning braille, but which have to be acquired. The list is not exhaustive and does not necessarily represent the order of acquisition. But it gives some idea of the patterns of inputs that are needed for the system to learn, and the connections these are expected to activate. In a computational model which could simulate the relation between input- and output-patterns, these inputs would have to be specified and weighted in relation to the existing patterns in the system. I have assumed a starting level of proficiency similar to the letter-by-letter reading shown by readers whom I have often called 'beginners' for convenience, but who were sufficiently skilled to be able to read continuous texts containing familiar words and contractions, at a reading rate from 10 to 30 wpm. The input patterns that would have to be 'fed' into simulated networks with differential weightings are as follows:

1 Segmenting familiar heard and spoken words into alphabetically defined phonemic sounds and connecting these with felt (new) dot density disparities in raised dot patterns;

2 Associating the same felt character with the sound and meaning of familiar whole words if, and only if, the pattern is flanked by blank spaces for single character contractions;

3 Decoding regular words sequentially and blending phonemic sounds to resemble word sounds that are associated with word familiarity tags and meaning;

4 Developing systematic line-keeping movements, using cues from hand-positions relative to kinaesthetic frame cues from body-posture, and

from tactual and movement inputs from scanning raised-dot textures of the scripts, and relating these to construing the meaning of words and gist;

5 Developing systematically-anchored place-keeping movements, involving connections between hand-movements, kinaesthetic frame cues, and verbal feedback in relation to an expanding vocabulary and semantic skills;

6 Connections between sound, meaning, orthographic knowledge, thematic knowledge and means of construing gist, and differentiating the functions of scanning movements by the two hands;

7 Exposure to orthographic and contraction rules through writing (using a combination of finger movements) and in reading; continued exposure to different patterns of activation from this source should produce further convergence in the connections that link the subsidiary (phonological–orthographic–lexical) network systems;

8 Connecting language systems in prose reading to active lateral scanning and producing habitual shear pattern activations on the fingerpad relative to the external layout, for frequently scanned words;

9 Learning patterns for some punctuation marks that are associated with the prosody of connected speech output, rather than with phonemes or words;

10 Differentiating the hands by assigning alternating verbal and spatial functions;

11 Integrating word meanings into prior context and using phonological–orthographic and contextual knowledge predictively;

12 Organizing scanning movements in response to task demands, prior to reading, to allocate attention to inferences and cognitive elaboration.

The fact that fewer skills of any kind are fast and automatic for young children means that learning requires maximum effort or attention for almost all the subsidiary skills that are needed for reading braille. The model assumes that the combination of immaturity and lack of knowledge of all kinds produces conditions resembling informational uncertainty. Two predictions follow. Young children are more likely to be disturbed by having to do, or to think of, more than one thing at a time, than older children. They will also need a great deal of redundancy in information for adequate processing. The predictions imply that it will take young children longer to learn the necessary association between the haptic and language processes. At the same time, the model predicts that the connections would also become functional or automatic earlier than learning the subsidiary organizations separately first.

The longer the connections are established, and continue to be reactivated, the more easily they are reactivated, and the more resistant they are to interference. Similar predictions, therefore, follow about the association of lateral scanning with reading for meaning. Learning two skills in conjunction with each other from the start would slow acquisition, but would facilitate the automation of the combined skill in later decoding tests. In terms of the dual task paradigm (Chapter 7), therefore, the question is whether learning to detect and say phonemes at the same time as learning to organize dot density disparities interfere with each other. The developmental assumptions of the model predict that learning the two forms of organization in association is slower and/or requires more trials, but that the association once learned also provides informational redundancy.

Another implication that has yet to be tested is that connecting the sound and pattern of a new letter is easier if both are associated at the same time with a familiar word. A character that represents a word as well as a letter should, therefore, be easier to remember if both are learned at the same time ('g' for GO; 'd' for DO). But these predictions need to be tested specifically (Chapter 8).

By contrast, adults who were previously fluent print readers should have no problems with phonemic segmentation, with English orthography, or with semantic, word, or world knowledge. Older adults may require longer training than young adults (Chapter 7). But the adults in the present studies were quite able to detect differences between isolated braille patterns, even if such detection was relatively slow. Apart from possible higher discrimination thresholds that can be off-set by sufficient practice (Chapter 7), there were two main differences between these readers and young braillists with similar reading rates. These were both connected with the difference in previous experience. One has to do with the very fact that former fluent print readers are accustomed to thinking of letters in terms of outline shape. Since braille patterns are inherently confusing (non-redundant), careful identification of shapes will be more useful for the detection of single letters than for continuous reading, though the faster new braillists attained a useful attenuated zigzag scan (Chapters 3 and 7). More important perhaps are the habitual associations between constituent language and orthographic–phonological habits by former print readers. The young readers were still developing habitual language–haptic/spatial connections, while former print readers also have to unlearn some habitual connections.

In terms of the network metaphor, interference from the activation of well-established connection patterns would be expected. If competent print readers depend on letter–sound associations in silent reading, having to substitute a new perceptual input should thus be more difficult than learning to associate new sounds with new patterns for them. Such predictions, too, require further study, especially with contracted forms. Modelling braille acquisition by former print readers, therefore, requires a different distribution of initial weights assigned to existing connections than for young beginners.

The difference between fluent braille and letter-by-letter reading cannot be described in terms of a single factor either. The progressive facility of processing that is evident in fast braille seems to apply to all the learned associations between different language and haptic processing skills. In terms of the proposed model, all network connections become habitual and streamlined with sufficient exposure to reactivation. Thus, in fluent reading of easy, clear, normally contracted texts, the scanning patterns and time-relations showed a smooth, relatively even uptake of verbal and spatial information from lateral scanning. There was rapid, skilled alternation of the hands for the verbal and spatial aspects of the text, respectively, in progressing to the next line. Competent readers scanned the spatial layout rapidly with both hands prior to starting to read, and had a good idea of the spatial layout of the text. They apparently also tagged or monitored the spatial location of significant portions of text, because they did not need to search through every previous word to find prior disambiguating texts when they come upon a perceptual or lexical difficulty. At the same time, decoding the verbal information progressed smoothly. Scanning became faster further down into connected easy text than at the start of silent reading, showing semantic influences on scanning speeds. Fast readers did not guess words from initial letters, although easily predicted morphemes at the end of words sometimes, though not invariably, took less (e.g. about 20 ms) time than other characters. The evidence suggests that fast readers pick up familiar words in context from rapid, lightly touched lateral shear patterns, suggesting temporal/spatial patterning of familiar words and forward predictions from context.

The range of skills on which competent readers can call when necessary was shown when there were difficulties. Perceptually degraded words elicited phonological, lexical, semantic and orthographic as well as perceptual skills by fluent readers, and these were interleaved with each other to construe the meaning of degraded words. Low frequency words that also contained infrequent contractions took longer and produced regressions, regardless of whether these violated syllable boundaries, provided they followed braille rules. Regressions, other than for perceptually degraded words, tended to be to prior, semantically relevant context. Unknown long names which could not be predicted from the context produced regressions which were similar to regressions over perceptually degraded words, and reduced reading speeds even by proficient readers to letter-by-letter assembled recoding strategies. Oral reading by competent readers is slower than silent reading. Oral reading seems to involve the planning as well as the execution of the prosodic patterns that express the meaning of the gist orally. The voice onset for a word lags behind the word currently being scanned by about three to four words in easy text.

The findings suggest that the question, which of the several haptic, phonological, semantic and orthographic factors 'win out' or become automatic with fluency, is probably misguided, at least for braille. The issue whether phonological recoding is automatically activated in silent reading cannot be answered by a simple assertion or denial. The prevalence and

time-course of grapheme–phoneme recoding depended on levels of proficiency, but also on word frequency. Recoding single-character contractions
into word sounds occurred in judging sentences that contained sound/sense
ambiguities. Competent readers showed no evidence of inner speech in
silent reading of easy texts from articulatory suppression, nor any effect
of syllable length for words that did not need to be remembered in text
comprehension. Similarly, contractions that violated syllable boundaries
had no more effect on experienced braillists than contractions that were
compatible with syllable boundaries, while word recognition by former
print readers was disrupted by contracted forms that were incompatible
with previous orthographic–phonological habits. The differences between
silent reading of easy and difficult texts by fluent braillists thus suggest
the close convergence and relative automation of all the subsidiary skills.
Silent fast reading implicitly uses predictions based on inferences from
the context, from syntactic markers, and from orthographic knowledge
and knowledge of contraction rules that were initially learned as explicit
rules. But these seem to become habitual associates of inputs from lateral
scanning. Reading for meaning makes use of inferences from previous
text to predict the type of information that can be expected. But with
difficult texts, speech-based phonological coding was evident under articulatory suppression also by competent readers. Perceptual difficulties elicit
recourse to inferences from the semantic context and from syntactic
markers in conjunction with perceptual clues. Unknown names that have
no semantic associates seem to reactivate letter-by-letter processes and
phonological and orthographic links. Such activation is unnecessary in
silent reading of easy text in which all connections have become quasi-
automatic and elicit streamlined procedures, including the smooth scanning and flexible use of the hands for different aspects of reading.

In terms of the proposed working model, changes in processing with increased ability can be explained without having to assume either that some
processes are always obligatory, or that some effects simply 'drop out' with
practice. The model assumes that the extent to which a learned connection is activated depends on the frequency and recency with which the connection has been activated in the past, and the strength of the connection
with the incoming pattern of activation. Precisely what connections 'drop
out', or are attenuated, in the process of streamlining or automation with
practice thus depends on the familiarity of the relevant connections as well
as on their relevance to a current task. For instance, fluent young braillists
do not mentally rehearse dot numbers of tactual patterns when reading or
writing braille, although they did so as beginners. Contraction rules that
initially have to be learned explicitly are used without conscious effort by
fluent braillists. But the streamlined pick-up of tactual information from
lateral scanning is disrupted when difficulties are encountered, just as in
driving a new car, failure for the hand to make its accustomed contact with
the gear lever elicits attention to a movement that had become habitual.

I am therefore assuming that interrelated network systems learn by increments from input patterns that are distributed over a relatively large network of connections, and that these become distributed even more widely with practice. More connections are activated with practice, because each input pattern differs from the preceding patterns by slight changes in context, and because of the changes effected by the previous inputs. Moreover, more repetitions with slight variations and linkages with existing connections are needed at the beginning of learning than towards the end of learning.

The model includes innately biased or dedicated connections in the networks. The frequency of exposure to particular input patterns is, therefore, expected to have major effects on processing in two directions. It alters the level of activation of previously activated connections. But it also activates other linkages in proportion to the difference in the specific experience of the particular event. Seidenberg and McClelland (1989), for instance, consider that word frequency effects may interact with differences in the frequency of exposure to the sound–spelling associations of regular versus irregular words. The differences in exposure interact further with levels of proficiency of readers, suggesting that fast readers treat more items as frequent or familiar. In principle, there is every reason to expect similar effects to occur in braille. The same assumption can apply to the availability of learned associations between, for instance, frequently encountered temporal shear patterns, speech sounds and their syntactic and semantic functions in a sentence. Weights would have to be assigned not only to the degree of longer-term exposure, but also to the recency of activation. For instance, encountering the contraction for the definite article (THE) repeatedly at the beginning of every line reduced processing time by a bright young student who had learned braille for a year to a much faster rate (0.64 s) for that contraction than would be expected from her normal reading speed (30 wpm). But the reduction in speed applied mainly to the article at the beginning of lines, and occurred much less for the same contraction in other contexts within the same script, suggesting that the specific location of the contractions, as well as the repetition of the graphemic–orthographic–phonological conjunction had been registered.

In principle, all the learned connections can become 'automatic' with practice. But equally, they are activated by the appropriate material and tasks. Which of the subsidiary skills in a given reading task is the more important or 'wins out' can therefore be specified by local conditions of legibility, word frequency and the simplicity of text construction, as well as by the level of proficiency in the subsidiary skills and state of the reader.

The criteria for determining when processing requires attention or conscious effort are controversial and vary with the type of task (Ryan, 1983; Schneider and Shiffrin, 1977; Shiffrin and Schneider, 1977). Theories of attention which are couched in what are sometimes called 'mentalistic' terms have used a variety of analogies. William James (1890) talked about the 'stream of consciousness'. Analogies with sudden illumination by a searchlight have been proposed. Attention has been compared to the intentional, deliberate control by a conscious pilot, as distinct from performance 'on automatic pilot'. However, it cannot be assumed that a single mechanism underlies all forms of 'attention'. For our purposes, automaticity and attentional demands in reading (La Berge, 1983; La Berge and Samuels, 1974) are best regarded as extreme ends of continuous changes in processing during the acquisition and performance of a complex skill. It is assumed that performance demands less monitoring with increased skill. More attention, or effort, or 'limited capacity' can, therefore, be devoted to other matters. Proficient drivers can hold an interesting conversation while driving. They are likely to stop talking when a squirrel suddenly dashes across the road.

As mentioned earlier, the main criticisms of connectionist (PDP) models have centred on the assumption that learning is described in terms of incremental effects of repeated input patterns. The more frequently the interrelated network is exposed to a given pattern of excitation, the stronger the effect will be. The question is, therefore, how these purely associationist assumptions can cope with such behavioural facts as learning in a single trial, making inferences on the basis of disparate pieces of information, recognizing similarities between inputs, learning and using rules, making conscious efforts, attending selectively to some aspect of the information rather than to all of them, and the fact that processing can vary due to task effects.

An interesting solution to one aspect of attention has been proposed by Whittlesea (1989) who implemented findings on attentional selectivity and the variability of processing due to task and context effects in a PDP model. The important difference is that the model replaces the usual assumption that learning proceeds by abstracting a common property of inputs, by the assumption that human sensitivity to the general structure of information depends on preserving particular experiences. Whittlesea claims that humans do not process individual components or summarize commonalities automatically. Tasks that operationally require analytic processing focus attention on components, while tasks demanding integral processing store and elicit memory for configurational information about the whole event. The only permanent impact of a stimulus is that the pattern of interconnectivity is altered. This changes the way the system will respond to another stimulus. Subjects encode stimuli as relatively integral units. The extent to which any or all parts of the network connections are activated depends on the composition of the next stimulus event.

The idea that particular experiences of events are encoded in a distributed form across an entire processing network, allows variable integration of processing. The specific assumptions of the model are implemented in a relatively simple task (Whittlesea, 1989; Whittlesea and Brooks, 1988), and do not include the initial and developmental biasing conditions which are needed in a realistic model of braille acquisition by young children. Nevertheless, the suggestion that coding particular experiences or events integrally (Whittlesea, 1989) accounts for context effects, selectivity of attention, and variability in processing with task conditions, fits the present data particularly well.

An important point about terms such as 'attention' is that the behaviours that they name can be defined by a number of operational criteria which are not necessarily co-extensive with each other, but are testable. One important criterion for 'automaticity' involves dual task performance. Processing is defined as automatic or as not requiring attention, if performance on that task is disturbed minimally, or not at all, by simultaneous performance on a second task, compared with performing either task alone. It is, therefore, possible to ask, for instance, whether the numbering method beginning braillists use becomes 'automatic' in the sense that it can be activated if necessary, or whether some strategies become redundant in skilled reading, and may not be activated at all.

Nevertheless, it will be obvious to the reader that in describing the convergent connections that a model of braille needs to incorporate, I have mainly used expressions such as 'attention to rules', the use of 'deliberate strategies' versus automatic processing, and the like. That also applies importantly to the processes involved in the integration of information into gist, and the constructive and predictive semantic/syntactic inferences that are implied by the findings (Chapter 5). The point is that the so-called mentalistic terms name behaviours than can be operationally defined and tested. Connectionist models usually include what are termed 'hidden units' in their systems. These are parts of the network that lie between input and outputs of the system and need to be assigned values for computational simulations to work. It is not clear as yet how far such assumptions can account for attentional, monitoring and inferential behaviours. I have assumed that, in principle, network models can re-describe these. But the general metaphor of convergent processing in active interrelated networks seems to account for the present findings better than traditional notions of invariant processing stages which exclude the development of perceptual organization which, in touch, is an integral part of learning to read.

4 CONCLUSIONS

The two questions asked at the beginning were how reading by touch is acquired, and how fluent braille reading takes place.

I have argued that the findings on braille are best described by the general metaphor of interrelated networks of active processes that converge in a variety of combinations. The model can account for the fact that pattern perception by touch is a constructive process which depends on the convergence of several inputs. It includes cognitive structuring and the effect of the verbal task on the perceptual pick-up, but also the perceptual support of verbal information by the fast and flexible use of the hands to sample information from different domains in parallel. For beginners, the connections of primary importance are those within and between the networks that are more specialized for processing inputs from touch and movement, on the one hand, and networks mainly specialized for processing language. Perception of braille patterns requires the progressive organization of inputs from touch and scanning movements at the same time as the patterns have to be associated with new (letter) sounds and speech outputs in the language. Contraction rules add further variability to the orthographic conventions and exceptions that link haptic perception and language processes.

The importance of familiarity, practice and experience was evident in tactual discrimination, the use of contractions and oral spelling, and in effects of long-term graphemic–orthographic–phonological habits shown by effects of auditory and tactual priming on words containing contractions. Similar conclusions were reached in considering individual differences between older experienced and new braillists.

An ideal connectionist model of braille learning and reading would provide computational implementations that specify the relative strengths of all incoming and existing patterns of connections to predict how they affect each other during the process of acquisition and in competent reading. I am very far from having the requisite evidence that could produce precise weightings for the connections that I have described. But I have given some indication of the relative strength to which they are likely to be activated during development. A learning rule is needed that works best with the maximum of redundant information early in learning, while minimal inputs activate existing connections with experience.

The working model proposes a series of hypotheses which explain the present findings, make predictions that need to be tested in the field and also raise further questions which will, I hope, be taken up by more people who are intrigued by the relation between language and touch.

References

Adams, J.A., Bodis-Wollner, I., Enoch, J.M., Jeannerod, M. and Mitchell, D.E. (1990). Normal and abnormal mechanisms of vision: Visual disorders and visual deprivation. In L. Spillmann and J.S. Werner (eds) *Visual Perception : The Neurophysiological Foundations*. New York: Academic Press.

Adams, M.A. (1981). What good is orthographic redundancy? In O.J.L. Zeng and H. Singer (eds) *Perception of Print: Reading Research in Experimental Psychology*. Hillsdale, N.J.: Lawrence Erlbaum.

Adams, M.J. (1979). Models of word recognition. *Cognitive Psychology, 11*, 133–176.

Allport, D.A. (1979). Word recognition in reading (Tutorial paper). In P.A. Kolers, M.E. Wrolstad and H. Bouma (eds) *Processing of Visible Language*. New York: Plenum Press.

Antos, S.J. (1979). Processing facilitation in a lexical decision task. *Journal of Experimental Psychology: Human Perception and Performance*, 5, 527–545.

Apkarian-Stielau, P. and Loomis, J.M. (1975). A comparison of tactile and blurred visual form perception. *Perception and Psychophysics*, 18, 362–368.

Appelle, S. and Countryman, M. (1986). Eliminating the haptic oblique effect: Influence of scanning incongruity and prior knowledge of the standards. *Perception*, 15, 325–329.

Appelle, S. and Gravetter, F. (1985). Effect of modality-specific experience on visual and haptic judgment of orientation. *Perception*, 14, 763–773.

Atkinson, R.C. and Shiffrin, R.M. (1968). Human Memory: A proposed system and its control processes. In K. Spence and J.T. Spence (eds) *The Psychology of Learning and Motivation*, Vol. 2. London: Academic Press.

Baddeley, A.D. (1979). Working memory and reading. In P.A. Kolers, M.E. Wrolstad and H. Bouma (eds) *Processing of Visible Language*, Vol. 1. New York: Plenum.

Baddeley, A.D. (1986). *Working Memory*. Oxford: Oxford University Press.

Baddeley, A.D. (1990). *Human Memory: Theory and Practice*. Hillsdale, N.J.: Lawrence Erlbaum.

Baddeley, A.D., Johnson, N. and Buchanan, M. (1975). Word length and the structure of short-term memory. *Journal of Verbal Learning and Verbal Behavior*, 14, 538–548.

Ballesteros, S., Manga, D., Navarredonda, A.B. and Reales, J.M. (1993). *Perceptual asymmetry in haptic discrimination*. Paper presented at the 34th Annual Meeting of the Psychonomic Society, Washington, D.C.

Ballesteros, S., Manga, D. and Reales, J.M. (in press). Haptic discrimination of bilateral symmetry in two-dimensional and three-dimensional unfamiliar displays. *Perception and Psychophysics*.

Ballesteros, S., Millar, S. and Reales, J.M. (in press). Symmetry in haptic and in visual shape perception. *Perception and Psychophysics*.

Balota, D. and Chumbley, J.J. (1984). Are lexical decisions a good measure of lexical access? The role of word frequency in the neglected decision stage. *Journal of Experimental Psychology: Human Perception and Performance, 10*, 340–357.

Bamber, D. (1969). Reaction times and error rates for 'same'–'different' judgments. *Perception and Psychophysics, 6*, 169–174.

Barron, R.W. (1980). Visual and phonological strategies in reading and spelling. In Frith, U. (ed.) *Cognitive Processes in Spelling*. London: Academic Press.

Barron, R.W. (1986). Word recognition in early reading: A review of the direct and indirect access hypothesis. *Cognition, 24*, 93–119.

Barron, R.W. and Baron, J. (1977). How children get meaning from printed words. *Child Development, 48*, 587–594.

Bartlett, F.C. (1932). *Remembering: A Study of Experimental and Social Psychology*. Cambridge: Cambridge University Press.

Becker, C.A. (1976). Allocation of attention during visual word recognition. *Journal of Experimental Psychology: Human Perception and Performance, 2*, 556–566.

Becker, C.A. (1980). Semantic context effects in visual word recognition: An analysis of semantic strategies. *Memory and Cognition, 8*, 493–512.

Becker, C.A. (1985). Do we really know about semantic context effects during reading? In Besner, D., Waller, T.G. and McKinnon, G.E. (eds) *Reading Research*, Vol. 5. New York: Academic Press.

Becker, C.A. and Killion, T.H. (1977). Interaction of visual and cognitive effects in word recognition. *Journal of Experimental Psychology: Human Perception and Performance, 3*, 389–401.

Berkeley, G. (1709/1974). An essay towards a new theory of vision. In D.M. Armstrong (ed.) *Berkeley's Philosophical Writings*. New York: Collier.

Berla, E.P. (1982). Haptic perception of tangible graphic displays. In W. Schiff and E. Foulke (eds) *Tactual Perception: A Source Book*. Cambridge: Cambridge University Press.

Berla, E.P. and Butterfield, L.H., Jr. (1977). Tactual distinctive feature analysis: Training blind students in shape recognition and in locating shapes on a map. *The Journal of Special Education, 11*, 336–346.

Berla, E.P., Butterfield, L.H. and Murr, M.J. (1976). Tactile political map reading by blind students. *Journal of Special Education, 10*, 166–276.

Bernbaum, M., Albert, S.G. and McGarry, J.D. (1989). Diabetic neuropathy and braille ability. *Archives of Neurology, 46*, 1179–1181.

Bertelson, P., Mousty, P. and D'Alimonte, G. (1985). A study of braille reading: Patterns of hand activity in one-handed and two-handed reading. *The Quarterly Journal of Experimental Psychology, 37A*, 235–256.

Berthoz, A., Vidal, P.P. and Graf, W. (eds) (1992). *The Head–Neck Sensory Motor System*. Oxford: Oxford University Press.

Besner, D. (1987). Phonology, lexical access in reading, and articulatory suppression: A critical review. *Quarterly Journal of Experimental Psychology, 39A*, 467–478.

Besner, D. (1989). On the role of outline shape and word-specific visual pattern in the identification of function words. *Quarterly Journal of Experimental Psychology, 41A*, 91–105.

Besner, D. and Davelaar, E. (1982) Basic processes in reading: Two phonological codes. *Canadian Journal of Psychology, 36*, 701–711.

Birren, J.E., Woods, A.M. and Williams, M.V. (1980). Behavioural slowing with age: Causes, organization and consequences. In L.W. Poon (ed.) *Aging in the 1980's: Psychological Issues.* Washington, D.C.: American Psychological Association.

Bishop, D.V.M. (1985). Spelling ability in congenital dysarthria: Evidence against articulatory coding in translating between phonemes and graphemes. *Cognitive Neuropsychology* 2, 229–254

Bishop, D.V.M. and Robson, J. (1989). Unimpaired short-term memory and rhyme judgments in congenitally speechless individuals. *Quarterly Journal of Experimental Psychology*, *41A*, 123–140.

Bisiach, E., Capitani, E., Luzzatti, C. and Perani, D. (1981). Brain and conscious representation of outside reality. *Neuropsychologia*, *19*, 543–541.

Boring, E.G. (1942). *Sensation and Perception in the History of Experimental Psychology.* New York: Appleton-Century-Crofts.

Bornstein, M.H., Ferdinandson, K. and Gross, C.G. (1981). Perception of symmetry in infancy. *Developmental Psychology*, *17*, 82–86.

Bornstein, M.H. and Krinsky, S.J. (1985). Perception of symmetry in infancy: The salience of vertical symmetry and the perception of pattern wholes. *Journal of Experimental Child Psychology*, *39* (1), 1–19.

Boswell, S.L. (1976). Young children's processing of asymmetrical and symmetrical patterns. *Journal of Experimental Child Psychology*, *22*, 309–318.

Bradley, L. and Bryant, P.E (1983). A causal connection: Categorizing sounds and learning to read. *Nature*, 301, 419–421.

Bradshaw, J.L., Nettleton, N.C. and Spehr, K. (1982). Braille reading and left and right hemispace. *Neuropsychologia*, *20*, 493–500.

Brady, S., Shankweiler, D. and Mann, V. (1983). Speech perception and memory coding in relation to reading ability. *Journal of Experimental Child Psychology*, *35*, 345–367.

Broadbent, D.E. and Broadbent, M. (1980). Priming and the passive/active model of word recognition. In R.S. Nickerson (ed.) *Attention and Performance*, Vol. VIII. Hillsdale, N.J.: Lawrence Erlbaum.

Bruce, V. and Green, P. (1990) *Visual Perception: Physiology, Psychology and Ecology.* Hillsdale, N.J.: Lawrence Erlbaum.

Bruteig, J.M. (1987). The reading rates for contracted and uncontracted braille of blind Norwegian adults. *Journal of Visual Impairment and Blindness*, *81*, 19–23.

Bryant, P.E. and Bradley, L. (1985). *Children's Reading Problems: Psychology and Education.* Oxford: Basil Blackwell.

Burklen, K. (1932). *Touch Reading of the Blind* (Transl. Merry, F.K.). New York: American Foundation for the Blind.

Campbell, R. (1987) Lip-reading and immediate memory processes or on thinking impure thoughts. In B. Dodd and R. Campbell (eds) *Hearing by Eye: The Psychology of Lip-Reading.* London: Lawrence Erlbaum.

Carpenter, P.A. and Daneman, M. (1981). Lexical retrieval and error recovery in reading: A model based on eye fixations. *Journal of Verbal Learning and Verbal Behavior*, *20*, 137–160.

Carpenter, P.A. and Just, M.A. (1983). What your eyes do while your mind is reading. In K. Rayner (ed.) *Eye Movements in Reading: Perceptual and Language Processes.* New York: Academic Press.

Carroll, J.B., Davies, P. and Richman, B. (1971). *The American Heritage Word Frequency Book.* Boston: Houghton Mifflin. New York: American Heritage Publishing Co., Inc.

Case, R, Kurland, D.M. and Goldberg, J. (1982). Operational efficiency and the growth of short-term memory span. *Journal of Experimental Child Psychology*, *33*, 386–404.

Cattell, J.M. (1886). The time it takes to see and name objects. *Mind*, *11*, 63–65.

Chapman, E.K., Tobin, M.J., Tooze, F.H.J. and Moss, S.C. (1977). *Look and Think:*

A Handbook on Visual Perception Training for Severely Visually Handicapped Children. Birmingham: Department of Special Education, University of Birmingham.

Chi, M.T.H. (1976). Short-term memory limitations in children: Capacity limitations or processing deficits? *Memory and Cognition, 4*, 559–572.

Chi, M.T.H. (1977). Age differences in memory span. *Journal of Experimental Child Psychology, 23*, 266–281.

Coltheart, M. (1978). Lexical access in simple reading tasks. In G. Underwood (ed.) *Strategies of Information Processing.* London: Academic Press.

Coltheart, M., Curtis, B., Atkins, P. and Haller, M. (1993). Models of reading aloud: Dual route and parallel-distributed-processing approaches. *Psychological Review, 100*, 589–608.

Coltheart, M, Patterson, K. and Marshall, J.C. (1980). *Deep Dyslexia.* London: Routledge & Kegan Paul.

Coltheart, V., Evans, S.E. and Trollope, J. (1990). Articulatory suppression and phonological codes in reading for meaning. *Quarterly Journal of Experimental Psychology, 42A*, 375–399.

Coltheart, V., Laxon, V., Rickard, M. and Eldon, C. (1988). Phonological recoding in reading for meaning by adults and children. *Journal of Experimental Psychology: Learning, Memory and Cognition, 14*, 387–397.

Connolly, K. and Jones, B. (1970). A developmental study of afferent–efferent integration. *British Journal of Psychology, 61*, 259–266

Conrad, R. (1964). Acoustic confusions in immediate memory. *British Journal of Psychology, 55*, 75–84.

Conrad, R. (1971). The chronology of the development of covert speech in children. *Developmental Psychology, 5*, 398–405.

Conrad, R. (1972 a). Speech and reading. In J.F. Kavanagh and I. Mattingly (eds) *Language by Ear and Eye.* Cambridge, Mass.: MIT Press.

Conrad, R. (1972 b). Short-term memory in the deaf: A test for speech coding. *British Journal of Psychology, 63*, 173–180.

Conrad, R. (1979). *The Deaf School Child: Language and Cognitive function.* London: Harper & Row.

Coran S. and Ward, L.M. (1989). *Sensation and Perception.* Philadelphia: Harcourt Brace Jovanovich College Publishers.

Corballis, M.C. and Roldan, C.E. (1975). Detection of symmetry as a function of angular orientation. *Journal of Experimental Psychology: Perception and Performance, 1*, 221–230.

Craig, J.C. (1977). Vibrotactile pattern perception: Extraordinary observers. *Science, 196*, 450–452.

Craig, J.C. (1978). Vibrotactile recognition and masking. In G. Gordon (ed.) *Active Touch: The Mechanisms of Recognition of Objects by Manipulation: A Multidisciplinary Approach.* Oxford: Pergamon Press.

Craig, J.C. (1989). Interference in localizing stimuli. *Perception and Psychophysics, 45*, 343–355.

Craig, J.C. and Sherrick, C.E. (1982). Dynamic tactile displays. In Shiff, W. and Emerson Foulke (eds) *Tactual Perception: A Source Book.* Cambridge, Mass.: Cambridge University Press.

Cratty, B.J. (1971). *Movement and Spatial Awareness in Blind Children and Youth.* Springfield, Ill.: Charles Thomas.

Crowder, R.G. (1982). *The Psychology of Reading.* Oxford: Oxford University Press.

Daneman, M. (1988) How reading braille is both like and unlike reading print. *Memory and Cognition, 16* (6), 497–504

Daniels, P.T. (1996). Shorthand. In P.T. Daniels and W. Bright, *The World's Writing Systems.* Oxford: Oxford University Press.

Davidson, P.W. (1972). The role of exploratory activity in haptic perception: Some issues, data and hypotheses. *Research Bulletin, American Foundation for the Blind*, *24*, 21–28.

Davidson, P.W., Appelle, St. and Haber, R.N. (1992). Haptic scanning of braille cells by low- and high-proficiency blind readers. *Research in Developmental Disabilities*, *13*, 99–111.

Davidson, P.W., Wiles-Kettleman, M. and Haber, R.N. (1980). Relationship between hand movements, reading competence and passage difficulty in braille reading. *Neuropsychologia*, *18*, 629–635.

Davis, C. and Forster, K.I. (1994). Masked orthographic priming: The effect of prime-target legibility. *Quarterly Journal of Experimental Psychology*, *47A*, 673–697.

DeCaspar, A.J. and Fifer, W.P. (1980). Of human bonding: Newborn prefer their mother's voice. *Science*, *208*, 1174–1176.

De Groot, A.M.B. (1984). Primed lexical decision: Combined effects of the proportion of related prime–target pairs and the stimulus onset asynchrony of prime and target. *Quarterly Journal of Experimental Psychology*, *36A*, 253–280.

De Groot, A.M.B. (1985). Word context effects in word naming and lexical decision. *Quarterly Journal of Experimental Psychology*, *37A*, 281–297.

De Renzi, E. (1982). *Disorders of Space Exploration and Cognition*. New York: John Wiley.

De Villiers, J.G. and De Villiers, P.A. (1978) *Language Acquisition*. Cambridge, Mass.: Harvard University Press.

Dodd, B. (1979). Lip reading in infants: attention to speech presented in- and out-of-synchrony. *Cognitive Psychology*, *11*, 478–484.

Dodd, B. (1980). Interaction of auditory and visual information in speech perception. *British Journal of Psychology*, *71*, 541–549.

Dodd, B. (1983). Visual and auditory modalities in phonological acquisition. In A.E. Mills (ed.) *Language Acquisition in the Blind Child*. London: Croom Helm.

Dodds, A. (1978). Hemispheric differences in tactuo-spatial processing. *Neuropsychologia*, *16*, 247–254.

Drewnowski, A. (1978). Detection on the word 'the': Evidence for the acquisition of reading levels. *Memory and Cognition*, *6*, 403–409.

Drewnowski, A. and Healy, A.F. (1977). Detection errors on 'and' 'the': Evidence for reading units larger than the word. *Memory and Cognition*, *5*, 636–647.

Duhamel, J.R., Colby, C.L. and Goldberg, M.E. (1991). Congruent representations of visual somatosensory space in single neurons of the monkey ventral intra-parietal cortex (Area VIP). In J. Paillard (ed.) *Brain and Space*. Oxford: Oxford University Press.

Durunoglu, A.Y. (1988). Repetition, semantic priming and stimulus quality. Implications for the interactive compensatory reading model. *Journal of Experimental Psychology: Learning, Memory and Cognition*, *14*, 590–603.

Ehri, L.E. (1980). The development of orthographic images. In U. Frith (ed.) *Cognitive Processes in Spelling*. New York: Academic Press.

Ehrlich, S.F. and Rayner, K. (1981). Contextual effects on word perception and eye movements during reading. *Journal of Verbal Learning and Verbal Behavior*, *20*, 641–655.

Ehrlich, K. and Rayner, K. (1983) Pronoun assignment and semantic integration during reading: Eye movements and immediacy of processing. *Journal of Verbal Learning and Verbal Behavior*, *22*, 75–87.

Eimas, P.D. (1975). Speech perception in early infancy. In L.B. Cohen and P. Salapatek (eds) *Infant Perception: From Sensation to Cognition*, Vol. 2. New York: Academic Press, pp. 193–231.

Ellis, A.W. (1984). *Reading, Writing and Dyslexia: A Cognitive Analysis*. Hillsdale, N.J.: Lawrence Erlbaum

Ellstner, W. (1983). Abnormalities in the verbal communication of visually-impaired children. In Anne E. Mills (ed.) *Language Acquisition in the Blind Child: Normal and Deficient.* Beckenham, Kent: Croom Helm.

Epstein, W., Hughes, B., Schneider, S.L. and Bach-Y-Rita, P. (1989). Perceptual learning of spatio-temporal events: Evidence from an unfamiliar modality. *Journal of Experimental Psychology, 15,* 28–44.

Ettlinger, G. (1967). Analysis of cross-modal effects and their relationship to language. In F.L. Darley and C.H. Millikan (eds) *Brain Mechanisms Underlying Speech and Language.* New York: Grune and Stratton.

Faglioni, P. and Villa, P. (1977). Topographical amnesia. *Journal of Neurology, Neurosurgery and Psychiatry, 40,* 498–505.

Fernald, A. and Simon, T. (1984). Expanded intonation contour in mothers' speech to newborns. *Developmental Psychology, 20,* 104–113.

Ferrand, L. and Grainger, J. (1992). Phonology and orthography in visual word recognition: Evidence from marked non-word priming. *The Quarterly Journal of Experimental Psychology, 45A,* 353–372.

Ferrand, L. and Grainger, J. (1994). Effects of orthography are independent of phonology in masked form priming. *Quarterly Journal of Experimental Psychology, 47A,* 365–382.

Fertsch, P. (1947). Hand dominance in reading braille. *American Journal of Psychology, 60,* 335–349.

Fielder, A.R., Best, A.B. and Bax, M.C.O. (eds) (1993). *The Management of Visual Impairment in Childhood.* London: MacKeith Press.

Finke, R.A. (1979). The functional equivalence of mental images and errors of movement. *Cognitive Psychology, 11,* 235–264.

Fischler, I. and Bloom, P.A. (1979). Automatic and attentional processes in the effects of sentence contexts on word recognition. *Journal of Verbal Learning and Verbal Behavior, 18,* 1–20.

Fisher, C.B. (1982). Effects of stimulus orientation and head position. *Perception and Psychophysics, 32* (5), 443–448.

Fisher, C.B., and Bornstein, (1982). Identification of symmetry: Effects of stimulus orientation and head position. *Perception and Psychophysics, 32,* 443–448.

Fisher, C.B., Ferdinandsen, K. and Bornstein, M. (1981). The role of symmetry in infant form discrimination. *Child Development, 52* (2), 457–462.

Fodor, J.A. (1983). *The Modularity of Mind.* Cambridge, Mass.: MIT Press.

Folk, J.R. and Morris, R.K. (1995). Multiple lexical codes in reading: Evidence from eye-movements, naming time, and oral reading. *Journal of Experimental Psychology: Learning, Memory and Cognition, 21,* 1412–1429.

Forster, K.I. (1976). Accessing the mental lexicon. In E.C. Walker and R.J. Wales (eds) *New Approaches to Language Mechanisms.* Amsterdam: North-Holland.

Forster, K.I. (1981). Priming and the effects of sentence and lexical contexts on naming time. *Quarterly Journal of Experimental Psychology, 33A,* 465–495.

Foulke, E. (1982). Reading braille. In W. Schiff and E. Foulke (eds) *Tactual Perception: A Source Book.* New York: Cambridge University Press.

Fozard, J.L. (1980). The time for remembering. In L. W. Poon (ed.) *Aging in the 1980s.* Washington, D.C.: American Psychological Association.

Fraiberg, S. (1977). *Insights from the Blind: Comparative Studies of Blind and Sighted Infants.* New York: Basic Books.

Frazier, L. and Rayner, K. (1982). Making and correcting errors during sentence comprehension: Eye movements in the analysis of structurally ambiguous sentences. *Cognitive Psychology, 14,* 178–210.

Frederiksen, J.R. and Kroll, J.F. (1976). Spelling and sound: Approaches to the internal lexicon. *Journal of Experimental Psychology: Human Perception and Performance, 2,* 361–379.

Frith, U. (1980). Unexpected spelling problems. In U. Frith (ed.) *Cognitive Processes in Spelling*. London: Academic Press.

Frith, U. (1985). Beneath the surface of developmental dyslexia. In K.E. Patterson, J.C. Marshall and M. Coltheart (eds) *Surface Dyslexia*. London: Routledge & Kegan Paul.

Funnell, E. (1983). Phonological processes: New evidence from acquired dyslexia. *British Journal of Psychology*, *74*, 159–180.

Funnell, E. and Davison, M. (1989). Lexical capture: A developmental disorder of reading and spelling. *Quarterly Journal of Experimental Psychology*, *11A*, 471–487.

Gaines, R. (1969). The discriminability of form among young children. *Journal of Experimental Child Psychology*, *8*, 418.

Galabruda, A.M., Corsiglia, J., Rosen, G.D. and Sherman G.F. (1987). Planum temporale asymmetry, reappraisal since Geschwind and Levitzki. *Neuropsychologia*, *25*, 853–868.

Garnham, A. (1985). *Psycholinguistics: Central Topics*. London: Methuen.

Gathercole, S.E. (1987). Lip-reading: Implications for theories of short-term memory. In B. Dodd and R. Campbell (eds) *Hearing by Eye: The Psychology of Lip-Reading*. London: Lawrence Erlbaum.

Gazzaniga, M.S. (1988). The dynamics of cerebral specialization and modular interactions. In L. Weiskrantz (ed.) *Thought without Language*. Oxford: Clarendon Press.

Gazzaniga, M.S. and Ledoux, J.E. (1978). *The Integrated Mind*. New York: Plenum Press.

Geschwind, N. (1972). Language and the brain. *Scientific American*, *226*, 76–83.

Geschwind, N. and Levitzky, W. (1968). Human brain: Left–right asymmetries in temporal speech region. *Science*, *161*, 186–187.

Gibson, E.J. (1969). *Principles of Perceptual Learning and Development*. New York: Appleton Century Crofts.

Gibson, E. J. and Spelke, E.S. (1983). The development of perception. In P.H. Mussen (series ed.); J.H. Flavell and E.M. Markman (Vol. eds) *Handbook of Child Psychology: Cognitive Development*, Vol. II, pp. 2–76. New York: John Wiley.

Gibson, J.J. (1962). Observations on active touch. *Psychological Review*, *69*, 477–490.

Gibson, J.J. (1966). *The Senses Considered as Perceptual Systems*. Boston: Houghton Mifflin.

Gibson, J.J. (1971). The information available in pictures. *Leonardo*, *4*, 27.

Gibson, J.J. (1979) *The Ecological Approach to Visual Perception*. Boston: Houghton-Mifflin.

Gill, J. (1974). Tactual mapping. *American Foundation for the Blind, Research Bulletin*, *28*, 57–80.

Gill, J.M. (1985). New Moon. *British Journal of Visual Impairment*, *III*, 85–86.

Gill, J.M., Muthiah, N., Silver, J.H. and Gould, E. (eds) (1996). *Tiresias: Research Information Handbook of Assistive Technology for Visually Disabled Persons; Volume 2: Equipment*. London: Tiresias Consortium.

Gilson, E.Q. and Baddeley, A.D. (1969). Tactile short-term memory. *Quarterly Journal of Experimental Psychology*, *21*, 180–189.

Gleitman, L. R. and Rozin, P. (1973). Teaching by use of a syllabary. *Reading Research Quarterly*, *8*, 447–483.

Gleitman, L.R. and Rozin, P. (1977). The structure and acquisition of reading I: Relations between orthographies and the structure of language. In A.S. Reber and D.L. Scarborough (eds) *Towards A Psychology of Reading: The Proceedings of the CUNY Conference*. Hillsdale, N.J.: Lawrence Erlbaum.

Glushko, R.J. (1979). The organization and activation of orthographic knowledge in reading aloud. *Journal of Experimental Psychology: Human Perception and Performance, 5*, 674–691.

Goldman-Rakic, P.S. and Friedman, H.R. (1991). The circuitry of working memory revealed by anatomy and metabolic imaging. In H.S. Levin, H.M. Eisenberg, and A.L. Benton (eds) *Frontal Lobe Function and Dysfunction.* Oxford: Oxford University Press.

Goodman, K.S. (1970). Reading: A psycholinguistic guessing game. In H. Singer and R.B. Ruddell (eds) *Theoretical Models and Processes in Reading.* Newark, Del.: International Reading Association.

Goodnow, J.J. (1971). Eye and hand: Differential memory and its effect on matching. *Neuropsychologia, 42*, 1187–1201.

Gough, P.B. (1972). One second of reading. In J.F. Cavanagh and I.G.Mattingly (eds) *Language by Ear and by Eye.* Cambridge, Mass.: MIT Press.

Goswami, U. (1988). Orthographic analogies and reading development. *Quarterly Journal of Experimental Psychology, 401*, 239–268.

Graziano, M.S. and Gross, C.G. (1994). The representation of extrapersonal space: A possible role for bimodal visual-tactile neurons. In M. Gazzaniga (ed.) *The Cognitive Neurosciences.* Cambridge, Mass.: MIT Press.

Gregory, R.L. (1970). *The Intelligent Eye.* London: Weidenfeld & Nicholson.

Grunewald, D. (1966). A braille reading machine. *Science, 154*, 144–146.

Haber, R.N. and Haber, L.R. (1981). The shape of a word can specify its meaning. *Reading Research Quarterly, 16*, 334–345.

Haber, L.R., Haber, R.N. and Furlin, K. (1983). Word length and word shape as sources in reading. *Reading Research Quarterly, 18*, 165–189.

Haber, R.N. and Schindler, R.M. (1981). Error in proofreading: Evidence of syntactic control of letter processing? *Journal of Experimental Psychology: Human Perception and Performance, 7*, 573–579.

Hamp, E.P. and Caton, H. (1984). A fresh look at the sign system of braille. *Journal of Visual Impairment and Blindness, 78*, 210–214.

Hanley, J.R., Hastie, K. and Kay, J. (1992). Developmental Surface Dyslexia and Dysgraphia: An orthographic processing impairment. *Quarterly Journal of Experimental Psychology, 44A* (2), 285–319.

Hardyk, C.D. and Petrinovitch, L.R. (1970). Subvocal speech and comprehension level as a function of the difficulty level of the reading material. *Journal of Verbal Learning and Verbal Behavior, 9*, 647–652.

Harley, R.T., Randall, K., Pichert, J.W. and Morrison, M. (1985). Braille instruction for blind diabetic adults with decreased tactile sensitivity. *Journal of Visual Impairment and Blindness, 79*, 12–17.

Hartley, J., Tobin, M.J. and Trueman, M. (1987). The effects of providing headings in braille text. *Journal of Visual Impairment and Blindness, 81*, 213–214.

Hatta, T. and Moriya, K. (1988). Developmental changes of hemispheric collaboration for tactile sequential information. *International Journal of Behavioral Development, 11*, 451–465.

Hatwell, Y. (1985). *Piagetian Reasoning and the Blind.* New York: American Foundation for the Blind.

Healy, A.F. (1980). Proofreading errors on the word 'the': New evidence on reading units. *Journal of Experimental Psychology: Human Perception and Performance, 6*, 45–57.

Heller, M.A. (1982). Visual and tactual texture perception: Intersensory cooperation. *Perception and Psychophysics, 31*, 339–344.

Heller, M.A. (1987). The effect of orientation on visual and tactual braille recognition. *Perception, 16*, 291–298.

Heller, M.A. (1989). Picture and pattern perception in the sighted blind: The advantage of the late blind. *Perception, 18*, 379–389.

Heller, M.A. (1992). The effect of orientation on tactual braille recognition. *Perception and Psychophysics, 51*, 549–556.

Heller, M.A. (1993). Influence of visual guidance on braille recognition: Low lighting also helps touch. *Perception and Psychophysics, 54* (5), 675–681.

Heller, M.A., Rogers, G.J. and Perry, C.L. (1990). Tactile pattern recognition with the optacon: Superior performance with active touch and the left hand. *Neuropsychologia, 28*, 1003–1006.

Helmholz, H. von (1866). *Treatise on Physiological Optics. Vol.3 (3rd edn 1926, translated by J.C.P. Southall).* New York: Optical Society of America. (1989) *Lectures on Scientific Subjects.* (translated by E.Atkinson). London: Longmans Green.

Henderson L. (1982). *Orthography and Word Recognition in Reading.* New York: Academic Press.

Henry, L. A. and Millar, S. (1991). Memory span increase with age: A test of two hypotheses. *Journal of Experimental Child Psychology, 51*, 458–484.

Henry, L.A. and Millar, S. (1993). Why does memory span improve with age? A review of the evidence for two current hypotheses. *European Journal of Cognitive Psychology, 5*, 241–287.

Herman, J.F., Herman, T.G. and Chatman, S.P. (1983). Constructing cognitive maps from partial information: a demonstrative study with congenitally blind subjects. *Journal of Visual impairment and Blindness, 77*, 161–166.

Hermelin, B. and O'Connor, N. (1971). Functional asymmetry in the reading of Braille. *Neuropsychologia, 9*, 431 435.

Hinton, G.E. (1989). Learning distributed representations of concepts. In R.G.M. Morris (ed.) *Parallel Distributed Processing: Implications for Psychology and Neurobiology.* Oxford: Clarendon Press.

Hinton, R.A. and Ayres, D.G. (1987). The development of tactile diagrams for blind biology students. *Journal of Visual Impairment and Blindness, 81*, 24–25.

Hiscock, M. and Kinsbourne, M. (1978). Ontogeny of cerebral dominance: Evidence from time-sharing asymmetry in children. *Developmental Psychology, 14*, 321–392.

Hitch, G.J. and Halliday, M.S. (1983). Working memory in children. *Philosophical Transactions of the Royal Society of London, B302*, 325–340.

Hitch, G.J., Halliday, M.S. and Littler, J.E. (1989). Item identification time and rehearsal rate as predictors of memory span in children. *Quarterly Journal of Experimental Psychology, 41A*, 321–337.

Hitch, G.J., Halliday, M.S., Schaafstal, A.M. and Schraagen, J.M.L. (1988). Visual working memory in young children. *Memory and Cognition, 16*, 120–132.

Hofland, K. and Johanssen, S. (1982). *Word Frequencies in British and American English.* Bergen: The Norwegian Computing Centre for the Humanities.

Hollins, M. (1989). *Understanding Blindness: An Integrative Approach.* Hillsdale, N.J.: Lawrence Erlbaum.

Horn, J. L. and Cattell, R.B. (1967). Age differences in crystalized and fluid intelligence. *Acta Psychologica, 26*, 107–129.

Howard, I.P. and Rogers, B.J. (1995). *Binocular Vision and Stereopsis.* New York and Oxford: Clarendon Press.

Howard, I.P. and Templeton, W.B. (1966) *Human Spatial Orientation.* New York: John Wiley.

Howard, L. and Polich, J. (1985). P300 latency and memory span development. *Developmental Psychology, 21*, 283–289.

Huey, E.B. (1908). *The Psychology of Pedagogy of Writing: A Review of the History of Reading and Writing and of Methods, Tests and Hygiene in Reading.* New

York: MacMillan. *American Journal of Psychology*, 9, 575–586; (1900), *11*, 283–302; (1901), *12*, 292–312.

Hulme, C., Maughan, S. and Brown, G.D.A. (1991). Memory for familiar and unfamiliar words: Evidence for a long-term memory contribution to short-term memory span. *Journal of Memory and Language*, *30*, 685–701.

Humphrey, N. and Weiskrantz, L. (1967). Vision in monkeys after removal of the striate cortex. *Nature*, *215*, 595–597.

Humphreys, G. (1989). Parallel distributed processing and psychology. In R.G.M. Morris (ed.) *Parallel Distributed Processing*. Oxford: Clarendon Press.

Humphreys, G.W. and Evett, L.J. (1985) Are there independent lexical and non-lexical routes in word processing? An evaluation of the dual-route theory of reading. *The Behavioural and Brain Sciences*, *8*, 689–705.

Hyvarinen, J. and Poranen, A (1978). Receptive field integration and submodality convergence in the hand area of the post-central gyrus of the alert monkey. *Journal of Physiology*, *283*, 539–556.

Hyvarinen, J. Carlsdon, S. and Hyvarinen, L. (1981). Early visual deprivation alters modality of neuronal responses in area 19 of the monkey cortex. *Neuroscience Letters*, *26*, 319–326.

Inhoff, A.W. (1987). Lexical access during eye fixations in sentence reading: Effects of word structure. In M. Coltheart (ed.) *Attention and Performance*, Vol. 12: London: Lawrence Erlbaum.

Ittyerah, M. (1993). Hand preferences and hand ability in congenitally blind children. *Quarterly Journal of Experimental Psychology*, *46A*, 35–50.

James, G.A. (1982). Mobility maps. In W. Schiff and E. Foulke (eds) *Tactual Perception: A Source Book*. Cambridge: Cambridge University Press.

James, W. (1890). *Principles of Psychology*. New York: Camelot Press.

Jared, D. and Seidenberg, M.S. (1991). Does word identification proceed from spelling to sound to meaning? *Journal of Experimental Psychology: General*, *120*, 1–37.

Jastrow, J. (1893). The perception of space by disparate senses. *Mind*, *11*, 539–554.

Jenkins, W.M., Merzenich, M.M., Ochs, M.T., Allard, T., and Guic-Robles, E. (1990). Functional reorganization of primary somatosensory cortex in adult owl monkeys after behaviorally controlled tactile stimulation. *Journal of Neurophysiology*, *63*, 82–104.

Johnson, P. (1982). The functional equivalence of imagery and movement. *Quarterly Journal of Experimental Psychology*, *34 A*, 349–365.

Johnson-Laird, P.N. (1983). *Mental Models*. Cambridge, Mass.: Harvard University Press.

Julesz, B. (1971). *Foundations of Cyclopean Perception*. Chicago: University of Chicago Press.

Just, M.A. and Carpenter, P.A. (1980 a). *The Psychology of Reading and Language Comprehension*. Boston: Allyn & Bacow.

Just, M.A. and Carpenter, P.A. (1980 b). A theory of reading: from eye fixations to comprehension. *Psychological Review*, *87*, 329–354.

Just, M.A. and Carpenter, P.A. (1987). *The Psychology of Reading and Language Comprehension*. Boston: Allyn & Bacow.

Juurmaa, J. and Suonio, K. (1975). The role of audition and motion in the spatial orientation of the blind and sighted. *Scandinavian Journal of Psychology*, *16*, 209–216.

Karmiloff-Smith, A. (1979). *A Functional Approach to Child Language*. Cambridge: Cambridge University Press.

Katz, D. (1925). *Der Aufbau der Tastwelt*. Leipzig: Barth.

Katz, D. (1989). *The World of Touch* (translated by L.E. Krueger). Hillsdale, N.J.: Lawrence Erlbaum.

Kelley, M.H., Springer, K. and Keil, F.C. (1990). The relation between syllable number and visual complexity in the acquisition of word meanings. *Memory and Cognition*, *18*, 528–536.

Kennedy, J. M. (1980). Blind people recognizing and making haptic pictures. In M.A. Hagen (ed.) *The Perception of Pictures*. New York: Academic Press.

Kennedy, J.M. (1993). *Drawing and the Blind: Pictures to Touch*. New Haven: Yale University Press.

Kessler, J. (1984). Accessible computers in the University. *Journal of Visual Impairment and Blindness*, *78*, 414–417.

Kimura, D. and Dunford, M. (1974). Normal studies on the function of the right hemisphere. In S.J. Beaumont and J.G. Dimond (eds) *Hemisphere Function in the Human Brain*. London: Elek Science.

Kintsch, W. (1974). *The Representation of Meaning in Memory*. Hillsdale, N.J.: Lawrence Erlbaum.

Klatzky, R.L., Lederman, S.J. and Metzger, V. (1985). Identifying objects by touch: An 'expert' system. *Perception and Psychophysics*, *37*, 299–302.

Klapp, S., Anderson, W. and Berrian, R. (1973). Implicit speech in reading reconsidered. *Journal of Experimental Psychology*, *100*, 369–374.

Kliegl, R., Olson, K.R. and Davidson, B.J. (1982). Regression analysis for studying reading processes: Comments on Just and Carpenter's eye-fixation theory. *Memory and Cognition*, *10*, 287–296.

Kliegl, R., Olson, K.R. and Davidson, B.J. (1983). On problems of unconfounding perceptual and language processes. In K. Rayner (ed.) *Eye Movements in Reading: Perceptual and Language Processes*. New York: Academic Press.

Kornhuber, H.H. (1984). Mechanisms of voluntary movement. In W. Prinz and A. F. Sanders (ed.) *Cognitive and Motor Processes*. Berlin: Springer-Verlag.

Krauthammer, G. (1968). Form perception across sensory modalities. *Neuropsychologia*, *6*, 105–113.

Kreiner, D.S. (1992). Reaction time measures of spelling: Testing a two-strategy model of skilled spelling. *Journal of Experimental Psychology: Learning, Memory, and Cognition*, *18*, 765–776.

Kosslyn, S.M. (1980). *Image and Mind*. Cambridge, Mass.: Harvard University Press.

Krueger, L.E. (1973). Effects of irrelevant surrounding material on speed of same–different judgments of two adjacent stimuli. *Journal of Experimental psychology*, *98*, 252–259.

Krueger, L.E. (1982 a). Tactual perception in historical perspective: David Katz's world of touch. In W. Schiff and E. Foulke (eds) *Tactual Perception: A Sourcebook*. Cambridge: Cambridge University Press.

Krueger, L.E. (1982 b). A word superiority effect with print and braille characters. *Perception and Psychophysics*, *31*, 345–352

Kucera, H. and Francis, W.N. (1967). *Computational Analysis of Present-Day American-English*. Providence, R.I.: Brown University Press.

Kumar, S. (1977). Short-term memory for a nonverbal task after cerebral commisurotomy. *Cortex*, *13*, 55–61.

Kusajima, T. (1970). *Experimentelle Untersuchungen zum Augenlesen und Tastlesen*. Neuburgweier: G. Schindele Verlag.

Kusajima, T. (1974). *Visual Reading and Braille Reading: An Experimental Investigation of the Physiology and Psychology of Tactual Reading*. New York: American Foundation for the Blind.

Laabs, G.J. (1973). Retention characteristics of different reproduction cues in motor short-term memory. *Journal of Experimental Psychology*, *100*, 168–177.

Laabs, G.J. and Simmons, R.W. (1981) Motor memory. In D. Holding (ed.) *Human Skills*. New York: John Wiley.

LaBerge, D. (1983). Spatial extent of attention to letters and words. *Journal of Experimental Psychology: Perception and Performance, 9*, 371–379.

LaBerge, D. and Samuels, S.J. (1974). Towards a theory of automatic information processing in reading. *Cognitive Psychology, 6*, 293–327.

Landau, B. (1983). Blind children's language is not 'meaningless'. In A.E. Mills (ed.) *Language Acquisition in the Blind Child: Normal and Deficient.* Beckenham, Kent: Croom Helm.

Landau, B. and Gleitman, L.R. (1985). *Language and Experience: Evidence from the Blind Child.* Cambridge, Mass.: Harvard University Press.

Lechelt, E.C., Eliuk, N. and Tanne, G. (1976). Perceptual orientation asymmetries: A comparison of visual and haptic space. *Perception and Psychophysics, 20*, 463–469.

Lechelt, E.C. and Verenka, A. (1980). Spatial anisotropy in intramodal and cross-modal judgments of stimulus orientation. *Perception, 9*, 581–587.

Lederman, S.J. and Klatzky, R.L. (1990). Haptic classification of common objects: Knowledge driven exploration. *Cognitive Psychology, 22*, 421–459.

Leinonen, L., Hyvarinen, J., Nyman, G. and Linnankoski, I. (1979). Functional properties of neurons in lateral part of associative area 7 in awake monkeys. *Experimental Brain Research, 34*, 299–320.

Leonard, J.A. and Newman, R.C. (1967). Spatial orientation in the blind. *Nature, 215*, 1413–1414.

Leonard, J.A. and Newman R.C. (1970). Three types of maps for blind travel. *Ergonomics, 13*, 165–179.

Levy, B.A. (1981). Interactive processes during reading. In A.M. Lesgold and C.A. Perfetti (eds) *Interactive Processes in Reading.* Hillsdale, N.J.: Lawrence Erlbaum.

Liben, L.S. and Downs, R.M. (1989). Understanding maps as symbols: The development of map concepts in children. In H. W. Reese (ed.), *Advances in Child Development and Behavior,* Vol. 22, pp. 145–201. New York: Academic Press.

Liben, L.S. and Downs, R.M. (1991). The role of graphic representations in understanding the world. In R.M. Downs, L.S. Liben and D, S, Palermo (eds) *Visions of Aesthetics, the Environment and Development: The Legacy of Joachim Wohlwill.* Hillsdale, N.J.: Lawrence Erlbaum.

Liben, L.S. and Downs, R.M. (1992). Developing an understanding of graphic representations in children and adults: The case of geo-graphics. *Cognitive Development, 7*, 331–349.

Liben, L.S. and Downs, R.M. (1993). Understanding person-space-map relations: Cartographic and developmental perspectives. *Developmental Psychology, 29*, 739–752.

Liberman, I.Y. (1973). Segmentation of the spoken word and reading acquisition. *Bulletin of the Orton Society, 23*, 65–77.

Liberman, I. Y., Shankweiler, D., Fischer, F.W. and Carter, B. (1974). Explicit syllable and phoneme segmentation in the young child. *Journal of Experimental Child Psychology, 18*, 201–212.

Liberman, I. Y., Shankweiler, D., Liberman, A. M., Fowler, C. and Fischer, F.W. (1977). Phonetic segmentation and recoding in the beginning reader. In A.S. Reber and D.L. Scarborough (eds) *Towards a Psychology of Reading.* New York: John Wiley.

Liberman, P. (1967). *Intonation, Perception and Language.* Cambridge, Mass.: MIT Press.

Lima, S. (1987). Morphological analysis in sentence reading. *Journal of Memory and Language, 26*, 84–99.

Lima, S. and Pollatsek, A. (1983). Lexical access via an orthographic code? The basic orthographic syllable structure (BOSS) reconsidered. *Journal of Verbal Learning and Verbal Behavior, 22*, 310–332.

Lindsay, P.H. and Norman, D.A. (1977). *Human Information Processing: An Introduction to Psychology*. New York: Academic Press.

Locher, P.J. and Nodine, C.F. (1973). Influence of stimulus symmetry on visual scanning patterns. *Perception and Psychophysics*, *13*, 408–412.

Locher, P.J. and Simmons, R.W. (1978). Influence of stimulus symmetry and complexity upon haptic scanning strategies during detection, learning and recognition tasks. *Perception and Psychophysics, 23*, 110–116.

Loomis, J. (1981). On the tangibility of letters and braille. *Perception and Psychophysics*, *29*, 37–46.

Loomis, J. (1990). A model of character recognition and legibility. *Journal of Experimental Psychology: Human Perception and Performance*, *16*, 106–120.

Loomis, J. (1993). Counterexample to the hypothesis of functional similarity between tactual and visual pattern perception. *Perception and Psychophysics*, *54*, 179–184.

Lorimer, J. (1962). *The Lorimer Braille Recognition Test. A Test of Ability in Reading Braille Contractions.* Bristol: The College of Teachers of the Blind.

Lorimer, J. (1977). *Neale Analysis of Reading Ability: Adapted for Use with Blind Children*. Windsor: NFER Publishing Company.

Lorimer, J., Tobin, M.J., Gill, J. and Douce, J. (1982). *A Study of Braille Contractions*. London: Royal National Institute for the Blind.

McBride, V.G. (1974). Explorations in rapid reading in braille. *New Outlook for the Blind*, *68*, 8–12.

McClelland, J.L. (1987). The case for interactionism in language processing. In M. Coltheart (ed.) *Attention and Performance: 12.* London: Lawrence Erlbaum.

McClelland, J.L. (1989). Parallel distributed processing: Implications for cognition and development. In R.G.M. Morris (ed.) *Parallel Distributed Processing: Implications for Psychology and Neurobiology*. Oxford: Clarendon Press.

Maccoby, E.E. and Bee, H.L. (1965). Some speculations concerning the lag between perceiving and performing. *Child Development, 36*, 367–377.

McCutchen, D. Bell, L., France, I.M. and Perfetti, C.A. (1991). Phonemic interference in reading: The tongue-twister effect revisited. *Reading Research Quarterly*, *26*, 87–103.

McGurk, H. (1976) Hearing lips and seeing voices. *Nature, 264,* 746–748.

Mach, E. (1897). *Analysis of the Sensations*. Chicago: Open Court Publishing House.

Mann, V. A. (1986). Phonological awareness: the role of reading experience. *Cognition*, 24, 65–92.

Mann, V.A., Liberman, I.Y. and Shankweiler, D. (1980). Children's memory for sentences and word strings in relation to reading ability. *Memory and Cognition*, *8*, 329–335.

Marr, D. (1982). *Vision*, San Francisco: Freeman.

Marr, D. and Nishihara, H.K. (1976). Representation and recognition of the spatial organization of three-dimensional shapes. Cambridge, Mass.: MIT Laboratory Manuscript.

Marsh, G., Friedman, M., Welch, V. and Desberg, P. (1981). A cognitive-developmental approach to reading acquisition. In T.G. Waller and G.E. Mackinnon (eds) *Reading Research: Advances in Theory and Practice*, Vol. 3. New York: Academic Press.

Marshall, J.C. and Newcombe, F. (1973). Patterns of paralexia: A psycholinguistic approach. *Journal of Psycholinguistic Research, 2*, 175–200.

Marslen-Wilson, W.D., Tyler, L.K., Waksler, R. and Older, L. (1994). Morphology and meaning in the English mental lexicon. *Psychological Review, 101*, 3–33.

Martinez, F. (1971). Comparison of two types of tactile exploration in a task of mirror-image recognition. *Psychonomic Science, 22*, 124–125.

Massaro, D.W. (1989). Review of speech perception by ear and eye: A paradigm for psychological enquiry. *Behavioral and Brain Sciences, 12*, 741–755.

Massaro, D.W., Cohen, M.M. and Gesi, A.T. (1993). Long-term training, transfer and retention in learning to lipread. *Perception and Psychophysics, 53*, 549–662.

Massaro, D.W. and Friedman, D. (1990). Models of integration given multiple sources of information. *Psychological Review, 97*, 225–252.

Meltzoff, A.N. and Moore, M.K. (1989). Imitation in newborn infants: exploring the range of gestures imitated and the underlying mechanism. *Developmental Psychology, 25*, 954–962.

Mewhort, D.J.K. and Beal, A.L. (1977). Mechanisms of word identification. *Journal of Experimental Psychology: Human Perception and Performance, 3*, 629–640.

Meyer, A.S. (1990). The time course of phonological encoding in language production. *Journal of Memory and Language, 29*, 524–545.

Meyer, D.E., Schvaneveldt, R.W. and Ruddy, M.G. (1975). Loci of contextual effects in visual word recognition. In P.M.A. Rabbitt and S. Dornic (eds) *Attention and Performance: V.* New York: Academic Press.

Millar, S. (1971). Visual and haptic cue utilization by preschool children: The recognition of visual and haptic stimuli presented separately and together. *Journal of Experimental Child Psychology, 12*, 88–94.

Millar, S. (1972 a). The development of visual and kinaesthetic judgments of distance. *British Journal of Psychology, 63*, 271–282.

Millar, S. (1972 b). Effects of instructions to visualize stimuli during delay on visual recognition by preschool children. *Child Development, 43*, 1073–1075.

Millar, S. (1975 a). Effects of input variables on visual and kinaesthetic matching by children within and across modalities. *Journal of Experimental Child Psychology, 19*, 63–78.

Millar, S. (1975 b). Effects of tactual and phonological similarity on the recall of braille letters by blind children. *British Journal of Psychology, 66*, 193–201.

Millar, S. (1975 c). Effects of phonological and tactual similarity on serial object recall by blind and sighted children. *Cortex, 11*, 170–180.

Millar, S. (1975 d). Translation rules or visual experience? Drawing the human figure by blind and sighted children. *Perception, 4*, 363–371.

Millar, S. (1977 a) Early stages of tactual matching. *Perception, 6*, 333–343

Millar, S. (1977 b). Tactual and name matching by blind children. *British Journal of Psychology, 68*, 377–387.

Millar, S. (1978 a). Aspects of memory for information from touch and movement. In G. Gordon (ed.) *Active Touch: The Mechanism of Recognition of Objects by Manipulation: A Multidisciplinary Approach.* Oxford: Pergamon Press.

Millar, S. (1978 b). Short-term serial tactual recall: Effects of grouping tactually probed recall of Braille letters and nonsense shapes by blind children. *British Journal of Psychology, 69*, 17–24.

Millar, S. (1979). Utilization of shape and movement cues in simple spatial tasks by blind and sighted children. *Perception, 8*, 11–20.

Millar, S. (1981 a). Crossmodal and intersensory perception and the blind. In R.D. Walk and H.L. Pick, Jr. (eds) *Intersensory Perception and Sensory Integration.* New York and London: Plenum Press.

Millar, S. (1981 b). Self-referent and movement cues in coding spatial location by blind and sighted children. *Perception, 10*, 255–264.

Millar, S. (1983) Language and active touch. In A.E. Mills (ed.) *Language and Communication in the Blind Child.* Beckenham, Kent: Croom Helm.

Millar, S. (1984 a). Is there a 'best hand' for Braille? *Cortex, 1984, 13*, 567–579.

Millar, S. (1984 b) Strategy choices by young Braille readers. *Perception, 13*, 567–579.

Millar, S. (1985 a) Movement cues and body orientation in recall of locations of blind and sighted children. *Quarterly Journal of Experimental Psychology, 37A,* 257–279.

Millar, S. (1985 b) Drawing as representation and image in blind children. *The 2nd International Imagery Conference,* University College, Swansea,

Millar, S. (1985 c). The perception of complex patterns by touch. *Perception, 14,* 293–303.

Millar, S. (1986) Aspects of size, shape and texture in touch. *Journal of Child Psychology and Psychiatry, 27,* 367–381.

Millar, S. (1987 a) The perceptual 'window' in two-handed braille: Do the left and right hands process text simultaneously? *Cortex, 23,* 111–222.

Millar, S. (1987 b). Perceptual and task factors in fluent braille. *Perception, 16,* 521–536.

Millar, S. (1988 a). Models of sensory deprivation: The nature/nurture dichotomy and spatial representation in the blind. *International Journal of Behavioral Development, 11,* 69–87.

Millar, S. (1988 b). An apparatus for recording hand-movements. *British Journal of Visual Impairment and Blindness, VI,* 87–90

Millar, S. (1988 c). Prose reading by touch: The role of stimulus quality, orthography and context. *British Journal of Psychology, 79,* 87–103

Millar, S. (1990 a). Articulatory coding in prose reading: Evidence from braille on changes with skill. *British Journal of Psychology, 81,* 205–219.

Millar, S. (1990 b). Imagery and Blindness. In P. Hampson, D.F. Marks and J.T.E. Richardson (eds) *Imagery: Current Developments.* Routledge & Kegan Paul, 1990.

Millar, S. (1991). A reversed lag in the recognition and production of tactual drawings: Theoretical implications for haptic coding. In M.A. Heller and W. Schiff (eds) *The Psychology of Touch.* New York: Lawrence Erlbaum.

Millar, S. (1994). *Understanding and Representing Space: Theory and Evidence from Studies with Blind and Sighted Children.* Oxford: Clarendon Press.

Millar, S. (1995). *Sound, sense, syllables and word length in prose reading by touch.* Paper presented at the scientific meeting of the Experimental Psychology Society, Birmingham, July 12, 1995.

Millar, S., Ballesteros, S. and Reales, J.M. (1994). *Influence of symmetry in haptic and visual perception.* Paper presented at the 35th Annual Meeting of the Psychonomics Society, St Louis, Mo, November 11–13.

Millar, S. and Ittyerah, M. (1991). Mental practice without visuospatial information. *International Journal of Behavioral Development, 1991, 15,* 125–146.

Miller, G. (1956). The magical number seven, plus or minus two: some limits on our capacity for processing information. *Psychological Review, 63,* 81–97.

Miller, G. and Nicely, P.E. (1955). An analysis of perceptual confusions among some English consonants. *Journal of the Acoustical Society of America, 27,* 338–352

Mills, A.E. (ed.) (1983). *Language Acquisition in the Blind Child.* Beckenham, Kent: Croom Helm.

Milner, B. and Taylor, L. (1972). Right hemisphere superiority in tactile pattern recognition after cerebral commissurotomy. *Neuropsychologia, 10,* 1–15.

Molfese, D.L. and Molfese, V.J. (1979). Hemispheric and stimulus differences as reflected in cortical responses of newborn infants. *Developmental Psychology, 15,* 505–511.

Monsell, S. (1987). Non-visual orthographic processing and the orthographic input lexicon. In M. Coltheart (ed.) *The Psychology of Reading. Attention and Performance 12.* Hillsdale, N.J.: Lawrence Erlbaum.

Monsell, S., Doyle, M.C. and Haggard, P.N. (1989). Effects of frequency on word recognition tasks, Where are they? *Journal of Experimental Psychology: General*, *118*, 43–71.

Moore, L.H., Brown, W.S., Markee, T.E., Theberge, D.C. and Zvi, J.C. (1995). Bimanual coordination in dyslexic adults. *Neuropsychologia, 33*, 781–793.

Morris, R.G.M. (1989). Does synaptic plasticity play a role in information storage in the vertebrate brain? In R.G.M. Morris (ed.) *Parallel Distributed Processing: Implications for Psychology and Neurobiology.* Oxford: The Clarendon Press.

Morton, J. (1969). Interaction of information in word recognition. *Psychological Review, 76*, 165–178.

Morton, J. (1979). Facilitation in word recognition: Experiments causing change in the logogen model. In P.A. Kolers, M.E. Wrolstad and H. Bouma (eds) *Processing Visible Language*, Vol. 1. New York: Plenum Press.

Munsinger, H. and Forsman, R. (1966). Symmetry, development and tachistoscopic recognition. *Journal of Experimental Child Psychology, 3*, 168.

Myers, J., Jusczyk, P.W., Nelson, K.B.G., Charles-Luce, J., Woodward, A.L. and Hirsch-Pasek, K. (1996). Infants' sensitivity to word boundaries in fluent speech. *Journal of Child Language, 23*, 1–30.

Neville, H.J. (1990). Intermodal competition and compensation in development: Evidence from studies of the visual system in congenitally deaf adults. In A. Diamond (ed.) *The Development and Neural Bases of Higher Cortical Development: Comparative and Cross-Cultural Perspectives.* New York: Aldine Gruyter Press, Hawthorne.

Neville, H.J. and Lawson, D. (1987) Attention to central and peripheral visual space in a movement detection task: an event-related potential and behavioral study. II Congenitally deaf adults. III Separate effects of auditory deprivation and acquisition of a visual language. *Brain Research, 405*, 268–283 and 284–294.

Newman, S.E., Hall, A.D., Foster, J.D. and Gupta V. (1984). Learning as a function of haptic discriminability among items. *American Journal of Psychology, 97*, 359–372.

Newman, S.E., Kindsvater, M.B. and Hall, A.D. (1985). Braille learning: Effects of symbol size. *Bulletin of the Psychonomic Society, 23*, 189–190.

Newman, S.E., Sawyer, W.L., Hall, A.D and Hill, L. G.J. (1990). One modality is sometimes better than two. *Bulletin of the Psychonomic Society, 28*, 17–18.

Newport, E.L. (1976). Motherese: The speech of mothers to young children. In N.J. Castellan, D.B. Pisoni and G.R. Potts (eds) *Cognitive Theory,* Vol. 2. Hillsdale, N.J.: Lawrence Erlbaum.

Nickerson, R.S. (1965). Response time to 'same'–'different' judgments. *Perceptual and Motor Skills, 20*, 15–18.

Nolan, C.Y. and Kederis, C.J. (1969). *Perceptual Factors in Braille Recognition.* New York: American Foundation for the Blind.

Norris, D.G. (1984). The effects of frequency, repetition and stimulus quality in visual word recognition. *Quarterly Journal of Experimental Psychology, 36A*, 507–518.

Norris, D.G. (1986). Word recognition: context effects without priming. *Cognition, 22*, 93–136.

Norris, D. G. (1987). Strategic control of sentence context effects in a naming task. *Quarterly Journal of Experimental Psychology, 39A*, 253–275.

Paap, K.R., Newsome, S.L, McDonald, J.E. and Schvaneveldt, R.W. (1982). An activation-verification model for letter and word recognition: The word superiority effect. *Psychological Review, 89*, 573–594.

Paap, K.R., Newsome, S.L. and Noel, R.W. (1984). Word shape's in poor shape for the race to the lexicon. *Journal of Experimental Psychology: Human Perception and Performance, 10*, 413–428

Paillard, J. (1971). Les determinants moteur de l'organisation spatiale. *Cahiers de Psychologie, 14*, 261–316.

Paillard, J. (1991). Motor and representational framing of space. In J. Paillard (ed.) *Brain and Space*. Oxford: Oxford University Press.

Paillard, J., Michel, F. and Stelmach, G. (1983). Localization without content: A tactile analogue of 'blindsight'. *Archives of Neurology, 40*, 548–551.

Palmer, S.E. (1991). Goodness, Gestalt, groups, and Garner: Local symmetry subgroups as a theory of figural goodness. In G.R. Lockhead and J.R. Pomerantz (eds) *The Perception of Structure*. Hillsdale, N,J.: Lawrence Erlbaum.

Palmer, S.E. and Hemenway, K. (1978). Orientation and symmetry. *Journal of Experimental Psychology. Perception and Performance, 4*, 691–702.

Pascual-Leone, A. and Torres, F. (1993). Plasticity of the sensorimotor cortex representation of the reading finger in braille readers. *Brain, 116*, 39–52.

Pashler, H. (1990). Coordinate frame for symmetry detection and object recognition. *Journal of Experimental Psychology: Human Perception and Performance, 16* (1), 150–163.

Patterson, K.E., Coltheart, M. and Marshall, J.C. (1985). *Surface Dyslexia*. London: Lawrence Erlbaum.

Pennington, B.F. (1989). Using genetics to understand dyslexia. *Annals of Dyslexia, 39*, 81–93.

Perfetti, C.A. (1992). The representation problem in reading. In P.B. Gough, L. Ehri, and R. Treiman (eds). *Reading Acquisition*. Hove, E. Sussex: Lawrence Erlbaum.

Perfetti, C.A. and Bell, L. (1991). Phonemic activation during the first 40 ms of word identification: Evidence from backward masking. *Journal of Memory and Language, 30*, 473–485.

Perfetti, C.A., Bell, L.C. and Delaney, S. (1988). Automatic (prelexical) phonetic activation in silent word reading: Evidence from backward masking. *Journal of Memory and Language, 27*, 59–70.

Pester, E. (1993). Braille instruction for individuals who are blind adventitiously: Scheduling, expectations and reading interests. *Review: American Printing House for the Blind, Louisville, Ky, 25*, 83–87.

Pester, E.J., Petrosko, J.M. and Poppe, K.J. (1994). Optimum size and spacing for introducing blind adults to the braille code. *Review: American Printing House for the Blind, Louisville, Ky., 26*, 15–22.

Pick, A.D. and Pick, H.L. (1966). A developmental study of tactual discrimination in blind and sighted children and adults. *Psychonomic Science, 6*, 367–368.

Podreka, I., Steiner, M. and Deecke, L. (1993). Increased regional and cerebral blood flow in inferior occipital cortex. *Neuroscience Letters, 150*, 162–164.

Posner, M.I., Boies, S.J., Eichelman, W.H. and Taylor, R.L. (1969). Retention of visual and name codes of single letters. *Journal of Experimental Psychology Monographs, 79*, No. 1.

Preissler, G. (1993). Developing communication with blind and with deaf infants. *Reports from the Department of Psychology, Stockholm University*, No. 76

Pring, L. (1982). Phonological and tactual coding of braille by blind children. *British Journal of Psychology, 73*, 351–359.

Pring, L. (1986). Orthographic effects of braille and print in the auditory modality. *Journal of Visual Impairment and Blindness, 80*, 993–998.

Pring, L. and Rusted, J. (1985). Pictures for the blind: An investigation of the influence of pictures on recall of text by blind children. *British Journal of Developmental Psychology, 3*, 41–45.

Probert, P.J., Lee, D. and Kao, G. (1996). Interfaces for multisensory systems for navigation for the blind. Paper presented at the EDVR Conference on Assistive Technology, Reading, July 1996.

Pufall, P.B. and Shaw, R.S. (1973). Analysis of the development of children's reference systems. *Cognitive Psychology, 5*, 151–175.

Pynte, J. (1974). Readiness for pronunciation during the reading process. *Perception and Psychophysics*, *16*, 110–112.

Rabbitt, P. (1993). Does it go together when it goes? The nineteenth Bartlett memorial lecture. *Quarterly Journal of Experimental psychology*, *46A*, 385–434.

Rabbitt, P and Goward, L. (1994). Age, information processing speed and intelligence. *Quarterly Journal of Experimental Psychology*, *47A*, 741–760.

Ratcliff, G. (1991). Brain and space: Some deductions from clinical evidence. In J. Paillard (ed.) *Brain and Space*. Oxford: Oxford University Press.

Rayner, K. (1983). Perceptual span and eye-movement control during reading. In K. Rayner (ed.) *Eye Movements in Reading: Perceptual and Language Processes*. New York: Academic Press.

Rayner, K., Carlson, M. and Frazier, L. (1983). The interaction of syntax and semantics during sentence processing: Eye-movements and the analysis of semantically biased sentences. *Journal of Verbal Learning and Verbal Behavior*, *22*, 358–374.

Rayner, K. and Pollatsek, A. (1987). Eye movements in reading: A tutorial review. In Coltheart, M. (ed.) *Attention and performance XII*. London: Lawrence Erlbaum.

Rayner, K. and Pollatsek, A. (1989). *The Psychology of Reading*. Englewood Cliffs, N.J.: Prentice Hall.

Revesz, G. (1950). *Psychology and Art of the Blind*. London: Longman.

Robinson, D.L., Goldberg, M.E. and Stanton, G.B. (1978). Parietal association cortex in the primate: Sensory mechanisms and behavioral modulation. *Journal of Neurophysiology*, *41*, 910–932.

Rock, I. (1973). *Orientation and Form*. London: Academic Press.

Rock, I. (1983). *The Logic of Perception*. Cambridge, Mass.: MIT Press.

Roy, E.A. and Elliott, D. (1989). Manual asymmetries in aimed movements. *The Quarterly Journal of Experimental Psychology*, *41A* (3), 501–516.

Royer, F.L. (1981). Detection of symmetry. *Journal of Experimental Psychology: Human Perception and Performance*, *7* (6), 1186–1210.

Rossano, M.J. and Warren, D.H. (1989). The importance of alignment in blind subjects' use of tactual maps. *Perception*, *18*, 805–816.

Rozin, P. and Gleitman, L.R. (1977). The structure and acquisition of reading II. The reading process and the acquisition of the alphabet principle. In A.S. Reber and D.L. Scarborough (eds) *Towards a Psychology of Reading*. Hillsdale, N.J.: Lawrence Erlbaum.

Rudel, R.G., Denkla, M.B. and Hirsch, S. (1977). The development of left hand superiority for discriminating Braille configurations. *Neurology*, *27*, 160–164.

Rudel, R.G. and Teuber, H.-L. (1964). Crossmodal transfer of shape discrimination by children. *Neuropsychologia*, *2*, 1–8.

Rumelhart, D.E. and McClelland, J.L. (eds) (1986). *Parallel Distributed Processing: Explorations in the Microstructure of Cognition*, Vol. 1. Cambridge Mass: MIT Press.

Rumelhart, D.E., Hinton, G.E. and Williams, R.J. (1986). Learning internal representations by error propagation. In D.E, Rumelhart and J.L. McLelland (eds) *Parallel Distributed Processing: Explorations in the Microstructure of Cognition*. Cambridge, Mass.: MIT Press.

Runeson, S. (1977). On visual perception of dynamic events. Doctoral Dissertation, University of Uppsala (quoted by J.J. Gibson, 1979).

Ryan, C. (1983). Reassessing the automaticity/control distinction: item recognition as a paradigm case. *Psychological Review*, *90*, 171–178.

Ryan, E.B. (1982). Identifying and remediating reading failures in reading comprehension. In G.E. MacKinnon and T.G. Waller (eds) *Advances in Reading Research*, Vol. 3. New York: Academic Press.

Sadato, N, Pascual-Leone, A., Grafman, J., Ibanez, V., Deiber, M-P., Dold, G. and Hallett, M. (1996). Activation of the primary visual cortex by braille reading blind subjects. *Nature, 380*, 526–528.

Sakata, H. and Iwamura, Y. (1978) Cortical processing of tactile information in the first somato-sensory and parietal association areas in the monkey. In G. Gordon (ed.) *Active Touch.* New York: Pergamon Press.

Salthouse, T.A. (1991). *Theoretical Perspectives of Cognitive Aging.* Hillsdale, N.J.: Lawrence Erlbaum.

Sandra, D. (1992). On the representation and processing of compound words: Automatic access to constituent morphemes does not occur. *Quarterly Journal of Experimental psychology, 42A* (3), 529–567.

Sanford, A.J. and Garrod, S.C. (1981). *Understanding Written Language: Explorations in Comprehension beyond the Sentence.* New York: John Wiley.

Scarborough, D.L., Cortese, C. and Scarborough, H.S. (1977). Frequency and repetition effects in lexical memory. *Journal of Experimental Psychology: Human Perception and Performance, 3*, 1–17.

Schacter, D.L. (1990). Perceptual representation and implicit memory. Towards a resolution of the multiple memory systems debate. In A. Dimond (ed.) *The Development and Bases of Higher Cognitive Functions,* pp. 543–567. New York: New York Academy of Sciences.

Schank, R.C. and Abelson, R.P. (1977). *Scripts, Plans, Goals and Understanding: An Inquiry into Human Knowledge Structures.* Hillsdale, N.J.: Lawrence Erlbaum.

Schiff, W. (1982). A user's view of tangible graphics: The Louisville workshop. In W. Schiff and E. Foulke (eds) *Tactual Perception: A Source Book.* Cambridge: Cambridge University Press.

Schiff, W. and Foulke, E. (eds) (1982). *Tactual Perception: A Source Book.* Cambridge, Mass.: Cambridge University Press.

Schlaegel, T.F. (1953). The dominant method of imagery in blind as compared to sighted adolescents. *Journal of Genetic Psychology, 83*, 265–277.

Schneider, G.E. (1967). Contrasting visuo-motor functions of tectum and cortex in the Golden Hamster. *Psychologische Forschungen, 31*, 52–62.

Schneider, W. and Shiffrin, R.M. (1977). Controlled and automatic human information processing, I: Detection, search and attention. *Psychological Review, 84*, 1–66.

Schriefers, H, Friederici, A. and Graetz, P. (1992). Inflectional and derivational morphology in the mental lexicon: Symmetries and asymmetries in repetition priming. *Quarterly Journal of Experimental Psychology, 44A* (2), 373–372.

Schwartz, A.S., Perey, A.J. and Azulay, A. (1975). Further analysis of active and passive touch in pattern discrimination. *Bulletin of the Psychonomic Society, 6*, 7–9.

Seidenberg, M.S. (1987). Sub-lexical structures in visual word recognition: Access units or orthographic redundancy? In M. Coltheart (ed.) *Attention and Performance: The Psychology of Reading.* Hillsdale, N.J.: Lawrence Erlbaum.

Seidenberg, M. (1992). Dyslexia in a computational model of word recognition in reading. In P.B. Gough, L. Ehri and R. Treiman (eds) *Reading Acquisition.* Hove, E. Sussex: Lawrence Erlbaum

Seidenberg, M.S. and McClelland, J. (1989). A distributed developmental model of word recognition in reading and naming. *Psychological Review, 96*, 523–568.

Seidenberg, M.S. and McClelland, J. (1990). More words but still no lexicon: Reply to Besner *et al. Psychological Review, 97*, 447–452.

Semmes, J., Weinstein, S., Ghent, L. and Teuber, H.L. (1963). Correlates of impaired orientation in extra-personal space. *Brain, 86*, 747–772.

Shankweiler, D. and Crain, S. (1986). Language mechanisms and reading disorder: A modular approach. *Cognition, 24*, 139–168.

Shankweiler, D. and Liberman, I.Y. (1972). Misreading: a search for cues. In J.F. Kavanagh and I.Q. Mattingley (eds) *Language by Ear and Eye*. Cambridge, Mass.: MIT Press.

Shatz, C.J. (1992). The developing brain. *Scientific American, 267* (3), 61–67.

Sherrick, C.E. (1991). Vibrotactile pattern perception: Some findings and applications. In M.A. Heller and W. Schiff (eds) *The Psychology of Touch*. Hillsdale, N.J.: Lawrence Erlbaum.

Sherrick, C.E. and Craig, J.C. (1982). The psychophysics of touch. In W. Schiff and E. Foulke (eds) *Tactual Perception: A Sourcebook*. New York: American Foundation for the Blind.

Shiffrin, R.M. and Schneider, W. (1977). Controlled and automatic human information processing: II. Perception, automatic attending, and a general theory. *Psychological Review, 84*, 127–190.

Smith, F. (1971). *Understanding Reading: A Psycholinguistic Analysis of Reading and Learning to Read*. New York: Holt, Rinehart & Winston.

Smith, P.T. and Groat, A. (1979). Spelling patterns: Letter cancellation and the processing of text. In P.A. Kolers, M.E. Wrolstad and H. Bouma (eds) *Processing of Visible Language*, Vol. 1. New York: Plenum Press.

Spencer, C. and Travis, J. (1985). Learning a new area with and without the use of tactile maps: A comparative study. *British Journal of Visual Impairment, 3*, 5–7.

Spoehr, K.T. (1978). Phonological encoding in visual word recognition. *Journal of Verbal Learning and Verbal Behavior, 17*, 127–141.

Spoehr, K.T. (1981). Word recognition in speech and reading. In P.D. Eimas and J. L. Miller (eds) *Perspectives on the Study of Speech*. Hillsdale, N.J.: Lawrence Erlbaum.

Spoehr, K.T. and Smith, E.E. (1975). The role of orthographic and phonotactic rules in perceiving letter patterns. *Journal of Experimental Psychology: Human Perception and Performance, 1*, 21–34.

Squire, L.R. (1987). *Memory and Brain*. Oxford: Oxford University Press.

Stanovich, K.E. (1981). Attentional and automatic context effects in reading. In A.M. Lesgold and C.A. Perfetti (eds), *Interactive Processes in Reading*, pp. 241–267. Hillsdale, N.J.: Lawrence Erlbaum.

Stanovich, K.E. and West, R. (1979). Mechanisms of sentence context effects in reading: Automatic activation and conscious attention. *Memory and Cognition, 7*, 77–85.

Stanovich, K.E. and West, R.F. (1983). The effect of sentence context on ongoing word recognition: Test of a two-process theory. *Journal of Experimental Psychology: General, 112*, 1–36.

Stanovich, K.E., Nathan, R.G., Vala-Rossi, M. and West, R.F. (1985). Children's word recognition in context: Spreading activation, expectancy and modularity. *Child Development, 56*, 1418–1429.

Stein, J.F. (1991). Space and the parietal association areas. In J. Paillard (ed.) *Brain and Space*. Oxford: Oxford University Press.

Stein, J.F. (1992). The representation of egocentric space in the posterior parietal cortex. *Behavioral and Brain Sciences, 15*, 691–700.

Stein, J. F. and Fowler, S. (1984). Ocular motor dyslexia. *Dyslexia Review, 5*, 25–28.

Stein, J.F., Riddell, P. and Fowler, M.S. (1987). Fine binocular control in dyslexic children. *Eye, 11*, 433–438.

Stevens, J.C. (1992). Aging and spatial acuity of touch. *Journal of Gerontology, 47*, 35–40.

Stevens, J.C., Foulke, E. and Patterson, M. (1996). Tactile acuity, ageing, and braille reading in long-term blindness. *Journal of Experimental Psychology: Applied, 2*, 91–106.

Sur, M. (1995). Maps of space and time. *Nature, 378,* 13–14.

Taft, M. (1979). Lexical access via an orthographic code (Boss). *Journal of Verbal Learning and Verbal Behavior, 18,* 21–39.

Taft, M. (1986). Lexical access codes in visual and auditory word recognition. *Language and Cognitive Processes, 4,* 297–308.

Taft, M. (1994). Interactive-activation as a framework for understanding morphological processing. *Language and Cognitive Processes, 9,* 271–294.

Taft, M. and Forster, K.K. (1975). Lexical storage and retrieval of prefixed words. *Journal of Verbal Learning and Verbal Behavior, 14,* 638–642.

Tallal, P. and Piercy, M. (1973). Developmental aphasia: impaired rate of non-verbal processing as a function of sensory modality. *Neuropsychologia, 11,* 389–398.

Taylor, D.A. (1976). Holistic and analytical processes in the comparison of letters. *Perception and Psychophysics, 20,* 187.

Thompson, R.F. (1967). *Foundations of Physiological Psychology.* London: Harper & Row.

Thorndike, E.L. and Lorge, I. (1959). *The Teacher's Word Book of 30,000 Words.* New York: Columbia University Teacher's College Bureau of Publishers.

Tillman, M.H. (1967). The performance of blind and sighted children on the Wechsler Intelligence Scale for Children. *The Education of the Blind. Study II,* 106–112.

Tobin, M. J. (1971). Touch: Braille and other tactual symbols. *Teacher of the Blind, 59,* 117–126 and 154–170.

Tobin, M.J. (1972). *The Vocabulary of the Young Blind Schoolchild.* Birmingham: College of Teachers of the Blind.

Tobin, M.J. (1981). An introduction to the psychological and educational assessment of blind and partially sighted children. *Occasional Papers (Vol. 5).* Leicester: Division of Educational and Child Psychology of the British Psychological Society.

Tobin, M.J. (1987). *Beginning Braille – A self-instructional reading scheme for newly blind adults.* London: Royal National Institute for the Blind.

Tobin, M.J. (1988). Beginning braille. *The New Beacon, LXXXII, 850,* 81–82.

Tobin, M.J. (1992). The language of blind children: Communication words, and meanings. *Language and Education, 6,* 177–182.

Tobin, M.J. (1995). Personal communication.

Tobin, M. and Hill, E, (1984). A Moon writer. *The New Beacon, LXVIII, 807,* 173–176.

Tobin, M.J., Burton, P, Davies, B.T. and Guggenheim, J. (1986). An experimental investigation of the effects of cell size and spacing in braille: with some possible implications for the newly-blind adult learner. *The New Beacon, LXX, 829,* 133–135.

Tooze, F.H.G. (1962). *The Tooze Braille Speed Test.* Bristol: The College of Teachers of the Blind.

Treiman, R. (1984). On the status of final consonant clusters in English syllables. *Journal of Verbal Learning and Verbal Behavior, 23,* 343–356.

Treiman, R. (1993). *Beginning to Spell: A Study of First-Grade Children.* Oxford: Oxford University Press.

Treiman, R., Fowler, C.A., Gross, J., Berch, D. *et al.* (1995). Syllable structure or word structure? Evidence for onset and rime units with disyllabic and trisyllabic stimuli. *Journal of Memory and Language, 34,* 132–155.

Treiman, R. and Zukowski, A. (1990). Towards an understanding of English syllabification. *Journal of Memory and Language, 29,* 66–85.

Treiman R. and Zukowski, A. (1994). What types of linguistic information do children use in spelling? The case of flaps. *Child Development, 65,* 1318–1337.

Trevarthen, C. B. (1968). Two mechanisms of vision in primates. *Psychologische Forschung*, *31*, 299–337.

Tulving, E. and Donaldson, W. (eds) (1972). *Organization of Memory*. New York: Academic Press.

Tversky, B. (1981). Distortion in memory for maps. *Cognitive Psychology*, *13*, 407–433.

Tversky, B. and Schiano, D.J. (1989). Perceptual and conceptual factors in distortions in memory for graphs and maps. *Journal of Experimental Psychology: General*, *118*, 387–398.

Ungar, S., Blades, M. and Spencer, C. (1995). *The British Journal of Visual Impairment*, *13*, 27–32.

Urwin, C. (1983). Dialogue and cognitive functioning in early language development of three blind children. In A.E. Mills (ed.) *Language Acquisition in the Blind Child: Normal and Deficient*. London: Croom Helm.

Vallar, G. and Baddeley, A.D. (1984). Phonological short-term store, phonological processing and sentence comprehension. *Cognitive Neuropsychology*, *1*, 121–141.

Vallar, G. and Cappa, S.F. (1987) Articulation and verbal short-term memory: Evidnece from anarthria. *Cognitive Neuropsychology*, *4*, 55–78.

Vallbo, A.B. and Johansson, R.S. (1978). The tactile sensory innervation of the glabrous skin of the human hand. In G. Gordon (ed.) *Active Touch. The mechanism of Recognition of Objects by Manipulation: A Multidisciplinary Approach*. Oxford: Pergamon Press.

Van Orden, G.C. (1987). A ROWS is a ROSE: Spelling, sound and reading. *Memory and Cognition*, *15*, 181–198.

Van Orden, G., Pennington, B. and Stone, G.O. (1990). Word identification in reading and the promise of subsymbolic linguistics. *Psychological Review*, *97*, 488–522.

Venezky, R. (1967). English orthography: Its structure and relation to sound. *Reading Research Quarterly*, *2*, 75–106.

Vennemann, T. (1988). *Preference Laws for Syllable Structure and Explanation of Sound Change*. Berlin: Mouton de Gruyter.

Villiers, J.G. de and de Villiers, P.A. (1978). *Language Acquisition*. Cambridge, Mass.: Harvard University Press.

Vurpillot, E. (1968). The development of scanning strategies and their relation to visual differentiation. *Journal of Experimental Child Psychology*, *6*, 632–650.

Walk, R.D. (1965) Tactual and visual learning of forms differing in degrees of symmetry. *Psychonomic Science*, *2*, 93–94.

Walk, R.D. and Pick H.L. Jr. (eds) (1981) *Intersensory Perception and Perceptual Integration*. New York: Plenum Press.

Walker, C., McKennell, A.C. and Tobin, M.J. (1991). Blind and partially sighted children in Great Britain. *The RNIB Survey*. London: HMSO.

Wallace, S.A. (1977). The coding of location. A test of the target hypothesis. *Journal of Motor Behavior*, *9*, 157–159.

Wanet, M.C. and Veraart, C (1985). Processing auditory information by the blind in spatial localisation tasks. *Perception and Psychophysics*, *38*, 91–96.

Wang, M.M., Merzenich, M., Sameshina, K. and Jenkins, W.M. (1995). Remodelling of hand representation in adult cortex determined by timing of tactile stimulations. *Nature*, *13*, 71–75.

Warm, J., Clark, J.L. and Foulke, E. (1970). Effects of differential spatial orientation on tactual pattern recognition. *Perceptual and Motor Skills*, *31*, 87–94.

Warm, J. and Foulke, E. (1968). Effects of orientation and redundancy on the tactual perception of forms. *Perceptual and Motor Skills*, *27*, 83–89.

Warren, D.H. (1977). *Blindness and Early Childhood Development*. New York: American Foundation for the Blind.

Warren, D.H. (1984). *Blindness and Early Childhood Development*. New York: American Foundation for the Blind.

Warren, D.H. and Rossano, M.J. (1991). Intermodality relations: Vision and touch. In M.A. Heller and W. Schiff (eds) *The Psychology of Touch*. Hillsdale, N.J.: Erlbaum.

Waters, G.S., Bruck, M. and Malus-Abramovitz (1988). The role of linguistic and visual information in spelling: A developmental study. *Journal of Experimental Child Psychology, 45*, 400–421.

Waters, G.S., Caplan, D. and Leonard, C. (1992). The role of phonology in reading comprehension: Implications of the effects of homophones on processing sentences with referentially dependent categories. *The Quarterly Journal of Experimental Psychology, 44A* (2), 343–372.

Waters, G.S., Seidenberg, M.S. and Brook, M. (1984). Children's and adults' use of spelling–sound information in three reading tasks. *Memory and Cognition, 12*, 393–405.

Watkins, M.J. (1977). The intricacy of the memory span. *Memory and Cognition, 5*, 529–534.

Watkins, M.J. and Watkins, O.C. (1974). A tactile suffix effect. *Memory and Cognition, 2*, 176–180.

Waugh, N. and Barr, R.A. (1980). Memory and mental tempo. In L.W. Poon, J.L. Fozard, L.S. Cermak, D. Arenberg,and L.W. Thompson (eds) *New Directions in Memory and Aging*. Hillsdale, N.J.: Lawrence Erlbaum.

Weber, E.H. (1978). *The Sense of Touch*. ('De Tactu', 1834, translated by H.E. Ross, and 'Der Tastsinn und das Gemeingefuhl', 1846, translated by D.J. Murray, for the Experimental Psychology Society.) London: Academic Press.

Weinstein, S. (1968). Intensive and extensive aspects of tactile sensitivity as a function of body part, sex and laterality. In D.R. Kenshalo (ed.) *The Skin Senses*. Springfield, Ill.: Charles Thomas.

Weir, R.H. (1962) *Language in the Crib*. The Hague: Mouton.

Weiskrantz, L. (1986). *Blindsight: A case study and its implications*. Oxford: Oxford University Press.

West, R.F. and Stanovich, K.E. (1978). Automatic contextual facilitation in readers of three ages. *Child Development, 49*, 717–727.

Whittlesea, B.W.A. (1989). Selective attention, variable processing, and distributed representation: preserving particular experiences of general structures. In R.G.M. Morris (ed.) *Parallel Distributed Processing: Implications for Psychology and Neurobiology*. Oxford: Clarendon Press.

Whittlesea, B.W. and Brooks L.R. (1988). Critical influences of particular experiences in the perception of letters, words and phrases. *Memory and Cognition, 5*, 387–399.

Williams, M. (1956). *Williams Intelligence Test for Children with Defective Vision*. Windsor: NFER Publishing Company.

Wills, D.M. (1978). Early speech development in blind children. *The Psychoanalytic Study of the Child, 34*, 85–117.

Worchel, P. (1951). Space perception and orientation in the blind. *Psychological Monographs, 65*, No. 332.

Zaidel, E. (1985). Language and the right hemisphere. In D. Benson and E. Zaidel (ed.) *The Dual Brain*. New York: Guilford Press.

Zakay, D. and Shilo, E. (1985). The influence of temporal and spatial variation on tactile identification of letters. *Journal of General Psychology, 112* (2), 147–152.

Zaporozhets, A.V. (1965). The development of perception in the preschool child. In P.H. Mussen (ed.) European Research in Child Development. *Monographs of the Society for Research in Child Development*.

Zeki, S. (1993). A Vision of the Brain. Oxford: Blackwell Scientific Publications.

Zhang, G. and Simon, H.A. (1985). Short-term memory capacity for Chinese words and idioms: chunking and acoustic loop hypothesis. *Memory and Cognition*, *13*, 193–201.

Zipf, G.F. (1935). *The Psychobiology of Language: An Introduction to Dynamic Philology*. New York: Houghton Mifflin.

Author index

Subject index

activation: automatic 140, 203, 293, 297–9; compensatory 21–2, 174; in interrelated networks 174, 278–9, 294, 297

active touch (*see* touch)

acuity in touch 15, 23, 24, 26–8, 30–2, 35, 38; and age 239, 246; in diabetes 149; 241; with experience and practice 30–2, 148–9, 241, 284; by recent readers 241; and the two-point threshold 30, 35, 239

affordances: 18–19 (*see also* information)

age (*see also* development, processing speed): and braille learning 239–45; and lateralization 216

alphabetic principle (*see also* phonology, spelling): in English orthography 2, 100, 181, 183–3

amodal perception 18–19 (*see also* crossmodal, intersensory)

analogy: in comprehension 222; phonological recoding by 101, 182

articulatory coding (*see also* phonological coding, working memory): and comprehension 113–6; errors in 281; loop 98–9; skills 218–19; and suppression 113–34, 285

assembled phonology (*see also* letter-by-letter reading): 109, 114–15, 135, 264; and word superiority 109

attention: 102, 132, 297–8; selectivity 298; to speech sounds in blind children 10, 216–19

auditory feedback and deaf babies 217

automaticity (*see also* attention): and experience 22, 100–1, 289–93

babbling 216; reduction in blind babies 218

beginning reading (*see also* teaching): as constructive processing 54; and dual tasks 54, 283–90; and hand use 83–4, 96; and haptic–verbal interrelations 283–90; and meaning 129; and phonological coding 115–16, 133

benders (*see* vibrotactile stimulation)

body-posture and handmovements 258 (*see also* movement, spatial organisation)

braille: 2, 26–7; alphabet 37; composition of 35–47; distinctive features 54; dot-density detection and holistic (global outline) coding 36–47, 110–13; and generalisation 47; perceptual basis 5, 17, 26–7; processes in acquisition 279–80, 290; shear patterns in fluent reading 87–9, 254–5; spatial shape organisation of 47–55, 283

brain (*see also* cerebral hemispheres, cortex): 27–8

CAPIN (convergent active processing in interrelated networks): working hypothesis 278; developmental assumptions in 279–81

cerebral hemispheres (*see also* brain, cortex): association areas 31–32; and hand advantage 67–73; in language 27, 216; and plasticity 30–2; in spatial coding 27–8, 32–5; and subcortical connections 28–9

cognitive factors 95–7; and braille 139, 243–5, 271–2; and low-level processing 89, 97; modulation by